Calmer Chameleon

Adventures of a songwriter

Phil Pickett

Calmer Chameleon

Adventures of a songwriter

Phil Pickett

WYMER
PUBLISHING
Bedford, England

First published in 2017
by Wymer Publishing
Bedford, England
www.wymerpublishing.co.uk
Tel: 01234 326691
Wymer Publishing is a trading name of Wymer (UK) Ltd

ISBN 978-1-908724-54-0

Transcribed and edited by Keith Hayward.

Every effort has been made to trace the copyright holders of the
photographs in this book but some were unreachable. We would
be grateful if the photographers concerned would contact us.

Front cover images © Andre Csilliag.
Back cover images © Barry Ryan.

Printed and bound by
Clays Ltd, Bungay, Suffolk, England

A catalogue record for this book is available from the British Library.

Cover design by The Andys.

To Ann,

My beloved and unwavering friend for sharing this crazy, wonderful and often scary joyride for whom no words could ever come anywhere near expressing my love and gratitude,

So I'll write you a song instead!

This book is also dedicated to my children,
Harry, Gus and Jack and to my grandson George Pickett

"A calm sea never did a skilled sailor make!"

- Anon

Contents

Foreword

As a pop-craved teenager in the seventies it was almost impossible to avoid the high camp of Sailor. One of those crazy indefinable pop groups that emerged from the cracks of Prog Rock and up between the legs of Ziggy Stardust. The noise they made was polished, layered and quirky. Banks of sweeping choppy harmonies with accordions and banjos. Songs like 'Girls, Girls, Girls' and 'Glass Of Champagne' fizzled into our lives and promised a life of vaudevillian decadence!

They were Camp with a capitol C even if they failed to see it themselves! It's amusing to read that years later, Sailor's keyboardist and songwriter Phil Pickett would find me a little eccentric.

Phil Pickett found his way into Culture Club towards the recording of our second album *Colour By Numbers*. We were having trouble communicating musical ideas and our producer Steve Levine decided to invite Phil to help us finish some rather potentially great songs. One of them being 'Karma Chameleon'. It wasn't long before he was sporting his old Sailor cap and joining us on the road.

I always had a great relationship with Phil, his wife Ann xx and boys and I never once stopped to consider what he thought of me. More importantly I take the view that what other people think of me is none of my business!

Marilyn, my friend from the eighties has always said, "there are three truths, yours, mine and the actual truth". I can't tell you if the parts of this book where I and my band feature are true or not. I have a selective memory but because of the Sailor reference I am reminded of a discarded lyric.

"Of all the pirates that I've known, you must be the best, you always lied about the past and covered up the rest!"

If Phil said it happened, then I guess it must have!

This book is a romp through the seventies, the eighties and beyond and Phil Pickett is at the helm sailing through a sea of discarded shoulder pads and platform boots.

Phil is a superb musician, a great songwriter and relentless storyteller and this book should be an essential part of your musical education.

Read it and weep glitter tears of joy!

Boy George x

Preface

I cannot believe my luck that I happened to have been born and grew up infused, enthralled and surrounded by the Rock 'n' Roll years of the mid-to-late twentieth Century; a period that future musical historians will look back on as the most tumultuous and revolutionary times of all, with some of the greatest characters and musical talents the world has ever seen. What's more, through my lifelong passion for music, I thank my lucky stars every single day that I actually ended up meeting, playing and working with many of my heroes. In truth, it was never just about the music with me though; like a moth to a flame I also was attracted by the pizzazz, glamour and style of pop culture and the amazing freedom it represents. Like the day when, transfixed, I watched Jagger, Richards and, in particular, Brian Jones, explode on to the stage at Birmingham Town Hall in March 1964.

That's where it really all began for me...

After a lifetime of playing gigs over five decades, 9 times out of 10 only the truly exceptional or the countless little episodes that made you celebrate, laugh, or cry are easily recalled. Or things that perhaps stand out for other reasons. What may be inconsequential to one person can often be profound to another. As Boy George himself says in his delightfully generous foreword to my book, truth is selective and invariably in the eye of beholder.

So, to my dear readers, friends and colleagues; please do not expect a blow-by-blow, day-to-day historical account of what were without doubt the most tumultuous and exhilarating years of my life, but instead, a great many personal impressions, reflections and insights gained from being an enthusiastic fly-on-the-wall throughout one of pop music's most fascinating colourful and controversial eras.

"Dreams are made of emotion" Boy George ('It's A Miracle')

I hope you enjoy my tale as much as I have writing, and living it!

Phil Pickett, August 26th 2017

Prologue

Thirty minutes earlier, Raöul, our Uber driver had picked Ann and me up from the sumptuous and legendary Bel-Air Hotel in Los Angeles, possibly the most luxurious hotel on the planet. It was August 24th 2016 and we'd been invited by Roy Hay to come to America and see Culture Club at the spectacular Hollywood Bowl, thirty years on from when I last played with the band. I thought, 'fuck it, why not'? 'Let's push the boat out one last time', (a very long way as it happened!)

I wanted to show Ann the kind of places we used to stay in whilst in L.A. back in the heyday of the band's eighties megastardom and this was, and have to say still is, one of the very best. Our car was not quite up to expectations however and the Bel Air bellhops had discreetly ushered the driver towards the back of the parking lot way behind the stylish limousines lining up like sleek black swans patiently waiting to transport their rich and famous clientele hither and thither. "Sorry sir", Raöul apologised in his Guatemalan brogue, "The whole town going to this show and we have to go over the hill. Freeways all blocked."

Culture Club were back on the road with a vengeance, my ex-1980's musical cohorts having patched up all manner of personal and business difficulties to make it possible; a glorious victory lap or two around the world for old times and pension funds' sake. Like many a fatal attraction, the saucepans were well and truly buried even though the odd handle may have occasionally been visible.

Now running very late, we finally made it around the back of L.A.'s most iconic venue and were deposited as close as he could get to the main gate. A few minutes earlier we were haring around bends as if being chased by cops in a B-movie high up in the hills overlooking the city, gazing in wonder at the glittering carpet of spectacular lights straight out of a Spielberg movie; a vast twinkling mirage of tinsel triumphs and shattered dreams and surely one of the most glorious sights in the world. All nerves, excitement and anticipation as we had come a very long way for tonight.

"Will the tickets be there?" (Yes, they were) "What about the special guest backstage passes?" (Yep, got those too) "Are the seats any good?" (You bet, right at the front!) Roy had done us proud, good lad.

Arriving under the canopy of stars, a jubilant and wealthy looking sold-out audience of 18,000 people were being serenaded "Last Night Of The Proms-style" by the majestic 80-piece Los Angeles Philharmonic Orchestra.

For a nail-biting moment I thought out loud; "Christ, we've come all this way and it's the wrong bloody night!"

"No, they're the warm-up act," Ann said. "Look, it says on the ticket. They're going to be backing Culture Club when they come on too!"

"Wow, really?" I couldn't believe it. All these people coming out to enjoy my ex-band and tomorrow night's show was sold out too.

We were now in our seats and I literally couldn't wait to see them play, this motley crew of outstanding and unique individuals that, in spite of all the trials and tribulations over the years, were like family to me, people I loved who all those decades ago had generously invited me to help them create the sound of Culture Club.

Could life really get any better than this?

A bottle of champagne arrived at our seat and popped just as the opening track, 'Church Of The Poison Mind' rang out. Exceeding every expectation, I was in heaven and chest-thumpingly proud of each and every one of them up there.

There was dancing in the aisles from the get-go and, along with the vast crowd, we were delirious with expectation. George was on fire and the audience were lapping up every bit of it. Hit after hit after hit, each and every song I'd played a part in, some I'd co-written, 'It's A Miracle', 'Move Away' and 'Karma Chameleon', probably Culture Club's most iconic hit. All of their songs written over thirty years ago sounded as fresh as the day they were recorded, and tonight under the August stars they were being supported by the magnificent 'L.A. Phil' (my nickname from that point on!)

I welled up at all those years ago having contributed my little bit to the musical provenance of the unique group of characters known as Culture Club. It was simply the best night of my life and frankly, I was a mess!

After the show, still basking in the glow of the occasion, we joined the line to get backstage with the likes of Naomi Campbell, Julian Lennon, Sting and most of the A-list movers and shakers of Hollywood out in force. In fact, it was just like the old days all over again, where coming off stage after a vintage Culture Club show in the eighties you never knew who you'd meet; John McEnroe, Torvill and Dean, Steve Winwood, Dustin Hoffman, Frank Bruno, Andy Warhol - always a crazily random 'who's who'! The social butterflies of the day always descended en masse.

Understandably nervous about meeting Roy, Mikey, Jon and George again in such gilded company and on such an important night for the band, I was beginning to think we were not going to get in to see them at all. There were so many people milling about and the security was extremely tight. "Look, let's go," I said losing my nerve. "I really don't want to scrabble around here with this lot, and anyway, I can try and call them tomorrow. They're gonna be really busy." But secretly I feared that Roy might have forgotten to arrange the correct pass, or perhaps was just too caught up with everything to remember. All sorts of things go through your mind when you're jet-lagged, and by this time, tired and emotional.

"Don't you think we should stay a bit longer Phil?" Ann interjected; "They do know you've come such a long way and would love to see you I'm sure."

We gave it another five minutes or so but as nothing seemed to be happening, somewhat reluctantly we turned to walk off down the hill. Thankfully however my self-conscious fears proved to be unfounded. "Phil!" I suddenly heard Mikey shouting from the stage door, who then quickly shepherded Ann & I out from the security line past the diamond-studded throng to warm and welcoming hugs of reunion with Jon and Roy; "Great to see you man! When d'you get in?"

"Only last night, we've come a very long way to see you guys!"

"This is Phil and Ann," Jon said, introducing us to his son Clive who was out on the road with his dad on a break from college; "He helped us write a lot of the songs and was really the 'fifth member' back in the day, weren't you Phil?"

"Well, I, er," mumbling modestly, but then I heard George calling my name from the other end of the packed hallway; "...and Ann!" he squealed enthusiastically waving us to come over.

"Well they made 'em up in Hollywood..."

George immediately - and considering where we were, appropriately burst into song by way of introducing me to P.K, his new manager and the assembled thronging celebrants with a famous song I'd recorded with Sailor in the seventies - 'Girls Girls Girls'; "... and put 'em into the moo... vies!"

"Phil used to be in a very camp band called Sailor who used to be on Top of The Pops all the time!" he jubilantly announced to all and sundry, (I couldn't believe that after all these years he was still so obviously impressed with one of my first attempts at pop stardom). "Anyway, they told me you were coming tomorrow night. Brilliant to see you though, did you enjoy the show?"

As long as the many calls on George's attention and his adoring backstage friends and fans would allow, we chatted briefly and amongst other things, asked us where we were staying.

"At the Bel-Air," I said proudly; "In fact, I thought you might be there too, like the old days."

"God, no," he said, "That's very 'Tony Gordon' (their ex-manager back in the day) but aimed with a knowing smile towards his new manager; "We're not allowed to do that bourgeois kind of thing anymore. This time we've got to make some money!" he chuckled.

I looked over at Ann as my hotel theory bit the dust. Still, we were, and for one last glorious night, in Hollywood.

George was in magnificent form, insouciant risqué cabaret at its finest, songs to die for and world-class comedy from a bottomless pit of a well-lived life of tiaras, triumphs and tragedies, from luxury to heartache indeed and now back again it seemed.

Earlier, the upscale L.A crowd had been eating out of his hand. The long wait to see Culture Club perform again had been worth it and a few decades on, this time having brought their kids along, they were re-living and re-loving every minute of it.

Seeing my dear mates again, I loved it, and them even more.

Things hadn't always been this good though.

Chapter 1
From Luxury To Heartache

Life, you'll notice is a story

*Life comes to us the way that a story does, scene by scene. You wake up.
What will happen next? You don't get to know - you have to enter in, take
the journey as it comes. The sun might be shining. There might be a tornado
outside. Your friends might call and invite you to go sailing. You might lose
your job... A year goes by like a chapter from a novel. Sometimes it seems like
a tragedy. Sometimes like a comedy. Most of it feels like a soap opera.
Whatever happens, it's a story through and through..."*
(From 'The Ransomed Heart' by John Eldredge)

I t's 4 o'clock in the morning on 7th February 2008 and I'm shivering in
sub-zero temperatures, teeth chattering in the grubby cab of a white van
parked at a pit-stop on a Belgian motorway desperately trying to get
some sleep.

Sound grim? Damn right.

I'd turned up a little early for the dawn ferry back to Blighty from Dunkirk
so had decided to grab some kip before turning up at the port. A very bad
idea as things turned out, but when you're stranded, cold and exhausted,
like the thousands of hapless British soldiers were, huddling together for
warmth on the beach in WW2 meekly awaiting death and destruction by
the advancing Germans, you don't always think straight. Anyway, like the
soldiers on the beach in 1940, I thought, 'what the fuck was I doing here in
the first place'? There must have been a good reason for buying this bloody
van weeks earlier but right now, trapped inside an ancient mobile fridge, I
couldn't for the life of me remember why. Oh yes. Now I do, the familiar dull
and aching abyss in the pit of my stomach. I needed to make some money,
and fast!

Up to just a few years earlier, or so it seemed, I'd been a successful
musician touring all over the world, writing hit songs - one of them closely
related to the title of this book and probably THE biggest song of the
eighties, a single that Quincy Jones himself had informed me was number
one in America and a pop classic that eventually, in Sir Richard Branson's
words, "became number 1 in every country in the world that had a chart!"

I'd toured with Culture Club throughout the world as the band's keyboard
player, sometime arranger and backing vocalist, helped them to get their
first record deal with Virgin Records and had played and sang on nearly

every one of their records. Among other songs, including 'Move Away' and 'It's A Miracle', with Boy George I happened to co-write 'Karma Chameleon', the group's biggest ever hit, a magical and serendipitous few moments of creation I will expand upon to be sure! For this achievement I was presented with two Ivor Novello Awards, a songwriter's greatest accolade, plus countless gold silver and platinum records for my work with the group and along with the Ivors, still some of my proudest possessions.

Earlier, in the Glam Rock seventies, my own band, Sailor, similarly though not quite as spectacularly, scaled the heights of international chart stardom with a number one hit, 'A Glass Of Champagne' and several other top ten records. Our boisterous and strident ditty, having held on interminably at number two for several weeks finally dislodged one of THE biggest singles of all time - Queen's 'Bohemian Rhapsody' from its coveted Number 1 position in the *New Musical Express* Chart. Even though we only briefly held on for a week, we'd finally got the massive hit we felt we deserved - and in the only chart that ever really mattered - the good old *NME*! (Henry still has his framed on his studio wall)

But things hadn't always gone that well. Far from it in fact! Right now for instance, where, from the driver's seat of a van stuck out on the freezing hard shoulder of a Belgian motorway, I found myself at 62, skint, down on my luck, clinically depressed and at end of the line career-wise - or so I thought - and all that happened before seemed a very long way down memory lane. Frankly, by now I was far too old to be given any kind of job other than shelf filling and taxi driving. Problem was, I considered myself almost the living embodiment of 'unemployable' and once you believe that about yourself, it can be an even steeper hill to climb back to where you belong. Anyway, hadn't I done too much in my life to deserve ending up here?

4.03 am… a deep, rumbling Pythonesque voice from the universe seemed to answer loud and clear; "No mate. Obviously, you haven't. Not yet anyway!" (By the way, said voice seemed to have a Brummie accent!)

Rewind just a few weeks earlier and in a spontaneous moment of madness spurred on by quiet desperation and blind faith, I pulled over when I saw the sturdy old Ford long wheelbase, 'Hi-Top' Transit van going absurdly cheap under one of the Brighton arches. I suddenly decided to increase my, about-to-be-terminated overdraft and bought the 11-year-old crate there and then. It felt like a good idea at the time and when something feels intrinsically right, I tend to go for it, besides, what was the alternative? We had to eat.

"You've done what?" Ann, my endearing wife, said when I arrived home, too numbed by the private hell of our recent financial Armageddon to put up much resistance. "I can make some money with this," I said somewhat feebly, a bus pass holder trying to sound like the invincible guy I once saw myself as. "I promise you, just wait and see."

What could possibly go wrong? Like now in Belgium for instance. I'd just delivered a van load of furniture to Brussels on the first of many pan-European jaunts, dog tired, unable to drive another yard and ruminating in the ice-cold cab exactly how, when and why the first-class express train of my former career had careered off the tracks. Forming my first band Sailor, in the seventies, I'd toured the world earning gold discs everywhere for songs like 'A Glass Of Champagne' & 'Girls Girls Girls'. I'd composed a West End musical, taught an 18 year old Robbie Williams to sing with Take That in my own recording studio, met Quincy Jones and worked with the late, great record producers, Arif Mardin and Phil Ramone; sang with Beach Boy Carl Wilson and Beatle, Paul McCartney; written and produced Malcolm McLaren and the incomparable Jeff Beck just to name a few. I'd also arranged McCartney's tribute recording in honour of his soul brother and co-writing partner John Lennon, performed by the former with his band Wings, to 4 billion people worldwide on the tenth anniversary of John's death outside the Dakota building in 1980. The list is endless, but all leading, in one way or the other, to over forty million records sold around the world, and unwittingly achieving a crazy childhood ambition of becoming a millionaire by the ripe old age of forty.

But all that seemed a long time ago. "What the fuck!" again I yelled out pathetically into the freezing night. But this time no one was listening. Lying across the bench seat in the darkness, hundreds of miles away from my warm bed back at home and looking up at the stars, I felt that things just couldn't get any worse. Could they?

Half dreaming with delirious, self-pitying thoughts and watching my breath forming crystals as I spat out another weary expletive, suddenly I stopped dead when I thought I'd heard the ominous sound of violent human activity somewhere out there, but not too far away in the darkness; a muffled but blood-curdling scream. 'What in heaven's name was that?

Nervously, slowly raising my head above the dashboard to see what was going on, to my ball-clenching horror, in the gloom, I could just about make out a group of men slowly walking towards the rear of my vehicle. They were in a strange V-shape, somehow recalling the not-so Magnificent Seven, like slow motion demented geese flying home, the biggest one at the front but all with a prowling, sinister and animal-like intent.

I can still taste the fear of a moment I will never forget. I knew in my bones that something sinister must have just taken place between the gleaming trucks, long distance ghosts, which on this dark night of the soul were being used to hide misdeeds and much unpleasantness from view. It was then it crossed my mind that perhaps somebody else might get their heads stoved in if some idiot in a van; 'er, that'd be me then'; was seen by any one of them witnessing the aftermath of the crime.

As quick as I could, I jolted my head back down towards the seat in an attempt to hide, desperately hoping I hadn't been seen. But my heart was beating so loud I thought anyone within 100 yards must have been able to hear it.

In the briefest of glimpses, hanging loose at the side of the biggest guy of the group slightly ahead of the rest, I made out what seemed to be an industrial-size monkey wrench; wait a minute, there was steam rising from the sweat on his arms and upper body! Built like Robert Mitchum in his prime, this gorilla was only wearing boots, jeans and a vest and it had to have been at least minus five out there in the darkness. Was I really witnessing this or could I still be asleep and it was all part of a dream? Whatever, I knew intuitively and without any doubt at all that wrongdoing of an extremely violent nature must have only just taken place.

Wide awake now but numbed with cold and anxiety, my petrified thoughts drifted into a kind of slow-motion animation of escapism and quite possibly, complete denial. I will never know. But by this time, no doubt courtesy of my drained synapses, incongruously my mind suddenly found itself drifting in and out of the smoke-filled ambience of Basin Street West, a warm, lively jazz dive in San Francisco's Long Beach way back in 1967, the 'Summer of Love' for many, and just a few streets away from Haight-Ashbury in the city where it all started.

to be continued...

Chapter 2
Mr. Ellington I Presume?

After effectively emigrating to America, I'd been drafted by the US Government to take part in the Vietnam war but for some time, had been on the run from the FBI who now urgently required my presence for a medical at the army base in Oakland just across the bay. In the very prime of youthful idealism, I was a draft dodger, conscientious objector and student of the radical peacenik folk-singer Joan Baez at her somewhat pretentiously named 'School of Non-Violence' down in Big Sur. But now I was in Basin Street, it was November 19th, 1967 to be exact, the night of my 21st birthday and I was deep in 'muso-hog' heaven, having just witnessed 'Sir Duke' Ellington and his legendary ensemble smoothly gliding into the glorious finale of the evening. My late mother Eileen, who'd flown over just a few days earlier to try and rescue me from the draft had disappeared into the bathroom, (I'd assumed), after Duke's sublime orchestra had wound up proceedings in typically tumultuous and triumphant musical complexity and harmony.

I sat there stunned with exhilaration at the performance in the bosom and bonhomie of my bakery workmates who'd taken me out on the town to celebrate with my all-time favourite musician. To my tongue-tied disbelief and absolutely typical of the spontaneous and irrepressible individual my mother was, bless her, she proudly returned to our table on the arm of the great man himself, who, smiling, placed his elegant silver cane carefully down at my table and sat down next to me. I couldn't believe my eyes. "Mr Ellington has come over to personally congratulate you on your 21st birthday, Philip, How about that?" she said, beaming with pride at her celebrity catch. "Congratulations young man," the legendary jazzman said. Then more thoughtfully; "Tell me, Philip, what have you been doing here in this great country of ours?"

My head, still spinning with the razzle dazzle of the club and the glorious musical moments I had just experienced, like the exuberant brilliance of Johnny Hodges at his best and the entire ensemble of the finest jazzmen on the planet, (and lest we forget, far too many 'Long Island Iced Teas!') haltingly I began to explain why it was I'd come to America in the first place; "I'm an apprentice baker sir, presently working on the night shift at David's Delicatessen on Geary Street just across town. I make cheesecake for the rich." I went on nervously, as if he would know or even care but whatever he thought, the great man stayed around for some time to have a drink with us and in any event, genuinely seemed puzzled that, by just being British, I could still be called-up to do my duty for the US Army.

I must say in retrospect however that my mother was still a striking looking woman in those days and one could detect a twinkle in those beady eyes of his. Whatever, what the hell, the man was sitting down at MY table. "I have a green card and apparently that automatically makes me eligible" I added. "Front-line fodder' in fact, or so I've been told, but the real reason I came to the United States was because I love American music and in my heart of hearts I suppose I would really like to become a songwriter; I guess, I don't know."

I went on to tell Mr Ellington that my father was a WW2 bomber pilot and a gifted pianist, who, before the war had played jazz piano, had met George Shearing a few times and was a contemporary of Britain's highly respected jazz outfit, The Hedley Ward Trio. But whilst on secondment for the RAF after the war, he was killed in Africa in a tragic flying accident on his 27th birthday when I was three years old.

Going into music professionally in England in the sixties just wasn't a serious career choice back then and even though I'd started writing songs and playing a few halls and clubs with my friends, I'd never really considered it something I could make a living at. More of an enthusiastic hobby I guess. So, for distinct and pertinent reasons that will become apparent later; I decided, instead, to go for the acceptable, if not rather dull occupation of a bakery industry apprenticeship, something that might pay the bills and provide a reasonable but no doubt, unprepossessing future.

Like many young people at that time, I was confused and ultimately unsure of what I really wanted to do with my life. Along with the imminent threats of nuclear devastation and the shocking assassinations of President Kennedy, his brother Bobby and civil rights campaigner Martin Luther King, evil and dark forces were abroad. But there was also the burgeoning possibility of a new world order and a 'times they are a' changin' mentality amongst young people that music spearheaded. So while some of my more academically gifted friends were university-bound, it was with a tinge of regret I resigned myself to go for the safe option of a trade in the bakery industry with one proviso; I would take a year out and hitch hike across America. But tonight, at last, I had more than an inkling that things might not work out that way after all.

So it came to be that at my 21st birthday celebration in San Francisco, arguably the greatest jazz legend of all time, paused, looked me in the eye and said quite deliberately and seriously the following words I have never quite forgotten; "Philip, listen to me, go back to England, follow your star and play music young man. This is why you're here."

Duke Ellington was at my table telling me what to do with the rest of my life and who was I to argue? It was a moment you really don't ignore, so I thought to myself; "Right I'll do that then! "

Chapter 3
Flight of Darkness

"She's mad, but she is magic.
There's no lie in her fire"
(Charles Bukowski)

"Look, darling, there's my picture with Mel Tormé in the newspaper," she proudly showed me one day after school, thereafter displaying the Birmingham Evening Mail glossy 10 by 8's in silver frames on the mantelpiece.

"Why is your hair purple mum?" I enquired flatly, as kids often do, at once pricking her innocent dreams of briefly entertained Manhattan sophistication.

One day in a chemist's shop a few days after being given the keys to a council flat in Walsall near Birmingham, Eileen, with me in tow like Paddington Bear, was approached by a stranger who told her in a very matter-of-fact manner that although he could not be seen, (describing my father down to the brass buttons on his RAF officer's uniform), he nevertheless was 'as real as day' and standing very close by. He wanted my mother and me to know, beyond doubt, that he would always be there for us both and that we would always be provided for. Although deeply unsettling at the time, the intervention by a complete stranger in a shop seemed authentic and a source of comfort to my mother and whether entirely genuine or otherwise, over the years this story became a powerful family myth.

From quite a tender age I became aware of how different she was and how others would regard Eileen whenever she walked into a room. Taking account of some wild Irish ancestry she could be as regal or as unpredictable as a Killarney thoroughbred, and at that time, only accentuated by what she saw as her unfairly reduced circumstances. But she was blessed with original thought, huge genuine warmth and uncompromising truthfulness. My mother also bore a more-than-passing resemblance to the pre-Hollywood Marilyn Monroe, and at times in manner and aloofness, perhaps more akin to a very exacting Bette Davis! I loved her with all my heart and still miss her every day.

During our stay in Walsall, for a short time, Eileen worked as a manicurist at the then highly fashionable Steiner's Hairdressers in New Street, Birmingham. Due to her looks and outgoing personality, my mother was immediately picked out as the model for a new hairstyle to celebrate the arrival of famous US crooner, Mel Tormé. In the days when everything from 'over the pond' was felt to be glamorous and exciting, Mel was appearing in cabaret in the Midlands and the extravagant hairstyle entitled "Velvet Fog" was created especially in honour of Mel's trademark smooth vocal tones.

Like some of her other jobs, this latest one didn't last very long. I'd be off school with some sort of ailment or other and taking the odd afternoon or morning off to look after me was not tolerated kindly, her being a single mother and all; not like it is today in the world of commerce, enterprise and sex equality. Eileen had a succession of dead-end jobs, usually having abruptly ended with the latest turndown of a male superior's inappropriate advances.

In post-War Britain when eligible men were either married or, for obvious reasons, in short supply, widows like my mother, especially of the more glamorous type, were either shunned and rejected by their jealous counterparts or 'hit on' by otherwise spoken-for males. In bleak post-war Birmingham, my mother stood out like a sore thumb. "Oooh she's lovely your mum, Philip, so elegant and glamorous like a film star," friendly Mrs Capewell told me once in the Edith Street corner shop. "Tuppence-worth of bloody paint, I don't know who she thinks she is," an old crone cackled on the 75 bus as she embarked, as if upon the First Class ramp of the Queen Mary, or just off the set of 'Breakfast At Tiffany's'. In reality, it was the grim rain-spattered Spon Lane bus stop to Smethwick.

What a difference a few years make. After WWII had taken its toll, our small family unit returned to England along with the thousands of other military personnel and their families, having lived in military accommodation in Germany. We were happy with our lot even though times were hard. My family initially stayed for a short time with my maternal grandmother at her house at 14 Edith Street in West Bromwich. My Dad was then posted to RAF Little Rissington, a beautiful Cotswold village in Gloucestershire where, due to extreme shortages of accommodation, we were billeted in a caravan up near the air base. To this, I shall return dear reader, as later in life, moved back there again for a few years but that, as they say, is another story.

My father applied for and was eventually offered, a much sought-after job flying for B.O.A.C. now known the world over as British Airways. As ever, and true to form, he came top of the class in every department. It was a good job because, as one can appreciate, there were vast numbers of pilots looking for jobs now the war had ended. First, he had to serve out a final year in the RAF, so to fill in time, took up a commission in Rhodesia teaching young pilots to fly for the Rhodesian Air Force. We were going to live in Bulawayo in what is now known as Zimbabwe. He was to be stationed at Heaney Air Force base just outside the town and detached accommodation, transport and servants were to be provided for his young family. Tickets were immediately booked on HMS Pretoria Castle on the Union Castle Shipping Line from Southampton to Cape Town, and a new life in a lovely house in Africa beckoned. The circumstances and events of my young life were already conspiring to ensure that for me, the life of a nomad and one of constant change seemed to be on the cards. My 'Karma' if you will.

My earliest memories, were of exotic animals, huge spiders bigger than my head, naughty baboons stealing from our brand new Fortnum's picnic hamper; my father lost in thought sitting upright on the edge of the bed in the dawn light; Amos, our servant boy's colossal smile as wide as the moon, the daily ice cream seller from the ice box on his bike, and Kudus, extremely large deer, (although admittedly at age 3, everything was huge), sticking their munching heads through our open nursery school window when we were supposed to be having our afternoon sleep in the intense heat of African daylight. Impressions gained from my mother over the years that were to follow were of enjoyable social gatherings, laughter in the sunlight, cocktail parties and mess hall dances with the other young service couples and their families. Everyone was thrilled and relieved to be so far away from the thin gruel of grim post-War Britain.

All that suddenly changed, however. On my Father's 27th birthday while teaching a student pilot to fly, the aircraft in which they were flying crashed killing them both instantly.

Back in 2011 in the middle of a Sailor tour of Germany, I'd just come off stage after a particularly good show in Essen. Leaving the venue on our way to the tour bus we signed the usual autographs and one of the fans, a woman, of around 30 or so, took me to one side and handed me a large and ornate-looking photo album. "Look inside Phil," she said proudly and I did. On the front cover was a picture of the Cathedral at Münster, Germany with the town's heraldic shield, and I immediately told her this was the town where I was born. "I know," she said with a smile, though a little disconcertingly I thought at the time.

"Turn ze page", (honestly, this is what she said), and again I did. This time it was a picture of a very old and imposing building surrounded by a beautiful park. It was a hospital; the B.A.O.R. (British Army on the Rhine) military hospital to be more precise. Surprised, I gave her a questioning look. The girl then said; "This is where you were born Phil" Then a pause; "Turn ze page!" Things were starting to get weird; I'd been to Germany countless times over the years and was quite used to the well-meaning intensity of some of the fans over there. On the next page was a close-up shot of a window on the outside of the same building, "Don't tell me" I said; "Yes" she interjected enthusiastically, "Ze very room you were born in!" "I really don't wish to know any more," I said, trying to make a joke out of it. But I was serious, as what would be next? 'Ze forceps' perhaps and god knows what else!

Eventually saying 'Auf Wiedersehen', getting on the bus with the rest of the chaps I turned and said; "If it had been a few days earlier I would have been born in Brussels!"

My mother and father met in the Midlands heavy industrial town of West Bromwich during the War, he, Flt Lt Philip George Pickett, a dashing RAF pilot home on leave from bombing missions over Germany, and she, Eileen Elizabeth Horton, a driver for the Red Cross Ambulance Service, tall, blonde and a real 'looker'. A German bombing raid had been in full flow over the High Street in 'West Brom' and among a few other stragglers who hadn't made it to the bomb shelter in time, they dived into a shop front arcade to dodge falling masonry, two attractive strangers suddenly finding themselves together and laughing at the madness of it all. The attraction was instant; they fell in love and quickly became an item, cutting a glamorous swathe through the otherwise extremely dour Black Country town.

Earlier in the war, Philip had flown low-level sorties on his bombing missions. The psychological impact of this type of warfare, as it was with many other young men in their early twenties who were taking such incredible risks every night, in addition to killing hundreds of people by their actions, was incredibly damaging. Sometimes these young guys, tortured by what they were being asked to do would beg their superior officers not to go up again; consequently, they'd have "LMF" stamped on their files; insulting and humiliating initials that stood for "Lack of moral fibre".

After this ordeal, they would be sent to teams of psychiatrists for assessment, and if necessary, treatment. Then just a few nights later, they'd be up there again going to hell and back. That is if they were lucky. A lot of them, the majority, in fact, weren't. It is impossible now to imagine the stress and fear those young men, like my father who was only twenty-two went through almost every night. He was a daredevil though, apparently, a swashbuckling character who would always drive the best cars and motorbikes, except no one, including his parents, ever knew where he got the money from. But get it he did, and always dressed in the finest clothes, was top in the class, that kind of thing. Definitely nothing like me at all!

According to my Uncle Mike who was just a young lad at that time and who hero-worshipped his dapper brother-in-law, Philip was quick-witted and always there with a succinct and well-timed phrase that was disarming, and usually very funny; more than a match, therefore, for his often fiery and independent-minded girlfriend Eileen. As if all this wasn't enough, to top it all he was a fabulous pianist, known in the local area and further afield as Phil "Body and Soul" Pickett due to his signature rendition of one of the classic jazz hits of the day.

Until the war came along, however, his parents, mainly his dad, insisted that he give up his musical aspirations and go to work at Kendrick and

Jefferson, the West Bromwich printing firm where my grandfather, Edwin Thomas Pickett had his sights on becoming a director.

My mother, on the other hand, was considered by Philip's father, an aspiring middle-class executive type, to be a little 'below the salt' although they looked so magnificent together, no one could deny them their happiness at being in love at such a dark time in history when every night could have been their last together. Eileen had endured quite a hard life up to meeting her husband-to-be. Her father, Bertie Horton, a political activist and conscientious objector who was partial to the odd drink - and Irish to boot, had walked out on his young family just before she was born, never to be seen again.

The infamous Bertie was my maternal grandfather therefore and the missing piece in my family jigsaw. Eileen desperately wanted to become an artist and seemed to possess an effortless natural talent for the subject, sailing through the entrance exam and was subsequently granted a bursary scholarship at Birmingham College of Art. She would have given anything to go, but times were brutally hard for the family and her mother refused to allow her to take up the scholarship, as, among other things, there was no one around to look after her younger sibling, Michael, a child by her mother's second marriage. Besides, at the end of each threadbare week, wages on the kitchen table were the only priority from everyone who was able to work just to keep the home fires burning. It was not all bombs and misery however; despite the fact the country was at war.

I will recount one story of their early life together, a little indelicate perhaps as apparently it was the night I was conceived, but which I suppose could be considered relevant, as, (a) the book is, after all about me, (b) is true, and (c) amusing and entertaining, in addition to, (d) revealing something of the kind of chap my father was, although you, dear reader will be the ultimate judge.

Very high up in the Top Ten of Pickett tales of family legend is the following story, which, in fact, only a few years ago whilst down in Cornwall, was verified by a third party. A, by now very old gentleman, who came from the same village and who then was a small boy, recognised me in the pub and vividly recounted this story about my old man as it had clearly caused a sensation back in the day and had got into all the local newspapers. The old boy even remembered the registration number on my father's motor car; 6 BRL (there was very little to do in those days!)

Temporarily escaping the smokestacks of The Black Country, Philip's young bride had travelled down to Cornwall on the train to "meet the folks" who had by this time, as they described it, 'left the rat race far behind' in West Bromwich and were now running the local village Post Office and general stores in Crowlas, near Ludgvan, close to Mounts Bay and Penzance. Towards the end of the war, my father had been on top secret 'ops' over

Germany and was planning to come down to Cornwall to take some leave and spend some 'rest and relaxation' time with his new bride. So, flying down to RAF St Mawgan (Newquay) in a huge noisy American Mitchell bomber, on the way down decided to surprise, and no doubt impress Eileen with an impromptu 'fly-past' skimming the rooftops of Crowlas High Street. Looking at a map, one can see that this is quite a diversion from St Mawgan! The RAF was very strict about these things, however, and 'number one' did not like their young pilots frightening the locals unnecessarily. Looking at the same map, you will also see that St Michael's Mount is very close by, a detail that is relevant to this story.

The low rumbling of a very large American bomber plane heralded its eventual arrival overhead by several minutes, suddenly roaring over the rooftops of Crowlas almost at a 90-degree angle from the vertical and my father jubilantly waving a map out of the cockpit window in his sweetheart's honour. Everyone in the village came out to see the spectacle after which he turned around and carried out a repeat performance. Naturally, Eileen thought this was hilarious and was terribly impressed, although some of the locals, not so. Many more enjoyed the spectacle though and finally, when banking away over Marazion, the warplane appeared to narrowly miss the iconic castle ramparts atop St Michael's Mount, whereupon its, by now, furious and apoplectic, occupant, Lord St Levan, immediately telephoned friends in high places at the War Office 'up Country' in the nation's capital. All hell broke loose for the young pilot on his eventual arrival at Newquay. Flt Lt Pickett was summarily hauled over the carpet by the RAF top brass and 'grounded' for a month - which on this occasion actually suited him rather well!

Almost exactly to the day, nine months later my mother was on her way to Brussels to meet her husband and give birth to 'yours truly' just after the end of the war. Due to bad weather, however, her plane was diverted to Münster in Germany, so I was born there instead; at the B.A.O.R. Hospital in Münster, Northern Germany, on November 19th, 1946 during one of the coldest winters in history.

Three short year's later when we were living in Bulawayo, it was my father's 27th birthday and consequently, he was in a dash to get home in his shiny red Willis motor car for a "surprise" party my mother had arranged. His many friends, neighbours and colleagues were hiding in various wardrobes and cupboards all over the place.

That day he had been teaching a Rhodesian Air Force student pilot named Beresford, a young chap of 21, to fly on instruments only. In those days this involved pulling a canvas hood over the cockpit to simulate night flying. By the time my father realised they were in serious trouble, ripping off the canvas cover and grabbing the controls, it was too late. Apparently, all he could do was narrowly avoid crashing into a school. Both pilots died instantly.

To add to the drama and catastrophe of this already tragic event, it turned out that Beresford, who earlier had failed his flying exam, waved my father down in his car just as he was driving out of the airfield gate on his way home and pleaded to be taken up "just one more time".

Philip relented and agreed to give the student another chance, this small act of compassion and generosity costing him his life, Eileen, her husband and this small lad in Africa, his dad.

Prior to returning to England, (hastily as the MOD, then as now, are notoriously unsentimental about the death of their personnel), my mother drove me to the edge of Victoria Falls, and as she once told me, would have ended it all for both of us had it not been for the low sunlight catching a smile in her small son's eyes sitting happily in the passenger's seat next to her. Relating this to my songwriter friend Simon Darlow (he of 'Slave To The Rhythm' fame) my tale eventually became the inspiration for a song we wrote together called unsurprisingly, 'Victoria Falls'.

At only three years old, however, I was far too young to have figured out for myself, or would have been told in those days, the enormity of what had happened. But no doubt I might have been dimly aware of an inexplicable and uneasy cloud of darkness spreading over what had previously been a happy, bright confident day on the African Veldt.

In the tragic aftermath, my mother Eileen was unceremoniously obliged only a few days later to fly far away from all the servants, civility and security of a colonial life in the African sun. She stepped down from the BOAC Stratocruiser with small dependent in tow and walked across the tarmac of Atlee's damp penny-pinched war-torn England to a threadbare widow's pension and a highly uncertain future.

Chapter 4
Romance Revisited

A round the early fifties when I was 6 or 7 years old in any one of a number of small rented digs we stayed in, sometimes in the middle of the night, my mother would wake me up by playing Gershwin's 'Porgy & Bess', a Sinatra, or a Billy Holiday tune on the gramophone, which is when I now realise, I must have become familiar with all of the musicals and hit songs of the day. She would often like to dance around the living room with a cigarette in one hand and a drink in the other, as often simply didn't want the night to end; no doubt contemplating the happy, and sad memories, all of which were brought back to life by the superb musical performances and songwriting of that time, even though, I have to say sometimes I just wanted to go back to sleep!

Later on in life, of course, I also realised this might have been considered an unusual way for a young lad to be brought up, but felt it totally natural at the time as one does in life and anyway, I always loved her to bits. She could do no wrong.

Now it was 1953 and I was seven. Eileen met a man called Philip Sutton. She managed to land a telephonist job at Bradford's Bakery - The Home Of Sunblest Bread, opposite the Albion's football ground in West Bromwich. Initially seeking a better-paid position as a typist, she was 'welshed on' by a jealous fellow employee as an unqualified impostor. Philip Sutton, the managing director of the company, became aware of her plight and attempted to console his betrayed and emotional employee. "This world isn't run by people who type" he assured my mother, "Don't worry, you do know how to work a switchboard don't you?" She didn't but there was a spark of something. She nodded affirmatively.

Son and heir to his father's bakery business, Sutton's of Coventry, Philip managed the entire Midlands Region but was already on his way to eventually taking over the whole of the UK Sunblest Group. He was an amiable, rotund, tough-but-sensitive man in his late forties, extremely successful, diligent and worldly. One day, and although respectably married with two grown-up daughters, he offered to give his new employee a lift home after work in his gleaming company maintained Rover 90 automobile to, in his words, "Save her catching the bus". They fell into an affair, a passionate, forbidden, and at times, difficult relationship that would endure for the best part of the next seventeen years. During this time he became the person who would change the landscape of both our fragile lives forever, and in the most part, for the better.

Known to me as 'Uncle Phil' and, although besotted with his Eileen, he also took a genuine interest in my development becoming a surrogate, although half-absent, father figure. Bringing his considerable powers of organisation to my mother's more fragmented and dysfunctional view of the world, he contacted the RAF Benevolent Fund securing me a private education. Philip then assisted financially in the purchase of a brand new house near the school. At arm's length, he hauled me out by my ears from a snotty-nosed, street-fighting, primary school in the arse-end of a dismal Birmingham suburb, depositing me in a pristine but scratchy uniform to my new seat of learning, 'Wylde Green College For Boys' in the leafy mortgage-free avenues of 'proper posh' Sutton Coldfield.

The clandestine and at times fiery relationship did, of course, raise a few eyebrows in post-war Birmingham causing 'kippers and curtains' to twitch in a more clenched and socially conventional era.

Most of the time I didn't pay that much attention to the fact he was already married, usually explaining him away to the more inquisitive and suspicious as a "family-friend" or "business associate" of my grandfather. In the end, he never left his wife and family to live with my mother permanently, as he often confided in me he would have chosen to, but rather maintained the status quo and artifice of the 'solid family-man' image essential to the ideals and company ethics of his billionaire mentor and boss, Sir Garfield Weston, owner of Associated British Foods.

In what now seems a far-off age, these family 'arrangements' were, perhaps much more common than the present day harsh scrutiny of an all-seeing, all-knowing and connected world would ever permit. There was 'wiggle-room' in those days. It was wrong of course and deceitful perhaps, but humans will always find a way to love one another and they did. Whilst growing up, therefore, I became the unlikely recipient of an extraordinary storehouse of his knowledge of business, and a personal philosophy of management and wealth-creation, which he was always attempting to share and explain to his 'bring-along' son. Whether I was ultimately successful in applying this wisdom to my life and business affairs will be left to the reader to judge, some no doubt with a wry smile

He often relished playing 'Mr Higgins' to his 'My Fair Lady' and her wide-eyed offspring, delighting in their un-jaded enthusiasm for his Pygmalion world, frequently being invited to share his other passions of musical theatre, ballet and foreign travel. Philip Sutton was an extraordinarily generous man to a fault. A certain healthy enjoyment and celebration of refined living developed over this period, throughout the late fifties & sixties which for better and sometimes worse - as my close friends would attest, seems to have expensively persisted to the present day!

After leaving College and already a huge music fan, particularly of The

Beatles and local band Spencer Davis, all I really wanted to do with my life was play and write music. At that time, however, it didn't really seem a viable career choice and therefore I decided, after Uncle Phil's powerful and convincing intervention, that my best chance for a future would be to enter management training and become an apprentice in the Bakery Industry.

A few years later, after returning from America with Duke Ellington's words still in my mind I did eventually decide to finally make my break into a music career. Uncle Phil took it very kindly and was; on the whole, very supportive, only ever seeking the best for me.

One bright summer's day in July 1970, I came home on the bus with my poet friend Mick Phillips from the Bull Ring Antique Market in Birmingham. I was looking forward to showing Eileen a 'stonker' of a bargain book of Napoleonic poetry by Longfellow and some other dead poets I'd found going for a song. It was leather-bound with a pretty engraving on the front cover and very, very old. I was very pleased with myself for having found it. On opening the front door, however, and seeing the stricken white face of my mother, my blood froze immediately sensing the worst thing in the world must have just happened: "Your Uncle Phil had a brain haemorrhage on holiday with his family in Elba" she cried out like a stricken animal. "He jumped into the swimming pool at the hotel and died instantly. I only had a card from him this morning. It was on the bloody news for Christ's sake!" She evaporated in convulsive sobs and physically appeared to diminish, folding in on herself against a cruel world. I realised that, of course, my mother was now a 'widow' for the second time in her life.

Walking around in a stupefied and grief-ridden daze for what must have been at least a couple of hours, I noticed I was still holding the poetry book, dispiritedly dangling half-open at my side. Vacantly my eyes gradually focused on the top of the page realising something deep in my unconscious must have randomly selected that place in the book. My heart nearly stopped and in a tingling shock, with hairs standing up at the back of my neck, I suddenly tuned-in to the words on the page. I couldn't believe my eyes. It was a poem about Napoleon's exile on a Mediterranean island written in the 'first person'. At the very the top of the page, the poem read...

"Though I die in this far off Isle of Elba..."

The book was sadly lost in the upheavals that were soon to come, but the long poem in the style of a letter written to a loved one, spoke of saying goodbye, urging its recipient not to grieve or reflect on what might have been, but rather recall the intense love and glories of a life well-lived.

Although still, a sunny July day dragged way down by the sadness and shock of the moment, a dark cloud deep in the soul almost imperceptibly appeared to lift; "Let's have a cup of tea Philip," my mother said.

Chapter 5
Leaving On A Jet Plane

"Take this radio Philip, you'll be able to listen to the men on the moon as you drive up to London". With strained jollity, my mother bounded out of the house with a transistor radio in one arm and a large white plaque under the other. "Oh and this sweetheart, you must take this as well. It was your Grandad's. It's an heirloom". She carried out the dusty old St George and Dragon relief that had been in our hall for years. My ancient sky blue 2CV shuddered at the sight of it, already heaving at the weight of all my worldly possessions swaying like a top–heavy wardrobe on a coiled spring.

"For God's sake mum, there's absolutely no more room. I bet the astronauts don't even have this much clobber. Look, I can't even change gear!" "Stupid bloody gearstick anyway" she observed. "Why can't the French make cars?"

Struggling, we vainly attempted to cram everything into my old Citroën, pushing and shoving like rush hour operatives at Tokyo Underground. Although managing to balance the radio on the dashboard, St George would definitely not be slaying any dragons in my new Battersea bed-sit for a while.

Both on the cusp of tears, all I really wanted to do was to drive off up the hill and get on with the next phase of my life, namely a job I'd been offered to arrange song demos at Chappell's Publishers in Bond Street, London.

The moon landing on this of all days had conspired to lend a heightened sense of emotion to the occasion and like the capital D in Destiny, made every thought word and deed in my hoped-for low-key exit pregnant with drama and significance. In the silence between the words, I recalled Kennedy's inspired prediction to put a man on the Moon by the end of the sixties.

That day, a bright blue hopeful morning 20th July 1969 had finally arrived and I was leaving home in Birmingham, England to seek fame and fortune in the big city. I couldn't believe I was finally escaping the orbit of a grey, mapped-out, predictable lifetime, a '9 to 5' slave in an industrial Midland town and taking a fearless leap into the unknown towards my real burning passion in life, music.

My previous attempt to leave home in 1967, when following my star to America on Cunard's Queen Elizabeth only led to me being obliged to return prematurely from America to Brum, my only alternative to Saigon, having been drafted for frontline duties in Vietnam. Whilst in the USA I'd ridden boxcars to San Francisco in a Kerouac inspired, journey of discovery, hitchhiking like a hobo and visiting on the way, a scene of almost mythical tragedy; Kennedy's assassination in downtown Dallas on 22nd November 1963. This had become one of the defining moments of modern history, and like the Holy Grail, I was moved to see it all for myself.

The following is an extract of a conversation with Keith Hayward at the Groucho Club London, September 2015:

"As a sixties teen I had an enormous passion for music. I started to follow bands around like The Spencer Davies Group, and Steve Winwood in particular, who I couldn't believe could be that good. His prodigious talent was beyond anything I'd ever witnessed first hand. It was such an exciting time in Birmingham; as well as the 'Spencers' we had Jeff Lynne and The Idle Race, Roy Wood and The Move, and The Moody Blues to name a few. There just seemed to be a real movement of music in the City, something really going on. I remember I went to see the Rolling Stones at Birmingham Town Hall in '64, it was one of the most exciting times of my life. It was like a nuclear explosion going off in my head. "Where did they buy clothes like that?" Anyway, it was on the bus to Tamworth College the next morning after seeing the Stones that I asked my friend Mick Robbins to join the band on bass, as had already earmarked Dave Peters, Paul Warren on drums and me on lead guitar and backing vocals. Going to record stores, like the Diskery in Birmingham with my mates and listening to music where Erskine T the DJ would play us stuff that we hadn't heard before. Dave Peters, who I grew up with, was a great influence turning me on continuously to new sounds and artists. Being relatively wealthier than the rest of us, he also had the best record collection which was a great source of material for the band. Howlin' Wolf, John Lee Hooker and Ike and Tina Turner were all amazing artists he introduced me to. He had a pretty decent voice too and played a mean harmonica, so a 'shoe-in' as the lead singer for my eventual band.

I remember hearing Tamla Motown at the Diskery and thought what the hell's that? The Beatles were very influential in that way too as they had recorded quite a lot of Tamla stuff on their first two albums. It was just a revolutionary time for a young person to be interested in music. It was special and we were just learning stuff. I thought, can I do this? It wasn't like a profession; it was a romantic dream and being a fan of the likes of the Beatles who seemed to release albums with great regularity 2 or 3 times a year. Stunning originality in quality and output and I just kept thinking, where did this all come from? It was a fascinating time so I thought that is what I'm going to do! So I formed my first band and called it The Blues Unit. R&B was all the rage then!

Well, enough about that.

I am a left-hander and I hadn't really sussed out how to play by reversing the strings on my guitar, but I was also starting to write songs, in an amateurish sort of way, and playing folk clubs. I saw myself as a budding songwriter really, so I decided that's where my future lay..."

***

When I got back to England in 1968, I continued following in my stepfather's footsteps as if by duty rather than real desire, but by now was a qualified baker having completed my apprenticeship. At first, I went back to working in bakeries again, just as my ex-band mates from The Blues Unit, Dave Peters and the others decided to go to university or to pursue proper careers in more sensible avenues.

I decided to soldier on, however, this time with my new friend and music partner, Paddy Maguire. Through this partnership, I sent some songs to Stuart Reid who worked for Edwin H Morris, a famous old New York Broadway Music Publishers in the Chappell's Building in London. This was in the heady days when the music business had impresarios and entrepreneurs with big offices and grand pianos and fresh flowers delivered every day. It certainly was a very different type of business to the one today and now reminds me of the transition between the music business of the forties and fifties, into the sixties and the era of the singer-songwriters like Lennon and McCartney and Jagger and Richards. Yes, we still had the traditional Tin Pan Alley songwriters churning out three-minute songs for music publishers to sell as sheet music, or for the likes of Tom Jones and Englebert Humperdinck who were massive stars, who relied on the songsmiths to write songs. But the times were changing.

I was forever sending songs to London and I'm sure I became quite a novelty. I can imagine the office boys saying to each other; "Hey, here's a song by that bloke Phil Pickett again - or is it a sponge cake this time?" as they laughingly opened the cake box I'd dutifully wrapped my latest reel to reel recording in. Whether it was the songs or my ability to bake cakes I still don't know, but I was eventually invited to London

"Yes me, I was going to London! The land of promise where the streets are paved with gold, to follow my dream etc." It seemed like a different world compared to the land where I lived.

***

Paddy was a real charmer, typical of guys of Irish extraction; a smoky charismatic voice, the gift of the gab and a physically imposing presence. My future sweetheart and the girl I was to later marry, (indeed who I was yet to even meet), was born in the house next door to the Maguires in Chevasse Road, Sutton Coldfield. Paddy and I formed a very effective musical partnership playing in many of the folk clubs and pubs in and around

Birmingham. I was always happiest writing the songs, singing backup vocals à la Simon and Garfunkel and teaching Paddy the chords and arrangements on some often quite obscure covers.

For instance, Paddy and I were one of the first to play Simon and Garfunkel's, 'America' locally and the tune, apparently written on Crewe Station at 3 am, was a real showstopper. So thus began for me, a real interest in the curation of material to copy or rearrange that would stand me in good stead throughout my career in music. Paddy was an incredible front man and performed lovely versions of 'Dirty Old Town' and 'The Wild Rover' in addition to songs of mine, such as 'The Gardener', 'Sit By You', 'Loser Takes All' and 'Harlequin and Palomino'. I was more than content to arrange and play the music, not as the 'star up front', but the one making it all happen 'back of house'. That was my role and the one I seemed to thrive in.

A breakthrough song I'd written and was desperate to record was called 'Time For Me', a mellow and wistful ballad that Paddy sang beautifully. I'd also started promoting my own folk club just outside Sutton Coldfield called The Showboat and even wrote a theme song, especially for the opening night. I decked the place out, as far as limited means would allow, to resemble the ambience and flavour of a Mississippi River Boat steamer, (just like the one used in the 'Karma Chameleon' video I now realise, but that's another story and fifteen years hence!)

Chris Barsby, my best friend at that time, was not musical in any way but was always a more than enthusiastic supporter of my early musical endeavours. He was a gifted artist so offered to paint a magnificent stage backdrop conjuring up the intended visuals and atmosphere perfectly. The idea was that I would book the headline acts then, every week, Paddy and I would support whichever artists I'd manage to cajole to come and play in Sutton Coldfield

The first artist I booked was an amazing young guitar player and vocalist, brand new on the scene but with a growing reputation, called Ralph McTell. Ralph was world-class; you could see that in an instant, even though he hadn't made it big at that point. Paddy and I were really nervous going on after him but the audience loved it, especially when Ralph rejoined us on stage for the finale. The debut night was a huge success. The following week I'd booked the Ian Campbell Folk Group, an established and respected outfit and 'the real deal' in traditional music circles. Their bassist was Dave Pegg, a rising star in his own right on the Midlands music scene having been in (or joined slightly after) the well-known Brum band, The Uglies with Steve Gibbons.

Anyway to me, a hopeful amateur, Dave was a celebrity and somehow I had a feeling that he might be able to advise me on how, when and where I might be able to record 'Time For Me' as I hadn't got a clue how to go about it. Nervous of bothering him, I realise now I shouldn't have worried as he was Brummie charm personified, incredibly approachable and couldn't have been kinder or more considerate. Dave Pegg immediately displayed the warmth and a deep friendship that has persisted to this day.

A few years later I went along with Dave to Mother's, Birmingham's famous club in Erdington, to see Fairport Convention. This was the night they offered him the bass gig for the Fairports. My hero, Steve Winwood had also just offered him a job too and Dave asked my opinion on which gig he should go for. Needless to say, as Steve was 'God' to me, I pushed him in that direction, but looking back, wisely he made the right decision by going with the Fairports, the band he still leads almost fifty years later.

Bearing in mind we'd never met before and that I was an obvious beginner, Dave not only gave me the number and address of the place we could record my song but even offered to come and play on it for free. I didn't know people like this existed!

After recording 'Time For Me' (with Paddy singing lead, Paul Warren on drums, Mick Kinsella, flute, Paddy and I on guitars & Dave P singing backing vocals), we sat around all night playing the track over and over again, congratulating each other on how well it had turned out. 'World musical domination' beckoned and this was by far the best experience of my life. I was convinced beyond doubt that the song would open all the doors, the Beatles would hear it and love it... it was all so easy! Well, none of this happened of course, but the experience of recording 'Time For Me' had the effect of filling up the tank with a million gallons of the highest octane fuel and would be more than enough (after a few more knock-backs!) to get me on to the next stage of my music career.

A friend of a friend heard the track in London (received 'natch' in the customary cake box!) and lo and behold, on the strength of it, a gentleman called Ian Ralfini, who ran Warner Bros Records, and his compatriot, Martin Wyatt, along with a tall and painfully polite chap who would eventually become a close friend, Yes's arranger, Tony Cox, were all coming up together from London to see Paddy and Phil (great name wasn't it?) in Brum.

We were fourth on the bill to an up-and-coming band called Fleetwood Mac at Mother's in Erdington - THE place to play for any aspiring band or artist anywhere north of Watford. Incidentally, I thought it strange at the time that the headline act, who'd arrived earlier dressed very smartly in Carnaby Street suits, changed into rough old denim before going on stage. Funny the things you remember sometimes!

I forgot to mention, and should add that in addition to Simon and Garfunkel's 'America' and a number of my own songs, I'd added a couple of new arrangements of then obscure songs I had curated from a record I'd found in a bargain bin in San Francisco. The album was called The Great Mandella by Peter Paul and Mary, from which Paddy and I covered the title track and one other. Playing bottom of the bill for an audience who had come to see shit-stonking R&B from their favourite blues band and way before Mac's later platinum record incarnations, we did okay but let's face it, the audience was pretty disinterested. But at least our renditions were good, although Paddy and I fretted it might have put our London visitors off having come all that way to see us. We needn't have worried though. In the dressing room afterwards, all three executives were beaming with enthusiasm and loved our show.

"What was that song, about three songs into the set, about a jet plane Phil?" Ian Ralfini asked, "Bloody fabulous tune, when did you write that one?" "Er," I stumbled, "I didn't I'm afraid, wish I had though. It's a track I found on an album by a folk music trio called Peter Paul and Mary when I was over in America. I rearranged the song for us. It's called 'Leaving On A Jet Plane'. Do you like it?" Martin and Ian exchanged knowing glances and looked very pleased with themselves. Being new to "the music business" I was a little confused. Ian looked over to Martin Wyatt and said, "Peter Paul and Mary, that's on our US label, isn't it? "Listen, guys, loved the show and will be in touch soon, "Ian said; "We must definitely get you guys down to London to do some recording. Thanks again." And they were out of the door.

That was the last we heard until a few weeks later when 'Leaving On A Jet Plane' by Peter Paul and Mary stormed into the charts and was suddenly all over the airwaves. After hearing my arrangement of the song at Mother's in Erdington, Ian and Martin at Warner Bros had gone ahead and released the track as a single which eventually went all the way up to number 2 in the UK chart.

In America meanwhile, inspired by its UK discovery, 'Leaving on a Jet Plane' originally written by John Denver, turned out to be Peter, Paul and Mary's biggest (and final) hit, becoming their only No. 1 on the Billboard Hot 100 chart in the United States. The song also spent three weeks atop the easy listening chart and got used in commercials for United Airlines in the late seventies. The song also topped the charts in Canada, Ireland and in many other countries.

"Ah," I thought.

Back to the Groucho Club with Keith:

"So there was obviously a lot of goodwill there from Warners towards us because I'd come up with this song that they didn't know they had and made it into a massive hit. It also revitalised all of Peter Paul and Mary's back catalogue and they made millions. So they (Warners) invited us down to London and told Paddy and I they had this song that Cliff Richard had been doing but it was "not quite right for him"; in other words he had rejected it, but we thought if it had been good enough for Cliff to consider, it was good enough for us. So we agreed to do it.

The song was called 'Baby I Could Be So Good At Loving You'. It was a sort of waltz. In the studio for the first time in Bond Street we really thought we'd made it. It was like "leave the car on the double yellow, who cares, this is it! I had never heard music coming out of speakers like that. It was orgasmic and I couldn't get enough of it. The tape machine was going round, 16 or 8 track (must have been 8 then I guess) and I just fell in love with the whole thing. Paddy did the vocal and made a pretty good job of it but they didn't put it out in the end. That was the first time I had been in a London recording studio.

Good to their word, Paddy and I eventually went down to London for a second time at Ralfini and Warner's behest and cost to cut a track in our own right. The song was to be William Blake's 'Jerusalem', the hymn that had affected me so deeply as a little boy on my first day of school in Cornwall and I didn't know why. Tony Cox came up with the idea and booked Advision Studio, then a basement in Bond Street. Again, the whole thing felt like a dream and was beyond exciting as Tony had hired some of the most incredible musicians I'd ever heard; Albert Lee on guitar (a Fender Telecaster of course), the saturnine Pat Donaldson on bass, Tony Kaye from Yes on Hammond and on grand piano, Brian Gascoigne, younger brother of Bamber (Original host of UK TV show *University Challenge*).

I can't remember who played drums but whoever it was, (possibly Pete Gavin from Heads, Hands and Feet and Vinegar Joe fame), he was incredible too. I was humbled that all of these gifted genius musicians were playing on our record. Also I hadn't thought our previous experience down the road at Chappell's studio could be bettered, but how wrong I was. These guys were sensational and it was agreed that the B-side would be a song I'd written called 'Doing The Best I Can' which, if anything, Paddy sang a lot better as knew the song and was not as intimidated as he had been on 'Jerusalem'.

Singing in front of these guys was a pretty awe-inspiring experience for him, I began to realise, and could feel the pressures incumbent on a "front man", which again, I was relieved not to be. However it was a little odd, as there I was, responsible for much of why we were there in the first place, but not actually playing or doing anything, apart, of course, from jumping up and down with enthusiasm like a demented cocker spaniel at everything I heard. Shortly afterwards though, we cut another tune of mine called 'Lay Me Down', a big, brassy gospel ballad in a style I loved to write in, and which was eventually chosen as our first single. (Georgie Fame later heard the song and recorded it, my first real cover by an artist I loved and who I had seen 'live' a few times when he'd come to Birmingham, so that was a real buzz).

We began to work more and more in the clubs around the Midlands.

Then one night when Paddy, a loveable rogue who I adored, but at times had a strange & obtuse sense of humour, proudly announced our next single.

To a packed audience in my hometown, amongst many of our friends, he announced it thus; "This is our first single, 'Lay Me Down' er, actually it's MY first single as the record company only want to sign me," he said. Then chuckled, looked around at me sheepishly and added; "What are you gonna do now Phil?" I was stunned and didn't know where to put myself but gamely carried on until the end of our set. "You bastard" I spat out as we came off stage immediately losing it. "When did you find all this out and why didn't you tell me?" Paddy gave me some flannel and said he thought I knew already but it turned out that Warners had sent him a letter and contract in the post clearly stating they only wanted him to sign on the dotted line, and not the two of us. What was he to do? etc.

It's probably best not to recount my reaction, but in fact, when I'd calmed down, of course, understood from his point of view what a difficult situation he had been placed in too. Truthfully I had felt like a third armpit in the studio in London and was trying to come to terms with exactly what it was I did and what role I would play in this music game. At least early on in my career, I'd had my first - and not to be the last brush with how brutal and unsentimental the music industry can be, and that it's always best, although easier said than done, not to take things too personally. Having said that, after the episode with Paddy and the loss of face involved, I could never bring myself to perform with him on stage again and, although still friends, as a professional unit we parted with the hatchet buried, but the handle still faintly visible in the ground!

Since I'd returned home to Birmingham from my American adventure, things had changed quite significantly in my home town. Drugs, mainly cannabis and LSD now seemed to be omnipresent at every social gathering. Smoking grass and hash had completely taken over the scene and everyone I knew was doing it. I didn't mind at first and, anyway, having lived in San Francisco and smoked my first joint in Haight Ashbury, how 'cred' was that? I initially enjoyed the experience, and I suppose, like all young people, saw myself as a bit of a rebel taking part in forbidden activity, differentiating us, the young generation, from 'grown-ups' and 'straights'.

But in my circle of friends, it was becoming tiresome to see how the ritual of the practice was becoming an end in itself, and the intensity and preoccupation of 'getting high" seemed to a large extent to have eliminated all of the good times and innocent humour we used to enjoy. Parties and gatherings quickly sank into intense concentration around the paraphernalia of weed, followed inevitably by complete communication closure, except perhaps for the occasional knowing goofy grin and a "Yeh... Ma'an", amidst rooms full of acrid smoke. As everyone in Brum knew that I was a baker by profession, several dealers began approaching me to make hash cakes and I even made one with opium once, a long story which ended very badly in the car park at The Belfry after seeing the Bee Gees. But it made me think; 'Hang on a minute, I've got to get out of here and away from of all this!'

Then I seemed to be losing friends left right and centre, as the inevitable experimentation with drugs, went to higher levels and overdoses, car crashes and personality breakdowns ensued, some never really recovering, which upset and disturbed me. What was happening to all my friends and the carefree fun days we had formerly shared together? Several years later I would even lose Paddy through depression brought on, I had always believed, by disillusionment and drug dependency. Eventually, my dear friend committed suicide by drowning in a lake in Sutton Park in 1976. So I made a conscious decision to escape Sutton, and finally, on the potential of the songs, (or so I thought), I landed an interview with Stuart Reid at Edwin H. Morris in Mayfair London.

I got the interview at about the same time as he'd heard my songs through local singer songwriter, Raymond Froggatt in Birmingham. I just went round to the singer's house. I didn't know who he was but it was about 1968 just after I'd returned from America. It was the sort of thing I would do - just turn up at people's houses. Froggatt was quite a big local star at the time and lived in Kingstanding. I found out where he lived, turned up and knocked his door with my cake box full of songs.

Luckily he let me in, made me a cup of tea and told me I should get in touch with Stuart Reid, his publisher. I didn't know what a publisher was then, but I sent the songs off anyway and soon received a letter asking me to come to London. Once again, I thought this was it. I was on my way. I'd written three or four songs by this time and went into Stuart's office with its big curtains and grand piano. I played the songs, but every time the song came to the chorus, his phone seemed to ring so the 'good bit' would be missed; every time. The song would come to an end and he said, "okay got anything else?" so I'd play him the next one and so on. It was frustrating and a bit of an anti-climax.

At the end of the meeting, he said he didn't like the songs at all. "I can see what you're trying to do Phil but you should leave that sort of songwriting to black people. Black people should write songs like that, not kids from Birmingham." (Honestly, that is how they talked in those days!)

He liked the way I arranged things however and said he was going to offer me a job. I was at once taken aback because he didn't like my songs, but he was still offering me a job! Go figure.

All the songs that I played him that day he would eventually hear again over the next few months and would say, "That's brilliant Phil, love it. What's that one called?" That's another rule of the music biz; no one knows what the fuck they are talking about!

Anyway with Reid offering me the job I moved to London. I remember the drive well because it was on the same day that Neil Armstrong had landed on the moon."

***

In common with the whole world, I had been shaken to the core by the constant grainy black and white repeats of Lee Harvey Oswald's deathly rain of fire, which came to represent the passing of all the youthful optimism of Kennedy's Camelot era. Evil was abroad and dark forces stalking the Earth were gaining the upper hand. In retrospect, it was only five short months after good had prevailed, through the steadfastness of the young President in the distinctly possible nuclear confrontation of the Cuban Missile Crisis.

Thankfully, however, today all was hope again in the powerful certainty that perhaps this moon landing would now become the greatest defining moment of that tumultuous decade. A human being was about to set foot on another celestial body for the first time in history. Maybe there could be a "bright new tomorrow" after all.

My mother broke the silence: "Your Nan said they should have gone up when it was full so they'd have more to aim at!" With moist eyes we hugged, no more words. I drove off up the hill London-bound to my new life.

Deciding not to risk the M1 with my fragile insect of ageing Gallic machinery, I took the A5 instead only hitting England's first-ever pristine motorway at Luton and stopped several times on the long journey to look up at the moon. It still seemed completely unfathomable that our species had achieved such a vast miracle of science, fuelled as ever by the dimly understood impulses of Mankind's inner space and with technology and computer power that a contemporary cellphone would dwarf.

It was a really hot day and I had it on the radio in the car all the way down, a very old 2CV that just about made it to London. They had landed on the moon practically as I left Birmingham so they were up there but had not yet got out of the capsule.

Finally crossing Chelsea Bridge, Neil Armstrong was preparing to clamber down the steps from Eagle his lunar module, a full six hours after landing at 11.17am GMT. One more time I stopped the car to look up in awe under the shadow of the upturned billiard table of Battersea Power Station in the golden light of late afternoon.

It was quite late when I finally went up the stairs into my one room bedsit within the mansion flat in Battersea carrying my small radio, suitcase and a mixed bag of emotions. I hurried up the small flight of stairs to turn the key in the lock. Placing my possessions down on the bed, I turned on the radio at the very moment, 5.17pm on 20th July 1969 that Armstrong's voice rang out through the static of space, the immortal words, "That's one small step for man, one giant leap for mankind."

Just at that very moment, it felt great. It was like it was meant to be somehow.

Chapter 6
A Willing Apprentice

S ome of my earliest memories, when I wasn't buried deep in the vaults of E.H Morris listening to tapes and arranging songs, was working with Stuart's assistant, cheery, cockney record plugger and song-seller, Mickey Clarke. Whether trying to get a song played by Ted Beston at BBC Radio 2 in Bond Street, just around the corner or an E.H Morris tune recorded by Cliff Richard, Mickey approached each task as one might selling rides at a fairground attraction. Mickey's malapropisms were also the stuff of music industry legend; quite political in his opinions and of a republican bent he once told me in all seriousness that we were "just prawns in their game."

"We've got a song for Rolf Harris Phil," Mickey said one day. "Come on, he's working over at Olympic Studios. I'll show you how it's done mate" he said conspiratorially to his young wet-behind-the-ears apprentice.

We arrived at the studio and saw ourselves in. Dwarfed inside the vast recording hall behind a bank of microphones was Rolf performing the vocal for a song called 'Two Little Boys', a classic song that soldiers sang in the trenches during the First World War. Mickey pressed the mic button walking past the studio mixing desk and, with an air of familiarity I found embarrassing even on the first day of this new job, said, "Hi Rolfie baby, have I got a hit song for you matey!" Ach, squirm. (This must be 'showbiz' I thought) "Okay Mickey," Rolf said in the terribly familiar Aussie accent, "Good to see you mate. Just let me finish this vocal and I'll be right in."

Rolf Harris sang the song all the way through in one take and after a short silence at the end, almost imperceptibly said, "Was that okay?" It kind of hung in the air until Mickey walked up to the desk next to the engineer again and hesitantly pressed the mic button; "Talking to me Rolf?" he asked the entertainer. "Yeh," Rolf answered, "Was that vocal alright?" Mickey looked over towards me and we both nodded affirmatively. "Sounded great Rolf," Mickey said, and as the engineer wrote on the tape box I noticed after 'Artist', Rolf Harris, and song title; 'Two Little Boys' - that under 'Producer' the session engineer, wrote 'Mickey Clarke'.

The major music industry publication at the time was called Music Week and every few months on the front page in bold writing they ran a 'Top Record Producers' chart. A couple of months after our visit to Olympic, at number three on the front cover, was Arif Mardin, at number two, George Martin and at Number One was... Mickey Clarke, as, it was assumed that the producer of Rolf Harris's massive hit 'Two Little Boys', which had now been at number one for a very long time - was him! Mickey was now an unassailable, platinum hot-property producer in black and white right there on the page, and who suddenly was getting calls from the likes of Diana Ross to come over to America and produce her next record. "You've got Neil Diamond on line one Mickey, shall I say you're in a meeting?" The poor deluded song plugger left E.H Morris in a flurry of newly-purchased chunky gold jewellery, a plethora of wide-boy mohair suits and in a puff of white powder was never seen or heard from again.

One of my favourite songs of that period, and one that appealed to my gospel sensibilities, was Percy Sledge's 'When A Man Loves A Woman', so I was in equal parts, elated and terrified when asked to accompany Percy on a white grand piano a few weeks later at a star-studded Mayfair private party to celebrate his record hitting the top spot in the UK chart.

By the time I sat down at the piano to play the song we had established a real connection and for some reason, I took the liberty to perform it in a much slower and more gospel-like and soulful tempo than the record. When his vocal came in the effect was mesmerising and the room full of agents, publishers, record company people and BBC producers fell silent at the power of the song performed in this new way.

After the show, Percy and I were like old friends and he took me around the room introducing me to everyone as "Wilson Pickett's soul brother". I don't know why but we really hit it off big time. I loved that guy. He was such a lovely character, very quiet and reserved but, like me had a similarly gregarious taste in the fashion of the day. Percy especially loved the bright pink Carnaby Street tie I was wearing. I was very happy to take it off there and then and give it to him, whereupon he did the same with his more sober offering. I don't think I've ever seen anyone quite so pleased and can still see the lovely toothy grin on his face. I've still got his tie somewhere at home.

Day and night it was music all the way and thinking back to the Basin Street Jazz Club in San Francisco, still, only three years earlier and Duke Ellington's timely word in my ear, perhaps his prediction was coming true and that music was really going to be 'it' for me.

One of the publishers at the party suggested I send one of my own songs, again a gospel-tinged ballad called 'Lay Me Down' to Georgie Fame. The song had already been recorded by my Birmingham buddy Paddy Maguire but although a great version, it had not been a hit. Fame was on the lookout for songs for a new album and I was a massive fan of his, having been to many of his gigs with my mates at the Flamingo Club in London's Wardour Street or back in my hometown of Brum at the Whiskey A Go Go.

The Whiskey was above Chetwyns on the corner of John Bright Street and Hill Street and was well-known for live Mod bands and for showing local bands such as The King Bees (who I also loved), Jugs O'Henry, The Moody Blues, Denny Lane, and, oh my God... the best of them all in my opinion, The

Spencer Davis Group starring sixteen year old Steve Winwood. (Here I go again!) Amongst other artists who appeared there (apart from my first band, The Blues Unit who once played a legendary all-nighter there) was The Small Faces, Long John Baldry & The Steam Packet and Gary Farr and The Knockouts.

Georgie Fame used to play virtually all night. They couldn't get him off the small stage until he collapsed with exhaustion, or what was described then as a "lack of stimulation". The place also booked great American acts such as Motown & R&B greats like Sonny Boy Williamson, Martha and the Vandellas and Ike and Tina Turner. All nighters were on Fridays till 8 am Saturday mornings and again on Saturday nights until Sunday morning. The owners Chris & Steve Healey were two great guys, who welcomed club goers dressed in jazz striped coats.

Great Brummie characters of the time frequented The Whiskey, a veritable who's who of Birmingham club goers, they used to pack in nearly 250 townies and mods (of which I was one) onto both floors in those days. (You had to be 'minted' to be a Mod though - in those days the fashions changed practically on the hour!) The place had no fire escapes and only a small front door with narrow wooden steps up to the first and second floors. Live bands were on the first floor and DJ's on the top floor. On busy nights many clubbers were turned away at the door if not considered part of the in-crowd.

People would fall asleep on the wooden floor after they tired from dancing at about 5 am, but the bands and DJ's played on till about 8 am the following morning. The Whiskey attracted people from all over the Midlands, including Coventry and from the London scene to dance and hear live music of the era. Birmingham was very ahead of pop culture in England at that time.

Back at E.H. Morris, I had the extreme good fortune to meet and work with a couple of brilliant songwriter/producers; Harry Vanda and George Young. At that time they were probably the biggest influences on my career to date. George and Harry were also signed to E.H. Morris, along with some other great writers, including lifelong friends, B.A Robertson and Scott English.

After their success with The Easybeats, the writing duo had just arrived back from Australia to work in London, where, (and I can still hear Harry's Dutch accent), "Everything was really going on man!" They were 'churning it out night and day and up to then, frankly, I'd never met such hard-working, totally cool inspired, songwriters and arrangers. We got on famously and the guys started to book me regularly to play the piano or Wurlitzer electric keys on their tunes, one of which was the original demo for 'Love Is In The Air'.

With those guys, it was all about the feel and they liked to keep everything ultra simple. George and Harry knew what they were doing more than anyone I'd ever met in those early London days. "Fuck the megacycles man!" George, in broad Glaswegian brogue, fag in mouth with his feet up on the mixing console, once yelled at a hapless sound engineer who'd had the temerity to suggest the level was probably a little too hot; "Get the fuckin' thing down on tape yer cunt!" (He had a way with words did our George!). But the track sounded bloody amazing, just like everything else they did. If it was funky, then it was the funkiest 'badass' track you'd ever heard. A smoochy ballad; then all emotion, soaring melody and luscious soulful symmetry. 'Beautiful and Black' was a classic multi-cultural anthem and a groove to die for, years ahead of its time, with lyrical contributions from David Hemmings, then the young Blow Up actor, a drinking mate of theirs, a couple of lines of which I never forgot;

I've seen Vermont on winter nights shake silver snowflakes from her hair,
But would the scene look half as good without a black night to compare
© Vanda and Young from 'Beautiful and Black', Copyright Control.

Hemmings also co-wrote some of the lyrics to one of my all-time favourite tunes of theirs; 'Pasadena' which became a huge hit down-under for John Paul Young. (Whilst in Sailor a new century on I had the great honour to perform 'Pasadena' on stage with John Paul Young in Berlin). With these, and on some of their other tracks, I believe George may have been the first producer to create drum loops. That is, splicing bits of tape together so that his obsessive drive to get the feel of a track just right was satisfied; namely, when there was no variation whatsoever in the tempo. This would be the precursor to dance tracks the world over in decades to come and fundamentally changed the way people made certain types of records.

One night while cutting one of their songs in IBC Studios in Portman Place, George and Harry took a call from legendary soul artist Isaac Hayes over in the States about a track we had cut only a few nights earlier. The two of them were blown away, as not only did Hayes want the song, but as he loved the groove so much, asked if he could use the track we'd cut the previous week. For a black American soul artist to use a Brit track as a basis for a record was unheard of in those days and a real testament to how Vanda and Young put their music together. 'Friday On My Mind', The Easybeats tune, was a classic of theirs and one of the very few cover songs David Bowie recorded.

George, even back then, would often talk about his ultimate ambition to put together and produce the ultimate rock 'n' roll band based on the same simplicity, raw energy and spine tingling riffs for which they were already famous. He didn't have to look too far! Harry and he would go on to produce George's younger brothers, Angus and Malcolm, unleashing AC/ DC upon the world, one of the loudest and heaviest rock bands of all time.

It is hard to overstate what a huge influence these amazing guys were to me and I relished any opportunity to play music with them as I always learned so much just by being in the same room. A decade or so later, after they'd moved back to Australia a second time (the Young family having emigrated first time round), it was as if time had stood still. Whilst on tour down under with Culture Club, in 1984, late one night I caught up with the guys (around 1 am after one of several sell-out shows we'd performed in Sydney). Predictably they were still hard at it down in the basement at Albert's recording studio, feet up on the mixing desk, fags in mouth laying down an absolute stonker of a track. These guys were just born to make music. "Congratulations Phil, we love Culture Club," Harry told me after we'd sunk a couple of beers for 'old times' sake; "Great feel on those songs man, well-done mate!"

A few years later and my path would cross with George's younger brothers, Angus and Malcolm when AC/DC stayed for over a year recording at my studio in Sheen. Those adventures deserve an episode of their own, but more on that later!

Back in 1970, whilst still working at E.H Morris by day, at night and at all other times whenever possible, I was beginning to make my way as a songwriter and session musician. In addition to meeting Vanda and Young, I usually just said yes to everything, a trait I would become known for in the music industry. I also worked with a weird and wonderfully diverse range of artists and projects, mainly through my friend, producer and arranger Tony Cox. Tony, being one of the trinity of music business impresarios who had been willing to venture out of London to come and see Paddy and I at Mother's in Birmingham, was incredibly supportive and helpful to my youthful ambitions in music. He constantly booked me for all manner of sessions. For instance, back at IBC, again he invited me to play the piano with a 60-piece orchestra on a number of tracks for Paul and Barry Ryan, a kind of early sixties version of Wham, whose huge and ponderous hit 'Eloise' was all over the charts.

Tony or "TC" as he was known, in addition to being a producer and ex-pop star himself, was a classically-trained arranger working with Yes and who was by now also managing bands and artists. Looking back, so many of my musical connections and influences came as a direct result of Tony's promotion of my talents, one of whom was Casey Synge, a tall, beautiful and imposing Irish lady with a stunning voice. Casey and I hit it off enormously and are friends to the present day, but our commercial endeavours to succeed in the music industry one would have to say peaked with a UK tour supporting Irish blues guitarist, the late Rory Gallagher. Our band included tablas and other exotic percussion supplied by David "Ned" Balen (another lifelong chum), and lead guitarist, Hugo Napier who is now a professional Brit voice-over king in Hollywood.

I was also invited to play guitar or keyboards on a number of projects for Tony at Sound Techniques Studio, such as for sultry and ultra-cool French songstress, Francoise Hardy, folk singer Mick Softly and through Tony's connection I also met Nick Drake, a singer songwriter who often frequented the Chelsea studio along with John Martyn and of the Fairports, Richard Thompson. After generously giving me my first ever break in the music business, I also rekindled my friendship with Dave Pegg, who, along with Dave Mattacks and the rest of Fairport Convention, are all friends to this day.

Tony Cox also introduced me to pop entrepreneur Jonathan King who along with Dave Pegg on bass, booked me to play lead guitar on Sakkarin's version of 'Sugar Sugar'.

It seemed that no sooner we were out of the studio than the pop entrepreneur's record began powering up the hit parade, finally getting as high as number 12 in the UK chart after our Top of the Pops appearance. It wasn't a song I was particularly proud of at the time but nevertheless working with Jonathan got me into the Top Of The Pops studio for the first of what were to become many times. With 'Leaving On A Jet Plane' this was now the second Top 20 record I'd been instrumental in helping to bring about and although I still hadn't written my first bona fide hit yet, I could feel the sweet smell of success in my own right tantalisingly closing in.

As much as I would prefer to forget it, no book of mine would be complete without a mention of my first and only attempt at a Eurovision song, 'The Bells Of Narbonne' co-written, prior to his forays into Hollywood, with my song-plugger turned record producer friend, Mickey Clarke. Before I knew Casey well (and after her performance on this song, I am surprised she still talks to me at all!) I booked her to sing on the demo, and upon first hearing her majestic rendition of lyrics such as; "The Bells of Narbonne they go ding dong ding dong" filled one with a sense pith and moment that is hard to describe.

Fortunately however there was no lasting damage to her career as Casey eventually achieved immortality as the founder member of Thunderthighs, the "doop-do-doop" backing vocal group on Lou Reid's iconic 'Walk On The Wild side' incidentally also recorded at Morgan Studios in Willesden. Later on, Tony also managed the band that Casey would go on to front after the demise of Casey and Friends. A fast and furious English prog-rock outfit called Gringo whose leader and excellent guitarist was Henry Marsh. As a co-founder member of Sailor, my best man, dear friend and co-conspirator in hundreds of other musical projects, Henry figures very prominently in this book and in my life.

Chapter 7
The Russian Prince

By far the most ground-changing event that happened during my time working for Stuart Reid at E.H Morris was the day I received a tape from a writer with the unusual name of Georg Hultgreen. Georg's voice, 12-string Gibson guitar sound and his production techniques blew me away and gave me goosebumps. Even though we still hadn't met, deep inside I knew I would one day make music with this man. Strange, but that's how it has always been with me. I just get a feeling about it.

On my strong recommendation ("You've got to hear this guy Stuart!"), Reid interviewed Georg and offered him a publishing contract there and then. A few weeks afterwards, whilst listening to Tony Blackburn's morning show in my bedsit flat on a very sunny morning in Prince of Wales Drive, Battersea, Georg's song 'Say Hello' came on the radio. That priceless moment sealed it for me. I didn't know him personally but through E.H. Morris I secreted away his phone number and called him up out of the blue. He was slightly taken aback at first, but being almost painfully polite and me in pushy Brummie mode, informing him it was I who had played a pivotal part in his publishing deal with Morris and thus the release of his single, he agreed to invite me round to his house and to hear what I had to say. "Georg, you don't know me at all but I can't tell you the effect your music had on me when I first heard it. I've got a very strong feeling we could work together successfully". As I'd pushed the boat out so far there was nothing else to do but go the whole hog; "Can we, therefore meet up and I'll tell you a little more about who I am?" "Sure Phil, why don't you come over for dinner with me and Christine tonight and we can discuss what you have in mind."

Everything about Georg was exotic, mysterious and foreign to me, which in addition to his approach to music, I found hugely exciting and a great inspiration. Coming from Birmingham I'd never met anyone quite like him before. Norwegian by birth, Georg had lived in Paris as an emigré and spoke fluent French. His aristocratic paternal ancestors had escaped Russia after the revolution and his mother, a well-known sculptress and associate of Picasso, lived in Mexico City. Georg spoke in a soft Canadian accent having lived in Toronto where his Japanese wife, Christine was studying. He'd already been in a band, which courtesy of Joni Mitchell was called 'Eclection' and had already achieved a reasonable degree of success as a live act. Therefore Georg was already considerably more experienced than I was and also a little older.

Fortunately, our first meeting went very well. We got on great and my intuition, usually a reliable friend, had been spot on. I respected Georg enormously and loved all of the songs I heard blasting out from his ingenious system of linked-up Beocord 'Heath-Robinson' reel-to-reel tape recorders. In fact, I couldn't wait to play on some of his songs and persuade him to form a band. He was very enthusiastic about the arrangement ideas I put forward on his material too, but somehow I knew he would be. Again I don't know why.

"But what about your songs Phil?" Georg enquired. "I think we should record them too, perhaps try a few things together." It may be hard to believe but doing my songs with Georg hadn't been the object of my quest at all. I loved Georg's music and thought I could add something to it, but at that time it hadn't stretched to doing any of my own material. So we tried a few things out together, Georg on 12-string and me on bass, guitar, keyboards, mandolin or Fender Telecaster guitar and as I had predicted, our two distinctly different approaches to music seemed to effortlessly gel. "Our styles are really compatible Phil and I'd be a lot happier if we could work on your songs too. What do you think?" When I got used to the idea, of course, I was thrilled.

Over the next few weeks we got together continuously and soon had what we thought, were some really strong tunes and inspiring demos under our belts, all of which had been recorded on Georg's ingenious system up in his tiny rooftop flat high above Little Venice. Christine's cooking was delicious and kept us going in perfect harmony. These were the very best of days of my life as a musician and songwriter to date. I had, after much searching, finally found the perfect partner and lead singer to work with.

One of the earliest songs I wrote, called 'Parachute' was directly inspired by Georg's method of dispatching the front door key down to ground level from the fifth-floor window of his flat at Clifton Villas thus saving him walking all the way down five flights of stairs and back up again. Typical Georg, he'd meticulously devised a key delivery system consisting of a weighted box containing the key attached to a large handkerchief in the manner of a parachute. It usually worked perfectly, but on windy days occasionally drifted off into next door's garden or even further afield. Georg was an introvert; meticulous, methodical and a true craftsman - the exact opposite of me; broad-brush, impulsive and out there but we complimented each other a treat and were a great team.

The songs Georg had written included 'Changes', 'Passing Time' "Movin' On' and 'Flying Machine' (a song which had already been recorded by Cliff Richard and a minor hit). My songs were 'Nature Man', 'Hometown Girl' (inspired by a new love affair!) and 'Chosen Wings' in addition to the above song, 'Parachute'. On choosing a name for our collaboration, I somewhat pushily suggested that Georg consider using his White Russian name of

"Kajanus' instead only because 'Kajanus Pickett' sounded better than 'Hultgreen Pickett'. Fortunately, Georg agreed!

Now that I had finally left E.H Morris I kept body and soul together doing session work, while Georg worked in a local pub, The Dover Castle, washing dishes. He also drove a delivery van for a greengrocer in Notting Hill. Through my previous job at the publishers, I'd met music mogul Lawrence Myers at GTO. One day without an appointment I turned up at his offices just off Oxford Circus with our tapes and persistently waited there until someone would see me. After several hours hanging around (probably I initially thought, just to get rid of me!), Don Powell Hunter, a very personable American management assistant, invited me into his office and play him our songs. He had been Stevie Wonder's personal manager for some time, was very musical and really seemed to know his stuff. Being a massive fan of Stevie, I was seriously impressed, even more so when Don reacted extremely favourably to hearing our demo recordings.

I'd never just walked in off the street into someone's office to try and get interest in a music project before, so was even more astonished and delighted when Don went out for a while and came back with Mr Myers himself. They listened to the tracks all over again. It seemed to be working. The two men looked very pleased and congratulated me on how strong they thought the material was. "We'd like to offer you a deal," Lawrence said. I was stunned but very happy. He wrote out a cheque there and then, handed me a contract and in words to that effect, said; "Go and make your record Phil and come back and play it to us when it's finished". That was it. It was as easy as that!

I went out of the GTO office into the spring sunlight, got on the tube at Oxford Circus and ten minutes later strode confidently from Maida Vale tube station to The Dover Castle pub. I tapped the little round window in order to get Georg's attention while he was washing his dishes and held the cheque up to the glass.

It was ten thousand pounds, a more than decent amount then, whereupon Georg threw his apron down and with a jubilant grin, casually walked out of the door never to return to that job ever again. Or come to that, any other job that didn't involve music.

Kajanus Pickett were well on their way!

Chapter 8
Midsummer Night's Dream

I had been in the grips of the music scene in London for about a year by now and had left the security of a steady wage at Chappell's to pursue the exciting prospect with Georg. (Come to think if it, that was my last proper 'job'!) However, even when life was busy, I never forgot my roots and made regular return journeys to my homeland in Sutton Coldfield to visit my mother whenever I could. One night, a night to remember as things turned out, I'd popped down to see a few of my old mates in The Royal pub, which is where I saw a wonderful sight for the first time. "Who's that?" I whispered to Paddy Maguire as she walked in the bar chatting & laughing with her friends, some of whom I knew but were not in my regular crowd. "That's Ann Sinsheimer, Phil", he said conspiratorially with a roguish Irish twinkle in his eye. "Her family lived next door to mine in Chavasse Road when she was a little girl". But seeing the look in my eye and how obviously smitten I was he added a cautionary note; "I think she's 'spoken for' though mate, they've been going out together for some time". "Hey, so am I" I said, "but it doesn't stop me having a look does it? She's bloody gorgeous!"

A perfect vision, petite of frame and delicate of feature with long strawberry blonde hair, a sunshine smile and an exquisite figure certainly made an impression over and above many of the girls in Sutton around that time, a provincial town that from far and wide had earned a reputation for its seemingly never-ending supply of lovely young women.

"Her father's American", my other friend Micky Jones chipped in. "Came over as a GI in WW2 and ended up looking after German POW's in Sutton Park", a bit of extra information that only added to her allure and exoticism as far as I was concerned and probably the exact opposite of what was intended. "He's a drummer too." "Ah well, you can't have everything!" I shot back, intending to disguise my intense interest with the time-honoured dig of a drummer joke, like; "What do you call someone who hangs around with musicians?"

She was 'accounted for' after all - and anyway I was going out with Madeline Turner, another Sutton girl, although my having now moved to London, cracks had started to appear in the relationship. So wide in fact that I later found out she'd been seeing Cozy Powell, another drummer, soon to be famous and apparently, for a few years at least, soon to be an "ex" friend of mine too!

As an only child, and courtesy of the RAF, having been educated at a private boys' school from the age of 10, (apart that is, from a brief stint at Tamworth College of Further Education) I was fascinated and in awe of the opposite sex, but with practically all one-on-one encounters evaporating in a form of shy awkwardness, hallmarked by either inappropriately intense moody and poetic behaviour that looking back was just plain embarrassing. On the other end of the personality spectrum, I might sometimes be inebriated with Dutch courage, brash and forthright, but which neither approach had been noticeably successful with "the ladies" on anything like the scale I would have preferred but had not yet developed the confidence to realise. I longed for the ease and sparkling repartee of friends like Chris Barsby, Mick Robbins and Pete Corcoran, all of whom had brothers and sisters and had grown up to more casually accept girls and their foibles. Unlike me who placed them delicately on glittering pedestals of rose-tinted untouchability and reverence. "Laugh them into bed Phil" Chris once told me was the secret, which patently, & frequently, worked for him.

Having been down in London for some time by now, however, thankfully there was a little more room for optimism in what Frank Zappa once described as 'the glandular arena" and although a gauchely inept 'late-starter' by now I was starting to get the hang of it. As well as being a little shy & reticent, at least, to begin with, there was also another factor. It's probably fair to say that my effortlessly glamorous mother Eileen might have inculcated in me, (so I have been told), a certain stylish flair for the kind of late-1960's attire I would throw on at the slightest excuse. This, added to the colourful and often effeminate Beatles & Stones-influenced fashion of the day and my fey pretty boy demeanour, (it was a VERY long time ago!), led some boys and girls to believe I might well have been gay, a word that was not used for that purpose in those days. "Oooh, you should have been a ladies hairdresser Philip" (imagine if you will, a broad black country accent), remarked Doreen, one of the white-coated young women in despatch at Stanton's: The all-night Bakery in the grim Black Country town where I worked driving vans around less-than-glamorous Wolverhampton and Bilston in the bleak freezing dawns. "Not working here in this shit hole anyway!" she chortled, delighted to take the proverbial out of the posh Sutton boy. "I'd get out of here as soon as I could if I was you, Philip!"

Well, a few years later, through sending my songs in cake boxes to London publishers, I had done just that and was by now proudly living in a one room flat at 20a Baker Street London NW1, a crumbling Dickensian hovel but a very fine sounding address. My musical dreams were coming together and Georg and I were avidly working, writing and recording songs for our debut album Hi Ho Silver for GTO and Signpost / Atlantic Records. With my talented and charismatic music partner, Georg Kajanus, practically every waking hour was caught up in the ecstasies of newfound musical discovery and fulfilment. So much so I guess that most of my thoughts were absorbed pretty much in my music and career and not on beautiful hometown girls up in Birmingham, or indeed helping to sort out some of my Mother's issues since her friend, Phil Sutton had unexpectedly died in Elba a few years previously.

At that moment, at The Royal in Sutton, I realised that I had been looking for HER, Ann Sinsheimer. That was why I'd driven all the way up the M1 but hadn't admitted it to myself, at least not with any kind of conscious thought process. I smiled inwardly upon realising I'd been drawn, as if by a magnet, to where I might bump into her again.

Through another Sutton friend, the late Paula Claddo, a larger-than-life character with a wicked sense of humour, who I absolutely adored and who also lived nearby in a flat in Paddington, I found out, to my more than passing interest, that Ann was in the process of moving to London herself and temporarily staying with friends. I was perplexed. Was she still going out with this guy or not? I had no idea, neither did Paula. However, she did tell me that Ann might be looking for a lift down to the big City soon. So without hesitation or trace of ulterior motive (promise!), I offered her a ride down to town and even picked her up with some of her things from her parents' house at Falcon Lodge.

Everything was cheery and polite on the way down and later on I asked her if she'd mind if I took a look at a small cottage I was thinking of renting just outside Bedford. She willingly agreed, but when we got there, was somehow led into being shown around the property with me. The landlady who reasonably assumed we were a couple, therefore, on anything pertaining to ironing, cooking or power points, where the vacuum cleaner was kept etc addressed all comments regarding such appliances to Ann for female approval. In reality, as she hardly knew me at all, this was hilarious in retrospect. She went along with it beautifully though, as didn't necessarily want to let me down in front of the owner, or give an impression of anything less than blissful future domestic cohabitation. There was a slight frisson of naughty possibility for a second or two that I secretly enjoyed, but no more than that, as I got the distinct feeling that this lady was definitely not about jumping the gun and ticking any cosy domestic boxes, far from it. But what I saw for the first time was a very dry sense of humour emerging, another aspect of Ann's that I found incredibly attractive.

When we finally arrived back at my flat in Baker Street, for some bizarre reason I cannot now recall, Anthea Joseph, the legendary and revered PR lady for CBS Records who knew Neil Young, Joni Mitchell and The Beatles personally and who I'd originally met through my Fairport Convention/Dave Pegg connections, had turned up at my flat out of the blue suggesting, after a few glasses of wine no doubt, that we all go out to the cinema together.

Imagine the scenario; Ann firmly believing that Anthea and I are an item and conversely, Anthea naturally assuming this lovely young blonde lady is my latest squeeze. But as the afternoon progressed, things became even stranger and more random; when in the middle of the film, which incidentally was Don't Look Back, D. A Pennebaker's fly on the wall documentary of Bob Dylan's 1966 UK tour, Anthea suddenly appeared up there as large as life on the silver screen right in front of us, her face the size of Harrods, talking and laughing in a very friendly and animated fashion with Bob Dylan for god's sake! Anthea smiled bashfully and the two wide-eyed Sutton kids, both fans of the Bard of New York were deeply impressed. For the sake of decorum, however, they were doing their damnedest not to show it too much. After all, meeting these kinds of people was what living in London was supposed to be all about!

The 'three's a crowd' dynamic was by now becoming a little intense however when all I really wanted to do was somehow get Ann on her own. But it wasn't happening and anyway she had to go back to do something or other at Paula's, where they were now sharing a small room within a larger mansion flat nearby on the Marylebone Road.

Rumours would later surface that Anthea had taken a bit of a sly shine to the fey-looking young Brummie songwriter and 'new kid in town'. But his head was way too far up in the clouds, preoccupied with other potential romantic scenarios, and in addition, of course, the ever-present burgeoning music career to even notice.

So we said our polite goodbyes outside the cinema in Baker Street in the dazzling glare and golden shafts of late afternoon sunlight and I went off to do some more writing and recording with Georg in Maida Vale. Days, or it could have been a few weeks later, not having seen or heard from Ann after the dream-like cinema episode, quite late one stiflingly hot summer's eve, I'd turned in for the night around 1 pm exhausted after a longer than usual session with Georg. I'd found that even the constant round-the-clock mighty roar of London's traffic only a few feet from my window could barely keep me awake. But on this night, there was also a tap, tap, tap coming from somewhere, very soft and gentle but definitely a tap, tap, tap. "What the hell is that?" I thought. Dragging myself out of bed and peering around the moth-eaten curtain to the pavement outside, and well, bless my boots, I thought. What do we have here? A 'Midsummer Night's Dream' no less.

It was Ann and she was outside on the pavement leaning over the railing and tapping my window with a milk bottle. "Sorry it's so late," she said anxiously, "but I don't know London very well at all and got hopelessly lost." "They all say that," I said, pinching myself and stifling a Cheshire Cat grin the size of the moon.

Sandra Turnbull, also from Birmingham who, fifteen years on would manage the Eurythmics and who was also a close friend of Madeline's, my ex, had offered Ann a lift back to Paula's from a party in Hampstead, or so the oft-repeated story goes. But with "Navbitch" and mobile phones still four decades in the future, in the dead of night, Sandra had dropped her friend off several blocks away from her intended destination. Now, on foot, Ann took another wrong turn, but as far as I was concerned, definitely and life-changingly, the right one! Scared and vulnerable, but suddenly recognising Baker Street again, Ann Sinsheimer from Sutton Coldfield, alone and lost in the big bad Metropolis found herself outside my door at one o'clock in the morning. But I certainly wasn't complaining, "You'd better come in then," I said.

> *To wake at dawn with a winged heart*
> *and give thanks for another day of loving;*
> *To rest at the noon hour and meditate love's ecstasy;*
> *To return home at eventide with gratitude;*
> *And then to sleep with a prayer for the beloved in your heart and a*
> *song of praise upon your lips*
> (Kahlil Gibran, 'The Prophet')

We fell for each other body and soul right from the get-go and lived together from that day in 1971 to this. Four years later we got married at Caxton Hall, the taxi taking us there frequently dodging the after-effects of the IRA's deadly Autumn bombing campaign throughout London.

During our very own "Summer of Love" whilst still furiously writing and recording with Georg, I felt I'd arrived at a blissful plateau of fulfilment and hope for the future. It felt great to be alive with everything going in the right direction at last. My love life, my new songwriting career, living in London, Georg, his wife Christine, Ann and I, were forging close bonds of friendship and shared musical interests. We frequently broke bread at Georg and Chris's tiny rooftop apartment in Little Venice, or over 'Char Siu' in Soho's Chinatown. While Ann was slowly coming to terms with working in London and her new partner's challenging domestic arrangements, Christine's superb recipes and home-cooked cuisine were just too good to resist, almost on a nightly basis after a hard-working day's recording at Georg's or at my place in Baker Street.

Later around 1971, Shelley Turner, Paul McCartney's American PA (a lovely lady who would eventually become one of our closest buddies) contacted me as I'd been recommended by her friend, Carol Martin-Sperry to audition for a new incarnation of Paul's post-Beatles band, the yet-to-be-named Wings. Carol, who knew quite a few people 'in the business' had spotted me playing the guitar and singing Beatles songs at a party in Megéve, and unbeknown to me at the time, I'd obviously made quite an impression.

This was at the time we'd driven through France at Tony Cox's invitation to see Henry Marsh's band Gringo playing in the town square of the French

Ski Resort (Incidentally it was only the second time I'd met Henry, from which point we became firm friends)

I'd met Denny Laine a few times and had seen him play with The Moody Blues on the Brum scene. In fact, I went to see the 'Moodys' support The Beatles at the Birmingham Odeon. It was there I noticed that Denny had been playing Lennon's black Rickenbacker during the Moody's support set and only a musical train-spotting geek like me would know that this signified deep 'matehood' amongst musicians. Therefore it came as no surprise that McCartney and he would have already been close friends, and although Shelley apologised profusely for wasting my time and building up my hopes, it was also no surprise to me whatsoever that Denny 'got the gig'. My big chance to work with Paul would come a few years later, however!

A few words on The Beatles. Seeing them live on stage in a small theatre for the first and only time I ever did was like having your brains plugged into the mains of what rock 'n' roll has only ever really been about. After watching them bounce onto the stage like young, uncouth Turks and tearing the place apart with their opener, 'Dizzy Miss Lizzy' I don't think I ever really got over the experience. But - in so many ways typical of my often perverse Karma - I needed to leave the show early that night, as guess what! 'The Blues Unit' was playing a gig at the Birmingham College of Food. The looks I received leaving a sell-out, heaving and screaming Beatles gig in full-flow were like... is this guy seriously OUT OF HIS MIND?

My band's music was as authentically bluesy and faithful to its roots as five nicely brought-up teenagers from a Midlands town could make a decent fist of. But unsurprisingly I suppose, after having just seen the Beatles, I realised then and there I wanted more of THAT!

Pop! Excitement, Glamour. Great tunes!

All things must pass and our Baker Street love-nest sojourn was sadly coming to an end. The estate agent had given me marching orders at a time when it was becoming desperately difficult, nigh on impossible, to find anywhere to live in London. After many disappointments, failed attempts and slammed doors in our faces over months trying to find something suitable, one day at breakfast Ann and I discussed trying a different approach; "Sod it, let's just bugger off somewhere, anywhere, and fly away from the problem for a while". So that's just what we did.

Ann had never been on an aeroplane before so we came up with the bright idea of going to the airport and taking the first flight we could afford going anywhere. We hailed a cab in Baker Street, asked the driver to stop off at the laundromat, and picking up our clean clothes in a bright blue laundry bag, headed straight off to Heathrow.

"We've got two hundred quid so what's your next available flight going anywhere?" I asked the bemused British Airways staff at the ticket desk, seriously showing off now. "Ibiza" she said. "Great, two tickets please, I'll pay in cash."

The excitement and joy in Ann's face was palpable. We were off on our first real adventure, the start of many more to come in our lives together, the wanderlust not ceasing when we arrived in Ibiza. We were sipping cool beers down on the quay and saw that a boat was shortly sailing to an even smaller island not too far away called Formentera, "Ooh, come on, let's go there!" she proposed, really getting the hang of this travel thing now. After an idyllic lazy cruise out to the island, to get out of the searing heat of a midday sun, we sought out a practically deserted bar in a tiny hamlet called San Francisco. Adjusting our eyes to the dark cool interior of the bar, the only other person in there was a guy wearing a cowboy hat over in the corner. "My name's Al," the immediately approachable Aussie said like someone out of a Clint Eastwood Western. "Did you just get in?"

We sat down over a cool drink and explained our predicament, that of having taken weeks and weeks of futile searching for a place to live in London, so far to no avail. "So we thought, bollocks to that, let's just fly off somewhere, get to know each other better, have a holiday and forget about it for a while," I said. "You've definitely come to the right place then mate," Al said intriguingly with a smile looking into his beer. "I just happen to have inherited an 8 bedroom property in Putney from an aunt," Al said. "I've been doing it up into flats for the last few months, came out here for a holiday, and next week I'll be renting the place out". "I've got a van too, when you get back I'll help you move in if you like!"

Chapter 9
Hi Ho Silver!

Georg and I keenly set about planning the recording sessions for our new venture at Morgan Studios in Willesden, while I still had to pinch myself realising I'd somehow secured a recording contract with the first company I'd walked into. Having secured a recording contract with GTO and through them, Arty Mogul's Atlantic subsidiary label, Signpost Records we were both raring to go and supremely confident about our musical future as a team. Georg and I could now call ourselves "professional musicians" as for the first time, didn't need to hold down crappy dead-end jobs in order to survive and pay the rent. It was an incredible feeling and I don't think I'd ever been as excited as I was about the prospect of finally recording with Georg in a proper recording studio.

The drummer on most of the Vanda and Young sessions I was involved in was Eddy Sparrow, an East End character of few words but with an awesome, rock steady, backbeat that the guys loved, so when Georg and I were looking for a drummer to play on our album I suggested we look no further. With part of the GTO advance we booked a tiny cottage in the wilds of Cornwall to go and 'get everything together in the country'. This may have seemed a rather strange thing to do, but 'de rigueur' in the early seventies.

I'd only just got together with Ann and being head over heels in love was already missing her like crazy. Therefore I asked Eddy, who owned an ancient grey minivan if he'd mind bringing Ann down to where Georg and I were staying after she'd finished work at the weekend. "Can I bring 'the lump' too?" Eddy enquired somewhat ungraciously with reference to his wife, who otherwise would presumably have to do without his charming company for an entire weekend back in Tottenham. "Er... no, I'm afraid that's not possible mate," I said perhaps too quickly. "There are only two tiny bedrooms and just a couch downstairs." "It's a bloody long way in' it?" Eddy noted. "'The lump' rolls my fags and not sure if the old van will make it all the way there, she's the only one who knows how to fix it." "Sounds like quite a girl," I said unconvincingly.

It was all starting to feel very *Withnail and I* again. "I'm sure Ann can help you drive" I proffered meekly, hoping he wouldn't change his mind. "Does she like gum?" he enquired bizarrely.

Apparently, all the way down to Cornwall and across Dartmoor in a dreadful storm, at Eddy's insistence, they both chewed copious amounts of gum, which every few miles he would grumpily get out of the van in the pouring rain and apply to a hole in the fuel tank to prevent them from running out of fuel. The rest of the time during this deeply unpleasant marathon, upon frequent request, Ann continuously rolled his fags and handed them to him as he was driving. Apparently, Eddie couldn't see very well either and the journey almost became an intolerable nightmare.

"I suppose that meant you must have quite liked me then!" I joked upon Ann's arrival in Cornwall and for years later.

After such an unpromising start to the proceedings, it was wonderful to see her and also to get down to the serious business of pre-production for our album. On Georg's recommendation, after having worked with star bass man Herbie Flowers on the Cliff Richard track, Georg's composition "Flying Machine", we decided to book Morgan, Herbie's studio in Willesden, along with a talented, taciturn engineer, Robin Black. It was quite close to where Georg lived and we set to work right away, every evening crossing like ships in the night with Rod Stewart, The Faces, Jeff Beck and Long John Baldry who'd been working in the studio all day. (We got the cheaper night session rates!) In the end, Eddy Sparrow didn't quite live up to expectations so we played most of the instruments ourselves in the manner of the original demos, but substituting washing up liquid bottles filled with rice and cardboard box bass drums with the real thing! The feeling of immense joy and satisfaction Georg and I felt on hearing the playback of our finished album "Hi Ho Silver" will stay with me forever and both Don Powell Hunter and Lawrence Myers at GTO (who hadn't bothered us, 'A&R'd' cajoled or tried to influence us in any manner artistically during the recordings) loved the album. Imagine that ever happening in today's music business environment!

David Bowie

Simultaneously, other-worldly and down-to-earth and with great personal warmth and charm, as we were signed to the same management company, GTO, David Bowie suddenly appeared on our radar and in our lives. Whilst Georg and I had been recording our debut album, I recall a bizarre but delightful evening spent in the exotic company of David and his wife Angie; she, wearing a beautifully cut man's pinstripe suit and he, elegantly attired in a tweed skirt, 'bipitty-bopitty' hat, Chanel jacket and pearls. Bizarre, not for the clothing, or even the transgender affectation, but that Ann and I had been invited, with the Bowies, (along with Georg Kajanus, his then wife Christine), to the Hammersmith Odeon to see and later meet, Diana Ross and The Supremes.

Whilst a more worldly Georg didn't bat an eyelid, much to my initial embarrassment, David immediately put me at my ease as true to gauche

Brummie form, I had mistaken him for his wife and vice versa! There we all sat in the back row of the Hammersmith Odeon watching the show; three couples enjoying a superbly random night out on the town. The humour of the situation escaped no one, particularly Bowie, who contrary to appearances did not take himself too seriously at all. He seemed to be someone who combined lofty artistic pretensions with a London cabbie's humour and was disarmingly funny and self-deprecating all evening. In retrospect, I often wondered how Boy George, at that time a teenage Bowie über-fanatic from Eltham, might have reacted had he been out for the evening with his hero way back in 1971.

"Like your songs man," David said just before we parted company. "Don Powell played me a couple of your things last week at GTO and they sounded great. Good luck with it all."

Subsequently we were invited to a few of his early shows in grotty London clubs around the making of Hunky Dory, (with producer Ken Scott at Trident Studios where The Beatles recorded 'Hey Jude') and witnessing his rocket-man ascent to worldwide fame at close quarters I became fascinated by the sheer single-mindedness of this amazing one-off impish genius in pursuit of his artistic vision who was well on his way to becoming one of the most influential artists of all time.

One of the early songs Bowie covered solo on 12-string guitar in a small club just off Oxford Circus, was Jacques Brel's 'Port Of Amsterdam', a searingly powerful showstopper of vile debauchery, prostitutes and drunken sailors on shore-leave, a particular performance of which, I always believed was a driving force and early inspiration of what would eventually become 'Sailor', the band Georg and I would eventually go on to form a year or so later.

Chapter 10
Pimps, Prostitutes and Sailors

In the end, it was hard for Kajanus Pickett to get the momentum and thus the recognition we needed. We went off to America to find a manager to try and solve the problem. We met one guy in the Brill Building in New York who told us that at that time we were merely, "the beneficiaries of others' good intentions" which wasn't entirely helpful. There were also others, such as Peter Asher in San Francisco, but all to no avail so we came back to London to continue our search for someone who could help us. Fate was to deal me another winning hand, however, when I found out that Steve Morris from E.H. Morris had moved over to London and was now running the family business. Although I wasn't working at the publisher's anymore, I had kept friendly with the family and having written several songs they were publishing, we were good friends. Steve approached me and suggested that if Georg and I got ourselves a bigger band, (rather than stay as a duo) he would manage us. I put it to Georg and he said it sounded like a very good idea.

After the experience of writing and recording 'Hi Ho Silver', the ease at which I'd managed to get us the deal with Signpost/ Atlantic Records, and the sheer joy and excitement of making what was my first record as a bona fide artist seemed charmed and therefore destined for success, sadly it was not meant to be.

In spite of some quite favourable reviews, Georg and I were finding it hard to gain traction on the radio, plus the limitations of being a duo in the mould of Hall and Oates, Gallagher & Lyle etc. proved to be a challenge when it came to performing live. We were intensely proud of our debut album 'Hi Ho Silver', having written all the songs, played each and every instrument and produced it ourselves, but throughout 1971/72 we began to think we'd have a better chance of success if we took the advice of Steve Morris and formed a proper band. I suppose that was the first time the idea for Sailor came about, although it did not have that name to begin with. Dennis Boyles, an American friend of Georg's who was a writer and published poet, suggested "KP Packet" as a new name, following on from where we left off in our previous musical venture, supposedly alluding to a steam ship and a household brand of nuts!

At the time, Ann and I were living together at 4 Holmbush Road, Putney at what, through my doubtful stewardship would become an infamous lodging house for itinerant musicians, students, artists, photographers and all manner of penniless budding creatives. The owner, that kindly Australian called Al, who we met in Formentera, clearly should have known better as he left me in charge of renting out rooms in return for a reduction in my own rent, whilst he went off globetrotting. I was a 'piss-poor' choice as a landlord and not 'cut out' for it at all, as renting, in my book, consisted of allowing most of my mates and their loved ones to stay entirely free of the vulgar folding stuff ever changing hands, one such resident becoming my friend and lifelong musical cohort; keyboard player and guitarist, Henry Marsh.

I'd met him the previous year whilst travelling across Europe on a Hunter Davies gonzo-style, stoned & crazed road trip, along with Tony Cox, and Rolling Stone US photographer Shep Sherbell. Already alluded to we were driving to Megève in the French Alps to see Gringo, a fast, furious and ultra-posh prog-rock outfit that Tony managed that featured an incredibly glamorous Irish singer called Casey Synge. The trip became a source of legend, at least those bits I could remember. Like a bad dream after a Peter Fonda movie, it involved copious amounts of illegal substances, tsunamis of cheese fondue, lashings of velvet trouser, long hair, snow, rambling and hysterical all-night conversations and nothing whatsoever played in 4:4. Henry was Gringo's lead guitarist. As far as Henry and I were concerned 'House on fire' and 'getting on' readily came to mind!

A few months later, however, (Gringo having split up), I played Henry the Hi-Ho Silver album at Putney and he loved it. He played guitar, keyboards and sang with great precision and verve in Gringo and was a very personable and lovely chap so I had no hesitation whatsoever in introducing him to my exotic nobleman friend Georg as a potential member of our about-to-be-formed new band.

Another of my mates, Paul Warren was a supremely gifted artist and the drummer of my first band from Birmingham days, The Blues Unit. Paul had similarly washed up on the forbidden shores at the den of iniquity known as 'Holmbush City Limits'. It hereby followed that the first rehearsal of the band that would eventually become Sailor quickly ensued down in our Putney basement flat, but the outcome was judged to have been "close but no cigar" according to Georg. I would have loved Paul to join, but, although Georg was convinced Henry was a perfect fit, his mind was not completely made up about my old pal from Brum. It just didn't really gel on the day and things can be like that sometimes I guess.

Georg rang me a few days later; "There's a guy I know called Grant Serpell who is drumming for Gino Washington's Ram Jam Band who works with a bass player called Mo Foster," he added. "Highly recommended, maybe we should go see them?" So Georg and I arranged to drive over in his ancient orange mini and meet them after their sound check at the famous swinging sixties club, Beatles & Stones hang-out, Scotch of St James in Mason's Yard.

Grant was a powerful, jazzy and economical drummer who had one of the best sounding Ludwig kits I'd ever heard, and although the funk and soul beats expertly provided for Gino were nowhere near what we were doing, Georg and I both felt it could work. Mo was a genius too, but we wanted to limit the band's line-up to four if possible. "Maybe you could play bass, on the keyboard Phil?" Georg said the first time it came up, taking me by surprise. Considering myself more of a guitarist back then, I also played keyboards, so the idea didn't seem too far-fetched. "I'll give it try," I said.

A few days later I met up with Grant and Henry and together we descended on Georg and Christine at their tiny but immaculate flat up in the rooftops overlooking Maida Vale near the canals of Little Venice. The four of us immediately clicked and seemed to share the same goals and aspirations, immediately hitting it off in anticipation of a brand new musical adventure. The new association was sealed and celebrated by breaking bread and enjoying one of Christine's legendary suppers. I was delighted as it had all seemed so easy with such a perfect blend of like-minded talents and personalities. Humour was also a key element, particularly between Henry and I, but overall the chemistry, although we all came from vastly different backgrounds, was key.

Sticking with Georg's earlier stipulation about the two of us as founder members having equal song writing, we began rehearsing four new songs, two of mine; 'Medallions' and 'Lost My Mode' and two of Georg's, 'Brag Brag Brag' and 'Traffic Jam', the latter having already been recorded for our previous project. Henry and Grant were thrilled to be on board as Georg and I were to have them in the band, but not contributing to the song writing (at the time) they needed to have a source of income guaranteed. At least in Georg's and my case we still had some coming in from our publishing deals with E.H. Morris, plus the vanishing remains of our earlier Signpost advance.

My arranger friend Tony Cox, who I'd first met when he came to Birmingham with Warner Bros to see Paddy and I perform at Mothers, (I think we know that by now!) happened to own one of the first prototype "Putney" synthesisers so we invited Tony to one of our early recording sessions where he played a catchy Bach-inspired riff on our new recording of 'Traffic Jam'. Checking out this early synth was a harbinger of things to come and gave credence to the earlier idea of me eventually playing a bass synth with my left hand, (instead of the more conventional bass guitar), whilst playing piano or synthesiser with my right. Added to this, Georg's 'Leadbelly' 12-string guitar style, Grant's minimally precise and powerful drumming and Henry's disciplined dexterity on piano, with every member also contributing to arranged four-part harmony vocals, we felt we were starting to carve out something truly unique.

The distinctive sound of Sailor could be heard in the room almost immediately and although each musician had come from different geographical, cultural, educational and musical backgrounds, an incomparable chemistry was undeniable right from the start. It was a thrilling experience and seemed to bode well for the band's prospects. I also discovered that I possessed a talent for vocal arrangement and harmony which in this brand new environment of the group that would become Sailor, seemed ideally suited to the task in hand.

Steve Morris paid for the initial sessions and also, as promised, stepped in as our manager, agreeing to take our demo tapes around the music business to shop for a recording contract. As Georg's and my publishers, he also agreed to pay Grant and Henry a retainer for their musical services out of Georg's and my royalty income until such time as a label was found to invest in the band. Time was marching on however and after a while it became obvious that it was taking Steve a lot longer to sell the band than he'd originally anticipated. Although we were confident we had something really special, not being snapped up inevitably made one feel a little nervous. Nothing was ever guaranteed or a foregone conclusion in this business though, and looking back over a long career, t'was ever thus. We were four ambitious musicians ready to take on the world and who now needed to get on and make it work. Steve was confident he would eventually get us signed provided we could be patient. We were becoming concerned that his laid-back 'California beach-bum' aura was perhaps not direct and pushy enough in the more down-to-earth UK market.

Against a backdrop of the desperate economic mess of the early seventies, three day weeks and rubbish piled high in the streets, many were feeling vulnerable due to so much industrial and political unrest at a time when the country was being brought to its knees by militant unions and socialist extremists grinding everything to a halt. In my own microcosm, my landlords were chasing me for rent and I was running out of cash fast. It was looking pretty obvious that something would have to give and that I might not be able to afford to stay on in London much longer while we waited for a deal that could change everything. But it didn't come. What I couldn't understand was that it had all seemed so much easier the first time around with Kajanus Pickett. Oh to be young again with the arrogance, certainty and entitlement of youth!

Meanwhile, Tony asked me one day if I would like to get involved in a remote residential recording studio venture he was planning up in Scotland, or anywhere, provided it was a long way from London. I asked him if he'd ever thought of Cornwall as a possible location, a place I'd always considered my spiritual home, and a county I knew well. A few weeks later, he'd found a derelict 17th-century water mill going cheap up a creek on the Fowey River in Cornwall and only accessible by boat. "Sounds perfect," I said. But in reality Tony needed no encouragement and the seeds of what would eventually become Sawmills Studio, now one of the most famous musical landmarks in the West of England, were well and truly planted.

On my return to London for a meeting with the band, to rehearse, meet and discuss progress on the deal, I was in for a bit of a shock, however. As a thrusting and feisty young songwriter from Brum who'd moved to London especially to find a lead vocalist and form my own band, the faît accomplit announced by Henry, Georg and Grant that day came like a bolt out of the blue. Whilst I had been up and down creeks in Cornwall, Grant and Henry had asked Georg if they could hear some of his material from a Threepenny Opera style musical theatre project he'd been working on, entitled 'Sailor'.

What I hadn't realised until then was the impact our earlier encounter with David Bowie had must have made upon Georg. Georg and I were speechless and particularly blown away by Bowie's emotional firestorm version of Jacques Brel's 'Port Of Amsterdam'. Georg knew the song, was a huge fan of Brel having become familiar with Brel's work whilst living in Paris in the sixties. He was intrigued and inspired by the seamy side of Parisian nightlife, and, who I later learned, had been writing a musical based on the streetlight stories of prostitutes, Madames and randy sex-starved sailors on shore-leave. The working title for this project was Sailor. Songs included 'Sailors Night On The Town', 'The Pimp's Brigade', 'Blue Desert' and 'Streets of Amsterdam' all of which captured the atmospheric and retro-sensibilities of the George Gershwin film; An American In Paris, with its elaborate dance routines of a more innocent bygone era of hope and romanticism, but in Georg's case, with a darker and more seedy twist.

Marvelling over Georg's theatrical inspiration, it was enthusiastically suggested at Sailor's meeting that instead of our current demos, the tracks that Steve Morris was still dutifully taking around the record companies, these new theatrical songs, solely written by Georg, should now form the basis of the band's musical direction, style, content and even our visual image, lock stock and nautical barrel.

Although I put on a brave face, inside I was devastated to discover that such a fundamental decision had been made in my absence. I am still not sure to this day if any thought had been given to what my reaction would be but, looking back, I was new to being in a band and perhaps a little naïve to the politics that also exist in this professional grouping. Being a huge fan and in awe of Georg's talent; after all, I had been the one to seek out and pursue him relentlessly in order to form a band, I realised that with Georg's encouragement and guidance I had also become a very ambitious songwriter myself. I really did try to be positive, although I had some genuine reservations.

"Does EVERY bloody song have to be about pimps, prostitutes and sailors though?" I beseeched, but to no avail, it looked like a done deal. My natural enthusiasm intervened as it always does in the end, but I did ask for a little more time to think about it; reasonably, I felt, under the circumstances. I loved Georg's songs and the quality and craftsmanship of his work, but still a part of me was deeply conflicted, and I suppose, for a while at least, I was quite angry, my writing dreams having been, (as I saw it then), cast aside. But in the end I accepted that the tide had moved against me, and by those I'd invited to take part. In hindsight and reflection, with a heady mix of experience and now years on, I don't blame anyone. More to the truth of it was that I hadn't yet arrived at who I would become as a songwriter at that time and that this new direction of Georg's writing style had a direct and inspired simplicity and completeness that I was yet to match.

"But I will one day," I told myself.

Excited by the new possibilities presented, Georg suggested that the title of his musical, 'Sailor', would also be a brilliantly simple and thus memorable name for the band, an idea which was enthusiastically carried, motion passed. "What about wearing sailor suits on stage?" someone else proposed. I inwardly groaned; "This train ain't stopping soon!" I thought. "YES. Like in South Pacific and An American In Paris? "We can get authentic sailor uniforms really cheap from Lawrence Corner, the old Army and Navy store near Euston." "How would you feel if we all had our hair cut really short, like Jack Nicholson in The Last Detail?" Georg said, with a look that suggested his mind was already made up, even though a style very much out of fashion at the time. "Great idea, it'll make us really stand out," said Grant, "I'm sick and tired of being in no-hope bands going up and down motorways that no one ever remembers and sleeping in the back of freezing vans."

He had a point; "You've got to have your own sound and a look that no one else has in order to make it or it's a total waste of time." Grant was passionate about this having already been in a variety of failed groups plus he was a little older than the rest of us and already had two kids.

Everyone agreed, and after all, they were right. I was new to this game and the only one in present company who'd never been in a proper professional touring band before. I bowed to the knowledge and experience present in the room. Georg was on a roll now and even suggested having tap dance lessons to enable us to do Fred Astaire-type routines on stage. To someone who considered his young, early seventies self, quite cool, even a bit of a dandy, ("A natural dresser" when referred to by Robert Wace, our eventual manager during the golden years), this was all getting very scary. What would my über-stylish mates think when they saw me tap dancing in a sailor suit and with short hair? Jesus.

I must admit I found a frisson of fascination in some of Georg's suggestions, the contrarian in me getting off on the idea that we might end up with a defined and deliberately camp image challenging the commonplace and predictable denim and long hair uniform of most bands of the very early seventies.

Georg suggested that we should also have an elaborate, fantastical and totally fictitious biography courtesy of his friend Dennis Boyles, in which each member was described as having first met in a Paris cafe called Le Pomme Flasques. It was barmy, provocative and threatening to fragile egos and still-forming identities, but something in the extreme discomfort of it all I also found quite risqué and refreshing. I can't for a minute think why except I've always loved dressing up and showing off!

But what was I going to do if I couldn't at least write some of the songs? The idea of tap dancing on stage screamed at every sensibility I possessed. We even went and had lessons and bought the shoes. Henry and Grant seemed okay with it all and Georg obviously loved the idea. "It scares me shitless" I confided to Henry one day. "Look at me! I'm more like Gene Autry than Gene Kelly". My cage was well and truly rattled.

I was twenty-five years old, just starting to make my way in my chosen vocation and, in the end, after many sleepless nights, finally decided to throw in my lot with Tony and instead pursue the Cornish recording studio venture hundreds of miles from London, where everything was bogged down in stress, problems and political strife. It seemed like a romantic and magical alternative to life in the big city, a challenge, yes, but I would end up co-owning a recording studio in a most beautiful part of the world. What could possibly go wrong? Anyway, it was many months on with still no deal on the table, and Tony's Cornish leap in the dark seemed like the natural thing to do, And anyway, to cap it all, we'd been kicked out of our flat!

The guys were disappointed and more than likely pissed off with me, but in the end, it all came down to what I really wanted: to write songs first and foremost. A large part of me knew that although Georg's writing was inspired, deeply personal and pouring out of him, I had a different furrow to plough and when all was said and done, I would be better off making my own way on my own terms within the music business, or so I thought. Some of those early chameleonic impulses were already stirring!

Chapter 11
1-2-3 Lets Go To Town

"Only those who attempt the absurd can achieve the impossible"
(Albert Einstein)

Having been down in Cornwall for what seemed like an age of hard work, no money, gruel and carpet sweepings and as yet, very slow business at the studio, a phone call from Steve Morris came through several months after he'd started approaching record companies with Sailor's demos. Exalted and relieved, he announced that Epic Records, part of the major CBS record label were hot to sign the band. They'd heard KP Packet's original 4-track demo tape, had passed it around the company and wanted to talk turkey.

"They really want to sign us Philip", Henry excitedly called me on the pub phone down at The Fisherman's Arms in Golant later that evening. "But I've left the band Hen," I said. "I'm not involved anymore am I? Anyway, I'm down here doing this now." "Er... well Phil," he stumbled, "Steve never actually told them you'd left so the record company still think you're part of it all," he admitted a little sheepishly. Then the bombshell: "But here's the thing," Henry said ominously, my loins now girded. I was all ears; "They want to come and see the band play live before they make a final decision, so Steve has arranged for them all to come down and see us play at Alastair Crawford's studio in Hendon next week". "Next week? What the fuck! Who are 'they'?" I asked, "The big boss man, Dick Asher, an A&R chappie, Dan Loggins, and Maurice Oberstein, the guy who signed Bob Dylan." "Christ," I said, or words to that effect. "Look Philip." Henry implored, "think about it man, you started this band and you should be a part of it. Anyway, if things progress, down the line you'll be able to write for the band, I'm sure." Thanks, I thought.

"Well, the music business hasn't exactly been beating a path to my door down here, that's for sure!" I said. Secretly, I was thrilled, however. A record deal for god's sake! It was a gig after all, and as I was beginning to find out; in a brutally insecure profession I was going to have to be adaptable in order to survive.

I wasn't a front man; never wanted to be and knew that I would always need to be part of a team. The realisation of this fact was liberating and not at all what I had feared. I resigned myself, that day to put my songwriter dreams on hold for the time being and my very best efforts, ideas and inspiration into Georg's songs and also behind a band I had, for all intents and purposes, played a very large part in creating. Plus I was finally going to get paid properly, a not inconsiderable factor!

"Okay," I said to Henry, "You're on!"

I drove up to London the next day to learn the songs and begin the all-important rehearsals, throwing myself into Georg's music wholeheartedly and with no reservations, harboured resentments or unintended puns. The label executives duly came down to meet us, seemingly having no idea of my having left the band at all, but Dan Loggins did ask why we were not performing the other tracks Steve had sent him. I was in the bizarre situation of telling CBS's A&R director who had heard my songs and wanted to sign us, that we were not doing those anymore.

"'Traffic Jam' won't be part of our repertoire anymore either now that we're doing this new material," said Georg to the battle-hardened music men in the room. They looked surprised. "We'll see about that Georg", the body language seemed to say. But whatever confusion there was over the name change and radically new musical direction was fleeting and temporary. The effect of seeing and hearing Sailor play Georg's peculiarly atmospheric and powerful songs with such distinctive and unusual instrumentation; military bass drums, fog horn synth bass, 'Nickelodeon', accordions and glockenspiels in such an intimate setting was an extraordinary, persuasive experience for the assembled music industry Titans. None of them had ever seen or heard anything quite like it before or since. The effect was instantaneous, dramatic and the deal was sealed. Smiles all round!

A few days later Georg, Henry, Grant and I were signed to a worldwide recording contract for six albums with Epic Records and we were on our way.

After the long wait and finally having now been signed to CBS / Epic, after what had been a precarious few months of being completely broke I wondered if I'd done the right thing by sacrificing my writing ambitions. It was a pleasant relief to be financially supported by the label and to be able to join in with my friends again with an endeavour which, whilst it may not have been perfect meant I could roll my sleeves up, back with the lads and do something I loved in a spirit of great and genuine camaraderie.

The sound of the band, now wholly concentrating on Georg's material for the debut album, was becoming more powerful every day. Playing together in rehearsals was a joy, meticulously arranging everything, Georg's 12-string Ovation guitar, my brand new synthesiser bass, (an ARP 2600 which we could now afford and, along with Stevie Wonder apparently the only act in the world using the magic box live for bass parts), Grant's amazing Ludwig kit, and two small Kemble upright pianos purchased from Samuels in Edgware Road, one for me and one for Henry. Georg was inspired now that he had "all hands on deck" again, the prodigal son having returned to the fold, and the atmosphere in the band was buzzing with an industrial intensity of wanting to get everything right.

Number one was that it had to be unique, if someone else was doing it, we'd try something different; no conventional bass guitar for us, it had to be fog horn synth bass; no bog-standard electric guitar, but a glorious bell-like Ovation 12-string; two upright Kemble pianos, accordion, glockenspiel, mandolin and military bass drum. Weird and wonderful is the way to describe it. I found that not being involved in writing any of the songs, in reality, gave me the freedom to be more objective in putting ideas forward, particularly with the vocal arrangements for Sailor.

Rehearsals took place at a large semi-detached house in Hendon, the home and studio of Alastair Crawford, an eccentric boffin but who resembled the 'Wild Man of Heavy Rock', once imagined to have been spawned into existence behind a row of Marshall stacks at the Roundhouse by an electrical short circuit, but who, in fact, was one of the sweetest and most gentle souls I'd ever met. Regal was the only way Al's demeanour could be described and indeed, rumour had it on very good authority that there were secret Royal connections somewhere in the Crawford gene pool, intimated to be the result of certain dalliances between Queen Victoria and her Scottish gardener, but we far preferred the Roundhouse theory of Al's first arrival on Planet Earth! Another great band, The Tourists, with Annie Lennox and Dave Stewart rehearsed at Al's on the days we weren't in.

One day Georg turned up with a blueprint sketch for 'The Nickelodeon', a sonic contraption that we hoped would eventually form the beating heart of the Sailor sound. What had been occupying our minds was how we could reproduce the sound of a huge swirling street orchestra with just four musicians on stage. No idea seemed bizarre or strange enough that we couldn't somehow find a way to incorporate it into our audio beast. The sounds that we had created as the main keyboard parts whilst recording the first album at Morgan Studios in Willesden were inspired by the jangly atmospheric melodies emanating from Parisian and Viennese music boxes played in the streets and squares of European cities; a little like The Third Man meets Edith Piaf.

Analysing the sound and breaking it down into its component parts directed all our energies towards finding a way to reproduce it for live shows. There was a resonating piano note for sure, slightly detuned, a shorter organ note, an early electronic synth sound from the ARP Pro-Soloist, a mandolin, and finally, a glockenspiel, all playing exactly the same note. The trick was how were we going to recreate this sound, along with complex harmony vocals on stage with only four people?

My mother had bought me a Black and Decker drill for my birthday the year before, (God knows why! I was always useless at any form of DIY), which Georg asked me to bring to the rehearsal one day. He immediately set about our beautiful Kemble uprights with scary authority drilling holes under each piano note, about two octaves worth. He then came up with the idea of attaching wooden dowels approximately 4 inches long to the underside of the piano keys, (here was the clever bit), the rubberised end of which pressed down on the exact corresponding key of a small ARP Odyssey keyboard bracketed directly under the piano keys. Then, for the organ note solution, Grant suggested we check out a device called a 'Piano-Mate' that he'd first come across while dodging fights and flying glass when playing in no-hope pub bands around Kilburn. Having located one, it turned out to be a ghastly cheap plastic attachment placed on the top of piano keys whereupon tiny pistons above every piano note, (well, about 24 of them), dropped whenever the corresponding piano note was depressed. The 'Piano-Mate' then emitted a sound roughly resembling a tasteless hybrid - something between a Rolf Harris 'Stylophone' and the agitated mating call of a gerbil being suddenly and unaccountably strangled. (Sorry to keep bringing Rolf into this!)

Strangely enough, when played with the other two sound sources; piano and synth and a degree of musical verve, it all started to sound reasonably impressive. Georg wasn't completely happy though as he felt there was still something missing from the overall sound. Not content with having invented a kind of mechanical 'midi' almost ten years before its time, (the development in electronic signalling that would practically define how most eighties music was produced), he arrived at rehearsals next morning direct from a hardware store having purchased no less than thirty door bells. The salesman probably suspected Georg was some kind of notorious slum landlord and not, in fact, a quietly spoken Norwegian and son of a Russian Prince.

With Alastair's assistance and under Georg's direction we began to attach circuit breakers to twenty-four of the piano hammers. Al, fag in one hand, was wiring them up to the doorbell mechanisms on top of the piano, the idea being that every time a piano note was played, (thus completing the circuit - am I losing you yet?), the bell hammer struck the exact corresponding note of a glockenspiel placed precariously on top of the piano. So, what came to pass, and the end result of this industry, was a detuned piano note, synth sound, 'piano-mate' and now, glockenspiel - four sound sources all playing the same note. Wow! When it actually worked, which as I recall took a very long time, Eureka! It was a Stanley Kubrick 2001 moment. You know, the one where the apes dance around the black obelisk, deliriously disturbed and throwing bones up in the air in slow motion. Seriously, when it all came together we couldn't believe our ears.

The stage was now set for our debut performance at The Nightingale Pub in Wood Green, North London, which had been decked out by the CBS staff in red check tablecloths and candles with all the girls wearing very fetching French red stripy tops and tight black skirts with black fishnet stockings.

Meanwhile, each member of the band quivered and shook with fear backstage in the dressing room prior to our first ever public performance. Were we raving mad? When you reach out for something unique, something to be proud of there is always a silent lurking fear that you may have just gone too far. But there was also a collective energy surrounding the four of us that seemed to be saying, "it's really going to work, it's unstoppable whatever anyone thinks." Thin as rakes, each wearing white bell-bottoms and genuine Lawrence Corner ex-Navy sailor tops, we were about to play a style of music that had never been heard before. We nervously arrived on stage having been given a huge build up by the big CBS mogul-man himself, Dick Asher, telling everyone how excited they were to have signed this somewhat unusual band. Everyone from the record company was coming to see us play for the first time and in the audience was Johnny Stewart, Producer of Top of the Pops and BBC2's In Concert, as well as most of the media movers and shakers of the day. (The significance of Stewart's attendance would come into play later on in the story).

CBS was a hugely successful label and seemed to be putting a lot behind their rather strange and theatrical new signing. My hands were shaking and I'd thrown up in the toilets minutes earlier, but we were here so we'd better get on with it!

1-2-3 "Let's go to town, ('let's go to town, let's go to town') down to the red light quarter, that part of town (that part of town, that part of town) where there is no such thing as law and order" - and we were away, the long voyage of Sailor had actually started and it was a riotous success!

At the end of the song, the reaction was quite extraordinary and we could tell right away from the stage that everyone was loving the unique sound of Sailor from beginning to end. The evening was a complete triumph and having been out on a limb, this was a complete vindication of all of the months of hard work, fears, group splits and financial worries. Although we knew we were playing to a partisan audience of record company, well-wishers, invited media people, a few close friends and loved ones, anyone could see we were on to something truly unique and amazing although there would no doubt be many tests, trials and tribulations to come.

Chapter 12
A Little Glass of Champagne

After our successful debut gig, Dick Asher, the European head of CBS Records, now wanted us to play in front of his entire worldwide organisation, so later in 1973 Sailor were invited to perform at their prestigious Los Angeles Convention. This was a big deal which meant that CBS staff from every country in the world would now be able to see the band.

It felt really good to be flying business class all the way to sunny California with Henry, Grant and Georg, as although we had yet to release a record, it seemed like the 'big guns' were all lining up behind us and we were now well and truly on our way. All of the clichéd trappings had been laid on for Sailor and a stretch limo dispatched to LAX to whisk us off to The Century Plaza Hotel, one of the finest in Los Angeles and part of the same building as the Convention Centre where we were billed to appear next evening.

My memories of dingy motels having hitched-hiked and rode box cars across America only five years earlier as a Vietnam draft dodger, and with the sage words of Duke Ellington still fresh in my mind, I strode confidently across the 5-star marbled magnificence of where I now found myself. In a quiet and self-congratulatory mood, it was satisfying to realise that through my love of music I was now experiencing a more opulent version of America than last time, some positive career prospects at last - and like everyone else in the band, taking full advantage of the 24-hour unlimited room service!

The England we'd left far behind was mired in the industrial conflict, misery and predictably depressing class warfare of the early seventies, so it was a huge contrast enjoying the California sun around the Century Plaza's swimming pool. Whenever we got taken anywhere in our constantly-on-hand limo, the awesome rich bass tones of immaculate Steely Dan and Eagles music on the stereo created a perfect sound picture of optimistic and all-powerful America of the era!

Getting ourselves ready to perform at the convention next day, yet again we were petrified, becoming a common thing these days, but also secure enough by now in the self-reliant four-man musical world we had created, that at the very least, we knew no one else out there would sound anything like us. The highly proficient US sound crew, familiar with more straightforward artists like Kenny Loggins and bands like Chicago were scratching their heads over our peculiar Heath Robinson 'limey' gear and instrumentation. Come the sound check, they were asking all sorts of questions; "Where's your bass guitar man?" "We don't have one", "Lead guitar and amp?" "Er, no sorry", "Why are you saying sorry?", "I don't know, it's a peculiarly British trait. Sorry", "What does this crazy fucking machine do man?" "That's the 'Nickelodeon' where most of our sound comes from, we designed it ourselves", "Uh huh."

But by now the crew were becoming concerned that the voltages of 'The Thing' would actually work at all on the night of the big show. As we were complete unknowns, the UK 'wildcards' of the evening's entertainment, we went on quite early to open the show in support of the big name headliners who would be on later; such as Kansas, Hall & Oates and, topping the bill, Barbra Streisand. So when our time came, in workmanlike manner, we bounded on stage trying not to let our nerves and jet-lag get the better of us.

Georg counted us in on the opening number, everyone looking at each other, too afraid to look at the vast audience out there in the darkness. After about eight bars or so, there was a strange and disturbing hissing noise, like tinnitus or loud static. For a moment I thought our speakers had blown. But seeing the huge grin on Henry's face looking across at me over the Nickelodeon, I looked to my left and saw that everyone in the room was up on their feet cheering and applauding the band. They'd never seen or heard anything like it before and were showing their appreciation right from the start. It was another new experience; seeing people clapping during the performance and not waiting to the end of the song like everyone else. In fact, it was exactly the same as the reaction at The Nightingale pub in North London a few weeks earlier. After the show, we got to meet CBS reps from all over the world, many of whom, like the South Africans, Australians and Dutch, were wildly enthusiastic about Sailor's music. So much so that the band would go on to have big hit records in all of those territories.

Meanwhile back in England, in support of our first album 'Sailor', Steve Morris had booked us on shows all over the country and also managed to get us a special guest slot on a substantial tour of the UK supporting Kiki Dee.

Our theatrical image and presentation, the weirdness of the instruments and 'look' may have put off some music fans. Especially those more used to regulation-denim and doctrinaire, post-hippy, rock 'n' roll, but usually after just two or three songs we would have the UK audiences in our pocket. Musical snobbery abounded though and the *NME*, *Melody Maker* and especially Bob Harris on his *Old Grey Whistle Test* turned their 'right-on' noses up at us, at least initially. The better we got we didn't give a shit though as we knew we were good. As I said before, I'd never been in a proper touring band like the others and an amusing episode happened when we were playing at a huge outdoor concert in Holland. I think it was the Pink Pop Festival, although it was a long way from being 'poppy'. Thirty thousand people were standing in the pouring rain waiting for the main act to come on but were aghast to see the four jaunty sailor boys leaping about all over the stage with their accordions and military bass drums. I got a perverse kick out of knowing they hated us, but in the end, with customary hopeless Brummie optimism, I quite enjoyed an experience I was still relatively new to.

"I didn't think we went down that bad at all," I said to counter the gloomy post-show backstage ambience of our damp caravan. "Well, what's that rotten tomato doing sticking to your arse then Philip?" Henry asked, as Georg and Grant fell about laughing.

With our own quirky stage set and lighting system, Sailor, in the early days, was considered more akin to a Brecht & Weill 'Threepenny Opera' theatrical review, rather than the kind of act we would eventually transform into an out-and-out seventies Glam Rock extravaganza!

In this regard the Kiki Dee tour was a useful, though not entirely pleasant learning curve as apart from Kiki, a self-effacing, sweet and charming lady with a fantastic voice, her band arrogantly rubbed our noses in it at every opportunity, reminding us of our lowly status on the bill whenever possible. This had the unintended effect however of making us even more determined each and every night to blow them off the stage wherever we could. The hard slog of these, and countless other dates around the country looking back was, I believe, part of our valuable '10,000 hours', a rigorous 24/7 musical apprenticeship that significantly contributed to the 'well-oiled powerhouse machine' that Sailor would go on to become.

A few weeks after this tour, influential TV producer Johnnie Stewart who had been seriously impressed by the band at The Nightingale, called Steve Morris and asked if Sailor would appear the very next day on BBC 2's prime-time In Concert programme. Due to bad weather in New York which had stopped The Edwin Hawkins Singers plane from taking off... Sailor's was just about to! The vocal group had been booked to appear on the show but now obviously couldn't make it. Therefore Johnnie urgently wanted to know if Sailor would be available to step in and do the show instead. Apparently Stewart, also the producer of the iconic Top Of The Pops TV Show was so moved by our London live debut, our first ever gig as it happened, that he'd put us in his little black book for future consideration.

Of course, we could not turn a magical opportunity like this down. At the same time however we realised that as the show went out 'live' to an audience of over eight million people, (and in the days when everyone watched TV!) - if we screwed up it would be curtains for any on-going career. No additions, post-production or re-doing anything, instruments or vocals would be possible. Live meant 'live'. A thirty minute, non-stop concert performance in which every twitch, nostril hair and bum note would be exposed for millions of people to see and hear. If I thought my nerves had been shredded at The Nightingale and the CBS USA Convention, it was piffle compared to this.

I showed up at BBC Television Centre at White City so fearful I could hardly speak. Or walk. Meeting Henry, Georg and Grant who were already there, I could tell we all felt exactly the same. This was the big one. An amazing opportunity, yes, but just how were we going to get through it?

Ann and her sister Julie, who had come all the way down from Sutton Coldfield had already taken their seats in the invited TV audience, as had Mitch, Christine and Susan; Grant, Georg and Henry's wives. We earnestly looked out in the studio gloom for a friendly face to latch on to while trying to look casual (we hoped!) while walking out like gladiators into the arena and the cameras. The studio was so quiet you could hear a pin drop, somehow making everything even more fraught in the silent atmosphere. In just a few minutes, on the other side of those cameras would be literally millions of people in their living rooms seeing Sailor for the very first time. We could all feel the power, of what was, to date, the most important moment of our careers coursing through our veins. If we could get through this, we could get through anything. Thank goodness we'd completed the Kiki Dee Tour and countless other dates, (around 170 shows in 1973-4 alone), as our playing was faultless and the show was in the end, an unqualified critical success.

Steve Harley was one of the millions at home watching us on TV that night getting ready to go out on his 'Make Me Smile (Come Up and See Me)' UK Tour. He was apparently so completely bowled over by our performance that early next day he contacted our management. "I want them on my tour" he said enthusiastically, "I love Sailor, they're the most unique band I've seen for years". This was by far the biggest tour we had taken part in to date and Steve and his band Cockney Rebel, including Jim Cregan and Stewart Elliot, stood side of stage watching our show practically every night. This was unheard of by a headline band and the highest praise a support act could ever wish for.

Steve and Cockney Rebel were huge fans of Sailor and loved everything we did. With all due respect to Kiki Dee, with Steve being one of the biggest stars around at that time and with his stupendous hit, this was a massive step in the right direction and our biggest and most important tour to date. It was also the perfect tour for us in other ways as when our eventual hit single 'A Glass Of Champagne' took off, it was patently obvious that many of the fans who had seen us on tour with Cockney Rebel had gone out and bought our record.

Steve's generous appreciation of our sound and stage act was reciprocated however as I often stayed late to watch him perform. It was a master class of how to enthral and entertain an audience. Although impeded by a physical condition, having suffered polio as a child (and one would have to say, not the most tuneful of voices in spite of these considerable and 'un-pop-star-like' setbacks), Steve transcended all difficulties and boundaries to become one of the most devastatingly powerful and charismatic performers I have ever seen on a stage. I'd literally never witnessed audience reactions like it, especially when he performed his song 'Sebastian'. It was a genuine 'tour de force' that I never forgot, and a benchmark to strive for when going on later to create and produce live shows throughout my career.

We were getting rave reviews for our live work but we were signed to a large international record label and up to the point of the Cockney Rebel tour our single releases from the first album had not charted in the UK or anywhere else. That is except for one country, bless them, Holland. The Dutch CBS contingent, who had been wildly enthusiastic out in L.A. at the CBS Convention, true to their word had put out 'Traffic Jam' as a single, which went straight to Number One in the Netherlands, guaranteeing our first ever Gold Album. The discs were proudly presented to us by Dutch CBS at an unusual press conference on a boat sailing around the canals of Amsterdam. Strange to think that Georg originally had not wanted this track, a hangover from our earlier Kajanus Pickett era, to be included on the album at all, but thrilling nevertheless to have received serious recognition in at least one major European country and something to show for all our hard work. Also a musician never forgets the first time he ever got a Gold Record!

Whilst the album had been enthusiastically and critically acclaimed - filed under 'promising' - and represented the simplicity, purity and atmosphere of Georg's singular musical vision, there were no other hits from the album and the record company was becoming very anxious. Also the relationship with our manager, Steve Morris, wasn't working out as well as we'd hoped. So after a brief 'courtship' period we decided to engage the services of Robert Wace, ex-manager of The Kinks and Stealer's Wheel, a strangely eccentric, but highly effective manager of whom several books could be written on him alone. At over 6'4", as thin as a stick insect and the subject and inspiration of 'Well Respected Man', the Kinks sixties hit song, Robert was 'old-school' personified with a cut-glass public school accent to match and a man who didn't mince his words. "We need a hit record or we're dead in the water", Robert told us one day at a meeting at the EMKA offices in Bond Street, "Oh and the image has got to change. The sailor suits are great, don't get me wrong but I think we should bring in some stylists."

EMKA was owned by the late Steve O'Rourke, manager of Pink Floyd, the most successful band in the world in 1974 and Robert's 'sleeping' partner in Sailor's management team. (EMKA also managed Marc Bolan, which is probably why one day whilst leaving the building, I quite randomly and unwittingly met Boy George, then a thrill-seeking teenage autograph hunter in drag. Ironic that he wanted my autograph then. But more on him later!)

Steve O'Rourke often said he far preferred coming to our gigs than Pink Floyd as not only did he love Sailor, (at least that's what he said), he also loved looking at the kind of attractive females who tended to come to Sailor shows, quite unlike (in his words), "The student types who frequent Floyd's gigs, they're all spotty blokes who live in bedsits!"

One night after a particularly rambunctious show in the Navy Port of Plymouth, still in our original Sailor suit era, and where we'd had 'stage divers' almost from the start, he'd turned up earlier, out of the blue, in one of his many cars, this time a beautiful Bentley Tourer, breezily telling us; "You know you've really 'made it' when everyone in the town dresses like you!"

Rather than having to travel all the way back to London in the back of a van, Steve kindly and generously offered us a lift in his car, but not too long on the journey, the otherwise magnificent automobile started to splutter and eventually petered out in what must have been, in pre-M5 and pre-mobile phone days - the middle of Dartmoor! We were all very concerned of course. But unperturbed, the multi-millionaire manager of the biggest rock band in the world got out a little black book from his pocket and uttered what would become, in Sailor folklore, the stuff of immortal legend; "I think I own a garage around here somewhere!"

Walking towards a village where he thought he'd seen some lights, O'Rourke returned not long after with some even more good news, he apparently owned a hotel nearby, and a very convivial establishment it was too!

Robert's 'stylist' ultimatum was quite a lot for us to take in, even though secretly I was relieved we might finally ditch the 'Sailorboy' image. Our resulting look was in many ways even more camp than our original Laurence Corner get-up. A bit like 'On The Waterfront' meets 'Casablanca', with lashings of make-up on the side. When one of our stylists earmarked an apache look for yours truly, I thought "Christ no, not again, what will it be this time, buffalo hides and feather headdresses?" But thankfully, she meant a Parisian gangster or street ruffian look, which, today I guess, would be more like the TV series 'Peaky Blinders', (coincidentally also from Birmingham) with cloth cap, collarless shirt, sleeves rolled up, and whilst also caked in make-up and rouge, the most threatening and provocative look my tiny teenage face could muster.

Georg looked convincing if not slightly menacing in his Brando leather jacket, fake tattoo'd cheekbone anchor, striped top and African Queen sea captain's hat. Henry meanwhile was rakishly dressed in a colonial suit and Panama hat, John Lennon wire glasses, silver cane, carnation buttonhole and could have just walked off the set of a Graham Greene movie about seedy intrigue in foreign parts. "How dare you" Henry probably said! Grant's 'look' ended up being slightly ill-defined, as sitting at the drums every night he felt he required something less cumbersome. But his sensitivities perhaps weren't immediately helped by Robert's typically robust comments upon entering the dressing room;

"Georg, you look amazing, a real 'lead singer' and a true 'star.'

Phil; you're a natural dresser. Very good looking boy, the outfit really suits you.

Henry: I love this look; it's perfect for you. You're going to be very rich."

Grant? You look like a cunt!"

This cameo, typical of Wace, was never taken personally, well, not much, in fact for some inexplicable reason every time Robert saw me in costume, I can still see him languidly exhaling cigarette smoke and exclaiming loudly, randomly and with a huge smile; "Jean Kent!"

The photo session for our second album Trouble was thus completed at Camden Lock, with our fussing stylists in attendance and judged by the label and everyone else to have been a great success. The cover shot on what would become our most successful album, featured Henry and I very much in the foreground and while it satisfied my considerable ego, I affected a degree of nonchalance about the choice, though the shot was unanimously agreed to have been by far the best, even by Georg.

Throughout this period of change we were still working our asses off on the road while Georg had been burning the midnight oil coming up with demos for our next record at his flat in Maida Vale. One day we showed up for a playback of his latest composition and, very modestly as was his way, Georg quietly unleashed a classically simple 'three chord bash' of a tune called 'A Glass Of Champagne' on his ancient creaking Beocord tape recorder.

The first verse went:

> *I've got the money, I've got the place*
> *You've got the figure, you've got the face*
> *Let's get together the two of us over a glass of champagne*

© Georg Kajanus, Morris / Sashay Music Publishing. Reproduced by kind permission.

Bang! Eureka! That was it, the whole thing right there in the first three lines, similar to many Beatles songs in its classic simplicity. Immediately we could tell it was a hit and realised Georg must have been taking CBS and Robert's words very seriously indeed. They needed a big record and boy were we going to give it to them. Initially I thought it may have been a teensy bit close for comfort to another well-known ditty that Georg had always had a crush on, (which shall be nameless), but quickly suggested a couple of arrangement changes on the spot which seemed to make the song even more of a sure-fire winner. Eventually, when the band put the song down at CBS's Whitfield Street Studios, (assisted by a sprightly and earnest young junior engineer named Steve Levine), the track featured Georg's distinctive 12-string Ovation electro-acoustic guitar with a highly disciplined metronomic feel throughout. My intrusive and raspy foghorn ARP 2600 bass synth played with my left hand absolutely straight on the beat with 'oompah-style' military precision, whilst 'first and fifths' only on my piano right hand; the simplest possible drum arrangement from Grant with no fills or frills whatsoever, and blistering unapologetic four-part harmony vocals on top. To cap it all, Henry's stupendously catchy Nickelodeon solo, a chorus in itself, which in the words of Rupert Holmes and Jeffrey Lesser, our new American producers; 'dotted all the i's', and the final finishing touch in making the track totally 'idiot proof'.

It was a pop masterpiece!

Rupert had also suggested that Georg perform the word 'Champagne' in a more pronounced fashion, like Steve Harley phrased key words in Cockney Rebel's 'Mr Soft' ("She makes me hap-poy!"). So later, in the studio, we encouraged a very shy and reserved Georg to sing 'A little glass of champoigne' instead of the more refined 'champagne'. We loved the effect but Georg, as ever the perfectionist, wasn't completely convinced. I hardly need say which version the producers went for when they mixed the track in our absence however.

A few weeks later, while we were still on the road in Norway, Georg not only loathed his voice affectation but also hated Jeffrey's finished mix of 'Champagne' which had been sent for our approval prior to release. It all seemed to be swamped in echo. Following his adamant stance, we disliked it too, but none of us quite as much as Georg; "We have to stop it being released" Georg declared, "We cannot possibly allow this mix to go out," he said defiantly with everyone nodding sagely in stern agreement. After all, we wanted our lead singer to be happy with the record. At the time we were in Scandinavia on a European tour but immediately flew back to London for a 'crisis' meeting with the label in an attempt to cajole them into allowing Georg to remix the track. But Dan Loggins, A&R Head at CBS, was having none of it and they went ahead and put out Rupert and Jeffrey's version of the single.

In November 1975 'A Glass Of Champagne' was thus released with the full might and manpower of a huge international record company machine firing on all cylinders well and truly behind it. Robert went into CBS's Soho Square offices every day terrorizing everyone in the building and reading the riot act, whereupon the single immediately began picking up radio play everywhere. All this activity was a new departure for us but as soon as I heard our song on the radio I could tell that Jeffrey and Rupert had really known what they were doing all along.

Just like the make-up and stage clothes of which, at first, I personally and subjectively felt were going to be grotesque and over the top in the eyes and ears of the public, the producers had just made our record sound larger than life in a similar manner; by over-emphasising and overstating certain sections. Accentuating the space and power by adding what we first thought was an excessive amount of plate echo, the producers had mixed the track specifically for radio and which, by now, was blasting out all over the airwaves. And guess what? It sounded utterly wonderful and so full of life and energy.

Up and up it went, cruising up the lower regions of the chart at first, which, in those far off days meant selling spectacular amounts of records at a time when even on a wet Tuesday morning in Scunthorpe you could shift thousands. Phones were ringing off the hook and we were everywhere at once, interviews, live radio, and almost every week Sailor seemed to be on TV, especially shows like Mike Mansfield's new kids' show, Supersonic on London Weekend Television, and on BBC TV's Basil Brush Show. Mansfield was a flamboyant and demonstrative TV producer who adored the band and said he would have had us on every week if he could.

We were also, by now, frequently appearing on Top Of The Pops, the biggest show of them all, so much so that I was on first name terms with the security guys at the gate; "Not you again, given you a job here have they?"

The reason for so many appearances on the show was that we'd been at 'number two' for weeks, as the record to beat was possibly the most successful and most played single of all time, Queen's 'Bohemian Rhapsody', which had been successfully fighting us off the coveted UK number one status week after nail-biting week. At practically any other time in pop history Sailor would have easily made number one and probably stayed there a long time, but Queen's 'magnum opus' was one of the biggest pop juggernauts ever.

One glorious day however, after what had seemed a frustrating eternity, Freddie's mighty operatic anthem finally ran out of steam after its ninth week at number one, and by the skin of our teeth, we edged up the home straight on the inside rail pipping Queen to the post in the NME Chart, albeit briefly at number one, but by God, we got there in the end! Legend has it that Freddie was overheard in the BBC bar later telling someone if he had to get knocked off by someone, at least it was a sailor!

As in Henry's words, "the world was now our lobster"; Sailor began a seemingly never-ending succession of UK and European tours, foreign TV shows and spectaculars; festivals; headline concerts; and corporate events. Every day was different but whereas before, when I always seemed to be climbing in and out of vans, it was now big black limos and First Class air travel everywhere. As in the unforgettable parlance of our dear friend, the late, great Reg Presley of The Troggs waxing forth on the joys of pop stardom, "Ere, this pop lark's great ain' it? What's it today Ronnie, pictures or pub?"

One evening after a sell-out 'Sailor Spectacular at London Dominion Theatre' followed by a glittering star-studded after-show reception arranged by CBS, the limo driver who had taken Ann and I to the party was still outside as we were leaving. "Great" I said, "can you take us home now please?" "Sorry mate" he said, I'm only booked until midnight but I can drop you off at Gloucester Road Tube if that's any good". Taking him up on his offer, the strange looks we got getting out of a huge immaculate limousine to catch the last tube home were something to behold.

Some of the contrasts between the quite phenomenal success the band was now enjoying and my personal life began to jar, not entirely made easier by the fact that Georg had moved out of his tiny flat in Little Venice now having bought an extremely fine house in St John's Wood with a gleaming Aston Martin on the drive. We'd bought our house down in Cornwall, prior to Sailor taking off in 1973 as part of my Sawmills Studio venture.

Golden Years

Champagne would be called for on other occasions this year too. It was Easter 1976 and I'd bought Ann an egg, the biggest one in the shop, made of Terry's dark chocolate, her favourite. It was a very special Easter as she was about to give birth to our first child. Earlier, knowing this day would finally arrive as sure as the tide would come up the Fowey River, I'd also hidden away a lovely necklace with purple stones from an antique shop in St Austell. "Oh Phil, it's gorgeous isn't it," she said. "Very expensive though, have I been a good girl?" "Yes, very good and it's your birthday in November, so let's wait and see shall we?" Later however I secretly went back to the shop on my own, I could just about afford it. The previous day I'd driven Ann to Treliske Hospital in Truro for a check-up as she was very close to having the baby, but they'd decided to keep her in. It was that close! It was a very bumpy journey in our decrepit Morris Minor.

A month or so previously; "I told you that you'd ruin your suspension with all that slate you brought back from Delabole" she said, "Yes, I'm sorry, but I really wanted to finish off the patio in time for the summer and our baby", I explained. There was a pause of reflection and then she added; "Leaving the car under five feet of water down on the quay, when you were too pissed to drive home didn't exactly help either!" "Shut up" I explained. A few weeks earlier, rather than drive a couple of hundred yards up the hill from our riverside pub, being considerably refreshed and over the limit, I'd left our car on the road by the quay. Next morning, overlooking the stunning view of the river from our bathroom in Golant, out of the corner of a bloodshot eye, reflected in my mirror whilst shaving; even with my blurred vision I noticed a small burgundy blob which appeared to be floating in the river just off the quay by the 'Fisherman's', "Hmm, wonder what that is", I thought. The previous night's car parking arrangements then dimly dawned through a classic head-thumping hangover, "Oh Christ, that's my bloody roof", I shouted in complete horror whilst running down the stairs and on down to the river, still only half-shaved. Miraculously, our local wizard mechanic at the Four Turnings Garage got the old banger going the same day I'll never know how he managed it, but he did, "You don't want to be caught in a remote Cornish village with a heavily pregnant wife and no wheels!" he said in a very Cornish manly way, Ann and I agreed compliantly.

Now, on our way to Treliske to have our baby, I kept apologising profusely, acutely aware of every single bump in the road and the impact it was having on the barely existing suspension of this ancient example of Oxford's post war automotive industry, "Don't worry, it'll probably make me give birth right here in a lay by, You'll be doing me a favour!" she said kindly as we drove towards Truro, "I don't think I can wait much longer though". Ann looked like a big beautiful egg herself.

Weymouth Wilson, the extremely capable midwife at Treliske Hospital, took one look at her on arrival in the maternity ward, "You're not going anywhere young lady," she said with mock sternness. "That baby of yours is obviously very happy in there, but we're going to have to move things along a bit faster now aren't we dear?" The nurses eventually came to tell us they were going to induce by breaking the waters next morning at 7:00am, Good Friday 16th April 1976. I was very nervous but Weymouth Wilson consoled me; "Don't worry Mr. Pickett, come back tomorrow around lunchtime and we'll see if that lazy baby of yours feels like joining us all for Easter. Where do these wonderful people come from I wondered and felt like hugging her on the spot.

Good Friday dawned and it was a beautiful Spring day as I drove alone along the deserted road towards Truro a little too fast. The moon was still up, the day heavenly and our baby was on its way. Somewhere on a narrowing promontory of land, on a watery planet, merely an atom spinning in deep space around a molecule, a tiny speck of human life keenly anticipated the arrival of its offspring with a love the size of the Universe. To steady my nerves along the way and still a little early, I pulled over into a pub I'd never been to and who should be in there chatting to the landlord, but George Luck, my friendly neighbour in Golant, the former chairman of the St Austell Brewery. On hearing of my mission he immediately ordered a pint. "Get that young man a drink, he's going to need it!" he said slapping me on the back, "Well, we're not quite there yet George", I said. But not very long after, I arrived at the hospital and went straight up to the maternity ward. Something inside told me life was never going to be quite the same again.

"Right, get your jacket off, Mr. Pickett and get these things on, you are going to help us deliver your baby, aren't you?" Weymouth Wilson spoke authoritatively, her commands never really mistaken for queries, "Come on, force of nature, let's go!" "Er, yes of course" I said gingerly not exactly relishing the idea. Ann's serenity never ceased to amaze me and, although quietly terrified herself having never given birth before, seemed more concerned about my state of mind; "You're not going to faint are you Phil?" I'd previously been known to keel over at the sight of blood and felt absolutely pathetic about it; I was now a man in a woman's world and within sight and proximity to the stalwart Wilson and my own courageous wife, so was absolutely determined not to let the side down and thankfully I didn't.

Much later, at 14 minutes past 4pm, Jack Philip Pickett was born (or 'Good Friday Jack' as he was known in the Fisherman's) to whoops of joy and a proud father's horizontal tears. It was the best moment of my life to date and felt like my greatest achievement as a human being. It was also a mighty relief to know that Ann had come through the ordeal intact, mother and new baby were doing fine.

Earlier there had been a small tent on the lawn outside the maternity wing where another of the fathers of the day, a young guy not much out of boyhood, was patiently waiting to see his child. He'd strolled down the drive with his girl the day before and now, together with new baby and rucksack in tow, the three of them wondered off with no fuss towards the main Truro-Penzance road, another brand new resilient family on their way in life. What a miracle!

Later, going home in the early evening, I seemed to be conscious that every blade of grass, every bush, and even individual leaves on trees were tinged with the same rich golden light of warmth and euphoria I felt inside. The sun was going down in the West behind me towards Lands End, my first son, Jack Philip had been born and my wife had come through her ordeal safely. Still on my own, but now with a family to look after, I drove back home to Golant on enlightened gossamer wings, my decrepit Morris Minor now a hovercraft of bliss.

Someone from the *Daily Mirror* called early the next day. "Hi Phil, congratulations. Is it a boy or a girl?" the journalist enquired. "A boy!" I proudly announced.

"Oh bollocks!" he said, "We were hoping to put you on the front page if you'd had a girl!" "Thanks," I said and hung up.

Sailor's follow-up to 'A Glass Of Champagne', 'Girls Girls Girls' was currently racing up the charts!

***

Primrose Mansions Lockdown

"I inched along the balustrade, crazy with fear and afraid to look down at the traffic speeding along Prince of Wales Drive far below. There was no turning back, no return to my prison inside the apartment six floors up without food, electricity or even a telephone to call out for rescue. My friend had obviously

been away for some time and had summarily been disconnected..."

Sounds like the start of a crime novel but it was June 1976 and unlike everyone else in the band, I didn't have a flat or bolt-hole in London to go back to, having been unable to sell our Cornish house due to the property crash of 1973 and the place halving in value. Therefore we had no choice when Jack came into our lives, other than for Ann to stay in Golant with him when I was often off on the road. This was no one's fault; it's just the way things worked out. I was quite envious of my band mates, all of whom could hotfoot home, put their feet up and relax seemingly oblivious of my plight, that of being obliged to find cheap accommodation or a friend's pad to crash until the next important date in the Sailor diary.

In this instance I'd just arrived in London to set sail for another tour. I was staying at Tony Cox's flat; "You're welcome to use the flat Phil but don't forget, the intercom buzzer doesn't work," he informed me cheerily. "Oh, and by the way, be very careful with the Chubb lock, it sometimes sticks from the inside and you can't get out".

It had. And I couldn't.

A few minutes earlier, realising the door was jammed fast, I'd shaken the handle violently, banging hard and hoping a neighbour might hear, but there was rarely anyone in the flat next door, in the eaves of Primrose Mansions, high up on the top floor. I picked up the phone to dial out and get help, continuous tone - nothing! Initially seeing the funny side or at least a wry smile at the all-too-familiar irony of my 'karma-drama' fate, seeping into consciousness came the grim realisation I might soon be staring, not just at the genital-tightening view down to the street below and far across Battersea Park, (I loathed heights), but also into hope-swallowing despair at the reality of my situation. There was absolutely no way of getting out of Tony's spartan flat, nothing to eat, and perhaps most ominously of all, impossible to communicate my plight to anyone. Oh, that and a trifling matter, I was supposed to be going off on a major, chart-topping, European Tour with Sailor in ten minutes time!

Why did this kind of thing always happen to me? The rest of the guys in the band seemed to live such uncomplicated orderly lives compared to mine. In fact everyone else I knew did. I sometimes thought there were strange forces at work in my life, patterns not of my choosing. It wasn't fair. I began to feel very sorry for myself, very high up, and very alone.

A re-occurring childhood dream came into my mind, not really a nightmare, but a disturbed empty feeling high above the earth perched on a thin diving board, sick with vertigo. Far below me was a tiny illuminated tank of water the size and shape of a penny piece and stretching down towards the pool, a long white ladder disappearing in perspective like a Tom and Jerry cartoon, except it was scary, not funny. Contrasted with a glorious roaring infinity of heavenly stars, I could hear my heart beat against an indifferent world, but also was faintly aware of organ grinders and merry-go-rounds from a fairground far below. (Was this perhaps a childhood premonition of Sailor?) The eager crowds were urging the circus-follower, a pale and thin boy, to jump off the board and way, way down, to dive into the tank like Houdini.

Just a few steps down the road, in Overstrand Mansions, was where seven years earlier on July 20th, 1969, I'd established my bed-sit base camp from where I would seek my fortune in London's Tin Pan Alley like Whittington's musical cat. At the very moment I dropped my suitcase and guitar down in the dark green room overlooking the lush park in summer's full bloom, Neil Armstrong had just stepped on the Moon and, in real-time, I heard his immortal words crackle out from the radio: "That's one small step for man, one giant leap for Mankind." But that was then, and meanwhile fear and trepidation were still having fistfights with hopeful outcomes inside my brain, and the bad guys were winning!

The day before Henry had telephoned. "We'll pick you up on the way to Heathrow tomorrow at 11 am Philipo," he breezily informed me, realising I was just about to endure the gruelling journey up from my home on the Fowey River. "They're sending a limo to pick us up, isn't it great?" He enthused. "It's going be an amazing tour, apparently we're a 'sell-out' everywhere". "In that case, I don't see why management won't agree to a bloody hotel for me in London. Everyone knows I live in Cornwall," I whined, somewhat mean-spiritedly pointing out the obvious. Still, it was no one else's fault I'd decided to buy a house in Cornwall I was unable to sell. Nevertheless, I'd asked our manager, Robert Wace, if the budget could handle a reasonable hotel before and immediately after these tours and TV appearances as it made things so difficult for me while I was trying to sell the place down there. "Not really Phil I'm afraid. The band feel it's not justifiable, but can't one of them put you up once in a while?"

I wasn't looking forward to the brain-numbing pre-M5 exodus all the way to London which, at journey's end, meant hauling my five weeks on the road bags up six flights of stairs, only to be rewarded by a night in Tony's sparse, hardly-visited ivory tower amidst the rooftops of SW11. "It's Primrose Mansions isn't it, Tony Cox's old flat?" Henry inquired.

But here I was stuck inside the sixth floor apartment, desperately looking up and down the road from the window of the substantial red-brick Victorian mansion block, when a few minutes early, I suddenly saw the sleek Daimler's shiny roof glide into view along the grand thoroughfare, regally pulling up outside the castellated entrance portico below. "Great! I'll shout down and wave out of the window. They're bound to see me," I mused optimistically.

Georg and Henry got out of the car and I could see them ringing the bell downstairs. But they didn't look up once. Why would they? "Hen, Georg" I screamed at the top of my lungs. "I'm up here, HE-LP!" But the noise of the traffic and jets screaming overhead (towards Heathrow, the destination I should now be travelling as if to rub it in) and even the sound of the wind in the trees opposite all conspired to drown out my futile cries into the ether. "Look up here you bastards!" I began to lose it. I'd never been so conscious of how bloody loud everything was in London. The tiny figures below couldn't hear me at all and were deep in conference with the chauffeur. Now I'm looking at my watch, removing grey peaked cap, scratching head, and looking up and down the road.

"I'm up here you bloody idiots, why, oh why, don't you just look up?" I yelled, now almost in tears of frustration and despondency. But they still didn't look up. Not once. Not one of them. Then a sinking feeling as I saw my bandmates shaking their heads and getting back into the lush Vanden Plas, clunking the doors expensively shut, and slowly gliding off in the direction of the airport.

"Why is Phil always late?" I could almost hear them saying to one another in the silent opulence of the car, annoyingly unaware of their bassist's unintended incarceration. I simply had to get out of the flat as not just my career but quite possibly my life depended on it. In reality my only chance was to try and make for the open skylight three windows along from Tony's; a 30-yard heart-stopping tightrope of terror. There was no choice other than to climb out on to the balustrade stretching along the entire length of the building to see whether it was possible to either call for help, or even attempt to break in and leave through another apartment.

Nervously and with extreme trepidation I edged out of the bedroom window, first confirming the ancient crumbly masonry would actually support my weight. Trying hard not to look down I shifted and shuffled along at snail-pace until, adjacent to the landing's skylight and only two more windows to go, my heart nearly gave way as I almost toppled off the ledge; a piece of the architrave I was grasping in my hand came away, crashing down on to the pavement below. As if in slow motion it seemed to take forever to reach the ground, instantly breaking up and ricocheting powdery white fragments between the cars across the road. "Fucking hell", I cried out in despair, my palms sweaty with vertigo and genuine terror. A mildly interested crow, my feathered partner in roof crime watching my perilous journey from his chimney-top, suddenly ruffled by the human's threatening expletive, slowly took off in the direction of the park. The street below was now deserted. The world had gone to work. I began to rehearse possible human contact scenarios inside my head; tap, tap, tap. "Er, excuse me. Um... I'm terribly sorry, and you probably think this a little weird, (disarming smile), but could I possibly come in through your window and I'll explain everything?" Mmm, perhaps not a good idea, especially, by now,

I was looking a bit like the 'Battersea Rooftop Murderer'.

I finally managed to arrive at the half open skylight; inside there was another dishevelled bedroom. Thankfully there was no apparent sign of activity in the flat but with nervous anticipation, I briskly tapped on the window three times, just in case. No, there didn't seem to be anyone in, thank God. So I put my hand through the smaller window above and attempted to lift the latch on the lower window to enable human access. My thoughts were conjuring up a Judge and Jury.

"So Mr Pickett, posing as a pop musician and TV personality, you are hereby accused of breaking and entering a complete stranger's apartment gaining illegal access, via the roof, like a common cat-burglar. I therefore sentence you to..."

"No Mi' lud, pleeee—ase! I can explain..."

Just as I was about to clamber through the window and jump on the bed below, I stopped dead in my tracks. Hang on a minute, what about my suitcase, my stage clothes for the tour, my passport, everything I needed for five weeks on the road. Was I raving mad? Even if I could get out of this place without being arrested, how on earth was I going to get back into Tony's apartment to get my stuff? From having been a prisoner inside Tony's flat, I'd now be locked out of it.

"OH, FUCKING BOLLOCKS!"

Still on the ledge, with a dull thud in the pit of my stomach, I came to the grim realisation that I'd have to go all the way back along the roof, climb back into Tony's flat, turn around and inch all my belongings back along the bloody 'precipice of doom'. "Okay there's no alternative, just do it!" I encouraged myself.

Returning along the tortuous route, I re-entered Tony's, gathered up my suitcase and guitar, and proceeded cautiously back along the outside of the building. Dragging the cases along the roof incredibly slowly was far more difficult this time especially now knowing, with certainty, I'd be seen as a burglar should anyone catch sight of me. However the ordeal was nowhere near being over as, due to my cumbersome and unwieldy possessions, it took several gut-busting minutes longer to reach my planned exit from this very real nightmare. Opening the window again I realised I could only go through with the plan by first throwing all my things onto the bed, and then, past the point of no return, gaining entry myself. It's strange the things that come into your mind at times like these; remembering my grandfather, who fought in the same First World War campaign, I recalled a quotation from General Foch, Commander of the French Ninth Army sending a message through to HQ during the Battle of the Marne in 1914: "My centre is giving way. To the left is certain disaster. My right is in retreat; situation excellent, I shall attack!"

Inspired by the folklore of Pickett ancestry and pumping up courage I smoothly carried out the operation with military precision, soft-landing on the unmade bed of a stranger who, if still having a bath, coming out of the shower, or perhaps in the kitchen making coffee, would probably kill me on sight, in fact no perhaps or probably about it! On the other hand, if the occupant was old and infirm, they would most likely die of heart failure and keel-over on the spot. But to my intense relief, hovering by the bedroom door, head cocked and listening intently, after a few moments I realised that, apart from my heartbeat, there was no sound of movement within the flat. Thank Christ for that!

Taking a deep breath I returned across the bedroom and closed the window making sure there were no tell-tale signs of a break-in. I knew I had to make my exit very quickly so I picked up the cases and, still in military mode, sharply made for the front door. Putting the lighter of the two down I attempted to open the Yale lock pulling hard, but the door wouldn't give. I threw the other case down twisting and turning the lock furiously, but to my complete brow-sweating horror, it simply refused to budge. I couldn't believe it! The door had been Chubb-locked too, but, unlike Tony's, this time from the outside! As Terry Thomas would have spat out, in one of his many, monochrome Brit movies; "BLAST!"

I was now a prisoner in a complete stranger's home along with all of my possessions; again I started to panic. What if they came back? How would I possibly explain my way out of this? But at least there was a telephone that worked. I dialled our number in Cornwall. It rang and rang, and rang. No reply. Then I remembered Ann was taking our baby son Jack for a post-natal check- up at Treliske Hospital in Truro. Slamming the receiver down, frantically I searched the kitchen drawers and cupboards, living room, anywhere there might be a duplicate key. I found an opened letter on the kitchen table addressed to the occupant asking how things were going at her new job. Briefly this illegal interloper entertained the idea of calling her at work and asking where she kept the spare key so he could let himself out of her flat.

But then again, perhaps not! I tried calling home again. This time, thank the lord, Ann picked up, "You'll have to slow down Phil, what do you mean, you're locked inside someone else's flat?" I was so fearful my words were tumbling out all over the place, but she could obviously tell I was in a parlous state of mind so tried to get me to calm down, "Look, take a deep breath, they're bound to have a spare one somewhere, everyone does" she said serenely, "Do they have a bureau or anything like our desk? That's where most people keep their spare keys." At the far end of the hall there was an antique roll-top desk, "There is one I said, thanks, I'll call you back." Eureka! I came across a drawer in the bureau containing some old keys. The problem was that there must have been about a hundred, but thankfully only ten were of the Chubb variety. Lo and behold I was delighted to find that the very first key I tried was the right one: "YES ! At last, a lucky break! I'm out of here!" I cried out, punching the air in victory.

Momentarily however, the bare-knuckle, white-water ride of adrenaline still coursing through my veins had made me feel sick, and I was also paralysed with exhaustion and relief. I flopped back down on the suitcase for a few seconds to reassemble my brain and internal chemistry. Then, gathering my bags quickly, I was out into the hallway like a dose of salts, finally slamming the door shut. The noise of my prison door reverberated for several seconds throughout the landings and stairwells of six floors and deep into my soul. I posted the key through the door, (what were they going to make of that?) and descended the staircase as if on air. Then I ran out into the street and hailed a passing black cab; "Heathrow please mate, I'm very late so can you step on it?" I implored breathlessly. "Sure guv'. Hop in." The cabbie squinted over his glasses, turning around, a flash of dim recognition: "Here, aren't you that bloke on the 'tele' with Pan's People and all that? 'A Glass of Champagne' isn't it?"

Oh to be famous.

Chapter 13
Prodigal Son

Growing up in Brum I believed that the most iconic and impressive venue in 'The Celestial City', in all of its ersatz Roman glory, was Birmingham Town Hall, and so this was a fitting place for my triumphant return as the prodigal son. Now armed with a huge hit record, I was destined to perform on exactly the same stage that, whilst growing up, I'd first seen so many of my heroes; The Rolling Stones, Bob Dylan, Moody Blues, Eric Clapton, John Mayall, Dave Brubeck, Spencer Davies and Stevie Winwood (even my beloved Acker Bilk), so this date was more significant than anything I'd ever done to date, so much so that I thought my chest might explode with pride and anticipation. My mother Eileen and Ann's mum and dad, Patricia and Bob, were coming to the show, as well as most of my friends, relatives, musician mates, ex's and rivals; they would all be there in the audience to greet the returning hero.

After seeing the Stones perform on the same stage on their first major UK tour, supported by The Nashville Teens and The John Barry Seven, the very next day, (after being unable to sleep that night!) I formed my first band with classmate Mick Robbins on the X99 Midland Red bus going to Tamworth College and called it The Blues Unit.

Now that Sailor was the chart-topping headliner, the whole building shook to its foundations and due to so many frenzied fans rushing the stage, security before, during and after the gig was extremely tight. Not tight enough however for a jealous female fan who managed to break through the cordon as we were leaving the venue, making a beeline for Ann and biting her hard enough on her arm to draw blood. Not for the first, or last time we both realised that amidst all the glory and excitement, pop could also be a messy and painful business!

Although a great performer, brilliant singer and in many ways the perfect front man, Georg, being essentially a very quiet and private person, could sometimes appear a little wooden on stage, and now that our audiences were getting bigger, more excitable and in their often lippy and typically British irreverent fashion, were sometimes a little hard to handle for the shy Norwegian. At the same time, trying to make up for the fact that both Henry and I were playing keyboards, not the most visually enthralling concept, looking, as someone once unkindly observed, as if we were 'standing at a gent's urinal', we began goofing around and playing up to the audience, showing off, if you will, as a counter to Georg's more formal and introspective manner on stage. With Georg playing the straight man, this frivolity between the pair of us went down extremely well with audiences and as our show progressed and refined, Henry in particular seemed to discover his true métier as an extraordinarily spontaneous, gifted and often wickedly funny 'MC'.

Germany, in particular, was also becoming a huge market for the band and we were a household name, a fact which doggedly seems to persist to the present day with practically every record we put out reaching Top 5 and achieving silver, gold or platinum status. Sailor was also by now the toast of German society appearing on every major TV show in the country of my birth, and also many others throughout Holland Denmark and Scandinavia. We were performing at huge events everywhere and being presented with cultural achievement' awards and commendations left, right and centre. One of them, in particular, was presented to the band by the former German Chancellor, Willy Brandt, while "Champagne" also hit number one in places as far afield as Australia and South Africa.

In contrast to what was, by now, much visible success being enjoyed by the band, there was a nagging feeling that financially things were not adding up, at least for Henry, Grant and me. For the amount of work we were doing and the time spent away from home, even though times were good generally, we were starting to wonder if we'd ever see any real money coming through, enough perhaps to buy a decent car, or go on a lovely holiday somewhere. This was brought home to us one day when Ann and I were travelling back down to Cornwall on a brief weekend break in her trusty but ancient and suspension-free Morris Minor, my car having given up the ghost long ago. We had to stop and fill up at a nearby petrol station. I was driving on this occasion and the male garage attendant's face lit up with celebrity delight as he recognised me as, "that bloke off the telly", but then his face seemed to go as dark as thunder and utter disgust, first looking at the car, me again, then back at the car as if for the first time; "'Ere, what in God's name are YOU doin' driving a car like THIS for? You're supposed to be a bloody POP STAR". The concept of having seen me on Top Of The Pops every week, but apparently driving this old banger, was almost too much for his strained belief system to endure, offending every sinew in his Cornish body. He walked back into his garage sullen and disillusioned, and frankly, insulted.

One of Sailor's last seventies appearances, prior to a disastrous USA Tour in 1976, was an unforgettable concert at Hamburg Town Hall. The band was at the utmost pinnacle of its success having just completed a sell-out German tour and the feeling in the Hall was something I'd never experienced to that degree before. The atmosphere was electrically charged from the opening note and the reaction of the crowd, throughout what was to be our final performance in our biggest market for at least seventeen years, grew and grew with each song until, at the end of the performance, the crowds simply refused to leave the building. I will never forget the sound they were making; an unstoppable Teutonic roar and it was actually quite scary to behold such power. Our loyal Hamburgers would not allow us to leave the stage!

Too many hysterically amusing adventures ensued that would fill several volumes, but one or two in particular stand out; for instance on one occasion when the band were sent off to tour and conquer America by Robert Wace and Steve O'Rourke. He believed, unwisely in retrospect, that we should sail away from our hugely successful markets in Europe where we were by now having hits all over the place, and instead, set our sights on America where there were vast amounts of money to be made touring 'to kingdom come' in vast stadiums, like Pink Floyd had. But just to be picky, there was the small matter of Americans not particularly liking our music at all, but we didn't know that then.

Upon our arrival in New York, however, our friend and enthusiastic mentor at CBS, Dick Asher, threw a party for us in the apartment of Walter Yetnikoff, who at that time was the most powerful recording executive on the planet. It was Walter who, along with Asher, was the subject of the best seller *Hit Men - Powerbrokers and Fast Money Inside the Music Business*, the explosive history of the extravagant business shenanigans behind the zenith of popular music. Walking around Walter's luxurious multi-million dollar apartment, champagne in hand overlooking Central Park and prior to going off on tour and having our dreams shattered, we still felt on top of the world with everything to play for. As Rod Argent, of Argent and formerly The Zombies, was also passing through town, the party appeared to be in his honour too so it was not, in fact, solely "Welcome To America Sailor", as the banner above Walter's ostentatious hallway would have had us believe.

That was okay though, we were relatively unknown in America at that time, in fact utterly unknown outside the skyscraper portals of CBS Records on 6th Avenue. Being a little cheekier than the rest of the band and now in the line to be awarded a piece of our celebratory cake by Walter himself, also perhaps as I was once a baker by profession, I couldn't help noticing that Rod Argent's cake was ever so slightly larger than Sailor's. Furthermore, it seemed to be decorated with a little more panache and fancy cream work than ours. Now at the head of the line and seeking to break the ice with the most powerful music business executive the world has ever known (and in his own apartment!) I inquired dryly, but still with the intention of projecting cheeky, northern working-class British humour; "Walter, why is Rod's cake bigger than our Sailor cake?" Bad move. Metaphorical alarm bells were going off left right and centre as Walter's and by now Dick's eyeballs were swivelling around in their sockets. With red faces and much steam emanating from their immaculate shirt collars and cuffs at the sheer brazen audacity of "What's this fucking guys name again?" highlighting the bleedin' obvious. Dick, never what you might call 'relaxed in his own skin', in fact as stiff as an ironing board, while addressing me in hushed tones spluttered and spoke very slowly; "Er, Phil? Er, um, I guess er, Rod's been over in the United States of

America a little longer than, er... Sailor has, and, er... ah" finally running out of road in answer to a question that was only really a joke.

What was it Churchill said about the USA & Britain being two countries divided by the same language? I couldn't have cared less actually but the episode had at least revealed that even at this exalted level of the business I had unwittingly discovered a phenomena that would forever be known as "cake hierarchy' and that a catering decision had obviously been taken at the very highest levels of the music industry.

Chapter 14
All Over Bar the Shouting

"You make your own luck, Gig.
You know what makes a good loser? Practice."
(Ernest Hemingway)

S ailor's final tour of America, at the insistence of Robert Wace and Steve
O'Rourke, was an unmitigated disaster on every possible level. Whilst not
without its lighter moments of fun and frivolity; never too far away if
Henry and I were sharing the same hotel or stage; financially, and more
importantly group morale was less than good, the seeds having been sown that
would, in the end, play a major role in the group's chapter one demise.
Inappropriately opening for acts like Charlie Daniels in Cowboy Country, and
Kansas in the deep Southern States did nothing to endear our quirky European
waltzes and Glam Rock pop played with accordions, military bass drums and
glockenspiels to US audiences; in fact quite the opposite. They just didn't get
it.

I can still see the look of pained incredulity on a soul brother's face after we'd
played our set at the mother-funkiest, whacked-out low-down R&B dive in
Philadelphia, which, at the end of our show, was less than a quarter full, the
regular clientele having left in perplexed, head-shaking confusion. "You
motherfuckers are crazy!" said a guy who looked just like Richard Pryor, staring
at us in bewilderment before wandering off as we were breaking down our
gear. "We'll have to fire Robert and Steve (our management) when we get back
to England", Georg said ominously, "This American tour has been a complete
waste of time."

He was right of course, but unlike the rest of us, Georg's conclusion had been
arrived at in the comforting warmth of financial security from his ever-
mounting songwriting royalties, whereas management was the only lifeline for
the rest of us in getting paid at all. But truth to tell, the whole idea had been an
expensive mistake and miscalculation for the band, which, in order to do the
tour at all, had been underwritten by CBS Records to the tune of tens of
thousands of pounds of our money with nothing really to show for it but air
miles, rancour, travel sickness and, in my case, a very realistic rubber moose
mask. Also, by now, I was desperately missing Ann and my new son Jack down
in Cornwall. The whole thing was becoming unbearable and I just wanted to
get back on the plane, put it all behind me and forget about everything for a
while.

One night at the very famous Troubadour Club in Los Angeles, Joni Mitchell
was watching in the audience. At the end of my tether with how badly the rest
of the tour had been going and what a waste of time it all was, I just felt like

being mischievous and naughty. I also thought Georg needed cheering up, so during our song, 'Girls Girls Girls', in which I always went up to perform the vocal harmony with him on the same mic. Just before the start of the song I'd put on the astonishingly lifelike, skin-toned moose mask that I'd earlier located from somewhere in Hollywood. I always enjoyed an ability to make Georg laugh almost uncontrollably, but on this particular night, perhaps because Joni Mitchell was in the audience, he definitely did not see the funny side of it at all. Not having noticed me yet during our rendition, but seeing members of the audience, including Joni, laughing their socks off, he glanced over at one point in the song and visibly paled in utter rage and horror at what I was doing. For Henry Grant and I, this made it even funnier as it seemed to sum up the utter insanity of what this tour had all been about. Several days went by however where Georg was still furious and refusing to talk to me. Finally on the third day after the event and being able to stand the silence no more, I uttered the immortal line (in Sailor folklore anyway) in all sombre seriousness; "Was it The Elk Georg?" at which everyone, including Georg, exploded with relief and hilarity.

From the wildly enthusiastic audiences of Northern Europe only a few weeks earlier to disinterested punters in Nowheresville, USA felt like a soul-destroying leap into the abyss and was definitely the straw that broke the camel's (and elk's!) back for Sailor.

Hindsight is always 20/20, but on a business level alone, deserting Sailor's hugely successful markets such as Germany, UK, Austria and Scandinavia, where we had hits and could sell out everywhere, to losing borrowed money playing in deserted bars in the American Mid-West, seemed to be an entirely new level of rock 'n' roll insanity. What were our managers thinking? As will by now, be evident from this tale and no doubt countless others, pop music can be a fickle mistress and by its nature, a disposable commodity; look the other way or go out of circulation for a few months and she moves on like grease lightning to the next shiny new thing that takes her fancy.

For instance, one day out of nowhere dark clouds appeared on the horizon in the shape and form of a certain Mr Johnny Rotten, uncouthness personified and whose wily puppet master, Malcolm McLaren, was never far behind. The same year, in fact, in December 1976 that Sailor had enjoyed two massive hits - 'A Glass Of Champagne' and 'Girls, Girls, Girls'. The future, at first quietly, then later ominously came knocking for us and many other bands from the Glam Rock era courtesy of an obscenity-ridden live TV interview of a band called the Sex Pistols on Thames TV's Today Show with the hapless (& soon to be jobless) Bill Grundy.

Symbolic at first perhaps and hardly noticed but even then, in one's groin you knew as a musician that big changes were afoot in the music-go-round and that the earth might be about to shift from under your feet. Not being allowed to write for Sailor during the most youthful and energised period of my career was the 'elephant in the room' I could no longer ignore. In spite of earlier hinting that he may at some stage relent, Georg was refusing to budge on the issue so I knew eventually I'd have to make a move if I was ever going to fulfil my own ambitions as a songwriter. I'd proved to myself and everyone I'd been a peerless supporter and promoter of Georg's talent, as much if not more than anyone else, but by Sailor's third album, it seemed that by having such free reign, if anything, seemed to have inhibited Georg's ability to write hit material.

Whilst on tour in the US, in a perfect world everyone other than Georg would have preferred to arrive at a workable compromise with management, but this was all blown out of the water when not long after our exhausted return to England, Georg unilaterally gave Robert and Steve their marching orders. So that, as my Gran used to say, "bar the shouting" plus a few months of fear, acrimony and aggravation - was that!

Little did we know then that fifteen or so years later, thanks to my chance meeting with a German multi-millionaire promoter in an airport lounge in Germany that, Phoenix-like, Sailor would dust off the ashes of the late seventies and rise again in glory playing to larger audiences and more people than ever before. But a lot more water would have to flow under the bridge first.

Later in 1978, our hopes and dreams of continuing as a major label band were, as we had feared, ruthlessly cast aside at the hands of CBS's 'new broom' and Head of A&R, Muff Winwood. Muff was the older brother of Steve Winwood and bassist of the band I'd worshipped and slavishly followed around Birmingham in my teens, The Spencer Davies Group. He decreed that Sailor was to be dropped from the CBS roster as a new musical era beckoned. Grant, who prior to Sailor was a chemistry teacher, returned to his profession, as ever the sensible member of the band. Georg, by now cocooned in his newly acquired St John's Wood wealth, built his own studio to start his solo career, but as Henry and I didn't have anything like these options, or any cash to fall back on we were pretty desperate, both of us having young families to support. In addition, Steve O' Rourke was now suing the band, jointly and severally, which effectively meant we couldn't earn anything from activities in music. Basically we were stuffed, but still putting on a brave face.

During this incredibly busy and at times very challenging period, the adventures, laughs and utterly ridiculous situations that Henry and I found ourselves in would fill several volumes, to which, dear reader, depending upon the success of this tome, will be enthusiastically returned to, subject to health, breath and reasonable expectations (as well as hopefully, copious of amounts of books sold!) in more graphic and entertaining detail later. But suffice to say that the Sailor adventure was an extraordinary chapter of my life that I shall never forget; have very fond memories of and would not for one minute change a hair of its head! (Even though I wouldn't mind getting a few of mine back!)

Chapter 15
Matterhorn of Filth

For many reasons that are by now, probably apparent to the reader I always felt that part of my soul was born in this far-off county by the sea in the West of England; Cornwall. This is why perhaps whenever times were uncertain or the future perhaps appeared temporarily bleak, I, and now we as a family, would return, over the Tamar River to regroup, rebuild and plan whatever was to be done next.

Back in 1950 my mother, fresh from Africa, a golden future and colonial life of luxury, servants, cars and cocktail parties, arrived in a state of bereft shock and sudden financial insecurity to a grey post-war, red-nosed and penny-pinched England. She stepped off the BOAC 'Stratocruiser' with me in tow like Paddington Bear, and we were met by her mother in one of the corrugated-iron mizzen huts at the eastern end of the runway over some fields at what eventually became Heathrow Airport. Well before Atlee's Government had got to grips with the enormous debts of war and Sir Ernest Bevan's still-to-come Welfare State, many widows had to mend-and-make-do to support themselves and their offspring. At a certain stage she must have got fed up with setbacks on the cruel rainy streets of West Bromwich and the continuous propositions of its ardent men folk and decided, upon invitation, to take me down to Cornwall to stay with my paternal grandparents in Ludgvan near Penzance where they ran the local stores and Post Office.

I was just coming up to junior school age when my mother applied for and got a job as the dinner lady in a prestigious boy's boarding school in Penzance, a position that also came with a delightful two-bedroom flat overlooking the harbour and St Michael's Mount Bay. Again, this occupation - for which I am not sure my mother was entirely suited, to be honest, nevertheless came to a somewhat abrupt end when the Headmaster insisted on some extra-curricular activities that would guarantee me a place in an establishment I would otherwise have had no chance of attending. Needless to say, it didn't work out, so my paternal grandparents suggested I go to the local school in Ludgvan instead.

She would deliver me scrubbed and blazered to the Western National bus every morning outside the Royal Hotel, next to the Railway Terminus in Penzance, for the three-mile hop to Crowlas, where my Nana would meet me. Then it was up Back Lane to my best friend Anthony's (not crossing any roads!) and finally trudging up School Hill together. Hearing Blake's hymn 'Jerusalem' being sung in Ludgvan School Assembly on my first day at school, filled me with a kind of ecstasy, although being so young I didn't know why I was crying my eyes out. Although I had no understanding of it, I think my musical soul must have come alive and the tears were those of joy on hearing for the first time the power of the melody and words of this song. So much so that my Nana, thinking I was just too upset and overwrought, took me home again!

When I was 5 or 6 years old I started to become aware, probably for the very first time, of who I was, where I fitted into the general scheme of things and a realisation dawned on how my life seemed very different to those around me.

The first friend I remember in my life was Anthony Carnell, a blond-haired child of an extremely happy and precocious disposition, one year my junior. It was at his home Carvossa House where we used to meet prior to ascending the hill to Ludgvan School every morning on those many damp Cornish days. On entering the kitchen of a healthy and rosy-cheeked Mrs Carnell, Anthony was inevitably tying a shoelace or finishing off a clotted cream and treacle sandwich. Or perhaps involved with the last-minute search for life and death school necessities, depressingly familiar with mums of small people the world over. Waiting for my friend, I was immediately taken by the warm friendly atmosphere of a large family house full of busy people on their way somewhere. This contrasted somewhat with the serene and dependable tick of a Grandfather clock in the formal polished hallway, a benign orderly Judge presiding over the comings and goings of a united family who knew who they were and where they were from.

Delicious warm baking smells emanated from the Aga range and typical of many Cornish kitchens, aromas of saffron, freshly baked bread and Cornish cream, made one's taste buds come alive creating a rich backdrop of domestic harmony. There was, as often as not, a tantalising bowl of cake mix to secretly dip your finger into whilst Mrs Carnell pretended not to look. Then suddenly turning round she'd catch us licking our lips and, tongue in cheek, scold us.

The ample sunny frame of Anthony's mother represented, for me, a world in which everything was in its place, food was in the belly, jokes and laughter filled the air and brothers and sisters looked on kindly at their younger sibling and his friend about to go up the hill to school. It seemed that, unlike me, they were bolstered against the world and its inconsistencies, living and thriving together in the place they and their forebears were born, secure in their own time and place in between the sea, the air, earth and seasons.

Meanwhile this only child, yours truly, had arrived on a bus much earlier in the day from rented rooms in an unfamiliar town, met by Nana at Crowlas bus stop, and had walked up 'Back Lane' by himself before arriving at 'Carvossa'. Even though I was surrounded by the love of a small but disparate family, they were still in shock and grief at the loss of their son and my mother, her young husband. I was not however made to feel there was ever anything untoward or lacking in the realities of my existence, but did begin to be aware of a feeling of looking in from the outside, consciously trying to fit in with different groups of friends and aching to be accepted as a local in the ever-changing scenery of my itinerant life. This feeling seems to have followed me like Peter Pan's sewn-on shadow and which many years later I came to understand and appreciate that Cornwall would always be part of my 'Karma' and who I was.

So back in the county again after the humiliations of Sailor's American tour, our management having been fired, and now careerless, after a few weeks, we were desperately running out of funds. Not having enough to go out in the evenings we were obliged to content ourselves watching, amongst other things, yours truly on one of the many repeats of Top Of The Pops or Supersonic. The irony of the situation was hard to avoid.

One evening over dinner with our neighbour, Bunny, at their rambling idyllic house on the other side of the village, we confided in her and husband Martin. They found it hard to accept that anyone who had been involved in such a successful pop band could so suddenly be down on their luck. Martin Minter-Kemp was a doughty, ex-naval commander of the SBS, the maritime equivalent of the most efficient fighting force the world has ever seen, the SAS. Soft-spoken and with impeccable manners, like Blackpool Rock he was indelibly printed to the core with characteristic true-Brit qualities of endurance, ingenuity and humour in the face of adversity. Stating the obvious, Martin piped up, "You need a bloody job old chap", and taking pity on my plight, kindly asked me to join him next day, 7 am sharp at Truro Dock. "The old boat needs a lick of paint and I could do with some help, especially from a Sailor!" he quipped, with a twinkle in his eye. Due to concert performances, TV and touring I hadn't done much manual work for a long time but did look forward, at least, to the novelty value of a few days of honest toil and, more importantly, some cash. Somewhat incongruously given the present situation I set off for Truro in my brand new Triumph Dolomite Sprint, driven out of a Berkeley Square Showroom only a few weeks earlier.

It was a warm sparkling morning when I arrived on the quay to find Martin and Doug, his First Mate, getting ready to leave. This surprised me, as I thought I was there to paint a non-moving object but, overriding this, was the shock of seeing the decrepit, rusting hulk in all its true glory, in glaring contrast to the previous evening's rose-tinted description. Overcoming all trepidation, however, we cast off in humorous form, many references to the band's name made in teasing, but good-natured fashion by Doug. It felt good to be part of this idyllic summer morning far away from band politics and concerns sailing seaward on the crystal river, with a chipped mug full of freshly brewed tea in hand.

"Here, what's that Babs in Pan's People really like? By God, I'd like to give her one. Bet you have, you bastard!" Doug jealously surmised, a broad West

Country smile disarming over-familiarity. But seeing me on deck wearing overalls and sticky paintbrush in hand, he was obviously having great difficulty making sense of it all, the fact that someone he'd seen 'on the telly' many times was now 'Second Mate' aboard 'HMS Shit-Heap' just didn't quite add up in his book. Momentarily confused and looking almost poignant for a second or two, he suddenly snapped out of it, quickly reverting to his cheery Cornish self. "Anyway, what's that Kenny Everett like? God, he's a bloody larf a minute!" he observed. "You ever met Roy Orbison?"

Doug naturally assumed that all those seen in the small brown box in his bed-sit in Mevagissey were on intimate terms with each other. I assured him this was sadly not the case, especially regarding Babs, and confirmed I'd not had that particular pleasure. The response almost seemed to invite apology and he was visibly disappointed. But the friendly banter at least whiled away the time daubing thick lead-based maritime paint on the rusty hull of Martin's pride and joy.

Whilst our antiquated vessel ploughed its weary furrow up the Fal, Martin, meanwhile, sat eccentrically in the middle of the deck in a rocking chair reading *The Times* and smoking a cigar. Up on top, protecting swarthy features and full head of grey-flecked hair, was an extravagantly large-brimmed hat of Australian outback origin. Usually reserved, Martin came alive, however, when keenly describing the next money-making adventure; ballooning across the Andes; top-secret nautical missions for MI6 along the Venezuelan coast; geodesic domes across Cornwall, (pre-dating the Eden Project by 25 years), were just a few of his most recent schemes. Indeed, we were presently aboard the latest dream child, namely an old tramp steamer which he had picked up for a song to take 'liquid waste effluence' from Truro Council out to sea and dumping it. Then, having persuaded Cornish farmers, a wary bunch at the best of times, that sea kelp would vastly improve their crops, on the way back upriver (Martin once described it graphically thus with a chuckle, "after dumping the unspeakable into the unfathomable"), he and Doug dredged kelp off the coast of Falmouth, lugged it back to Truro in the hold, bagged it up and sold it to the 'horny-handed sons of toil'.

We made our weary way back upriver in the early evening after a hard working, but blissfully peaceful day at sea; me exhausted, sunburned and filthy. Being obvious that the tide would not quite carry us back to Truro, Martin planned to spend the night grounding his flat-bottomed ship on a mud bank. The idea of Ann at home in a clean warm lovely bed was very obviously more appealing than the bare planks and oil-stained mattress of my cold and increasingly damp bunk space. Martin took one look at me, sympathetic. "Why don't you take the tender and outboard and go home tonight?" he said generously. "There should just be enough tide to get you back to Truro, and we'll meet you on the quay in the morning".

I didn't need asking twice and as the light started to fade we lowered the tender into the water. Martin handed me the battered looking Seagull outboard engine and an oily can of two-stroke. He hurriedly explained the eccentricities of starting the engine, the tide now flowing briskly in the opposite direction of my intended travel. I pushed off and was alarmed at how quickly I seemed to be carried back towards the sea. Pulling on the starter rope, once twice, three, four... nine times, there was no sign of life. Turning a bend in the river and losing sight of the mother ship I began to worry that perhaps this was not such a good idea after all. I realised that I would not be able to row against the now very strong tide. To cap it all, the battery in my torch was fading and just at the point of giving up, I gave it one more desperate pull on the rope with blistered fingers. To my massive relief, the flimsy contraption splurted angrily into vigorous life like a demented and suddenly disturbed wasp. I didn't care about the noise, I was going home and felt overjoyed that tender, outboard and I were now biting against the run of the river and proceeding at a rate of knots towards Truro, my waiting pristine car and a warm welcome home. It was a good twenty minutes before I rounded the bend again to even reach the spot where earlier I had cast off. Downing a twilight beer on deck, it caused Doug no end of mirth, "You back already then; she kick you out?" he laughed into his bottle. It was around 10 pm by now, and Martin had already retired to captain's quarters.

It was getting much darker and my battery had finally bitten the dust. By the light of a full moon, however, I could see towering mud banks glistening high above me on each side. The river was dramatically narrowing and flowing fast against my hull, impeding progress significantly. I prayed there would be enough water to round the next bend, when, with an unpleasant jolt, the outboard suddenly and uncontrollably sprang up as it hit bottom. The engine stopped.

Once more, peaceful and complete silence reigned on the river broken only by the sound of a distant heron. It was, however, merely a fleeting consolation against what was to become a night of almost mythical reckoning. Attempting to navigate into deeper patches I started to panic as it was patently obvious I'd eventually run aground. There was nothing for it but to jump overboard and try pulling the tender over towards some trees where I could at least tie her up for the night. I made out what appeared to be the dim light of a window through dark trees on the north side of the river and, as my craft was definitely not going anywhere, for the time being, took off my shoes, rolled up my jeans and stepped out of the boat into what I assumed was a firm and shallow river bottom.

Wrong!

I was suddenly petrified to find myself sinking fast into vile thick, sucking mud, almost to my waist and from that moment I knew this was all getting far beyond a joke; on the contrary, it was turning into a life-threatening nightmare. With extreme and serious effort, I just about managed to clamber back aboard and luckily found the riverbed harder on the other side, allowing me to disembark again and pull the tender in, on what was only now, a trickle of water over toward some trees. I tied the rope as secure as I could to an overhead branch. Lord knows what Martin would think tomorrow morning as he chugged back up river to find his pilotless tender tied up to a tree, but in truth, at that moment, I didn't much care.

I ventured towards the light with the thought of asking at the house if I might call home. Unlatching the gate and timidly walking up the pathway to knock the door, I jumped back in shock as a fierce dog sprang out like the Hound of the Baskervilles, barking viciously and chasing me barefooted out of the gate, which I only just managed to close in time. My heartbeat must have been audible in Truro when finally, pausing for breath back at the tree, realised I still had to walk another mile or so back up river and cross the other side to my parked car. Once again I gingerly stepped into the darkness along the bank, my bare feet cut by sharp stones and my legs stung all over by unseen nettles. Finally, I could actually see my car on the dockyard and, at last, civilisation.

A little too hastily now I attempted to find a spot to cross the river and after several more messy sinking and stinking episodes eventually found myself at the foot of what appeared to be a mountain of household rubbish, old washing machines, fish heads and supermarket trolleys. I realised I still had to scale this Matterhorn of filth before I could win back the wheels of my glistening chariot and speed homeward. At this point, I broke down in uncontrollable laughter, both in the intense relief at still being alive and for getting myself into this mess in the first place.

Slowly clambering up the pile of rotting waste, exuberantly now, unvanquished by cruel nature, tides, darkness and hostile elements, I was about to grimly discover that the long night - and my trial by ordeal was not yet over. Within clear sight of the summit, I suddenly lurched back as the blood-curdling scream of a huge white apparition sprang up in front of me, breaking the still night's silence and stopping my heart yet again, the creature's wings knocking me headlong back down the slope and deep into the garbage.

After the initial shock, I realised I must have disturbed some kind of giant seabird and once again, defiantly laughed to the sky at the utter madness of my predicament. Climbing up on hands and knees one last time, exhausted and wretched, I finally reached the quay just a few short steps from my vehicle. For what seemed like minutes I lay on my back looking up at the stars, reflecting on my ordeal and how out of nowhere can things go so badly wrong. As sailors have often been known to say; "Worse things happen at sea", I thought. Mentally I was also recovering my equilibrium for the drive home; walking up to the car, opening the door and smelling the brand new lustre of leather and wood. At once I became acutely aware of my own rank odour, a not-so-subtle combination of a rubbish tip, mud bank and fish farm. Worse still was how I must have looked; soaking wet, covered head-to-foot in mud, bits of garbage (and worse), clinging to the remains of what used to be known as my clothes.

I decided to strip down to my underpants throwing jeans, shirt and sweater into the boot. I then climbed into the immaculate interior, started her up and at long last, finally sped homeward into the night. There was hardly any traffic on the dark twisty road between Truro and St Austell and I was just getting used to the feel of the pedals on my bare feet, when, pulse quickening, I passed a police car in a lay-by. The sight of what looked like, no, in fact indeed was, a stark naked man, black-faced, driving a brand-new car, at speed, in the middle of the night must have been, even for Cornwall, worryingly strange.

Of course, they slowly pulled out on to the main road and were soon following me. Recklessly, I almost put my foot down hard on the board but, luckily, thought better of it as they pulled closer. They went to overtake and drawing alongside, indicated for me to pull over. The two policemen parked some distance in front and at first, stayed in their car, one of them on the radio and the other not taking his eyes off me. Eventually getting out one of them very cautiously walked up to my driver's side. Feebly, I attempted a nonchalant and disarming smile, as if to say, "Hey, there really is an innocent explanation for all of this officer", and "isn't life strange" etc. But looking like a demented cross between Harold Steptoe and a Black and White Minstrel and half-naked to boot, they really weren't in the mood. "Is this your car Sir?" one of them said, straining at politeness by a mere Cornish thread. "Yes officer" I tried to explain, "Look, er..." "Then would you mind explaining why you're driving around in the middle of the night in your underpants... Sir" he interrupted, emphasising the last word pointedly. I was reminded of the customary patronising monotone tinged with slight sarcasm that must be drummed in from Day One at the Police Academy. But I suppose he did have a point!

In my delirium, I had tried to rehearse what I was going to say, but what came out seemed to be: "Look, officer, I've had a very long night and just want to go home." He replied, "Yes Sir, so would we". Impatient now; "Would you mind getting out of the vehicle and putting both hands on the roof where we can see them?" He didn't say "Sir" this time. I quickly complied. When finally satisfied I wasn't the 'Penzance Axe Murderer' I showed them my rotting heap of clothes in the boot and also luckily managed to produce my driver's licence. I also had a couple of Sailor albums in the boot. "That' me," I said. "My day job!"

After a few minutes their justifiable caution turned to hilarity; "We thought, who's this bloody pervert then?" said one of the boys in blue; recounting what had happened, we all fell about in hysterics, one of them sagely advising, "If I were you, sir, I'd have a bath before you climb into bed with your wife tonight.

Pardon me but you don't harf' bloody honk!" After this episode, the boys in blue kindly escorted me all the way back to Golant, and still laughing, with thumbs up at the top of the village, bid me good night, turned around, and drove back towards Truro.

Not possessing a door key and at three o'clock in the morning, an undressed, mud-encrusted man holding a dirty bundle of wet clothing, nervously tapped on the back window at 3 River View. A bleary-eyed Ann finally opened the door a few moments later, and seeing the unsightly spectre standing before her, said, "Hello darling; been to a party"?

***

Adding irony upon irony, whilst I had spent the day painting Martin's ship, Ann greeted a pack of intrepid German Sailor fans who had travelled to England and had made it all the way down to deepest Cornwall via planes, trains and automobiles on a quest, *"to find ze house of Phil Pickett".* After asking after me in the Fisherman's Arms, our local pub down by the quay, the disciplined and organised gaggle of 'Autogrammjäger' finally found their way up the steep hill to a little alleyway around the back of our house overlooking the River Fowey at Golant. By now and much to Ann's initial trepidation, however, the party of Germans were peering in through our kitchen window. As soon as their quest had been explained Ann took pity on the youngsters and invited them into our house. Nervously, but very pleased with themselves, the small party shuffled in for tea and sandwiches and much inquisitive, but respectful, conversation ensued in that serious, direct and earnest manner common to those whose birthplace I share. When one of the party asked if she could use the bathroom, Ann suddenly remembered that our stair carpet, probably first purchased before World War One, was so threadbare and old it had swastikas featured predominantly in the design. Prior to the 1930s this symbol was universally associated as a sign of peace and harmony until rudely collared into the service of the Third Reich. God only knows what the poor little German fans would think if they saw it; possibly that Phil Pickett was a little closer to his German roots than they'd previously imagined, but not in a good way!

Upon finally bidding farewell one of the more well-to-do teenagers of the group, whilst taking a last glance at our somewhat modest surroundings and not meaning to be patronising remarked, in that slightly arrogant German manner; "It's funny Ann. You know for some reason I thought that Phil Pickett would be living in a much bigger house than this".

Without missing a beat and for years the stuff of Sailor legend, she remarked, "So did I."

Chapter 16
Maharishi

" There's this chap called Mark Leighton, a Transcendental Meditation teacher at the Balham Centre, who is also a builder and decorator by day" Henry called me up one day to tell me; "He's putting a new roof on at the Centre and says we can go and work for him; says he'll pay us cash!" "Sounds good," I said, "When do we start?" "Tomorrow. Can you make it Philip?"

The next day, I couldn't believe what I'd so casually agreed to the previous evening. We were up steep ladders on a bloody roof in Balham, and boy it was cold! We soon nicknamed Mark "The Sarge" as although a renowned teacher of Transcendental Meditation, he always seemed to be barking instructions to the two of us like some kind of spiritual Sergeant Major. Another job was steaming and scraping vile ancient Victorian wallpaper and a hundred years worth of muck and slime from the walls of a cold and decrepit house overlooking Clapham Common. When the weather would allow we also painted the rails outside black.

It was during the winter and unremittingly grim. "He gives you all the cushy jobs!" I complained to Henry one day, "I always get sent up the bloody ladder when you're just asked to hold it steady". "You know I hate heights Philip," Henry said meekly but, as usual, we both collapsed in mirth at the utter ridiculousness of the situations we constantly found ourselves in.

One day during our decorating activities, Henry informed me out of the blue that Mike Love from The Beach Boys was arriving at Heathrow the next evening from California and as I lived out near the airport, would I go and pick him up? Mike was a leading light of the Transcendental Meditation movement in the States in those days and although they'd only met briefly, they shared a number of mutual friends and associates through TM. "I don't know him at all Hen, how is that going to work?" "It's fine," Henry assured me, "he'll be okay. He's a really nice guy and The Beach Boys love Sailor apparently". "Wow," I said, "I grew up listening to their music." I was chuffed to bits to hear this, as couldn't have been a bigger fan of the group, especially having worn out at least three copies of *Surf's Up*, my favourite album of theirs. Prior to forming Sailor with Georg, that record was probably our biggest inspiration by far, especially when it came to vocal arrangements. "We'll also be meeting that guy I told you about, Ron Altbach, who has invited us out to meet Mike. It'll be great fun," Henry added. I was dimly aware of that conversation and that Ron was also the keyboard player for The Beach Boys and yet another TM teacher. Ron had asked both of us out with Mike for an Indian meal at Khan's in Notting Hill.

I'd been obliged to sell my car a few weeks earlier, but a close friend, Dave Peters from my Birmingham school days and the lead vocalist in my first band, generously offered to allow me the use his ancient white van-like Renault 4. The car was so old that moss, tiny mushrooms and fungus had healthily adapted themselves to the damp environment around the windows of the automobile; the design of which was one of stubborn Gallic eccentricity. Parts of the road were clearly visible through the floor under the driver's seat. The closer I got to Heathrow and my celebrity pickup, the more acutely conscious of it I became, and of course, it was pouring with rain to boot. The windscreen wipers, like tiny frantic chopsticks, were futile against the wintry deluge.

Mike, suntanned, radiant, extremely rich and wearing a Beach Boys tour jacket, would earlier that day, no doubt, have been dropped off in a Cadillac or some such vehicle, in style and in time for his flight from a sunny Californian airport. On his arrival in London, it was freezing cold, pissing down with rain and was now being invited by me to get in on the wrong side of a rusting fungus-ridden vehicle, probably the size of his chest of drawers back home. The singer of 'Good Vibrations' looked confused, perhaps even a little scared, but still displaying Californian cool as we rode off into the night, wipers going like the clappers to no avail whatsoever. He hesitantly inquired, "Er, what kind of... 'car' is this Phil?", "It's called a Renault 4 Mike," I said slowly so he could hear above the din of wipers and road. "It's French" I exclaimed hopefully, by way of explanation. "A Ren - what?" he said, never having heard the word before. I told him again.

Silence. Then, remarkably, still crouching forward as if not allowing himself to relax in my strange tiny vehicle, bizarrely, while staring ahead into an uncertain night, Mike began to sing the well-known Beach Boys classic, 'Surf City', as we were driving along the Westway in the rain towards Notting Hill to meet Ron and Henry at Khan's. "I bought a '30 Ford wagon and we call it a 'Woodie', Surf city here we come."

***

A few years earlier, in 1973, after being steadfastly opposed to the idea, Ann talked me into, or probably closer to the truth, tricked me into going along to the Albert Hall with her to the see the late Maharishi Mahesh Yogi who was giving a talk on Transcendental Meditation, an ancient Vedic practice of calming the mind and relieving stress. I was then of the mindset that all great art, poetry and music essentially was wrought from the soul, involving copious consumption of cigarettes, Scotch whisky, grass and anything else to hand. Even though Henry and his wife Susan, at the time living upstairs from us at Holmbush Road, were an attractive and successful advertisement for their newly acquired technique of 'TM', for me it was more a case of, "No thanks man, I must suffer for my art and anyway, don't need anything like that."

As I recall, Ann was convinced that we too would both benefit from TM, and somehow she got me into the Albert Hall on the sly pretext that it was a jazz concert we were going to; Mose Allison or someone like that, but once inside the building, I secretly admired her doggedness in getting me to go at all so I felt obliged to stay for a while. We sat there for what seemed an interminable age of long dull talks from grey men in suits wearing sandals with no socks (not a look I admired!), who were saying "Jai Guru Dev" a lot. Who was this "Dev" anyway I thought? Eventually, I became claustrophobic and an intense desire to leave the packed auditorium overcame me. The Maharishi, meanwhile, a sweet tiny man in a white robe and bare feet sat on a raised podium of flowers and garlands and seemed to chuckle a lot between the constant drone of his monotonous and earnest Western followers. But when he did speak it was about a new 'Age of Enlightenment' that was dawning, although I couldn't understand most of what he was saying in his high-pitched Indian sing-song voice. "Come on," I whispered to Ann, "let's get out before the rush", a habit I'd acquired at gigs I wasn't enjoying. But not wishing to appear rude to the Maharishi, I hovered around by the very furthest exit from the stage until he'd finished speaking, already contemplating a lovely frothing pint of bitter at the pub around the corner within minutes.

Just at the end of his talk, as I was turning to bolt out of the door, the little Indian holy man, approximately 100 metres away, suddenly got up from his dais to bow and bless the audience. The next thing that happened, even now I still find very hard to explain. It felt as though my heart had expanded out of my body in a startling and inexplicable flash of light, which although I hesitate to describe the sensation, is the closest I can get.

If anyone else had tried to explain it I'd probably still be running for the metaphorical door! I'd always had, what I considered to be, a healthy cynicism towards the esoteric and in many ways still do. But within just a few seconds, it appeared that both Ann and I had run the entire circumference of the enormous building to arrive by the Maharishi's departing car. In fact, we found ourselves practically inside his vehicle and were offering him a flower.

"Beautiful," he said with a huge smile, "Jai Guru Dev."

***

Every day after the long hard slog with Henry and The Sarge, up ladders and down holes, Ann had somehow managed to get a job on nights at Heathrow Duty-Free. Most evenings, therefore, she would meet me to swap the Renault and three-year old Jack, outside Hammersmith Odeon, where we'd drive out to the airport together in our clattering wardrobe on wheels and then say goodbye until 4 am next morning. Jack and I then went home for supper, after which I'd read him a story and put him to bed. Then later, when the house was quiet, I'd write songs.

To help him get to sleep one night I wrote a lullaby called, 'Starlight', then other songs like, 'Danger On The Titanic', 'Don't Send Flowers', 'Feast Or Famine' and 'Private Eye'. Pretty soon I had a whole album's worth of songs. Bottled up as a writer for so long in Sailor, the ideas just seemed to flow out of me.

I had no idea what the next step would be but felt that I had to keep doing what I loved most if I was ever going to get us out of the deep hole we now found ourselves in. Although circumstances looked bleak, we were happy in the knowledge that we were, at least, being proactive and not wallowing in "woulda, coulda, shoulda" territory.

Verses in the writings of Florence Shovel Shinn on abundance seemed to be working in our lives as was TM, although it was still early days. On Friday nights, all the money we'd earned that week was placed on the dining table and allocated in little piles to individual debts, current requirements, cinema, the babysitter, this and that.

Henry was very enthusiastic about my songs and demos and unbeknown to me, after a performance he and I gave at the Balham TM Centre one evening to raise more money for the roof, he'd given a tape of my songs to Ron Altbach. Hen and I were planning a post-Sailor musical venture with a very talented brother / sister duo I'd met down in Cornwall called Gavin and Virginia (Ginny) David, but so far, as songs were pouring out of me, we hadn't written anything together. We had also approached Grant to be involved in our new venture but in the end, he was unenthusiastic, preferring to go back to his teaching activities having found the last chapter of Sailor particularly demoralising. Although sad, as he was such a great drummer and brilliant bloke, I couldn't say I blamed him!

In the breaks between The Sarge's building jobs, Henry and I also tried our hand at mini cabbing, this time at my instigation, (incidentally at a poky cab firm next door to Maison Rouge Recording Studios, which, although entirely unconnected, would later on become quite significant in my story.) "Your cars are frankly too old and scruffy to take passengers", the no-nonsense manager said bluntly, "Plenty of parcel work though, take it or leave it, there's plenty who will". We took the job and immediately found ourselves darting all over stiflingly hot London in a heatwave for very little money, but as ever, adventures galore.

One afternoon Henry delivered a small parcel to an address in Clapham, at which, mysteriously, all the curtains were drawn even though it was broad daylight; "Ah, we've been expecting you, come in," a sombre looking Greek man said to Henry on the doorstep. "But, I..." Henry went to intervene; "No, no, come in, it's best to deliver it personally to the recipient", the man said. So Henry, obligingly, followed him into the hall. "He's in there," said the gentleman, "leave the gift for his family on the table please", at once ushering Henry through the doorway, who not wishing to disappoint, entered the darkened room. In the centre was an open coffin containing an exceptionally dead man staring heavenwards, "Er, listen..." Henry again went to explain, but again the Greek man interrupted, "I'll give you a little time to say your prayers, pay your respects to the deceased, and then you can leave," he said quietly but firmly, closing the door behind him - leaving Henry and the dead stranger in the room of a house he'd never set foot in before.

"Take this package up to the West End would you Phil?" the manager asked me one hot afternoon. "Traffic's biblical today, there's some royal bollocks going on," he said, "It's got to go to the Robert Stigwood Organisation" scribbling the address on a piece of paper. This was back in my world, or at least my ex-world as Stigwood, and his close association with the Bee Gees, *Saturday Night Fever*, The Who, Tim Rice and Andrew Lloyd Webber, was one of the biggest pop impresarios around. It took me over an hour to get up to town with most of London at a complete standstill. To my surprise having finally delivered the package, the veteran camp comic entertainer Frankie Howerd was standing on the steps outside Stigwood's impressive office building in Mayfair. "Are you my cab?" he said in his unmistakable voice, "No, I only do parcels, I'm just dropping one off", I explained, "Anyway I'm not allowed to take humans, the car's a bit crap". "Ooh," he said looking me up and down, "I don't mind, anyway dear, my last two cabs haven't shown up. Are you going anywhere near Ken High Street love?" "I could do if you don't mind the state of the car," I said; whereupon he happily hopped into the passenger seat of the Renault up front with me.

The traffic was still crazy and we were moving at snails pace, but he was so easy to talk to. Frankie Howerd was part of the fabric of British comedy, along with the Goons and *Round The Horn*, with a direct line of provenance all the way back to the British Music Hall Theatre era. Later, a star of the *Carry On* films, and a character who'd always made me laugh in my *Dandy* comics growing up. Having established I was similarly in the trade, even though at present, as Frankie noted, resting, we got on like a house on fire. "I love Sailor, especially, what was it? 'Girls, Girls, Girls', "I've got a part in one of Stigwood's films," he said with a flourish, "Sgt Pepper's Lonely Hearts Club Band" and said he'd been at Stigwood's office to tie up the contract. "Ooh, it's ever so good," he said, "I hope it's a success!"

When we arrived outside his house and after declining his very generous offer of payment, (the sparkling conversation having been ample reward!) right out of the blue and apropos nothing at all, Frankie Howerd asked me if I'd ever tried 'the homosexual thing', just like that. "It's very nice," he said welcomingly, "Anyway, would you like to come in for a cup of coffee then?

It's the least I can do to thank you for my lift home," the entertainer said suggestively. "Er, no thanks Frankie, it's not really my thing, anyway I've got another parcel job in Fulham." I lied. I told him I was married and we had a baby boy at home; thanked him and said he might have been forgiven for trying it on having seen me on TV, admitting that Sailor had looked as camp as a row of tents! "Ooh, suit yourself then dear" I can imagine him saying but was more than likely just conveyed in a look.

It was now the hot summer of '78 and Henry and I were working on a crumbling three-story house near Clapham Junction. The Sarg had gone off to another job somewhere but had left instructions to remove some cornice work high up on the building and I'd already gone up the ladder a few times inspecting what had to be done. It was excruciatingly hot and I was already exhausted and feeling quite depressed at my lot. There was also a foul smell emanating from somewhere very close. Was it me I thought? "Hen", I conjectured, "Do you think when you do these types of crap jobs and are really poor, after a while you actually start smelling like shit?" Henry fell about laughing, immediately realising I must have trodden in some dog do and then gone up and down the ladder a few times. The stuff was all over me and, as if that wasn't bad enough, worse was to come.

Having washed and cleaned myself up I was now right at the very top of the ladder, three stories up, with Henry about half way, allowing enough weight distributed evenly along the ladder to ensure my safety. Meanwhile, I was having difficulty with a section of the cornice above my head that wouldn't budge. Giving it an extra hard tap, the whole section suddenly broke off hitting my head extremely hard and dazing me, the other half landing on Henry's head who'd been looking up towards me. He just about managed to stagger off the ladder through a second-floor window and, climbing gingerly down again, eventually, so did I. Both of us, steeped in pain and humiliation, just lay there on the bare floorboards in the bright sunlight contemplating our fate for quite some time. But this time, we weren't laughing, "Hindu holy men say that when you get a sharp blow to the head like that, you can often pay off 'thousands of years-worth of karma', Henry said quietly after we'd lain there an hour or so. "Judging by the lumps on our heads, we're probably enlightened then," I said. "But whatever. I don't think I can take much more of this. Shall we call it a day today?"

That night after supper Henry called me. "Philip, remember me telling you I'd given a tape of the songs to Ron Altbach", "Yes" I said, "Well, it turns out he knows a famous record producer called James William Guercio in the States, who manages Chicago and Blood Sweat and Tears and also has The Beach Boys signed to his label, Caribou Records", "Wow, go on" I said all ears, "Anyway, Ron sent him the tape and when he heard 'Danger On The Titanic' he flipped apparently and wants to come over here and sign us!"

"What was that you said about karma again?" I asked Henry.

Chapter 17
Cowboy Angel

James William Guercio's limo pulled up outside our drive on a February morning in 1979, exceeding the width not only of our house, 39 Lock Road, Ham, but also that of my neighbour's semi. Nervously peering round the side of our twitching curtain we first glimpsed the tiny American walk up to our humble front door, the liveried chauffeur politely standing by his gleaming black car. "JWG" wore a ludicrously ostentatious full-length fur coat, obligatory ten-gallon hat and appeared the epitome of rock 'n' roll cowboy-land millionairedom. As producer and manager of huge rock bands, Chicago and Blood Sweat and Tears, as well as being the owner of Caribou, the world-famous ranch, legendary studio and record label of The Beach Boys, as well he might. Urban myth would have us recall later on that he was actually wearing spurs on this occasion, but I may have been a little overawed and prone to exaggeration in the re-telling. Suffice to say that Jimmy, as we later came to know him, was more importantly to us on that day, an angel in cowboy clothing. Sent from somewhere heavenly to fly us all, family and I, far away from decorator's hell, financial grind and nasty-surprise-ridden brown envelopes full of English Winter, to somewhere over the rainbow, seas, clouds and mountains and his 3000-acre ranch way up in the Rockies above Boulder Colorado. This is where he had built his residential recording studio, at that time, the best in the world. Spitting on the path outside before entering the house, (a tobacco-chewing ritual and habit, that, over time, though not exactly learning to love, we got used to), it was patently obvious he had never set foot in a house as small as ours. "Jeez, you couldn't swing a goddamn mouse in here!" he observantly and somewhat undiplomatically noted, but adding for good measure: "Hi, I'm Jimmy Guercio and I love your music Phil", as we shyly exchanged introductions. Contrary to the brash, flash and extremely grand entrance, we eventually came to know him as a quiet man with a big heart, originally from a very poor Sicilian-American background and not usually given to the extrovert behaviour attributed to the cliché of the US Mid-Western wealthy. Back on the ranch, however, he always wore spurs!

"Ron Altbach played me some of your tunes and I just had to come over and meet you guys and see for myself", he said enthusiastically. "Howdya like to come over to Colorado and make some records?" Jimmy bore a certain resonance and uncanny resemblance (in every aspect but height) to the movie actor Robert Mitchum. I instantly felt the warmth of our initial exchange and together with his expressed enthusiasm for my music, I knew that we were going to get along just fine.

Later I learned that he had given up all musical activities since the untimely death of Terry Kath, his soul-mate buddy and genius guitarist/leader of Chicago, who had shot himself in a tragic freak accident at Caribou only a couple of years previously. 'If You Leave Me Now' was the last record Jimmy had produced and had played on, according to Ron, that is until he'd heard some of the demos I had recorded in Ham. "I think you write great songs, Phil," he said quietly, "and I can help you make them into hits."

Who was I to contradict him?

It was a joyous moment and the culmination of many months burning gallons of midnight oil in my front room writing and preparing demo recordings on my humble tape deck, usually late into the night after returning from the gruelling decorating job with The Sarge and Henry. What seemed remarkable about such benign serendipity was that it was all a million miles away from the regular and well-worn music industry pathways and contacts, but nevertheless unarguably at the highest level of the music business. Thank goodness Henry had given Ron the tape. If I'd sat down and attempted to engineer a meeting with one of the most successful producers of all time, I probably would have stood no chance whatsoever. But the spontaneous and innocent means of introduction, as it turned out, was far preferable and much more of a surprise as it had all happened quite naturally. As a consequence, it was plain for all to see that Jimmy was definitely on the hook.

"I'd also be honoured to play bass on your music if that's okay and I've found a great drummer, James Stroud, who will be ideal, he's a really tight player from Nashville and loves the songs," he exclaimed in his Mid-Western drawl. "Now, what kind of deal you lookin' for?" Jimmy inquired in good old-fashioned 'lets get-to –the-point' plain speaking.

After dropping this bombshell, he immediately scanned the room looking unsuccessfully for the next place to spit. Neither Ann nor I were entirely sure about the etiquette involved in these matters but tried not to show it. Otherwise, it was all just too good to be true! Ann and I had spent so many months crossing each other like zombies on the doorstep, or meeting up underneath the flyover by the Hammersmith Odeon to exchange our decrepit fungus-ridden Renault 4 containing baby son Jack after my hard day's labour in the freezing cold, prior to her (all) night-shift at Heathrow Airport's Duty-Free. At the end of each week, we would place our meagre earnings on the dining room table playing 'Jesus feeds the 5 thousand', dividing up and appropriating various small piles of cash to each debt in order of immediate priority. Had all that time spent reading the books of Florence Scovell Shinn actually paid off? Now, over the same tiny dining table, we were being asked how much we wanted to pay off all of our debts and go and play music in the best studio in the world, in the lap of luxury and excitement for the next six months. What was a poor boy to do?

Vainly attempting to appear nonchalant and unfazed I tried to respond casually; "I think I have something down on paper in my office. I'll just go get it for you to look over," I said haltingly, realising I'd given it no thought whatsoever until that moment. In truth, I hadn't really believed he would even turn up, let alone be talking dollars this soon. Sticking a sheet of virgin white in the Olivetti, I began to type furiously while Ann put some music on in the living room to drown out the noise of the typewriter. Also at the same time making tea, both her and Henry engaged our illustrious guest in a polite conversation about horses, something I knew they knew absolutely nothing about. Making it up as I went along, what came out on the page apparently was the following, which somewhat baldly and simply stated:

Proposed Recording Contract
With Caribou / CBS Records and James William Guercio
Album 1: Advance £50,000.
Plus: Recording costs, accommodation and flights to the USA for my entire family, Henry's family & Ginny and Gavin David.
Plus: New keyboards, equipment and guitars.
Terms: Contract territory, duration and royalty to be discussed and agreed.
(Nice of me!)

Future Recording Options
Album 2 £75,000.
Album 3 £125, 000 doubling up' on each future option...'

Fearing he'd probably walk right back out the door to a waiting car, airport, Concorde and a very large US Ranch back home upon reading the contents - I snatched the paper from the machine and marched back into the living room. With nervous anticipation, and still attempting to appear relaxed, I thrust it into his hand. "Here it is Jimmy. Sorry to take so long but it was hidden under some tapes" I lied unconvincingly.

In my mind's eye, from that point, the script might well have been as follows; that our benefactor went red in the face, dropped the paper to the floor and exclaimed: "Are you out of your fucking minds? What a goddamn cheek you crazy limey sonofabitches! I'm outta here! Perkins, get the car!" But in reality and after looking at "the deal" for no more than a couple of seconds, he carefully folded it up and put in an inside pocket, and said quietly, "Sure, okay, that's all agreed. Now when can you come out? In a coupla' weeks?" Swallowing hard, flabbergasted and elated at the same time, all the faces in the room especially mine broke out into a huge Cheshire cat grins. "I think that might be okay," I said as I felt my head was about to explode with joy and relief.

A few weeks later, Henry and I asked our driver to stop the Suburban high up in the Rocky Mountains wilderness on our way to Nederland and beyond, to the famous Caribou Ranch. Our 747 had been delayed due to very bad snowstorms and, after having been diverted to Dallas, we finally arrived at Denver late at night. The peace of the deserted mountain road in the dark starry night was breathtaking, made even more so by a thick blanket of virgin snow which seemed to cushion all thoughts and emotions deep in that clear silence and also in the promise of what was to come. A huge warm glow of relief and happiness filled my entire mind and body. Spontaneously, we both dived into the snow and rained down a hail of snowballs on each other, truck and driver. He must have thought the two limeys he'd just picked up at Denver after a six-hour wait were not at all like his usual star- studded clientele and were barking mad! We didn't care though. We were just having a good time after finally realising we were here at last, alive and kicking and after one or two of the usual hiccups, it was all definitely going to happen. After what had seemed like a continuous and undignified, cold grimy struggle back in England, now, already thousands of miles away, this moment was indeed one to savour.

We finally arrived at James William Guercio's majestic four thousand acre Caribou Ranch, nine thousand feet above sea level and high up in the Rocky Mountains of Colorado. Passing through the wooden log security gates, it was still a further half an hour's drive, through dirt tracks and snow driven canyons, before we entered the compound. This was a continuation of what, only a few weeks ago, would have seemed an impossible dream. Around the last bend, in the light of a full moon and the unspoiled wilderness of a thousand cowboy movies of old, we suddenly came upon Jimmy's legendary mountain retreat, a small hamlet of homesteads, smoking chimney-stacks, log cabins and larger wooden outbuildings; one of which was the world-famous studio and Jimmy's private cinema. Another housed his vast collection of RV's, off-roaders, Cadillac's and Harley Davidsons. Finally the Mess Hall, the meeting greeting and eating place and the heart and soul of Caribou Ranch. Every night around these tables you never knew who you'd be breaking bread with at sundown.

On our arrival, we were taken to meet Jimmy and Ron Altbach, now installed as our new manager, amidst much man-hugging celebration. Later we met the studio personnel, housekeepers and cooks and our official introduction to the Caribou staff was complete. A warm welcome fit for Kings to the not-so Wild West.

Exhausted after the epic journey from London, but relieved and elated at having been granted another shot at a music career, Henry and I were finally transported via snow buggy to our individual log cabins which, in reality, although technically built from logs, were super-luxurious two-storey, three bedroom, dwellings with fridges overflowing with a cornucopia of dietary delights; TV's in every room, (rare back then) all connected to Jimmy's central supply of "every goddamn Hollywood movie ever made", four-poster beds in all bedrooms and a grand piano in every cabin.

From the toil and struggle in grimy South London building sites, literally scraping shit from my arms only a few weeks earlier, we had somehow wound up at the most celebrated and exclusive rock 'n' roll studio on the planet, with a book full of songs and a bank full of cash.

Whenever people shall gather, look back and speak fondly of the long-forgotten golden glory years of rock 'n' roll - this was truly it - a gold-plated Nirvana in the eye of the hurricane, and we had truly arrived!

Much mirth ensued as Henry and I compared the ex-wildlife in our respective cabins, a disturbing plethora of gruesomely stuffed animal heads with decidedly pissed off expressions protruding from every wall; moose, caribou, (naturally), stoat, bison, deer, hog; you name it and the poor thing had been hunted, shot, stuffed, trophied and hung up to dry. After all, this was pure 'huntin', 'shootin', fishin' cowboy territory.

After I don't know how long, I awoke as one might from a coma, jet lagged out my brain, not knowing the time or even where I was at first. But I could just make out the magnificent snow covered peaks, a river flowing into a nearby lake and the beautiful Christmas card scenery around my silent cabin. I figured it had to be just before dawn. The quietness was comforting, cushioned even more by giant snowdrifts against the cabin. How the hell had we managed to pull this off? In a dreamy, pre-dawn, moment I thought of Ann and Jack so far away back in England and wished that they could both be here to share the experience; marvelling at how just a few ideas, words and songs, written and recorded in our tiny front room at Ham, had somehow transported us here and had already changed all of our lives for the better; given us some hope for a future.

Bandmates Gavin and Ginny David were flying out from England a few days later and after that, Ann and Jack, Susan, Henry's wife and their little boys, Thomas and Oliver. Jimmy was true to his word making it financially possible for our families to join us but wanted us to get started with pre-production first prior to their arrival. We met early next day over unlimited coffee in the Mess Hall, followed by a slap-up American breakfast. Were there ever finer moments than this? "Got James Stroud who's down in Boulder, comin' up to the ranch later", Jimmy said. "Best drummer I've heard for years. He's from Nashville and let me tell you, he really hits 'em hard". Jimmy also told us that Dick Asher, from our old label, had called as CBS was, unbeknown to Henry and I at the time, also the parent company of Jimmy's Caribou label. So, lo and behold, we were back on CBS Records again, albeit indirectly. Asher, however, had also told Jimmy, in no uncertain terms, "Hell, if Henry and Phil are part of it, the band must be called Sailor!"

Up to that point, not only because the music we intended to record was entirely different from Sailor of old, in fact, it felt good to be breaking away from what had become quite a rigid musical format, we also had designs on a new name, although nothing had leapt out and knocked our socks off at this stage. Jimmy and Ron pitched in and said they thought Sailor was a great name, with great provenance and we should definitely consider carrying on with it. Especially so as great bands like Fleetwood Mac had endured frequent and fundamental changes of personnel and musical styles over the years. "Besides, Carl Wilson who lives up here on the ranch loves Sailor. You guys are one of the Beach Boys' favourite bands," Ron was pleased to tell us.

Therefore after much thought, Henry and I soon agreed to call ourselves Sailor once again.

One evening over dinner Ron told us a very touching story about Jimmy. He was so devastated after the Russian Roulette, drug and alcohol-fuelled death a couple of years earlier of Terry Kath, his closest friend, that he'd since given up all desire and interest in music and recording, preferring to concentrate on his ranching and mining interests instead. He just couldn't bring himself to play music again, that is until Ron played him the songs written while I had been working for The Sarge. "I gotta do this," he apparently told Ron, "This is the first project I've heard in years that's made me want to go into the studio again."

The plan was to record the backing tracks with just the four of us initially; James Stroud on drums, Henry on guitar, me on synth keyboards or piano and Jimmy on bass, (in his case a very old Fender Precision with the same strings he'd had on there since the early sixties). We were honoured to have him play with us, especially as he'd arranged and produced so many hits; 'If You Leave Me Now' by Chicago was the latest, still on heavy rotation on the radio while we were in residence at Caribou. As an accomplished musician himself, Jimmy had played most of his life in dives, prisons and gin joints, before getting his major break touring incessantly as part of the backing bands for many of the greats. The guy was a legend and was also celebrated in Hollywood as an influential movie director known for directing the classic film *Electra Glide In Blue*.

When the basic rhythm tracks felt good and were signed off, the plan would be then to record vocal overdubs and final arrangements with all lead guitar work to be added by Jerry Donahue, an anglophile American and an amazing player I'd first met in my early London days recording with Dave Pegg, Dave Mattacks and the Fairports at Sound Techniques in Chelsea. Jerry was gentle charm personified, so much so he'd been re-christened 'Captain Nice' and was simply one of the finest players I'd ever met. It was a privilege to have him on board and Jimmy was blown away by our choice of player.

Later on in the proceedings, when James Stroud got called to return to Nashville, another old friend and touring partner, Stuart Elliot, Cockney

Rebel's and also by now, Kate Bush's drummer flew in to join us in the rarified atmosphere of our Rocky Mountain retreat to help complete the tracks. Stuart was a 'quiet riot' and a very funny guy, who reminded us of a dinner we once attended at Georg and Christine's beautiful house in London, to which Georg had also invited his sister Eva. Eva was, at that time, one of the most renowned dominatrices in New York, where she had her own well-attended and gruesomely equipped dungeon. Henry, Stuart and I, being slightly reserved about these matters and very British were agog listening to some of her stories, which chiefly involved whips, manacles and all manner of accoutrements. By now, her stories were getting wilder as the night and the drink wore on. Sensing Stuart's apprehensive shyness and teasing him a little, Eva asked if he would ever be interested in trying out anything from the list of incredibly expensive perversions on offer. "I might be," he said promisingly, "but I couldn't afford any of that fancy stuff. How much do you charge for a clip round the earhole?"

Gavin was the official bass player of the band and a very accomplished musician, but having Jimmy take over that role, as well as producer, hit maker, studio boss and éminence grise, was understandably difficult for him to accept at first. Later on, however, when it came to recording Sailor's trademark four-part harmony vocals, Gavin's role shone to the fore, proving to be a vital component and key part of the sound. Ginny meanwhile, possessed the voice of an angel and could have easily carried the band as lead singer on her own.

One of the first tracks we recorded was 'Don't Send Flowers', a tune I'd written about Kerry Hatton, a friend from our Birmingham days, who had died in a car accident driving the wrong way down a one-way street in France. This stark and shocking fact we only learned about by reading the Sunday papers early one morning. His manner of checking out seemed to sum up his brief but eventful life entirely, and I took the title from his parent's request before the funeral.

> *Kerry run to the other side*
> *Have some fun on the other side,*
> *You were always trippin' on your feet,*
> *You went the wrong way down a one-way street.*

© Phil Pickett. Reproduced with permission of Imagem Music Publishers.

Although I'd written nearly all of the songs and it was intended that I would be the lead singer of the new Sailor, after I heard Ginny sing "Flowers" there was really no contest. Also, I was never completely comfortable in the role of the frontman and Ginny's was a captivating and beautiful performance of the song. Jimmy, in particular, was greatly enamoured and the track was eventually chosen as our first single. A little later, through my publishers,

Johnny Stirling and Stewart Newton, the tune was picked up by producer Chris Neil and recorded by Sheena Easton on her debut double-platinum hit album, Take My Time, which, being the opening track on her first LP, awarded me my first significant recognition as a hit writer.

Vocals can be a strange thing, especially when assembling harmony groups. For instance, you could have four of the most technically brilliant vocalists in the world, but putting them all together in a group didn't always come off. Henry and I had spent years touring by now, and were both of the; 'if in doubt, belt-it-out' mentality. Whilst individually it might sound a little severe, when put into a group arrangement, the power and resonance of having that kind of voice mixed in with the others, often resulted in an edgy and more distinctive sound. Sometimes Jimmy recorded voices individually, sometimes in groups, but while recording Henry on his own one day, he had obviously never encountered this type of sound before. "Jeezus!" Jimmy implored, taken aback at the ferocity of the sound coming out of Henry's mouth and back at him through his million dollar speakers; "You could cut down trees with that voice!"

The studio piano, an old Steinway Grand, had a wonderfully crunchy and toppy sound, which Henry and I were delighted to discover, was the very same instrument from CBS New York's Studio One on which Simon and Garfunkel's 'Bridge Over Troubled Water' had been recorded. The acquisition of this wonderful keyboard had apparently been the eleventh-hour deal-breaker in Jimmy's negotiations with CBS Records. Jimmy's ancestors were from a certain part of Italy where all kinds coercion and brinkmanship were often employed in one's business affairs. Guercio's methods, in the nicest possible way, were sometimes more akin to the plot of a Mario Puzo novel, (cue sombre marching band and mandolins). Meanwhile, Asher and the CBS legal executives during the negotiation were crying tears of frustration, and also, by now, tearing out the remains of their hair, pleading with Jimmy to "just sign the fuckin' thing!" But the tiny Italian was already walking out of the door and halfway down the hall when, before stepping into the elevator, famously turned around to the hapless throng and said; "I ain't signing nothin' 'til you throw in the CBS Studio One Steinway Grand!"

They capitulated of course but he got his way... and the piano! Amongst all the artists who had recorded on it since its relocation to Caribou were; Elton John, Michael Jackson, Billy Joel, Chicago, Earth Wind and Fire, John Lennon and The Beach Boys - but now it was apparently our turn to play this incomparable and provenance-laden instrument half way up a mountain in Colorado.

Ron Altbach, the chief architect of bringing this life-changing experience to our door, was also a devoted TM teacher, as well as an extremely brilliant musician himself. As we had met through the TM movement and not through normal music business channels, the practice of regular meditation seemed to have become an important facet of the group and an activity we wished to pursue. I for one was wide-eyed and grateful for how everything had come together in such an effortless manner and all seemingly out of the blue, although I often suspected there was far more to it than that. Under Ron's guidance and supervision, therefore, we commandeered one of the cabins for non-compulsory, but often very pleasant and effective, daily group meditation sessions, teasingly tolerated by Jimmy, a firm non-believer.

Between recording sessions and on days off, Henry and I, when not playing hours of table football with Gav, Ginny and the studio staff, waiting for Jimmy's inevitable call up the spiral staircase; ("Vocal people!") indulged every one of our Lone Ranger cowboy fantasies. We often picked out our favourite horses from Guercio's stables and rode out high up on the ridge, along dry riverbeds, through forests and up to an ancient silver mine, an hour or two's ride from the Ranch. As there were bears and the odd coyote occasionally causing trouble, it was insisted upon that we would take turns in carrying the handgun, just in case of emergencies. On our long rides together we reflected on what a far cry it all was, not just from our previous incarnation as Glam Rock TV Gods a couple of years back, but a little later as the dice rolled, our experiences up ladders and down on our luck on South London building sites with The Sarge. In this crazy business, I considered myself hugely blessed to have such a wonderful friend and collaborator along for the ride and which, almost every day, in bad, or good times like these, so often resulted in not even being able to stand up for laughing so much at some observation or other; or in many cases, at ourselves. I have long since been absolutely convinced that as regularly as possible, crying tears of uncontrollable laughter mixed with playing and writing music every day of one's life will keep anyone perennially young whatever their age.

***

Carl Wilson

One night, everyone on the Ranch, including Jimmy and his wife Lucy, all the staff and engineers, Ron, the band and our friends all decided to go down to a bar in Boulder, around thirty miles down the mountain to see The Teardrop Explodes, a band which, at that time, was on its first tour of America. I wasn't feeling too great that evening so took a rain check on the proceedings, but in any event had to urgently finish off lyrics for the next day's vocal session for 'Danger On The Titanic.' As it began to get dark, and by now all alone in the Mess Hall, the realisation dawned that I was now the only person on the entire Ranch. A vehicle's headlights suddenly appeared, snaking up the mountain road. From my recollection, it was still around a twenty- minute drive away, but definitely heading at speed towards the Ranch. I don't know why but I suddenly felt uneasy and vulnerable like I was in some kind of outback wilderness Stephen King movie. The lights got nearer and closer still and, becoming obsessed with them, finally, I made out it was a Station Wagon with darkened windows approaching the gate. It flashed past the Mess Hall and abruptly parked around the back of the building; the crunch of tyres on thick snow; a door slamming and then... eery silence, apart from a distant animal cry.

Too scared to go and look for myself, I froze to the spot and sat there wondering what to do. This was ridiculous. There had to be an explanation, but perhaps my irrational fear was due to a combination of factors; the extremely high altitude, exhaustion after singing my lungs out all day and deadline stress over finishing lyrics, all of which were crowding in on me and making me panic. Then I heard the footsteps coming into the kitchen, large hulking great steps; then before me the enormous bulk, height and size of a man's silhouette just on the other side of the swing doors. It was like a Western Movie saloon bar scene just before the shootout. The doors swung open and I thought I was going to have heart failure. The scary stranger said; "Got any bananas?"

"Wha...? Yes, I think so, er, in the fridge, yes there's some in the fridge" I said almost whimpering with relief at such a random request from the tall bearded stranger from out of town. It wasn't the "Here's... Johnny" axe murderer after all! "My name's Carl Wilson, I live in the next valley," he said humbly, I nearly fell out of my chair but immediately got up, shook his hand and clumsily introduced myself. Then we went off around the kitchen together on a banana quest. What a way to meet one of the ultimate vocalists of all time, the beyond heavenly voice on 'God Only Knows', Darlin'', 'Surf's Up' and some of the finest vocal renditions in the history of rock 'n' roll - the soundtrack of our lives. "Heard you guys were up here and really like the music you're making, Phil," Carl said, so politely. "Jimmy played me your demos man, they're really cool." I told him how much that meant to me, as it would to everyone in the band. I timidly asked if he might be interested in coming and singing on one of our tracks, "I'd be really honoured to," he said giving me a few dates he'd be around. We carried on talking for a while, about all the great records The Beach Boys had made over the years and what was happening in music right now. Everything he said was deeply considered and serious and even on a first meeting, one could see that Carl was a shy and introspective man with perhaps a few scars. A bona fide died-in-the-wool artist through and through.

In the end, the track he said he'd like to do was 'Whatever's In Your Heart', to this day, Ann's favourite song of mine. Carl chose the 'third-above' harmony to my lead vocal on the choruses and once again, privately, would have much preferred it if he'd just sang the whole song with me doing the back-ups! When his voice came in, first take; it was complete and utter magic. He couldn't help it; the sound was just there like some divine natural creation.

Understandably when the track came to be mixed by Jimmy and his doughty chief mixing engineer Wayne Tarnowski, we kept asking for more and more of Carl's voice in the final mix, so much so that the end result sounded more like a duet.

> *You ask me why the road is long and narrow*
> *And are we all the dreamer or the dreamed?*
> *Just take my hand and we'll try to play the truest part*
> *And you must believe, whatever's in your heart*

© Phil Pickett. Reproduced with permission of Imagem Music Publishers Ltd

I'd written so many songs and by now, Henry and I were also writing, but due to Jimmy's future time constraints, plus, in his own words "we were all having so much goddamn fun making music", he decided he wanted to record a second album, almost back to back with the first, so we'd have two albums in the bag before we went off touring. After returning to England, therefore, we were soon making plans to go back out to Caribou for a second visit.

Whilst back home I co-wrote a song called 'The Real Me' with Florrie Palmer, who lived just around the corner in Ham. A singularly brilliant writer who had penned 'Nine To Five - Morning Train', Sheena Easton's only number one hit in the States. As we had the same publisher in London, Johnny Stirling, and as I'd already got a song on Sheena's album, 'Don't Send Flowers' he had put us together to write. Almost immediately, after sending the song off, we received a telegram from Quincy Jones's office in L.A. telling us he intended to cut the tune with Donna Summer, considering it to be "one of the most commercial songs I've heard in a very long time." I was overjoyed but glad I hadn't gone out and ordered a brand new Bentley, or any Bentley come to that, as when it came to recording her lead vocal, due to the inconsiderate woman having just recently turned religious, she refused point blank to sing Florrie's lyric.

As I recall it was about party-girls having fun in nightclubs and doing their own thing. So this meant we were dead in the water. Drowning our sorrows in the local pub in Ham, I suppose we had to accept it was yet another case of rich or poor, every songwriter's ultimate truth, "It's never final 'til it's vinyl!" The introduction to Quincy, however would stand me in good stead a little later on in my career.

Jimmy, meanwhile, never put a foot wrong as far as making millions and millions of dollars was concerned. He was as rich as Crassus and getting richer by the day and now at a stage of his life, having been raised in relative poverty and struggle, where everything he touched turned to gold. When we were out in Colorado, on our first trip, he told us of a little ole idea he'd come up with called CMT - Country Music Television – which, by the time our second visit to Caribou came along, he'd already sold to the Westinghouse Corporation for 86 million dollars. Then, having bought some land to build a few properties and a golf resort down in Boulder as an investment, while the engineers were excavating the plot, they discovered a huge natural gas reserve. Naturally! One hell of a lot of it and bingo, again the man could do no wrong. He loved music as much as anyone I've ever met, but also as a student of the Law of Attraction taught me that money is an energy, a current which either flows towards you or is repelled out of your grasp. As I had always experienced a reasonable amount of the latter in my life to date, I was very interested to meet someone like Jimmy who hopefully might show me a way to the former!

The mood and atmosphere between us all while making our music at Caribou was incredibly special and the closest thing to idyllic that one could ever enjoy as an artist, or indeed as a human being. The camaraderie, laughter and good times of one big, happy and creative family were among the best of my life. I will also be eternally grateful to Jimmy for allowing us to share such a 'Rocky Mountain High' experience with our families, especially after all the ups and downs of a tumultuous decade that we all had, in one way or another, collectively experienced.

At the end of our first album's recording sessions, Jimmy and Ron packed us off to yet another ranch he owned near Santa Barbara in California for some more glorious and adventure-filled R&R time, inviting us to take his super-luxurious Caribou RV off along Highway 1 to San Francisco after a few days if we wanted to. We did want to! We wanted to do it all, and we did!

All good things must come to an end. As our first album; *Dressed For Drowning* (titled by our old friend, journalist and poet Dennis Boyles and based on our epic track 'Danger On The Titanic') had just been released and just as we were completing our second, *TV Land*, a devastating revolutionary cull, the largest corporate annihilation in CBS's history dubbed the 'Night of the Long Knives' and as brutal as any Godfather movie, took place. Almost half of the CBS A&R staff's careers disappeared overnight. Tragically for us, it included all of the personnel and departments that were previously supporting and working on our *Dressed For Drowning* album. It looked like the experience of a lifetime, and the year-long 'Westworld' adventure that Ron and our Cowboy Angel, Jimmy Guercio had made possible, was now sadly coming to an end.

Chapter 18
Foot in the Door

"I can't carry on with it any longer I'm afraid Philip" Henry informed me one day, which came, as these things often do, like a bolt out of the blue. He was talking about our now defunct musical partnership. "I'm really sorry mate, but after Caribou and all that, Susan decided we should sell up. She's intending to move us all up country to a slip road on the M6 in Skelmersdale," he joked thinly to soften the blow. "Where the fuck's that?" I politely enquired. I must admit I was taken aback, "Are you sure about all this?" I said, although could tell he had made up his mind or at least had had it made up for him.

My erstwhile Sailor buddy and partner in crime, Henry Marsh, had accosted me with the news that they'd decided enough was enough with the music biz and that he and Susan were imminently intending to leave rundown and filthy Clapham to move to a clean-living, family orientated, TM meditation community in Lancashire. We'd conquered the charts together, toured the world and shared many musical triumphs and disasters, but it was now time for him to weigh anchor. "What will you do Philip? Why don't you move up there too?" Even though we had both been committed TM Maharishi meditators for almost ten years, I wasn't inclined to ditch my aspirations as a songwriter and in any event, didn't feel temperamentally inclined or comfortable with the idea of living in a commune. "No Hen, not for me mate, I'll be okay, but you should go for it." I tried to sound more supportive as, in a way, I understood Susan's impatience with the deprivations at the thin end of a Chapter 1 rock 'n' roll career. "Anyway, you know how much I hate brown rice! Good luck though and say a few mantras for me 'oop north!"

Although concerned about losing my music partner, I didn't have the heart to be mean about it and anyway knew it wouldn't make much difference. I couldn't in my heart of hearts blame Henry since we'd both crashed back down to earth again after the phenomenal experience of our stay at the famous Caribou Ranch Studios up in the Rockies of Colorado. We'd recorded two albums, mainly of my songs, with legendary producer and filmmaker, James William Guercio, through whom we were lucky enough to work with some amazing world-class musicians on our tracks, including the late Carl Wilson of The Beach Boys. 'Don't Send Flowers', the opening track on Sheena Easton's massive debut hit album *Take My Time* was now selling in millions, which afforded me a measure of financial ballast and badly needed encouragement, such as several new Gold and Platinum discs to hang on my walls, that at least enabled me to call myself a professional songwriter again after Sailor had been dropped, (now for the second time), by CBS Records.

A few months later, Steve Levine, that young engineer/producer I had known from my Sailor days, turned up unannounced at our house in Ham, Richmond, brandishing a small flight case containing a mysterious object I'd never seen before. He called it a Linn-Drum machine, the curse or saviour of eighties music depending on which way you looked at it, but definitely the former if you happened to be a drummer. Steve was the second engineer at CBS's Studios in Whitfield St London, the place where Sailor had recorded its hits and all but one of its five albums. Being second engineer was a humble occupation involving brewing copious amounts of tea, sharpening pencils and for bands, other than Sailor, more than likely rolling spliffs.

I'd always marked Mr Levine's card as an upwardly mobile chap who barely concealed his ambitions as a 'hot-shot' producer. He was definitely going to make it one day. "This little box is the future and it's going to change everything in our business," Steve told me. "You sound unsure," I said. As if to prove the courage of his predictions he'd sold his car, (an ancient hideous orange Morris Marina), to get enough money to buy the innocuous- looking black box. Consequently, he was now on foot. I was, as ever, hugely impressed with his 200% self-belief in his own ideas and opinions, a must for any budding producer/entrepreneur. At the same time, I thanked my lucky stars I wasn't a drummer.

We'd kept in touch in the intervening few years since Sailor, with Steve encouraging me to make a few bob doing sessions now that my partnership with Henry had run aground. I began to assist him on a motley succession of pierced punk bands, New Romantic upstarts and fluffy pop acts including Sham 69, Fatal Microbes, Honey Bane and others. Having been recently dropped from my label and feeling a bit low I was flattered by Steve's belief in my talents, which usually involved helping the budding young producer come up with interesting bass lines, keyboard riffs and motifs, especially for the groups who couldn't play very well, or who might need a bit of help on vocal arrangements, (most of them come to think of it!) I'd sometimes even "ghost" the lead vocal track too. I was, in his words "a one-stop shop" and I greatly appreciated the new lease of musical life Steve was offering me.

One day in the Spring of 1981 Steve called and asked if I would come down to Maison Rouge Studios in Fulham, (at that time owned by Ian Anderson of Jethro Tull). There was a new band he'd been asked to produce called The Sex Gang Children, where I was to assist with the usual keyboards, sounds, and possibly backing vocals, as there was only one singer in the group. His name was George. Steve warned me that I wasn't to be put off initially by George's manner, or more particularly by his outrageous appearance. "Don't be too shocked Phil, he looks a sight for sore eyes and lives in a squat so can be a bit smelly to be honest", I was taken slightly taken aback by Steve's candour, "but he's a big fan of Sailor and would love to have you on keyboards."

Apparently, George had approached Steve a few days earlier to ask if he "knew the guy who used to play keyboards with Sailor on Supersonic? They were soooo camp!" Contrary to rumours over the years, this was not the intended effect of our 'on the waterfront' image but looking back at old video footage, a hardly surprising comment. We were as camp as a caravan site, all tight trousers, wan expressions, heavy makeup and sailor suits. What did we expect? As ever the 'chameleon', only a few months earlier, I'd been up a Colorado Mountain playing mid-western harmony ballads with twangy guitar solos in check shirts and cowboy hats.

So having frequently worked together and kept in touch, Steve was immediately able to produce my phone number which, as I later learned from George, impressed the band no end. Not wishing to appear uncool or fazed in any way, I didn't inquire further as to why I might find the apparition greeting me at the studio disconcerting. On the contrary, I was quite accustomed to some of the more extravagant punk and burgeoning New Romantic acts, many of whom, through Steve, I'd been working with by that time.

This was the brand new era of outrageous clubs like Taboo, Beat Route and Dial M For Dolphins and, unbeknown to me then, in the style and outrageousness stakes, George was already a rising star. "So what day do you need me, Steve?" I asked, diary open at the following week. "Can you come over right now?" he replied: "We've just started a track I could use you on". This drop everything approach was to form a pattern over the next few years and, as I would soon find out, was something I might have to get used to. I dived into the car and arrived at Maison Rouge Studios in Fulham an hour or so later, laden with my still gleaming Prophet 5 keyboard, I self-consciously shuffled into the control room where the band was all quietly waiting. Without introduction, I saw George the confident and charming Maître D and hanging back shyly across the far wall, his three musical musketeers. I'd got it in one. Steve politely introduced me to everyone and I was immediately struck by the contrast between George's friendly and disarming manner peering out from a matted manifesto of manky dreads, (but was he a bloke or a girl? I really couldn't make it out). A slightly menacing, vertically-challenged but devastatingly handsome drummer, Jon Moss, looking like a teenage Tony Curtis eyeballing me with insouciant punk suspicion. Then there was hyperactive, stick-thin Billericay beanpole, Roy Hay, and coming up at the rear, regal and diffident black bassist, Mikey Craig completing the unlikely quartet. Indeed, as Jon would later famously sum them up in one of their first interviews; "A Jew, a Black, an Anglo Saxon and an Irish Transvestite."

The dirty and torn T-shirt outrageously worn by George depicted a scene of homosexual activity which, whilst not entirely subverting an avowed hetero's sensibilities, did, however, cause one to actively avert the eyes. I put this at the back of my mind and bravely soldiered on while they watched me set up my gear in the control room. That moment of turning up to a session to play with a band for the first time, (sometimes the last), can be quite a harrowing ordeal for the uninitiated.

My approach was always to be as friendly as possible to everyone in the room so that even if they hated my playing at least, hopefully, they wouldn't mind having me around for a couple of hours. But George had me perplexed right from the word go. Without looking like a gauche idiot, how could I possibly come out in the open and ask him, or anyone, directly about what gender he/she was?

I kept thinking I'd cracked it, only to become suspicious, a moment or two later, when perhaps a word, expression or mannerism suddenly betrayed the stone cold certainty of the previous assumption. Again I realised what a sheltered life, in middle-class suburban Richmond, I must have been leading since Sailor went into dry dock. But, in common with millions all over the world during the years that were to come, without a shadow of a doubt that whoever he or she was, I knew I had just met the most entertaining, excruciatingly funny, irresistible, irrepressible and possibly the most controversially original human being I had ever met in my entire life. Looking back, as I write, although dressed like a homeless person and not yet the Boy George that everyone on the planet would soon come to know and love, he was already an icon. I had landed on my feet again!

Then there was 'The Voice'.

The song they had invited me to play on was called 'Do You Really Want To Hurt Me'. I sat at the Steinway Grand piano while Jon, Roy and Mikey ran through the tune, showing me the chords and arrangement, then George came in from the control room with a flustered "let's get on with it shall we?" demeanour. He stood at the microphone behind a screen just to my left and through the headphones, I heard his voice for the very first time. As all musicians who would deafeningly discover over the years, George was an artist who liked his vocals ear-splittingly loud in the headphones and monitors. The track started and soon I was enveloped and carried along by a vocal tidal wave filling my head with colours and reminiscences of all of my favourite singers rolled into one; shades of Elvis, Buddy Holly, Smokey Robinson, Roy Orbison, Marvin Gaye and even Marilyn Monroe's breathy sweet vibrato all magically conjured up into one unique and soulful voice. My God, the connection was immediate and seemed to go straight to the heart and soul of the listener, the hallmark of a truly great vocalist; amazing to think that it all came so naturally without having had any vocal training whatsoever. The sound was just there and it was so effortless. Shivers went down my spine in the quiet irrefutable certainty that once again, I'd arrived at the right place and at the right time. I wanted to appear cool but couldn't stop a huge grin spreading across my face. Punk had happened, come and gone, and now this was the start of the eighties and I knew I'd just caught a wave of whatever was going to come next, with a voice like that they would conquer the world. It could only be a matter of time.

Right from the start, I was one of the few who predicted "Do You Really" would be the hit, although I understood that, as a ballad, any young hotshot band would probably prefer a more up-tempo club track for their first hit record. The group would, no doubt, learn as time went on, as I had in Sailor, that you can never second guess your audience. It is them and them only who decide. Well before even being considered as a contender, Mikey's friend, young toaster, Amos, agreed; "Peter Powell play it and it reach to Number one, Virgin dem a-cut it and it sell a mill-ion!"

I was convinced that this track would be the one to break them in the UK and when their first single, 'White Boy', a searingly melodic dance groove, with a tumultuous sax solo from Nick Payne, didn't make the grade, I approached George and Jon to recommend they reconsider "Do You Really" as a single as, to me, the song stood out head and shoulders above the rest. "Nah," said Jon, George looking on; "We're going with 'I'll Tumble For Ya', we don't want a ballad." George adding that he thought the song too personal. George constantly and hilariously played to the gallery with whoever walked into the room, usually to the detriment and at the expense of his already long-suffering band-mates. His car-crash, ego-on-steroids and Teflon personality utterly and effortlessly dominated proceedings, leadership fitting him like a silk glove as if, to the manor born, without even breaking a sweat. Even in these early days, when he looked like a homeless person, I noticed that few attempts were made to usurp his shining crown of wit. As, in any event, not many were up to the task of taking him on verbally, except perhaps Jon, but that was to come later and not on this first impression. "I'm the statue of taking liberties!" he/she loudly and camply declared to all and sundry.

It suddenly occurred to me that I was only yards away from the greasy mini-cab office where Henry and I had delivered packages only a couple of years before after having been unceremoniously dumped by our label, CBS Records when punk burst on the scene.

George meanwhile, oblivious to my previous career setbacks, was continuously curious about my having been in a successful band that had achieved a coveted Number One record and whether or not, I thought Sex Gang Children would ever make it. "Oh my God Phil I just can't tell you how much I want to be famous, honestly, what's it like to get to number one?" George beseeched me in words to that effect, almost whispering, in the soon-to-be-famous husky asthmatic voice and hardly containing himself in anticipation of what I, too, was starting to feel was a foregone conclusion.

I think I was able to impress on him and all of them, that it could only be a matter of time and that in every department, the songs, the image, George's voice, the whole package was going to explode onto the scene. It was quite touching, for that brief time before they were to become famous, that George and the band seemed to see me as some kind of rock star deigning to attend their sessions, no doubt having been chauffeured in from a mansion in the shires. In reality, albeit in glamour-glow, that delusion was already in the rear view mirror. Having already been dropped on two occasions by CBS Records and on the contrary, chauffeur-less, I had just driven to the studio from a semi-detached cottage in Ham in my ancient but elegant Daimler V8.

Back then, their attitude was quite incredulous and innocent prior to their inevitable breakthrough, and I enjoyed the flattery of their mistaken assumption I was some kind of millionaire ex-rock god doing them a huge favour, when in reality the exact opposite was the case. I needed a job and a chance to carry on playing music and writing songs and here it all was on a heaped plate. So I did little to quell the illusion and in any event, at that stage of a band's development, you need all the encouragement you can get, which I certainly offered in spades and which I know they appreciated at the time.

Everything about George from the get-go was shocking, unique, supremely entertaining and hilarious. Every outrageous comment about a rival was delivered with blatant and delightful innocence, all the time looking at you, (in on the joke), directly in the eyes, mischievously inviting conspiracy. You simply couldn't help being totally fascinated by his innate and unerring sense of making everything happen around him. (You may have noticed I am now referring to him as "him" as that evening I called Steve and asked him outright - just to make sure once and for all). Insatiably, he wanted to know any gossip I might be able to reveal about Mark Bolan and David Bowie, realising I had, at various times, been signed to EMKA and GEM, the aforementioned's management companies. Of course, now it all made sense, I remembered meeting a very young and freaky George hanging around outside the Top Of The Pops studio and also at EMKA's office in Bond Street in the late seventies. One of the many kids we referred to as the EMKA Scruffs dressed in drag as a Mohican Boadicea or bodacious nun waiting to button-hole Mark Bolan for his autograph. Or, come to think of it, anything else that might have been on offer. George had even asked for my autograph once, which we thought was hilarious.

After I'd completed a few more keyboard overdubs on that same first day when 'Do You Really Want To Hurt Me' was recorded, the atmosphere noticeably warmed with the rest of the band, as I now realised they had been just as nervous as I was. The track sounded very special indeed and although it was the first song I'd ever heard George sing, its still, in my opinion, one of the very best vocal performances of his career. What interested me even more about this strange and incongruous unit was a kind of arrogance and standoffishness, signifying their post- punk attitude which, along with the voice, could only really mean one thing; Eventual World Domination!

I found myself, later that evening intensely looking forward to being in his company again, instinctively drawn to such an intoxicating and unique personality. He was just so much fun to be around. There was definitely something to love about George, his truth and unabashed honesty made it very clear to me that, along with the voice, this appeal would carry him and his unlikely quartet around the world many, many times and boy did I aim to be along for the ride. Consequently, I was thrilled to be asked back over the next few days to play on the rest of *Kissing To Be Clever*, the band's debut album. In particular and much to the chagrin of Mikey and Roy, who rather fancied themselves as vocalists but were firmly kept in their box by George, I was also invited by Steve and George to perform and track-up all the male backing vocals.

Up to this time in my career, I'd only been familiar with the more diplomatic, public school manner of my bandmates in Sailor when it came to question which musical parts should be played or whether or not one's vocal harmonies were appropriate.

For instance, it might have played out like this; "I'm not quite sure if that note fits Phil, you might like to try something like this. Do you mind awfully? Thanks". With The Sex Gang Children, who thankfully, during the course of these early sessions, changed their name to Culture Club and from George O'Dowd to Boy George, it was refreshingly, if not insultingly, entirely a different matter. "Oy! That's fuckin' awful Phil, can't you play something a bit less clever?" said Roy, albeit accompanied by the cheeky and disarming Essex chuckle. I'd never really been known for clever but, on the other hand, did nothing to dispel their impression and henceforth tried to keep everything I played ultra-simple, which they seemed to like a lot.

Noticeably absent from this chapter at least, I was still yet to meet and work with Helen Terry and to hear her astonishing vocal contribution to the early Culture Club tracks, in particular on "Do You Really", but will return to this incomparable lady and her talents later.

As time went on George, to my genuine embarrassment often would generously sing my praises to the others, which understandably pissed them off royally. "No, Phil's gonna do the backing vocals, your voice sounds like shit!" he opined diplomatically, shooting Roy down like a Sergeant Major from hell. "Anyway, fuck off munchkin!" George answered his critics, "He's been in a hit band and you haven't, wanker," George chided in a purring and demure Monroe drawl through fluttering lashes to poor old Mikey, who also vainly harboured ambitions as a backing vocalist but found them suddenly dashed against the rocks of George's relentless willpower. Understandably this directness didn't exactly go down too well with the others. Occasionally during band discussions over differences of musical opinion George, usually interrupting someone and would bluntly pipe up, "Let's see what Phil thinks, after all, he's been on Top of the Pops and you haven't, you spotty dwarf!" (I couldn't for a second guess who he might have been referring to here!)

Mr O' Dowd could never be accused of being in any way half-hearted or vague about what he was thinking. Like quicksilver, it came straight into his mind and out of his mouth to amuse, vilify, tease, or merely dismantle others' fragile egos or pretensions. In later years, in particular, having obviously taken on and dealt with many of his demons publicly or otherwise, he could spot, root out and seek and destroy bullshit or dysfunctional behaviour in a heartbeat like a heat-seeking missile, and from a hundred miles away. George's huge personality, turbocharged by the stamina equivalent of several large healthy oxen, quickly dominated any given situation and all pretenders to the throne would, in short order, be subjugated by his seeming effortless wit and camp cruelty; followed characteristically by the loveable, and by now familiar, asthmatic cackle. So whenever, on occasion, George's promotion of my ideas in preference to the others took place; during rehearsals, or later on, in writing sessions, I often prayed for the earth's crust to open up and swallow me whole. Usually, the rest of the group took it in good heart, however. We were getting on well and it was both exhilarating and fortunate to be working with such a bunch of talented young musicians, the next pop generation on from the one I'd enjoyed in the seventies. Moreover, I seemed destined in some way to be part of it all whether I liked it or not and so far I liked it very much.

At 36 I hadn't realised how much I'd missed my former life on the road with a successful pop band, as I was now almost certain would soon be the case with Boy George and Culture Club. Some of my more mainstream music biz friends and muso mates were less than impressed, however. "Er, yes, he's only 19, from Eltham and wears makeup, dreadlocks and a dress," I'd say defensively, "But just wait until you hear his voice! Honestly, I'm telling you, Culture Club is going to be the biggest thing in the world!" Amidst howls of derision and "no chance mate!" I resolutely assured everyone I knew that this particular tranny would soon be on every transistor from Shanghai to Timbuktu. "Yeh, right Phil!"

Jon was a fascinating character with some very original perceptions and ideas; everything seemed black and white with him. Contrary to the camouflage of his Damned, working class vowels, (a band he'd briefly played in), it was patently obvious that Jonathan Aubrey Moss had benefited from an expensive education and was clearly the commercial brain behind Culture Club. He quietly took me to one side on the last day of recording, it becoming increasingly obvious that underneath the chippy East End matinee idol exterior beat the heart of a very sharp businessman. Although not immediately forthcoming, "Look Phil," Jon said one day while giving me a lift in his VW Golf; "You're probably far too busy and we can't afford you, but we're going off on a UK tour in a few weeks and would love you to come and do the shows with us, okay?" "Oh, and could you help with the driving?" he added as an afterthought; "I'm the only one with a driving licence and we'll need help driving the van." I don't think I let on, but was secretly thrilled to offer my services for a minimal daily per diem in the full and confident knowledge that a massive future for the band beckoned. A fact I was, possibly, one of the first people they respected outside of their immediate circle to confirm. "Don't worry," I said, "You'll be able to afford me a lot sooner than you think". "Do you think so?" he replied with great charm and genuine modesty.

Years later when Boy George's book, *Take It Like A Man* came out, I was interested to see how George looked back on these early sessions at Maison Rouge and their importance, if any, in getting the band off the starting grid in the first place. For instance, I hadn't realised that in spite of having been under the noses of all of the labels and A&R men for some time, the band were still not signed, which was obviously becoming a source of concern for all of them. According to his book, the turning point came when they decided to hire Steve Levine, who, by bringing me and others on board to help improve their sound it seems that this may have done the trick. Up until these early *Kissing To Be Clever* sessions at Maison Rouge, Culture Club were not being taken seriously by the music industry and a vital recording contract had eluded them to date. But immediately after these sessions with Steve, Culture Club was signed. In George's words, "Steve Levine gave us a bigger sound, adding brass, and keyboards played by Phil Pickett adding a worldly sophistication. Phil had been a member of the seventies pop group Sailor... I was excited, I'd bought Sailor records when I was a teenager. It seemed mad that he was playing for us; we now sounded polished and professional."

During the next few days, after hearing the tracks that Steve had produced at Maison Rouge including the song that would go on to be their first number 1 record - 'Do You Really Want To Hurt Me' - Culture Club were immediately signed to Virgin Records and the rest is history.

On the way out of Maison Rouge at the end of the first day, George approached me to ask if I could lend him a fiver for some fags and to get the tube back to his squat in Carburton Street, Fitzrovia London. Out of the corner of his eye, Roy had noticed me proffer the crumpled note, later whispering in my ear, "You won't see that again, mate!" as usual book-ended with the familiar Billericay chuckle. He was right, I never did.

But over the next few years, being part of Culture Club would be, beyond all doubt, the most rewarding, challenging and dramatic of my entire life.

Chapter 19
Dressing To Be Clever

About to turn up for my first rehearsal with one of the hippest and most dangerously fashionable bands of the early eighties, I decided it would be a good idea to get a haircut on the way into town and at least put some modicum of effort into looking the part. As these were the very earliest days of Culture Club, it was a long way from being mainstream and except for the elitist of the fashionable elite, the most far out gatekeeper tastemakers and London tranny scene of the day, not many had heard of them yet, but this only added to the eclectic band's growing underground mystique.

The early eighties post-punk and New Romantic scene was awash with strutting, as yet undiscovered, flamboyant peacocks, such as Pete Burns and Haysi Fantayzee, all trying to outdo each other in outrageousness and style, including the 'chosen one' lining up on the inside rail who would eventually emerge from London's fashion and musical underground to indisputably claim the world-wide crown of unassailable gender-bending aristocracy.

Just around the corner from where Ann & I had once lived together in our 8' x 5' rented room within a flat just off Berkeley Square, (where she worked at über-trendy nightclub Morton's), was Crimpers, a stylish and renowned hairdresser for upwardly mobile upstarts and hipsters of the day. Holding my breath, I booked myself in for a ludicrously expensive trim, internally signifying, I suppose, the so far unconscious feeling that, as gigs went, this could be a very important day for my music career. A stylist was selected for the challenging task of fashioning, what even in those far off days, was a volume challenge. But Tracy, as it happened; from Basildon near to where Roy Hay lived was doing a capital job of making me feel, if not look, reasonably presentable. Inevitably, as discussions from the hairdresser's chair go, the conversation turned from "been anywhere nice this year?" to what the customer did for a living. So when asked, I was quite chuffed to tell her that I'd been part of Sailor in the seventies, (which her Mum would have remembered, blah!), but that I was now working with a very hot new band called Culture Club and a singer called George.

The attractive young stylist shrieked with delight; "Oh, they're amazing!" she said, getting really excited; "I haven't seen them play live yet but I met their drummer, Jon Moss, last week at a club in town, he was lovely," she said emphasising the last word considerably, whilst suddenly coming over all dreamy and bashful. Then a little quieter, revealed, "In fact, he drove me home afterwards in his white Golf". At this point in the conversation any details of further events were unforthcoming. Snapping out of the mood however, now more cheerily, she asked me to send her love to Jon if I was seeing him later, "Oh yes, I will be" I said. "Can you give him my number then? Here it is, I forgot to give it to him the other night," handing me a shiny Crimpers card with her number scribbled on the back. "Pleased to" I said.

Later on I turned up at Nomis Rehearsal Studio, (named after Simon Napier Bell who owned the rehearsal rooms; his name spelt backwards) in Shepherds Bush for the 1pm start. Prior to the arrival of the rest of the band I began to beaver away wiring up my recent Prophet 5 acquisition, that and an older Roland Juno 60, making sure the vocal mic worked adequately and checking my monitors. Both of these instruments were used on the *Kissing To Be Clever* recording sessions. Jon and Roy arrived a little later and were soon boisterously setting up their gear, laughing and joking like hooligans on speed. All was industry, laughter and noise and then when completely satisfied with their sound, the two began to riff like The Wild Men Of Rock they certainly were never destined to be in this band. George entered the room suddenly, without warning, disrupting the mood and carrying several large designer bags. Finding a microphone to make himself heard above Roy and Jon's raucous din, he shouted at earsplitting level, "Shut the fuck up Roy, who do you think we are? IRON MAIDEN? "YOU SHUT UP GEORGE!" Roy answered defiantly but chuckling, "We're just havin' a larf, anyway you're late! Been shopping again have we?" Culture Club's lead guitarist added with heavy sarcasm. Inviting agreement to his point of view by looking over at me and around the room, George said over the mic to no one in particular; "I hate rock, it's so dated. Anyway, if you want to be a Rock God you're in the wrong band!" upholding the position that, in regard to his group's musical direction, style and taste dictated even out of hours. "Come on guys" interjected Jon, the stern adjudicator, "Time is money, let's get on with it shall we?"

"Who put you in charge Napoleon?" George came back camply, albeit this time fluttering his eyelashes and in a Monroe 'come-hither' drawl, accompanied by a disarming chuckle which, as many would come to know and love, was pure trademark George. "Edgy, this lot", I thought to myself, but so far an entertaining, interesting, if not challenging introduction to band life with Culture Club and clearly setting out, for the first time, the parameters of what would become a familiar blueprint on their activities where making music was concerned. As indeed was the following tableau: "Where's Mikey anyway?" George asked, "I dunno, fucking shwartzes!" sneered Jon, "He's probably been on another one of his ganga binges."

Murmurings of discontent followed by stoic resignation ensued upon the realisation that Mikey would only show up "when he did", and that "that was Mikey". Apparently their bass player's tardiness at keeping appointments was legendary, not only missing them by hours, but sometimes even several days would go by before he turned up.

"Well, we've only got today and tomorrow to get this right so let's start without him", interjected Roy, now adopting a Famous Five's 'can-do, let's do the show right here and now with rubber bands and string', disposition. The other session players, saxophonist Nick Payne, Terry 'trumpet' Bailey and I exchanged looks. What were we getting ourselves into with this bunch? But then Roy immediately suggested we start proceedings with 'White Boy'. Shouting out the key above the din, Jon rolled the Revox tape and began the count in; "1 - 2 - 3 -4..."

The opening strains of the dreamy keyboard intro, Jon's dramatic Simmonds drum fills, Roy's 'Nile Rogers' funky guitar and the stabbing brass riffs suddenly all ground to a halt when the studio door slowly and almost apologetically crept open. A sheepish Mikey, bass guitar case in hand, was peering inside the room to check the vibe. Hard to imagine that a black man of such beauty and leonine countenance could be compared to a sheep, but in this company, a lamb to the slaughter he undoubtedly was. "Sorry guys" he proffered pathetically, "but I wa..", "Yeh, yeh Mikey" interrupted Jon unsympathetically, "Look, can we talk about this later?" he implored, "We've only got Phil and everyone here for today and tomorrow and we've just got to get on with it now, okay? Mikey, suddenly relieved of having to make a painfully detailed, laboriously recounted, and more than likely, completely fictitious explanation, leapt into action, immediately providing the magnificent bottom-end to the sound of Culture Club. Thankfully for him everyone in the room could immediately feel and experience the heart and soul underpinning the music of Culture Club. The last piece of the jigsaw had been added and the sound was finally complete. For a brief moment there was peace in the land, a relief and satisfaction that everything was going to sound just fine on the night. The band was rocking at last and I was elated to be part of it all and by god, when everything came together, you could tell it was going to be one hell of great band!

Although decisions and changes were being made on arrangement ideas, left, right and centre, normal in any rehearsal situation, during the *Kissing To Be Clever* recording sessions some questions were being aimed in my direction by George, much to the visible annoyance of Roy and Jon. "Let's ask Phil what he thinks. He's a grown-up and has done all this before and we haven't", George said, somewhat undiplomatically but which again, as the afternoon wore on, made me feel a little uncomfortable. I tried, as a newbie, to step as lightly as possible and to be fair, if an idea worked musically, which most of them fortunately did, then from whoever it had come from was quickly forgotten. Anyone who is familiar with the way I work, in that kind of creative environment, would probably say I throw loads of opinions and ideas into the mix and am usually quite good at getting them across. In the main, however, the impression gained from these very early stages of Culture Club was what exceptionally gifted musicians Roy, Mikey and Jon were in their own right. A lot of the other bands Steve Levine had introduced me to prior to these guys could barely even play, let alone sing properly. I sometimes felt that George, not being a musician himself, might not have always appreciated just how good his band mates were at the time. In fact it was easy to forget that, being not much more than half my age, these young guys, from very different backgrounds, could nevertheless play with fluent proficiency.

George, meanwhile, often became impatient with musical deliberations and arrangement cul-de-sacs and clearly expected results immediately or would often become sulky and irritated. "Look, I hate all this, can't you work it all out before I get here?" he implored. "God, I hate muso's, they're so boring!" He had a point. Musicians, the world over always like to riff together and have some fun warming up, but if you were a vocalist, it could be tedious at times. George's forthright pronouncements on backing vocals also didn't help my exposure to what was beginning to be seen as favouritism toward someone who, after all, wasn't "even in the fucking band," especially as Roy and Mikey clearly saw an important role beckoning within the future of their sound, that of being the principal backing vocalists of Culture Club. On this and on many other matters, however, one could only feel a little sorry for them. George's mind was made up.

As mentioned previously, this first rehearsal and UK tour did not yet include the amazing vocal gymnastics of Helen Terry, so dependable backing vocals were obviously going to be required as part of the on-stage sound and anyway, I'd sung on most of the album tracks.

"Look, come on George, we know all the songs so why can't we sing these parts?" pleaded Roy. "Because you can't. Your voice sounds like a wasp in a jam jar that's why," George fired back with finality, not missing a beat; "Phil's gonna do them coz he's had hit records and you haven't!" "You sound unsure George", Roy responded, but this time a little crestfallen having been worn down by George's singularity of purpose and the inevitability of his 'force-of-nature' attitude to life, music, fashion and also, it would appear, backing vocals.

Apart from an awkward and edgy directness I was simply not used to, what I was beginning to love about this band and their individual characters, (as well as their irreverent honesty and humour in spades), was how quickly these sudden outbursts of quite vile, but it has to be said, straight-talking and truthful exchanges, gave way, almost instantaneously to the evolution of songs, sounds, arrangements and ideas that were incredibly effective and fresh-sounding. However harsh and critical the insults were, in both directions, it never seemed to affect the ongoing mood for more than a few minutes at most. Above all, although deeply uncomfortable some of the time, it was very refreshing in comparison to anything I'd known in the past.

To accommodate some of the aspects of the sound that were not possible to reproduce with such a limited line-up; for instance to enable Jon to stand up at his Simmonds kit so he could be seen and therefore more visually effective, it was decided a Revox tape machine would be used to provide the few missing elements of the on-stage sound. The Linn bass drum, snare, hi-hat and some minimal, but effective, strings and effects were all pre-recorded which meant the tempos were set and therefore it was of vital importance to know when the track had started so you knew where to come in. This was Jon's job, a task which he normally performed admirably, but God help us all, as happened on a few notable occasions, if he'd counted us in at the wrong place as the result could be disastrous.

Later in the afternoon, everything now cooking along nicely, the 4+3 piece mini-orchestra worked on 'I'll Tumble 4 Ya', 'Do You Really Want To Hurt Me', 'You Know I'm Not Crazy' and the first single, 'White Boy'. Although we could have used a lot more rehearsal, always the case with most bands, everyone seemed happy that the set was starting to sound quite polished and professional. On a break during the second day when I was feeling on top of everything my end, and while the band were quietly chatting away, in an attempt to ingratiate myself with Jon, who, although superficially friendly, I felt was the group's most unreadable character, I thought I'd mention something; "Oh Jon, by the way, I met someone called Tracy at my hairdressers this morning. She says she met you the other night; really nice girl, very pretty", I smiled in a wink-wink, blokey, knowing kind of way. Jon immediately froze, his eyes shiftily darting around the room, suddenly more a man hunted than 'one of the lads', or a flattered recipient of female attention. Had I said something out of place? Out of nowhere the temperature in the room seemed to drop twenty below zero and a hazy inexplicable gloom descended. Confused, I was nevertheless committed to the social gambit I'd started and, as if with my own spade digging the hole even deeper, humbly proffering the crumpled card by now withering in my hand. I valiantly soldiered on; "Anyway, ahem, I've got her number here. She says she'd like to give you a ca..", "Who's Tracy Jon?" interrupted George glaring in Jon's direction, his voice full of controlled menace, whilst still at the microphone. I hadn't seen this side of him before, but then it was still very early days. Roy, his back to George but with his guitar and lead still plugged in to his amp, walked over towards me at the keyboards, on the way mouthing the words soundlessly but emphatically, a ventriloquist in reverse; "SHUT...THE... FUCK... UP, PHIL!"

"Come outside Jon" George bellowed, "COME OUTSIDE!" at which Jon, angrily, slammed his sticks down on the snare drum, the two of them urgently making for the door like dogs to a fight. From my viewpoint, I could see the whole scene strangely being played out in slow-motion, Jon's sticks bouncing up from the drum, revolving like the cavemen's bones tossed into the air in Kubrick's *2001*. I was terrified and naturally thought, "Well, there goes my gig!" Although the adjoining room was soundproof, the level of shouting and screaming going on and the muffled thuds of what was obviously knuckle on flesh seemed to permeate the entire building. Also it was now crystal clear to the assembled motley crew that whatever had created this huge falling out with my employers was clearly my fault, although still for the life of me I hadn't yet worked out what was going on, or indeed why everything seemed so knife-edge and volatile with this band. But I was about to find out.

Mikey chuckled nervously whilst Roy, no doubt feeling sorry for me, came over to the keyboards and said, more sympathetically this time; "Look Phil, don't worry, you weren't to know". Then looking around at the other 'sessions' said; "Well, I guess that's it for today guys!" Although still oblivious to my part in this mayhem I felt dreadful. Roy went on to explain; "George and Jon are an item you see, anyway the band has to live with it, it's all a bit crazy but, you know, it works most of the time. Sometimes it can be fucking awful though, like today!" he said, suddenly back in his default Billericay 'pearly-king' persona and typical Roy; "Nah, mate, don't worry about it. Whaddya gonna do?" Laughing his head off like a madman; "You'll still come and do the tour with us though won't you?"

I took my gear out to the car, still deep in thought at what had happened and noticed that a very large bird had crapped all over my windscreen, alongside a horrible yellow parking ticket. Great! Driving back home I further mulled over the implications of what I'd learned that day, how appearances often weren't everything and how consequently things might or might not play out in the future. Had I blown it? If so what a shame, as in all other ways this gig seemed so full of promise and I did not want to miss out. What I was soon to discover was at the very epicentre of the beating heart of Culture Club was a white-hot, deeply passionate love affair, 'forbidden' not only in the sense that Jon appeared in all other respects with his matinee idol good looks and 'one of the lads' repartee, to be avowedly heterosexual, but also I understood that if George and Jon's love life had been revealed publicly at that stage, it would almost certainly have damaged the image and thus have adversely affected their commercial ambitions in the pop marketplace.

Even by the eighties, some aspects of what would be considered totally acceptable these days in terms of gay relationships just weren't back then. Although in the decades to come George would be a catalyst and leading light in articulating and redefining the boundaries of misunderstanding surrounding gay consciousness in society. But right now there was just too much at stake to let the secret out and nothing would stand in their way. Culture Club were deadly serious about 'making it.'

Crossing Chiswick Bridge towards Richmond some late afternoon sun suddenly burst through the dramatic clouds forming two beautiful rainbows; at the same time a few specks of rain had mingled with the shit on the screen temporarily blinding me enough to pull my ancient Daimler V8 over. One thing seemed certain; at the end of this first proper rehearsal, Culture Club would only last as long as Jon and George's tempestuous relationship; the raison-d'etre and inspiration behind most, if not all, of its music, would allow it to. This realisation made me feel instantly more sympathetic towards Mikey and Roy's situation, although of course they must have known it too. As has been well documented, the lyrics to every Culture Club song, words which George wrote in their entirety, (and woe betide anyone to put words in HIS mouth!) were either directed at, or about Jon; lyrics that dealt with insecurity, lust, joy, heartache, betrayal, pleasure and pain. Love songs therefore that everyone who was, or had ever been in love could instantly relate to.

But in George's case, the words to his songs seemed to be supercharged with a darker, insatiable twist. In retrospect, the narrative of his obsession with Jon unknowingly delivered an emotional authenticity in the band's music that, coupled with George's searing and heartfelt vocals, was both its crowning glory, directly responsible I believe for the band's phenomenal worldwide success. But it was also the Achilles heel that would lead to their ultimate and all-too-public downfall. There would be no half measures with this bunch. One could almost feel and predict the glories and accolades that were to come, but also a sneaking suspicion that Culture Club would never just fade away like other bands. A hair's breadth away from triumph would always be a full on Greek tragedy of earth-shattering proportions - A bonfire of the sanities - or nothing at all!

This secret marriage of inconvenience; one minute a peaceful and benevolent burning star of creativity collaboration and love, the next, an unpredictable, masochistic lava-spewing, hydra-headed beast, was the very sun around which the scurrying planets of; a superlative hit-making machine, the magic dials and faders of producer Steve Levine, Richard Branson's record and music publishing companies, armies of photographers, PR's and journalists, an entire fashion and merchandise industry, countless millions of fans around the world and lastly, the band itself would all revolve and depend on for survival - on a volatile, paranoid and incandescent love affair. This was what would be required to maintain the artifice of Culture Club and its fantastically successful orbit. There'd be a lot of fun to be had on the way however, that is until the whole edifice would eventually collapse in on itself, forming a black hole into, or out of which nothing could escape.

Then there were the bad days!

Chapter 20
Tears, Tours and Tantrums (Part 1)

So it came to pass that the day of Culture Club's first ever UK tour dawned. It was a fine summer morning in June 1982 that the band and crew assembled at 9.30am at what was to become the regular launch pad for each and every forthcoming UK, European, and international tour that the band would undertake throughout its meteoric rise to worldwide fame during the early eighties. All personnel had been instructed to meet outside the legendary art-deco portals of the Hammersmith Odeon, now known less auspiciously in the age of sponsorship & product placement as the Eventim Apollo.

It was one of London's most iconic rock venues, having hosted The Beatles, The Rolling Stones and over the years, every major act on the planet. I also had several unforgettable memories of playing in this theatre when Sailor supported Steve Harley and Cockney Rebel on their barnstorming 1974 tour. Then after 'A Glass Of Champagne' dislodged Queen's 'Bohemian Rhapsody' from the NME Number 1 spot, we headlined the prestigious venue in our own right. (Only a year or so later Culture Club would fill the theatre out several times over with police escorts to and from the venue - but we weren't to know that just yet!) But now it was a new decade. I was with a brand new band and it felt like striding out to the crease on a bright confident morning, and a second innings.

Ann and I had dropped off Jack, then 5 years old, at his Montessori School in Richmond before driving on into Hammersmith to say goodbye for a week or so, neither of us knowing where this was all going to lead, but somehow with a feeling that things were at last on the move again in my career. Meeting the other musicians, nerves seemed a little on edge at first, understandable perhaps as this was the new line-up of the four, plus me, Terry Bailey on trumpet and Nick Payne on tenor saxophone. Like any new unit going out on their first tour, more likely than not under funded and under-rehearsed as we were, whatever gloss you try and put on it, you're crapping yourself at least until the first gig is out of the way. Roy, as I recall, was his lively and irrepressible self, and Mikey had surpassed all expectations by actually being on time for a change. When we pulled up outside his mum's house in Hammersmith he said, "Good morning chaps, shall we do it then?" addressing his van mates pleasantly, as ever the gentleman. Then on through heavy traffic up the Edgware Road to Finchley Road Tube Station to pick up an uncharacteristically quiet and taciturn George and smooth, affable and business-like Jon.

Polite greetings exchanged and packed in the van like sardines, the incongruous crew, now complete, finally set off for Nottingham University. Hardly the fashionable, über-cool, venue one might have imagined as a suitable debut for such an eclectic and groundbreaking ensemble, but a 'gig' nevertheless and hopefully a good warm-up slot for the more trendy establishments eagerly waiting for us later in the tour. "Don't worry, they're all just dreary socialists in cardigans and beards", mused Jon witheringly; "and that's just the women!", he added trying to cheer George up, but with the look that flashed back, failing miserably. Sitting next to the driver up front, as would always be his want throughout the next few years, the lead singer of Culture Club was clearly apprehensive about the tour but soon warmed up, first joining in the banter and then, true to form, completely taking over when north of Watford. I was relieved. Everyone seemed to be friends again and although possibly over-sensitive, the thermo-nuclear war I'd almost caused during the rehearsals last week now seemed merely a line drawn in water.

The first Culture Club UK tour did not include the incomparable singer Helen Terry, which, as rumour had it, allegedly may have been due to a last-minute spat over wages and terms with manager, Tony Gordon. As Helen would later recall cheerfully (the first of a number of disputes having been dealt with by the time the second UK tour came along), she'd clearly seen several anorexic moths flying out of the manager's wallet when the bill came for tea and biscuits at The Richou Café, Tony's favourite, (if you were paying). That and possibly a certain bolshy abrasiveness, for which Helen, a proud lesbian woman in a man's, and now a 'trans' world would infamously become known for as the tears, tours, and tantrums wore on.

On the last day of rehearsals, a week or so before, (and on every subsequent tour), George showed up with a bag containing a quantity of strikingly original stage costumes, the likes of which I'd never seen before. The outfits looked amazing, revolutionary and cutting edge and I was thrilled when I realised that the 'sessions' i.e. Terry, Nick and myself, were also expected to wear the clobber. The jazzmen weren't keen at all, mumbling nervously, ("what would our mates think, etc?"), but I didn't need asking twice. It made total sense, having already been part of a band where, in many ways, the image was almost as important as the music. Getting in early with my choices, I bagged a terrific combination of Rasta camouflage pants in green, covered in all kinds of hobo symbology; a white and yellow shirt with striking visual patterns and a Casey Jones-style US train driver's hat.

George once said that the designs represented cultural pilfering on an industrial scale, but it all worked together fantastically well. The entire collection was so fresh and unique it could have been a contemporary art installation at the RA or the Tate. I was dying to try everything on when I got home and felt the 'bee's knees', instantly looking the part. After all, when music had turned serious again in the late seventies, secretly I'd missed the dressing-up showbiz outrageousness of the Glam Rock era which had always appealed to the show-off in me. Now, in the early eighties, it seemed like George was about to bring it all back again with a vengeance, or at least for Culture Club, a completely new kind of fashion statement. As I was a part of it all, albeit vicariously, I found it all terribly exciting. Sue Clowes was George's gifted designer and friend. Her designs were fresh, stylish and highly innovative, featuring stars of David, smiling black children, roses intertwined with warplanes and graphic designs with phrases such as 'tarabat agadar', Hebrew for 'movement of all cultures' with obscure Romany gypsy signs, symbols and such.

Although not yet aware of its significance, we were witnessing the beginnings of a unique restyling of British multiculturalism, a phenomenon that George and Sue were apparently pre-empting by several years. Gradually the realisation hit me that while all manner of industry and activity had been focussed on the musical content of Culture Club by day, George and Sue had in addition, also been hard at it staying up, night after night creating the all-so-important look of the band. The designs were like a breath of fresh air and the flip-side of an often pretentious, preening and self-conscious New Romantic look prevalent during the style changeover after the visual nihilism and bleakness of punk had all but petered out.

An early eighties style smorgasbord was patently up for grabs, with bands like Adam and the Ants, heavily influenced by designers such as Vivienne Westwood, partner of Malcolm McLaren, at their 'Seditionaries - Clothes for Heroes' emporium on the ultra-trendy King's Road. The shop window and interior was styled on a lurching sixteenth century galleon with low ceilings, slanted floors and the exterior, all drooping slate gables with a huge clock displaying thirteen hours, its hands rapidly travelling backwards. It all harked back to an Elizabethan age of highwaymen, dandies, and buccaneers. This was after McLaren, (who I'd eventually meet and record with) as ever the pop visionary, a prime mover in the creation of the Punk look and ethos during the seventies had implored his wife to "do something romantic - look at history" for the eighties.

Spandau Ballet meanwhile were all kilts and quiffs, again looking backwards in time for visual inspiration while other groups like Duran Duran were Anthony Price smooth-suited Brummie bootboys hanging off Caribbean yachts with supermodels and obviously content with northern bourgeois clichés such as, "Look at us, we've made it!" Throughout these style wars, meanwhile, burning the midnight oil in a W1 squat, Kensington Market and at the Foundry, where George had worked as a shop assistant for the innovative Sue Clowes. The two now joined forces to come up with more futuristic creations for Culture Club, combining symbolic and revolutionary styles that would appeal to the misfits, left-outs, and freaks; in short, the vast majority thus far ignored and un-catered for, namely those who would never stand the remotest chance of fitting in with the flawless demographic of pop aristocracy on the cover of *The Face* magazine. The concept was pure commercial genius in retrospect, as it had simply never been done before. With this aspect and on so many other levels, it was beginning to dawn on me that ambition in this band literally never slept and that a lot more was going on behind the scenes than I could have ever imagined.

These thoughts and many more were spinning round in my head as Jon and I took turns to drive "oop bloody north" on the M1. George, as would become customary, if in the right mood, set about establishing his verbal dominance over the group, as usual breaking the ice with the subtlety of a rhino peeling a grape. He began by poking good-natured fun at the shy, retiring Nick Payne, having noticed how much the sax player resembled the Colorado hippy crooner, John Denver. Nick, at first embarrassed and perplexed, had to admit that he bore more than a passing resemblance to the American folk singer, particularly with regard to the hairstyle and First World War Lennon prescription glasses. This observation stuck and gave rise to much George-full mirth, often accompanied by enthusiastic renditions of 'Rocky Mountain High' in his breathy Marilyn Monroe voice. His humour, whether directed at others, or most of the time at his own expense, was infectious, disarming and full of mischief, but overall I was experiencing, through George's utterly unique observations on life, sexuality, music, everything, a glimpse of a new and fascinating world that now, as a 36 -year old musician living out in leafy Richmond-on-Thames, I'd barely known existed. It was a very welcome wakeup call and I was revelling in it.

For instance, by this stage, long having been a student of pop, I was hearing first-hand, the interaction and animated gossip between George and a young band who were obviously going places. Pop manoeuvring in the dark and business strategies by day, occasionally throwing in my three ha'pence worth when (frequently) asked was the way things developed for me. I was hearing music industry gossip a decade on (but could have been a century) from where I'd achieved success in the music industry first time round. George, meanwhile and prior to making it was intrigued and always wanting to hear about my Top Of The Pops & LWT's Supersonic experiences, also relishing every behind the scenes tale of Bolan and Bowie I could muster from the time when Sailor had been signed to the same management companies. From the point of view of someone who had been there and done that as he saw it, George would interminably ask my advice and opinion on everything about the music business in those very early days, but in reality, not only was I was bowled over by George's overwhelming personality and ego-on-stilts, I was also drawn to how he and the band seemed to be reacting to and dealing with the brand new music environment of the early eighties.

Finally arriving at Nottingham University, Dai, the band's Welsh road manager, began setting up the gear on stage in the Students Union. It was a very dull, grey and ordinary building and Jon's predictions seemed spot on. If anything, the students milling about were even drearier than he had predicted and worse, totally disinterested. "Dated fellow" mused Roy sarcastically as if from another planet, sizing up one young chap in particular sporting a tweed sports jacket, grey flannel trousers and tie. "Why are we playing here Jon?" George wanted to know; "No, seriously, what a bunch of tossers and freaks, can't we forget the whole thing and go home?"

The positive mood in the van on the way up to Nottingham drained away as reality dawned that this was a "soft" gig, a term in the industry which meant that as there was, as yet, no real demand for Culture Club, at such an early stage in its career, the booking agent had quite obviously booked one or two shows that would already have their own built-in audience, like this one in a students' union bar, therefore it could have been Culture Club or the Krankies, no one would have really cared that much. "Sod it, we'll treat it as a warm-up then," said the ever-upbeat Roy, who, one felt, still couldn't quite believe his luck at having been invited to join the band in the first place. Meanwhile, it seemed to have already dawned on George that he would have to grit his teeth and experience quite a lot of these kinds of gigs until Culture Club made it into the charts.

Once the sound check was completed, the band piled back into to van and set off to look for the hotel, Dai directing Jon in the driving seat to a very unpromising, dark decrepit hovel on the outskirts of town. "What's it like?" the band asked, as Dai returned to the van with the room keys, having checked the touring party in. Back came Dai's stock answer in a flash, an expression he would repeat whether, (eventually), The Plaza, 5th Avenue New York, or, in this case, Hotel Shit-Heap, Nowheresville; "Best one yet boys!" a strange response, on reflection, as it was only the first night of the tour, but a catchphrase that still persists to this day. At least I was lucky not to be sharing, but the sight and smell of the room as I opened the door almost made me heave. The curtains were half hanging off the rails, a single light bulb from the ceiling sizzled before expiring; the bed, so dishevelled and grubby-looking Tracy Emin would have wretched. The room so small, you'd have to go outside to change your mind. You could almost see the bed bugs standing to attention, licking their lips in anticipation at their new sorry prey. If all of this wasn't enough, then there were "the stains". Whatever had gone on, or had more than likely gone off, in these sheets, hours or perhaps only minutes before I'd arrived on the scene, left very little to the imagination, damp patches everywhere, pubic hair, the lot. It was disgusting.

Like many other musos who had frequently toured the world, I liked my creature comforts but was also quite used to roughing it when circumstances and the tour budget demanded. But this place was on another level of filth and degradation, so I decided, there and then, that whatever happened, I could not possibly spend one more minute, let alone a whole night, in this room. With extreme prejudice, I strode angrily back to the lobby intending to complain bitterly, but met George, who was at the check-in desk trying to locate a hair dryer; he asked me what was wrong and told him I couldn't possibly stay in the room I'd been allocated, adding for good measure a graphic rundown of the reasons why, but not to worry himself at all as I was going to sort something out. Launching, into what I felt was a justifiable tirade of public outrage at a hapless hotel management, I was surprised to see how embarrassed and uncomfortable George became upon witnessing the vehemence of his keyboard player, even trying to pacify the situation. "You can have my room, Phil, honestly, it's quite nice, I've already been up there", he said kindly, pouring oil on troubled waters so as not to cause a fuss. He said that he wasn't bothered by the surroundings at all. Thinking about it, this made sense as, after all, his current home was a commune squat in W1, that would probably make this place seem like The Savoy. I found George's intervention quite sweet actually, revealing, as it did, another side of his normally invincible and dominating personality - that of a mother hen looking out for one of her brood. Unworldly and quite naive, he obviously hadn't been used to dealing with mundane problems like this in life so far and the whole thing, travelling, group politics, staying in hotels, was all very new to him. In years to come, I was quite sure he'd soon learn, in short order, to perhaps not suffer fools and knaves and crap hotels, quite so compliantly. I didn't take him up on the offer, of course, as anyway the chastened hotel staff moved me to something that was a marginal improvement, which at least had some clean sheets!

An hour or so later I made the lobby call on time with the rest of the band and set off for my first ever Culture Club gig. George emerged with Jon from their room, having freshly made up and in the full majesty, pomp, and circumstance of his overwhelming Boy George magnificence. It was going to be a very interesting night.

"Let's get it over with then," George said in a resigned tone, getting into the van.

Chapter 21
Tears, Tours and Tantrums (Part 2)

Nottingham University Students Union Common Room may not have been the most auspicious venue at which to roll out the live entity that was now Culture Club, but after a few days of proper rehearsal and the introduction of experienced professional musicians, such as Nick, Terry and myself going on tour, was a gesture to prove to the world and themselves that they were now taking this aspect of their career seriously.

A few months earlier, as newcomers on the scene, the Sex Gang Children had taken part in one or two shambolic attempts at playing live, one of which George spoke about in an interview with *The Guardian* at the time; "When we first started playing gigs we were terrible, so bad we were brilliant; we did a gig in Chadwell Heath and got heckled by this builder who called me a fucking queer. I walked off without finishing the gig and the band were screaming at me!"

Jon was very aware that it didn't matter how great the songs and the image were, it would never be enough; the only real way to show that the members of Culture Club "weren't just fashion plates" was to get out there and do a proper tour. As time would prove beyond doubt, George then, as always, applied exactly the same minute attention to detail and time, care and effort on his appearance, whether at some drab hall in the back of beyond, like tonight, or later on in his career at Wembley Arena or Madison Square Garden, when Culture Club was number one in every country in the world. His commitment and professionalism in this regard, if nothing else, was, in my experience, unparalleled right from the get-go.

As another hero of George's, eternal cult figure Leigh Bowery once said, "Dress as though your life depends on it or don't bother." George's look, as he once described it, was, "A miracle of cosmetic engineering and fashion camouflage". It was as devastating as it was mesmerising, magically rendering an otherwise indifferent body shape; large frame, big bum and short arms, via a Houdini-like transformation into a stunning and beautiful transgender artifice. But tonight this towering magnificent presence was an outrageously camp peacock in full bloom, looking every inch a world superstar in the making. He might just as well have arrived from outer space as far as the provincial Nottingham audience were concerned; a number of whom were still clearly having trouble categorising their, thus far, limited student perceptions of exactly who and what this apparition was before them; an oversize 6'6" (in heels), Geisha mannequin wearing full makeup, androgynous threads with ribboned dreads topped by an orthodox Jew's wide-brimmed black fedora hat. It was clearly far too much information for many of the poor young souls, still searching and, in many cases failing, to find a viable identity for themselves.

On such a relatively historic evening therefore, a drab, badly-lit, half-filled room greeted Boy George and Culture Club as the band finally made their debut on stage, with one or two young people in the audience even smoking pipes! The place seemed less a hotbed of revolutionary, cutting-edge learning for tomorrow's world, than a self-regarding fogeyish Conservative club full of young people already looking old, (and a thought occurred to me that maybe it hadn't been such a bad idea not going to university after all, even if they'd have had me in the first place, which in retrospect was extremely doubtful).

Waiting to go on, I was full of time and tour honoured Sailor bonhomie and "chocks away chaps, let's make it a biggie!" back slaps and thumbs-up action which I thought might ease the tension backstage. But on the contrary, I only garnered an incredulous look of lip-curling punk derision from the quartet. I won't do that again, I thought! George and the audience didn't exactly get off to a good start either, with him returning to the power of ten, any hostility or jokey insults about his appearance of which, in fairness, there were many. The trouble was that although some mild heckling was emanating from a cheekier minority within the audience and a good number were still visibly shocked by George's appearance and demeanour, they didn't have access to a microphone so their comments were relatively inaudible to most. But George did!

As justified as it may have seemed to some in countering such impoliteness, his caustic and insulting repartee was amplified through a powerful PA at full volume, so NO ONE there could possibly mistake his extreme prejudice. He did not like being up there and boy was he letting the audience know it. "You should get out more often, tosser", he spat out insultingly at one comment or another. The problem was that it had the effect of spraying a can of shit mist over any enthusiasm otherwise beginning to develop in the room, each and every audient naturally believing his bitchy vitriol was aimed at them personally. This could become a problem I thought.

Although still new to performing and developing the masterly stagecraft skills that would in time become apparent, choice quotes from Mae West, Marilyn Monroe and his favourite, Tallulah Bankhead, which communicated spikey camp attitude or variations thereof, were often employed in this type of situation. Even if at the time were patently untrue, such as; "I earn more in a day than you do in a year by dressing like this, wanker" (although he may have embellished Tallulah's quote somewhat for local effect), "What would you like to drink George?" someone yelled from the back, "Blood" he replied instantly. Nevertheless a few songs in, one could see, by now, that a growing number, in spite of having been raised on middle-class, middle-of-the-road indiscriminate radio one rock and pop were appreciating the spectacle, if not even actually starting to enjoy the music. After all, it was not perhaps as inaccessible as first appearances may have led them to believe.

During 'I'll Tumble 4 Ya', Jon's Revox tape machine suddenly stopped mid-song due to a power cut, bringing the whole performance to a crashing but temporary halt. But, strangely enough, when the power came back on again shortly afterwards, the machine was quickly discarded; the unintentional hiccup only seemed to have served as a catalyst in breaking the spell of an understandably nervy and defensive opening night. Without the machine to fall back on, the musicians were galvanised into displaying their chops much more freely. And this band could certainly play their asses off! The show and general confidence picked up mightily from that point, although it could not have been said the evening was a total triumph, far from it, in fact. George couldn't wait to get out of the building. But still there was always Hotel Shit-Heap to look forward to and a drive to Manchester in the rain the following morning.

Back in my threadbare digs and on my own again, dark thoughts were swirling around my head; although we did reasonably well under the circumstances, I was depressed. After all that initial promise, my excitement at having met George and really believing they had what it took to break through, what if I was barking up the wrong tree? George's approach on stage, in the way he looked and acted, started to concern me. Even though he'd clearly been provoked, surely he was always going to attract such comment and reaction from certain parts of the crowd? What did he expect? What if he genuinely couldn't handle it? I wasn't being paid on this trip, the band couldn't afford it anyway, and I'd offered my services in good faith to show them just how much I believed in their future success, but, having been in Sailor and experienced how professional a band has to be in every single department to make it, maybe I was making a big mistake. Perhaps my music business friends had been correct in their dismissive observations ("what on earth are you doing with this lot Phil?") and Culture Club wasn't going to make it after all.

Arriving in Manchester, we pitched up at the too-cool-for-school Hacienda Club, where we were definitely made to feel like the, "fuckin' southern bastards", playing an away fixture to avoid relegation at Manchester United on their own pitch. The Manchester crowd, as George recalled, were, "bored and anorexic", but in fairness, it was only 25% full the night we played and in the end, we went down pretty well. Especially when we played 'White Boy' which, unsurprisingly as it was a pretty cool club track, a lot of the crowd seemed to know well. Better than Nottingham anyway!

The next night at the Bluenote in Derby, however, Culture Club absolutely smashed it; not only was the show, by now three nights into the tour really finding its feet, but the young mixed crowd was bursting at the seams and going mental. The Derby kids were much more relaxed and less up themselves than was the case at the painfully self-aware Hacienda. George was in his element. This was the first time I got more than an inkling that he was emerging from the chrysalis of London's fashion scene and had everything it took to become a world-class performer in his own right. Perhaps I hadn't been so hasty after all!

Leaving the hotel the next day, which Dai had, again, confidently confirmed was definitely the "best one yet boys", we set off for Southend and were now quite close to Roy's neck of the woods. For some reason, although highly illegal and uninsured, Roy somehow managed to get behind the wheel. We were running a bit late and as he approached a large traffic island in the vicinity of the gig and from the depths of the very shallow recesses of Roy's mind, for some slapstick amusement known only to himself, he missed the exit for Southend Central and went round the island a second time. Then, inexplicably, a third, this time guffawing loudly. Every time he completed a circuit, naturally, we thought he would just take the correct exit next time. Wrong! Not seeing the joke at all, George became quite angry; "For fuck's sake Roy, stop acting like an idiot. JUST STOP IT, OKAY? You're so fucking stupid, it really pisses me off!"

He was not amused at all, which only seemed to increase Roy's manic merriment, going around the island yet again, a third then a fourth and now a fifth time. Older readers may recall the stupid faces pulled by comedians like Norman Wisdom (hat on backwards) and Tommy Trinder, which these days might be interpreted as educationally subnormal; Roy's crazed demeanour, that day, brought back the entire slapstick genre of Music Hall Theatre. Perhaps it was the sea air and being back in Essex that did it. I counted 17 times around the island before he got bored and finally succumbed to a van-full of robust abuse!

The second and third to last shows at Southend, followed by Brighton went by in a haze, but the last show, at London's Heaven was, I believe, the first great moment for the band, a triumphant return to the nation's capital and to a club now owned by Richard Branson, head of their record label and publishers, Virgin Records and Virgin Music.

Entrepreneur Jeremy Norman first opened Heaven - what was to be an entirely new form of Gay club in 1979, becoming more and more open and outrageous into the early eighties, as gay lifestyles became more acceptable within society and culture. Originally a run-down roller-disco called Global Village, the club is still housed in the arches beneath Charing Cross railway station. Heaven was seen as the London equivalent of New York's famous gay club, The Saint and prior to that, most gay clubs in London were hidden or down in furtive cellar bars or pub discos. Heaven brought gay clubbing into the mainstream of London nightlife, therefore it was obvious that this venue could not have been a more perfect showcase for Culture Club at that time, but there was a huge risk involved.

The club could accommodate over 1200 paying customers, but how many would turn up to see us? Hardly any tickets had been sold in advance and the band's credibility and reputation would have been dead in the water if, as seemed likely, only half the tickets were sold or, even worse, hardly anyone turned up for their home-town UK tour finale.

As soon as we arrived at the venue that afternoon for the sound check all anxiety in that department immediately evaporated, there was a huge palpable buzz in and around the club, with touts already offering tickets with huge mark ups in the middle of the afternoon. This was the hottest ticket in town. All kinds of weird and wonderful folk were trying their luck to get in but the show was already sold out. The day was exceptionally memorable, not only because Ann was coming to see the show for the first time, but also my late mother, Eileen, who, upon seeing him for the first time, said to a startled and compliant George; "Come here, let me see you; you look fantastically gorgeous darling", proceeding to grab him by the shoulders and swivelling him around on his heels to get a better look. It wasn't too often George was speechless, but up to that time, I don't think he'd met anyone quite like her. "Who's that Phil?" he said laughing, "I'm sorry, that's my mum," I said, "She's a bit of an extrovert, but she loves the way you look."

As wives, girlfriends and mums had guest passes, yet another side of George's nature revealed itself for the first time, similar to the hotel episode only a few days earlier. On our way to the dressing room, George shouted out ahead of us; "Wait! Don't go in there yet, let me go in first, thanks," whereupon, he went in, closed the door and turned all the gay soft-porn pics to the wall in order not to subvert or shock any of the band's friends and guests. George, who could be shockingly outrageous himself (as has been well documented), was nevertheless considerate and in a charming way, even quite prim about the often risqué behaviour associated with band life on the road, especially as he was so new to it all. Drugs of any description were completely out of bounds, as was overindulgence in alcohol and number one priority, if anyone associated with the band, sessions, crew or record label was caught using their position with Culture Club to take advantage of impressionable females of any description, they needn't bother coming back. George exerted a moral authority over louche behaviour that would have put Mary Whitehouse to shame. I firmly believe he would have fired anyone on the spot had we have ever remotely given him the chance.

Musical Youth supported us and went down really well. The atmosphere in the by now, heaving club, was electrifying and extraordinary. The set was blistering, especially so on this night, as all of the band's proud families, friends and their hometown peer group (or in George's case, as noted by his tranny friend and mentor Philip Sallon, his "queer group"), were all out in force to cheer on Culture Club's triumphant homecoming. You could also see lots of other bands of the day furtively milling about, checking out the opposition and seeing what all the fuss was about. George, in his own words, was "effing and blinding like a fishwife" and was in magnificent form, quite frankly having the time of his life.

They had taken a big risk in booking such a large place for their London debut, but boy, had it paid off big-time. Roy, Jon, Mikey and George, as well as me and the rest of us, were now well and truly blooded after, what in the end was a credible, memorable and very effective tour of England. Up on stage, I'd never felt heat like it and everyone's clothes were drenched through. Hundreds of pre-pubescent girls were screaming their heads off between songs, incongruously mixed in with an older more decadent and androgynous, New Romantic crowd; many dressed like variations of George. It was manic, crazy, phenomenal and obviously working. Radical, polysexual subversion side by side with tearful tiny teenyboppers. None of us, or anyone, in fact, had ever seen anything like it. God knows what would happen when the band actually had a hit record. I saw Ann's smile from the back of the room, even before I saw her; "I think I know what you're going to be doing the rest of the year," she predicted.

Although I didn't know it at the time, this was the last gig before Helen Terry would augment the sound with her powerful, soulful voice. On this first tour it was, basically, George backed only by me on vocals so by the end of the Heaven show, and their first UK tour, my voice gave up the ghost completely, but it had been one of the most exciting gigs I'd ever done in my life. Neil Tennant, in those days a journalist & critic, before taking up his own pop career, had written something scathing and bitchy about Culture Club referring, (in a nerdy NME muso-snob derogatory fashion), to the use of tape recorders on stage. Later when the Pet Shop Boys launched their own career, we at least expected he would have real musicians on stage (not their entire sound on backing tapes). Mikey, for one, did not take too kindly to him being in the audience and after a couple of choice words with noses only an inch apart, Tennant left the building in a hurry never to return.

Not too long after selling out Heaven, Virgin arranged a show for Culture Club at The Lyceum on the Strand, which Richard Branson attended; no doubt to come and see for himself what all the fuss was about with his newly signed controversial quartet. None of the band, including George, had actually met their label's owner yet, the day-to-day running of the company being left to others like Simon Draper and Ken & Nancy Berry. I'd already met Richard quite a few times from my Sailor days where he would often hang around outside our gigs, leafleting the crowds leaving our venue, either for an act he was promoting or for his lesser-known ventures, such as selling student magazines advertising, among other things, urine tests and the like. I'd also once been to a wild rock 'n' roll party with Fairport Convention at The Manor Studios near Oxford which he owned, but that's another story.

He'd seen the show anyway and as usual, dressed in a shabby old green sweater, threadbare corduroys and looking more like a homeless person than a record company impresario, had somehow shambled his way into our dressing room ahead of me, with George following on behind after just coming off stage. "Who the fuck are you? George demanded angrily of the bearded stranger, "Piss off out of here!" I tried to interrupt, "Ooh, just a minute George..." I said, "This is our dressing room", George said to Branson really losing it now, "What are you doing in here and who the fuck are you anyway?" he demanded. "Er, I'm Richard Branson, George," he said almost inaudibly, (Richard spoke very quietly, still does). The noise from the gig downstairs was still quite deafening. "What? I can't hear you", I grabbed the moment to interject immediately and save the day; "George, this is Richard Branson, he owns the record label that you and the guys are signed to."

"Well, why didn't he fucking say so then?"

Chapter 22
"No Mermaids, Sailors or Drag Queens"

That's definitely me out of the video then, thought I, when finally, (and at last, as far as I was concerned), Virgin decided to put out 'Do You You Really Want To Hurt Me' as the third single from *Kissing To Be Clever*. A video was urgently commissioned and fearing George's overpowering creative influence on the visual storyboard, Jon, Roy and Mikey got in early with the director, Julien Temple, to lay down some ground rules, with the succinct directive of the chapter heading above. What they definitely did not want was George to run with it and bus in coach loads of campness with every tranny from Eltham to Watford coming on board. Quite a cheek on Mikey's part, in retrospect, as perhaps the missive also should have read "And NO Mikey" on the forbidden list, as the bassist never showed up on the day, or even the day after the shoot, thus missing out on appearing in his band's first ever video. Mikey's absence was due apparently to excessive indulgence of a herbal nature enjoyed at a West London party on the night or nights before the video shoot. But thankfully his bacon was saved by brother Greg, who stood in for him at the last minute. But in the annals of Culture Club provenance and legend, this was a defining incident which would return to haunt Mikey again and again up to the present day.

Julien wanted the film to be, "about being gay and victimised for your sexuality, for which George was an emblem". A satirical send-up of the bigotry and hypocrisy of the many gay judges and politicians who had enacted anti-gay legislation. Controversially he blacked up the members of the jury sitting in judgement of George in the courtroom scene. Although Americans may have been shocked at the reference to their racist past, in England the idea of blackface was more acceptable as it had been part of its extremely robust Music Hall tradition. The video shows Boy George as an outsider getting kicked out of different places in various historic settings.

'I'm Afraid Of Me' the second single after their first release, 'White Boy', had similarly bombed. An indigestible fact made painfully worse in George's mind, especially as their contemporaries and rivals, Haysee Fantayzee's debut single, with its randomly perverse title; 'John Wayne Is Big Leggy' was getting loads of plays on Radio One and looked like becoming a sure-fire hit. In pop music, as in other competitive fields, you don't mind seeing your friends do well, but for Christ's sake not THAT well! With George however and by now having got to know him better, I suspected that Gore Vidal's pithy observation for the even less generous of spirit seemed much more appropriate; "Every time a friend succeeds, something inside me dies."

I was a stuck record on the first UK tour, always going on about the hit potential of 'Do You Really Want To Hurt Me' to George, Jon or anyone who would listen. Not just because it was the first song I'd played on. I'd be flattering myself if the ultimate decision had, had anything to do with me, which of course it didn't. Anyway, up to that point, George always felt the lyric, as ever, about his tempestuous and masochistic relationship with Jon, was far too personal and downbeat. Also, as is often the case with ambitious recording artists starting out on their road to fame, the group probably thought they could second guess their audience as far as which track would, in the end, the public would go out and buy in their multitudes. But I'd already learnt in Sailor that no one really knows exactly what the secret is that would fire up the herd mentality of Joe Public and which magical ingredient would guarantee a hit record. I suppose we'd all be rich if we knew that one! But from first the day I heard 'Do You Really Want To Hurt Me', in fact, the day I'd played keyboards on the song at Maison Rouge, something inside told me this record had whatever that fairy dust was in spades.

George's vocal rendition was heartfelt and sublime, Mikey's bass part was/is probably one of the most distinctive reggae bass lines of all time, and to cap it all Steve Levine's production was so deft of touch I just couldn't see how the record could fail. On top of it all was the priceless vocal contribution of Helen Terry, particularly with her lush, soulful and unique textured harmonies. In my mind, this was the finishing touch to what was, and still is, a classic and timeless record. Helen's voice effortlessly enhanced the sound of George's lead vocal in a much more original manner than would have been the case had they used any other of the countless female backing vocalists around at that time; girls who were used on everything going.

Helen gave Culture Club an incomparable sound signature, rare for a backing vocalist no matter how good they were technically. George had only just recently met her outside Heaven and auditioned her there and then on the street, a blast of her Big Mama Thornton voice rooting him to the spot. When it turned out she was one of the "doop-di-doop" girls on Lou Reid's iconic 'Walk On The Wild Side' this casually introduced, but impressive, nugget of information, apparently sealed the deal. Years before I'd already sung with some of the best session singers on countless vocal sessions. With legends such as Sue and Sunny, (who were featured on Joe Cocker's 'With A Little Help From My Friends'), Madeleine Bell, Rosetta Hightower & Lesley Duncan, (The Stones's 'You Can't Always Get What You Want' & Blue Mink). I also met and worked with an amazing Irish singer called Casey Synge, whose three-girl group Thunderthighs backed Lou Reid on his massive hit. That record became a calling card for hundreds of aspiring female vocalists at that time trying to score work in a hugely competitive environment, many of whom, cheekily, used the über cool association of the Thunderthighs brand on their CV's, one of whom was obviously Helen.

But as there were only three girls in the group, Derry, Karen, and Casey, all of whom were close friends, I knew for a fact Helen couldn't have been involved. Also whilst making the Kajanus Pickett album, I'd even been at Morgan Studios when Lou Reid was cutting the track.

"But who cares?" I told Helen, her face stricken with guilt when we met for the first time at Maison Rouge Studios outside in the corridor. "Look, name one member of this band who isn't a rock 'n' roll imposter, we're all reinventions. Look at me, I'm no exception!" "Anyway, I'm not going to say anything" I promised her. "I was mini-cabbing & delivering parcels only a few months ago just over the road, so really who gives a shit?"

Painfully shy and introverted at the best of times, Helen, who over time I would come to know well, often disguised an initial lack of confidence by speaking incredibly fast, her words tumbling out like a waterfall and at first, treating most people, myself included, with a kind of aristocratic, arm's length, haughtiness stopping just this side of mild disdain. In other ways she wasn't one of your average 'session singers' either; female accessories, often employed as much for their looks as their vocal abilities. Ms Terry could be awkward, tetchy and uncompromising; an out-and-out feminist, hammering against the walls of what, in fairness, was in most cases, the patriarchal domain of a male-dominated music industry of which she was clearly determined not to be yet another female, downtrodden by-product. Good luck to her, I thought. It was and still is a very tough business for a woman, but by God when she opened her mouth at the microphone she could sing like voices of angels and in retrospect, the fact she was short, large and lesbian only made her an even more perfect choice for the revolutionary type of band George was trying to assemble. His group would be aimed at all the misfits and freaks with less than perfect body shapes; the unchosen, those usually left in the long cold line outside the nightclub. And that was its unique selling point. Culture Club was never going to exclude anyone from the party George intended to have!

As I got to know Helen better over the next few years I came to appreciate the wicked bonds of a shared sense of humour and mutual professional interests. Underneath the bolshie affectation of left-wing bluster, class conscious, dropped vowels and East London banter; as with Jon, I suspected there was a solid, middle-class education lurking somewhere in Helen's hinterland. I later learned that she was a direct descendant of the provocative bohemian Victorian actress of legend and notoriety, Ellen Terry. Of course, it all started to make sense. Not part of the inner molten core of the group, nevertheless we were two independent planets in our own orbits of increasing influence on the sound and songs of Culture Club. Despite being opposites in character, outlook and politics, we got on famously touring the world, swapping notes and exchanging gossip, hers always far more interesting than mine, whilst negotiating the various love twists and turns of Jon and George's increasingly stormy relationship. We often exchanged intelligence in the lobby on any latest reports from the front. "What's on the cards today number one?" I asked her one morning; "Heard anything overnight"? "Yes, number two, reports of a low depression on its way in from the Atlantic" she vouchsafed. "Sightings of flying crockery across the corridor just before dawn, batten down the hatches today me thinks," all delivered in crisp, RAF-style stiff-upper-lip monotone. "Damn this leg, wish I was going with you" I responded", in similarly clipped tones but knowing damn well, whatever happened, I would be. I was loving this new life of mine that by chance and a stroke of huge luck I'd somehow landed in. Saxophonist Steve Grainger had replaced Nick Paine who, along with Terry 'Trumpet' Bailey were now the two-man brass section on our second UK tour and, for some daft reason, the officers mess terminology caught on: "Cripes, Pickett's bought it over the Channel sir, he just went too far with that keyboard solo last night, poor beggar!" This was now the settled line-up of "the sessions" that would go on to help Culture Club conquer the world throughout the next three tumultuous years, with only one more change a year or so later when 'Gentle Giant' Ron "Jazz trousers" Williams replaced Terry Trumpet. Buddhist Ron came straight from the RAF to join the band, so his droll one-liners and typical brass player's humour fitted in a treat.

Back at Maison Rouge and Red Bus Studios, having recorded backing vocals with Helen, my voice was pitched up somewhere in the midrange, as it had been when I'd provided the ballast to some of the great star vocalists previously referred to. Having had that experience, as well as the vocal harmonies I contributed to on Sailor songs, made me very quick on the uptake where vocal harmonies were concerned. "I like your voice Phil", George said one day during the *Kissing To Be Clever* sessions. He looked pleasantly surprised. "It's really bland and 'white' sounding isn't it?" Damned with faint praise, I waited for the killer pay-off insult, but none came; he was flattering me, he actually did like my voice. "It's really poppy", he noted; "I really like the sound of everything." "Thanks, George", I said, carrying on under his and Steve's, direction and completing all the male backing vocals while Roy and Mikey, hopes again dashed, disconsolately looked on. I knew I would have hated that had it have been my band.

Helen, an artist in her own right, seemed much more like a fundamental part of the group's sound and at one time George suggested to the others they should perhaps consider her becoming a fully-fledged member of the group. Roy and Jon put their feet down decisively, one might say understandably, not wishing to add more outsiders to the group's inner circle of trust, thus further diminishing their own influence by taking on any new partners in the group's affairs and decision making. My initial impression was that George didn't really mind or care that much about how many people were involved in the Culture Club project, at least not at first. All he seemed to strive for was curating the various talents involved to create hits; for instance in the songwriting, which I would later be invited to take part, his principal, overall objective was to make everything sound unique and above all, successful, whatever it took. In fact, very much like his magpie approach to the painstaking assembly of his clothes, styles and 'looks'; a pinch from here, a steal from there.

Having Helen on board in any capacity now made the band a truly formidable vocal line-up. Even though I thought we'd done pretty well on the first tour, with Helen's vocals now having been added into the mix, soaring above on the highest parts and adding her explosively incandescent set-pieces of pure soul, vocally Culture Club were now a major force to be reckoned with. The majestic three-part harmony vocals we were now able to produce on stage were a joy to behold and a real treat that I looked forward to being a part of every night.

So it was later in 1982, on 14th October, again, from Hammersmith Odeon, that we embarked on our second UK tour, this time with ten shows to look forward to all over England and Scotland; unofficially to promote the release of 'Do You Really Want To Hurt Me'. This time the tour could not have been timed better. As usual, all of the hotels, according to our road manager, Dai, would be the "best ones yet boys" (actually some of them were!) and right from the start of the tour one could sense that the crowds were not only growing, but their reactions were becoming much more enthusiastic, especially now that the word on Culture Club was spreading fast. 'Do You Really Want To Hurt Me' slowly began its steady ascent up the chart, but very few outside of the band's inner circle had realised what a close-run, knife-edge thing this was. There was an awful lot riding on this record, for in spite of the underground buzz in an influential but tiny London clique of artists and fashionistas, Culture Club still hadn't had anything approaching a hit record and time and money was running out fast. With marketing and recording costs as high as they were, and now with the huge extra costs of having to make expensive videos to promote their acts, labels frequently dropped artists if they weren't seen to deliver the goods from record one. The real pressure was now on.

The initial press reviews and reactions from BBC radio were also lukewarm at best, with the influential *Smash Hits* magazine describing the single as, "weak, watered-down fourth division reggae", and many other publications, like *NME* and *Melody Maker*, similarly deriding the track, many preferring to make fun of George's music and image. The omens didn't look good to begin with and, furthermore, BBC radio informed Virgin Records, disrespectfully and in no uncertain terms that, "We can't promote this record, what is 'it'? Is 'it' a bird or a plane? Is 'it' a drag queen? Anyway, we don't interview transvestites!" Can you imagine any of them saying that today? The worldwide impact that George would subsequently go on to spearhead by representing the cause and understanding of Gay Rights would be impossible to overestimate. But this was still 1982.

In my own world of fellow musicians, some music executives I knew and even a surprising number of my closest friends knowing the kind of career I'd enjoyed up to this point, thought I'd really lost the plot this time. I always knew in my heart that I was right about Culture Club though and that the naysayers would, in the end, all prove to be wrong. In my experience, when things were this good, regular punters didn't always get it right away. Like the Beatles and Stones, there was something a little awkward about them at first, simply because it was all so new. The look, the sound, everything. George's voice and personality could not fail in my view, even though things weren't always on an even keel. When they were, which was quite often, the sheer enjoyment, honesty, diversity and humour of being around this group of resilient and incomparable characters was infectious. Like a love affair you never wanted to end. But who, in God's name, would have thought that such a controversial, poly-sexual and subversive outfit, as shocking as the group and lead singer were at the time to their many critics in the mainstream media, would receive their first major, rocket-powered, breakthrough moment courtesy of the most middle-of-the-road, old-fashioned, combed-over, post-dated disc jockey of them all?

Completely out of the blue, BBC Radio 2's 'Diddy' David Hamilton, on the housewives and pensioners station selected 'Do You Really Want To Hurt Me' as his 'Record Of The Week'. 'Diddy' David turned out to be the gatekeeper who would single-handedly fling open the doors to Culture Club's future pop music world domination. 'Record of the Week' status guaranteed powerful plays across the entire BBC radio platform. Without such endorsement, it would have left the band skating on very thin ice indeed, career-wise. Three failed singles from a debut album no doubt would have raised some very serious questions at Virgin, as the days of record labels standing by their artists, no matter how many releases and however long it took, were already long gone. Although it was great news, in the larger scheme of things, the image and idea of Radio 2 playing their record, and not Radio One, like Hayzee and the rest, was nevertheless an insult and reality-check on their ambitions. "Who listens to fucking Radio 2 anyway?" Roy bitterly complained. "Well, a hell of a lot of people", I thought to myself, and beggars couldn't be choosers.

Another magic ingredient in the synchronicity of Culture Club's beckoning destiny, which would prove to be a game-changer, was the sudden illness of Shakin' Stevens on the eve of his Top of the Pops TV performance. It allowed George's band an unexpected last minute and highly coveted appearance on the UK's most influential hit-making TV show. Happy accidents and magical serendipity have played their part in the initial breakthrough of a huge number of artists including Sailor. Thankfully with the resulting furore and notoriety this performance ultimately caused, Culture Club would be no exception.

As we finally set off on the road for our second UK tour, the band's memorable first ever Top Of The Pops appearance was still the talking point of the entire nation. With gender bending androgyny and "was 'it' a boy, or a girl?" the currency of every newspaper headline the day after their appearance on the show meant that the record suddenly shot up to number three in the chart. People were talking about it all over in the country; in offices by the water coolers and in school playgrounds everywhere. Suddenly Culture Club and Boy George were on everyone's lips and radar.

Once again we picked up George and Jon in Hampstead on our way up north, this time in a bigger and better van which, thankfully I wasn't called on to drive anymore, the bewildered and out-of-his-depth Dai, now having taken over that role. What's more, I was now being paid properly on this and all subsequent tours. An abundance of deep joy and peace now reigned supreme in the land. In addition, everyone in the touring party and crew was quietly aware of how well the record was doing after the legendary Top Of The Pops appearance, so we had more than an inkling it could go all the way, perhaps even on this tour. After all, this was what the pop industry was all about.

Almost from the first show at Leeds Polytechnic, you could feel the levels of audience hysteria starting to kick in massively. Apart from one notable exception, wherever we played the stage would quickly become a shrine of flowers, teddy bears, George dolls and knitted characters; sweets raining down on our heads, love letters and drawings of their favourite band member, usually George. Bubbling, just under the surface, a brand new phenomena, 'Culture Club Mania', was underway which pretty soon would crash over the UK like a tsunami.

In stark contrast to these palpable undercurrents of excitement suddenly breaking and how brilliantly everything was progressing on the career front at last, George and Jon's relationship sadly seemed to be on a downward spiral. Although from the earliest days, they positively seemed to relish each and every interview opportunity (George and Jon being the principal spokespersons for the group), now that their schedule was becoming more intense as the band's popularity was exploding, the two of them were now spending much more time together around the clock. Also, some of us began to realise that stage-managing their relationship in front of an inquisitive but as yet unsuspecting world may have started to take its toll. Apart from the odd spiteful and sarcastic comment flying around the van, at the hotel or backstage of which there never seemed to be any huge effort to conceal, at first I wasn't too aware of what was going on. Although Helen, by knowing

George and some of his friends much better than I did, always had more of the low-down on what was really happening behind the scenes. Suddenly and dramatically, however, on the 17th October 1982 after our show at Cardiff Nero's the night before, while on our way up to Sheffield's Leadmill Club, things suddenly burst out into unpleasant, open warfare and decidedly took a turn for the worse.

On a driving break, Helen and I were a little late into the motorway café near Bromsgrove on the M5, where Roy and Mikey, seated at one of the tables, were visibly downcast, whilst Jon and George were hammering it out in the midst of a very loud and public altercation. The argument abruptly ended when George, slowly and deliberately, as if in a Laurel and Hardy movie, poured a whole pint glass of orange juice over Jon's head. An act so outrageous as to leave Jon speechless, and very wet, but still bolt upright in his chair, not moving an inch. "Cunt, I hate him", George spat out as he whisked past Helen and me, a mass of dreadlocked outrage already on his way back to the van, whilst Jon attempted to clear himself up, choosing to ridicule his lover in front of all of us rather than berate him over what had just happened. "I think he's going mad actually," said Jon quietly, "No, seriously man! He's completely losing it all the time, it's fucking ridiculous!" Tensions were thus very high on the way to the gig, but later on, the show went surprisingly well. Sheffield, after all, was home to The Human League so was definitely a town where the upstart southerners fully intended to pull-out all the stops to seriously impress their cool and stylish northern rivals, so obviously, for the duration of the show, all internal divisions and fighting were briefly forgotten; very briefly as things turned out.

The next couple of days would prove to be the very best and the worst in Culture Club's brief and incident-prone history to date. On the long drive up to Glasgow from Sheffield, George was clearly out of sorts and upon arrival, missed the soundcheck preferring to rest up in the hotel, thus saving himself and his voice for the show. When we finally went on stage a few hours later, very late as it happened as George had kept everyone waiting, interminably fussing about this and that, his voice sounded awful and he wasn't hitting many of the notes. Three or four songs into the set, he gave up the ghost entirely and after apologising to the audience about sounding "like Joe Cocker", abruptly disappeared off stage leaving the rest of us up there while the bad tempered Glaswegians jeered; "Canna fuckin' sing, yer fuckin' southern nancy boy."

The aggrieved and clearly unsympathetic jocks howled, possibly, even more wound up than usual, after being made to wait before George had deigned to appear in the first place. Glasgow can be a real horror show when it wants to be, I thought, recalling a few of my Sailor and Mott the Hoople memories, the night the latter cancelled our tour. Eventually, following George back into the dressing room there was another bitter argument raging. I felt very sorry for George; his voice was so bunged up, croaky and asthmatic he could hardly speak, the last few days of angst, constant interviews, travel and tiredness having obviously got the better of him. But none of his band appeared to want to offer any support or sympathy. On the contrary, they were deeply critical and to my mind, very uncaring towards their lead singer. "Just get up there and do it man, for fuck's sake! What's the matter with you?" They seemed to speak as one. "I can't, I just can't", George said almost crying by now, "I sound like shit!" and pleading with Jon or anyone to go and make an announcement to the crowd, who were, by now, booing and jeering. "Tell them we'll come back and do the gig later, please Jon."

I could only think back to the camaraderie and mutual dependency with Sailor and what we would have done in this situation; without doubt, or question what seemed to be going on here would never have happened. One of us would have just got out there and covered it, told a joke or something. I felt quite angry. "Someone should go out and speak to the audience", I said, assuming the veteran muso role in the proceedings; "George shouldn't have to do it, it's getting really ugly out there." Roy and Jon looked at me blankly, but then turned to George again; "YOU do it George - just get out there man. You tell them!" (in other words, 'mind your own friggin' business' thought I).

It was unbelievable; George simply had no choice but to go back on stage, on his own, feeling like death and explain to an extremely hostile crowd why he couldn't sing, promising that Culture Club would return and honour the date when his health improved. In the end, I admired George's courage in the face of such mean-spirited opposition, both from the audience and his own bandmates. "Don't bother, you're fuckin' crap"; the crowd booed, jeered and barked back at him, sealing what was one of the darkest and most depressing show nights I have ever experienced before or since. George looked suicidal on the way back to the hotel. No one in the band seemed prepared to take his side at all, which seemed callous and cruel, almost sadistic. What was it about these guys when everything else seemed to be going so well for them?

Exhausted and weary after a very long and demanding day, I slept long and hard, whilst unbeknown to me, or many of us, a vicious and violent punch-up had been going on in George and Jon's room just down the hall, which, according to Helen a number of days later, was several notches up on any previous fights. This time Jon had allegedly threatened George by holding a broken glass up to his face. It must be something they put in the water in Glasgow. No one apart from the two of them would have known about it next day in the van going to Edinburgh however. The atmosphere, although subdued if anything was reasonably pleasant as everyone was pleased to be getting away from Glasgow and that dreadful club, now being referred to as "Night Mares".

Another reason the for the upbeat mood was that everyone knew this was the day of the brand new weekly chart run-down on Radio One, the 19th October 1982. So just before 1 pm, Dai pulled over on the hard shoulder of the old A8 Glasgow-Edinburgh road so everyone could listen to Tommy Vance's final three chart positions...

"...Musical Youth's 'Pass The Dutchie' has slipped from pole position to Number Two. ...AND THE NEW UK NUMBER ONE IS... CULTURE CLUB with - 'DO YOU REALLY WANT TO HURT ME', the DJ announced, jubilantly. Whereupon, amidst handshakes and hugs, we got out of the van and danced a little jig in celebration by the side of the motorway. It was a sweet moment to savour; even though some of the band had received a nod and a wink, we were all together on the road hearing the news like everyone else in the country, officially, for the very first time. These moments are the deeply symbolic and highly memorable events, the time-honoured, touchstone moments in every musician's life. At least those lucky enough, as we were, to have contributed to the song's provenance in some way.

George, bless him, after the ordeals of the night before, looked pleased too, joining in, smiling and celebrating with the rest of us, although I thought it odd at the time he was not his usual cascading, gregarious self, whether fighting fit or, as he was that day, fighting a cold. It wasn't until a few days later that I would appreciate why his mood had been so subdued on the day he'd finally achieved his ultimate ambition.

The next day in Edinburgh I got up especially early to walk into town to buy some underwear and socks and was surprised to find George downstairs in the lobby. "I need some stuff too, can I come with you?" "Yes, great," I said, happy to spend a bit of one-on-one with George, empathising on how dreadful Glasgow was the night before last and gossiping and exchanging info on yesterday's amazing news.

We walked along the street chatting, never difficult or haltingly with George, and distinctly recognisable from the clothes he was wearing. A few people in cars driving by were tooting their horns and smiling and waving at him enthusiastically. Everything seemed to have happened so fast, but having strangers recognise him was something very new which tickled him immensely.

Still quite early in the morning, the store only just having opened, we ascended in the rackety lift up to an almost deserted creaking top floor and on to the makeup counter where he began to buy a few things from a bashful and wide-eyed female shop assistant. She'd clearly never met anyone quite like George before and it was still only 9 o'clock in the morning. I stood by patiently as he tried a few things. But then suddenly, out of the corner of my eye, I could see and hear some girls gathering at the far end of the floor shouting to each other and then, slowly at first, starting to descend upon us like a herd of wildebeest along the aisles. "Och, it's him off the telly, c'mon, let's git his autograph!"

The ancient concave wooden floors of the building shook and roared as more and more of them clomped along adding to the main throng gaining speed along the central aisle leading up to where George and I were. I couldn't make out where they'd suddenly all come from. "Come on George, quick, we've got to get out", I shouted above the din, guiding him towards the nearby stairwell exit. Some of the faster movers were already grabbing at him trying to steal his hat and tear bits off his hair and clothes. The terrified shop assistants looked on as we hurtled off, in an undignified fashion, towards the exit, not even completing the purchase. It had been so quiet only a few seconds earlier.

I just about managed to get him through the door while I tied my scarf around the glass door handles to keep out the teeny, tartan terrorists, who were, by now, screaming their heads off and banging on the door, "Gi's an autograph will ye George? Och, come on!" They knew his name! Some of them were now crying, their quest to literally rip their celebrity prey to shreds having been cunningly thwarted. At the foot of the stairwell, miraculously, there was a cab outside which I immediately grabbed, opened the door and unceremoniously shoved an obviously stunned and shocked George into the back seat. "Drive!" I shouted dramatically, and, at that very moment, the familiar dreamy opening chord sequence of 'Do You Really Want To Hurt Me', the nation's Number 1, started playing on the cabbie's radio. The driver had just realised what was happening and was beaming in his rearview mirror. George smiled, he was strangely mute, sitting back in his seat looking very pleased with himself. He appeared to be looking into the far distance out of the window, "That's it then George. You finally got what you wanted" I said. "From this point on, nothing in your life will ever be the same again." And it certainly wasn't!

Chapter 23
Frenzy Factor

As the tours and shows with Culture Club progressed after 'Do You Really Want To Hurt Me' hit the top spot, turbocharging the quartet's pre-meteoric ascent to eventual world domination, everything was now going exceptionally well. But although their stage show was developing in confidence, compared to previous experiences I'd had, their showmanship, in the early days, often seemed shambolic and unprofessional, and therefore in my mind was achieving nowhere near the crazy reactions from sell-out crowds I'd experienced before.

From where I was standing, (behind a bank of keyboards), there was still something lacking in the audience 'frenzy-factor', which, in my view, was running at around 75% of what it should have been. Culture Club deserved better and I knew in my bones something wasn't cutting it. George was always great value, an engaging performer and the perfect front man. That is, if he wasn't hassled and rattled by hecklers who could often affect his mood, which, true to form, he never cared to disguise that much. In the end, I felt that it might be more about the pacing of the set and the running order of the songs.

Having performed hundreds of gigs I knew that before you'd achieved your first hit or, even better, had several under your belt, the crowds would be generally supportive, but the reaction changed mightily when they could latch on to a huge radio smash. For instance, before 'A Glass Of Champagne' took off in the charts, we meticulously designed the set around dynamics and pacing, where to put the quieter songs in relation to the up tempo tracks for maximum impact, keeping continuity really tight, carefully building the show's performance up to the climax and the hit, and not to 'shoot one's bolt' too early, excusing the obvious analogy.

In the early days of a band, you might have a minority of hard-core fans who knew the album off by heart, whereas the majority were there to see what all the fuss was about and frankly, just to see if you were any good. Culture Club's stagecraft, at first, often veered towards anarchy; harking back more to the punk era than the polished, professional hit-making machine the group was well on its way to becoming. On the early tours, Jon gave a heads-up as to what the next song would be, seemingly at random. It could sometimes then degenerate into open differences of opinion on stage, so I figured the running order and pacing of the set just wasn't something they considered that important.

George's playful and confrontational banter and repartee, meanwhile, confronting the audience with camp badinage, such as, "How many POOFS out there tonight", usually got a laugh but often thinly so and on a few occasions was met with awkward silence. After all, we were still in the very early days of gay liberation and on both sides of the Atlantic, Culture Club audiences were, at first, bewitched, bothered and bewildered by George, not really knowing how to react. Especially in America, where even in the trendiest East or West Coast venues, audiences were surprisingly conservative, uptight and if anything, even threatened by George's unconscious embodiment of the bawdier and sexually subversive traditions of British Music Hall Theatre.

Watching the audiences, you could see that George was just too full on for them at first. From my perspective, I enjoyed how he disrupted everyone's preconceived notions of what a gay pop star, songwriter and transvestite could be. After all, in 1982 it was still only fifteen years since the decriminalisation of homosexuality in England and Wales, (but not until 1980 in Scotland and two years after that in Northern Ireland). When the music and fashion movement, known as New Romanticism came alive in the early eighties, Boy George eventually emerged as its unofficial cheerleader, going on to probably do more to promote the cause of British gay equality than anyone before or since. By mischievously telling *Smash Hits* that he "much preferred a cup of tea to sex", guided by Jon and Tony, he as good as ensured that all the mums, grandmas and Radio 2 listeners of middle-of-the-road Britain would adore him by deftly camouflaging his overtly sexual outrageousness. They'd always loved queer entertainers in Britain, as long as, Jon often said, it wasn't "shoved in their face", to coin a phrase.

Suddenly, post-George, everywhere you looked pop appeared to have been taken over by gay artists; Bronski Beat, The Pet Shop Boys, Pete Burns & Dead Or Alive, Steve Strange, Marc Almond and of course, gay royalty themselves, Elton John and Freddie Mercury. Also much to the chagrin and in the end, open hostility from Boy George, who knew beyond doubt (he often complained), that his friend George Michael was gay, his bitter criticisms of Michael's faint-heartedness and betrayal of the gay cause during those years was an open secret in the business. In George's often vehemently expressed opinion, the young Greek singer skulked away in the closet for much longer than he needed to.

All but a few of the above stars, however, couldn't have stood a ghost's chance without their trail having been well and truly blazed in the previous decade by the godfather of colourful ambiguity, bisexuality and androgyny himself, Mr David Bowie. Boy George and everything he represented, far from being risqué and deviant to a new pop generation coming of age, felt like a breath of fresh air to a musical youth grown weary of constant heterosexual phallic posturing; male strutting and rutting, tight leather trousers, amps turned up to 11 and absurd permed hair. That was all now consigned to the bygone age of the dinosaur!

George was initially very smart about concealing his more brazen gay sexuality but, in any event, was verbally kept on a very tight leash by Tony Gordon and particularly by Jon. "They don't want Widow Twankey or Larry Grayson, George, just be very cool and enigmatic about it all, keep them guessing!" Jon said. Very good advice as it turned out and for most of the time, George became an adept master of subterfuge and PR savvy, stuck to like glue, thus rubber-stamping the deceit of his harmless, sexual credentials to the media world, most of whom were now eating out of his hand.

Writing this book and looking back over the years I realise that, although a 'calmer chameleon' and an only child, who at times could be a bit of a loner, I was always drawn like a magnet to larger than life characters like George - iconoclasts who disrupt the cosy status quo with original and unconventional thought. My mother, Eileen, was very much in that mould, which is probably why they always seemed to get on so well whenever they met. Whilst conducting an interview with a major US TV network in L.A. at which I was present, on a conversational foray into gayness and, more specifically, how Quentin Crisp was first received in America, George astounded me, (and the interviewer!) by baldly stating live on TV; "Actually, Phil Pickett's mum is the campest person I ever met!" Personally, politically and professionally, I seem to come alive around such luminous characters, even though the other side of the coin at times could often be something darker and less approachable.

The first time the band flew anywhere was up to Glasgow to honour the previously cancelled show after our dreadful night at the 'Night Moves' club. On a packed plane full of sniggering grey-suited business men, the boldest one of whom in the cheap seats and suits sneeringly asked George, "Why do you have to dress like THAT?" George, without missing a beat, in full makeup, rabbi's hat and hobo mannequin dress delivered his stock reply in his campest Marilyn Monroe drawl; "I earn more in a day than you do in a YEAR looking like this!" Not strictly true of course but the now-cowed worker drone was firmly back in his grey little box where he belonged. Hard to fathom now, but George, back then, with the way he looked, who he was, and what he said, still represented a revolutionary assault on most people's senses and sensibilities.

Every offstage moment around him was spectacularly alive, dramatic and hilarious, but during the performance, things could still be quite ropey and unpredictable. "What do mean, you don't think we are going down well enough?" George protested archly when one day I decided to approach him and Jon on the subject; on our second, or could have been third UK tour and on our way to Margate in Kent. "I didn't say that George. The band ARE going down well, don't get me wrong, but I think we could blow the roof off every night if the running order was changed slightly, that's all I'm saying". "I think you're wrong Phil," Jon said defensively, "We're going down great; No seriously, look, not everyone knows all the songs yet and anyway audiences are a lot cooler and self-conscious now than they were in the seventies" (which I suppose could have been interpreted as 'shut the fuck up' old man, but I chose not to).

I still held to the view that the reaction to the shows could be vastly improved, mentioning my theory to Mikey and Roy. But again the blank looks and impervious shrugs seemed to be saying; "Mind your own business mate". So I thought I'd better back off the ancient mariner role a tad. Nevertheless, I did have one last little go at Jon. "Look, it's your band, but what have you got to lose?" I asked him, "Just let me try something, for one night, and see if it makes any difference, I want to change things around a bit in the set, for instance, to put 'Do You Really Want To Hurt Me' nearer the end of the show and make a few other changes beforehand". "Go on then" Jon reluctantly conceded. Later, in the dressing room, he announced, with camp sarcasm to the rest of the band; "Phil's doing the setlist tonight girls, okay?"

Granted there could have been an element of serendipity, coincidence even, at having chosen this venue, The Theatre Royal Margate to tender my showbiz thesis. But as the gig progressed, the reaction of the audience became hysterical to an embarrassing degree. Fans were fainting in the front row and throughout the auditorium, many were being carried out by the clearly overstretched St John's Ambulance staff. Towards the end of the show, the ancient venue was literally shaking to its foundations. Fans were rushing the stage left right and centre, screaming like tearful banshees, making a grab at Roy and Mikey as they were desperately trying to get off stage; George having already departed the mayhem.

The next day's newspapers were full of some of the earliest reports of 'Culture Club Mania' and of the number of fans who had passed out or had required medical attention. In other words, it was exactly the kind of crowd delirium I'd prayed for. Above the tumultuous din of the euphoric crowd, I just managed to catch George's eye as he was going offstage; "That's what I was talking about George!" I shouted over to him.

Although everyone was visibly shaken by the electrifying reverberations still going on in and around the theatre, backstage and in the eye of the hurricane, no one referred to my set-list manoeuvrings at all. In any event, who knew if it had any bearing on what we'd just witnessed? After all, it could have just been a coincidence. But I couldn't help noticing that from here on in, the running order resolutely and emphatically stayed the same for the rest of the tour and which no one seemed to question after Margate. The brass players, Helen and myself celebrated alcoholically even more than usual that night. That kind of reception from fans could only mean one thing, "Ker... ching! Loads more gigs and "The Curly Fish!" But more on that later.

Chapter 24
Essex Boy

('Chimera': 1. a thing which is hoped for but is illusory or impossible to achieve. 2. In Greek mythology: a fire-breathing female monster with a lion's head, a goat's body, and a serpent's tail)

S pring was here again, a very hopeful year full of professional promise and whilst settling into more tours and one-off gigs, there were occasional days off and therefore a little time for social and recreational activities. As Roy always was and still is, a very keen sportsman, one fine day I invited him to, "Phil's posh club dahn Chiswick" - The Hogarth Club, no less. At the time it was one of London's very few 'Health and Racquets' clubs, first opening during the early 1980's. It was here, over many hard-fought games of tennis and in spite of our age difference and backgrounds, I got to know Roy a little better. He appreciated getting out of the tiny North End Road bedsit in Fulham that he shared with his then girlfriend and later wife, Alison Green. Unbelievably wiry, very quick and with a blistering serve, I'd like to think that Roy and I were evenly matched as I'd played loads of tennis touring around the world with Henry Marsh when in Sailor. In truth, though it was very rare I could take a set from the Billericay whippersnapper!

New to pop stardom but by all accounts briskly getting the hang of it and before tsunamis of dosh had started rolling in like an unstoppable tide, upwardly mobile Roy appreciated the affluent affectations and surroundings of the exclusive members' club. Especially, so he told me, as had only ever played at school and on concrete municipal courts before. Introducing him to Jon Lind one day, one of my dearest songwriting buddies and also a keen tennis player, bedazzled the young guitarist no end. Especially upon learning that Jon had written 'Boogie Wonderland', one of Roy's favourite tracks. Behind the cheeky, mischievous Essex banter and surreal slapstick sense of humour, Roy was an extremely likeable character who, the more I got to know, the more I could clearly see was a seriously determined, talented and ambitious young guy, well on the rise.

To some extent he was confused and frustrated by having to merge his preconceived dreams of pop stardom and all the trappings he'd reasonably assumed this entailed, with the reality of becoming famous in a band whose lead singer was a controversial gay icon, conducting a clandestine and volatile love affair with their conflicted drummer, who, in George's own words had been, "screwing and strangling their way across the map." The realisation expressed in our rest breaks between ends, (which I was glad to milk for all they were worth), had already dawned on the poor lad long ago, that the chimera of his greatest ambition might, at any time, suddenly evaporate into thin air like a Will-o'-the-wisp at the drop of a Rabbi's hat. Nevertheless, success was in the air and so close he could almost taste it.

Self-assured, streetwise and opinionated, especially when it came to music, the fact that his burgeoning pop career was utterly dependent on the fiery volatile relationship between two mercurial and bombastic cohorts, Roy nevertheless accepted his uninvited 'karma' with a blue-collar, subjugated, but essentially cheerful 'cockney' resignation. Although clear by now he'd hitched his wagon to a unstable and unpredictable star, albeit one that was definitely going places, little did he or any of us know back then, in the carefree spring sunlight on a Chiswick tennis court, just where in an unfathomable universe this wagon of dreams would take him - and in our disparate ways I suppose, all of us.

In the studio, in rehearsals or on stage, when playing the guitar, Roy exuded an air of great musical authority for one so young, bearing in mind that he was still only twenty or so at Maison Rouge when we first met. In a self-taught and idiosyncratic style, Roy is also a consummate pianist, although guitar was his main instrument in the band.

From the earliest days of Culture Club, I was impressed at how much commitment and, at times, daredevil abandon Roy threw into his playing, an aspect of his personality that, especially on guitar, invariably produced parts and arrangement ideas that were edgy, exciting and unpredictable. These are qualities of the instrument that many, including myself, consider of paramount importance in making a track come alive. In life, however, this devil-may-care approach can sometimes produce precarious results!

It must be said that out of everyone in the band, Roy in particular openly seemed to resent George's attempts to promote me, an outsider, or anyone else come to that, into the musical decision-making process of Culture Club. Even more so later when George invited me into the songwriting inner circle of the band. Having already been in a group myself, one I'd in fact put together but where I had been excluded from the writing process, I probably sympathised with him more than he knew.

To a certain extent, Jon shared Roy's protectionist intent although I figured in the drummer's case it was more to do with the business angle of having to dilute their royalties with another hand in the pot. Mine. Mikey meanwhile was always affable, tending towards generosity of spirit and equivocal about my contributions to the emerging sound of Culture Club. Then again he could have just been stoned. George was dominant, however, one day telling Roy, "Look, it's better to have 20% of a hit than 25% of something shit and Phil's input is only adding to what we've got. We need help so what is your fucking problem?" As usual with this kind of peppery conversation, everything was out there in the open for all to hear, see... and feel! Ouch! I didn't blame Roy though. The music business is rough and tough enough with so many people you have to pay. In many cases, a nest of vipers blithely ripping you off while smiling in your face. George and Jon, however, seemed to be more objective, having realised, perhaps with wisdom beyond their years and their egos, that for the important second album to succeed big time then the songs would have to surpass anything they'd done before.

Things very soon turned a corner for me however when, at a band rehearsal at Nomis, Roy chilled out, stood back a little, and allowed me some creative space to come up with the chords and arrangement ideas for a song originally called 'It's America', but which later evolved into one of the mainstays of Culture Club's show - then and now - called "It's A Miracle".

George had written the lyric on our first visit to America after we'd played at the Palladium in New York and whilst staying at the Warwick Hotel on Sixth Avenue. The band's publicist at Virgin, Ronnie Gurr, on the tour bus one day, hinted that perhaps singing about 'America' and how brilliant it all was might be taken the wrong way by their jealous UK fans. George, never really hung up on creative issues like that, didn't bat an eyelid and immediately changed the title to Ronnie's suggestion. It was a cool, eclectic and upbeat tune with sophisticated chords and while working them out, I could tell that Roy absolutely loved what I'd come up with for the song. Also now knowing how much Roy liked Earth Wind and Fire, I tried to angle the arrangement more in that vein. "I wouldn't have thought of those changes Phil, it's a real step-up mate, well done," he said, generously shaking my hand. While I still didn't have carte-blanche or anything approaching it, co-writing and arranging this track, (in fact the first song of Culture Club's to which I'd actually contributed) opened the door to later successful collaborations and co-writes with the band, and separately with George. Mikey's bass part was, as ever, masterful, funky and melodic and the tune was so much fun to play. More than that though, it sounded like a smash.

A year or so after our Hogarth Club tennis matches, when the more clichéd aspirations of Roy's pop stardom were kicking in big time and when he was clearly 'coining it in' grand style, Ann and I were invited to his and Alison's pre-housewarming, to celebrate the acquisition of their first rockstar crib.

In their case, it was the otherwise unprepossessing detached ex-home of Alan Williams, another Essex boy done good. He of the dog-torturing castrato voice of the hit record, 'Sugar Baby Love' and his white-capped, suited and booted Rubettes. The 'Rubies' were like Sailor, in that they were an ensemble of pop's previous decade, with whom I had shared the same stage many times and no doubt entertained similar pop dreams of an earlier era; platform boots, star-spangled guitars, makeup on men and doubtful hairstyles.

The baton of music stardom and symbol of status the house purchase represented, was, quite literally, being passed from one pop generation to the next; down the disillusioned snake and up the aspirational ladder. Out of date, out of style and clearly out of cash, the previous owner's man-pad was yet to be subjected to Alison's exquisitely grandiose decorative taste. In what could almost have been the backdrop to Abigail's Party the overwhelming sense of orange, brown and vomit green shag pile carpets, gruesome avocado bathroom suites and as one of Roy's aunties noted, "some lovely (tongue-in-cheek), pine woodwork", sent all sense of current 1980's style aesthetic into a tailspin. Drowning in a seventies sea of Dralon ostentation internally, bad taste also reigned outside, in the shape of an absurd grand piano-themed swimming pool in the back garden. This amused Roy no end which, in a bizarre and surreal fulfilment to an unconscious fantasy, seemed to fit the bill perfectly. For all I know, it was probably why he'd bought it in the first place!

Chatting to his amiably humble Dad over nibbles in the kitchen, the family was obviously thrilled at Roy's new-found success, but also detectable was faint parental anxiety about the changes their talented Hay junior was eagerly inviting into in his life. The latest of which was just now, spluttering and roaring like a demented Italian beast, onto the drive outside. Roy, revving the engine and beaming with Essex pride, was behind the wheel of a shiny new Ferrari and laughing like a lunatic. This really was "it" and why not? He'd made it and what better way to show his friends, his family and the world. Not bad for an ex-hairdresser and insurance clerk from Southend.

His dear old Dad shuffled off outside ahead of everyone else to admire his pop star son's latest acquisition and to inspect the fearsome machine at close quarters. The guests, meanwhile, including Ann and I, mingled and mumbled above the racket and followed on. Clearly overawed and a little shaken by such an overt symbol of unimaginable wealth, his Dad offered the sage advice that any parent who'd spent an honourable, working-class lifetime of limited means and frugality might: "You'll have to watch it there son, petrol's really pricey these days." "I don't care, Dad," Roy said, walking confidently over the threshold into his new house and his new life. And he didn't!

As we recently talked over tea at the Groucho Club, about the balmy Chiswick days of tennis almost forty years on, I told Roy how fortunate I'd considered myself to be during the 1980's, in that no one else in the band knew how to play tennis. This meant that I got to go and play in some of the finest places on the planet; on top of New York skyscrapers, on lush green courts of Beverly Hills and at luxurious resorts the world over.

Once, after a three-set game in Tokyo, Roy told me that, in order to keep a very bored Alison amused on the long afternoons while we were hammering balls all over the court, she was hammering their credit card to tiny pieces in the shopping malls. "Glad I won!" Roy said the day after we'd been invited to play at the prestigious Sydney Olympic Park Centre on Rod Laver Drive. Oz's version of Wimbledon had been opened especially just for the two of us. "That bloody game set and match yesterday cost me over five thousand quid!" he said laughing away, as our driver took us back to the hotel. With a wry smile at the Groucho recently we also reflected on the intervening years since Montreux, Switzerland, where in 1986 I had helped the band write and record their fin de siècle *Luxury To Heartache* album with fabled producer, the late, Arif Mardin.

Arif was like a Godfather to me, having worked with him on a number of occasions in the studio and who I'd, therefore, recommended to Jon and George when they were reaching out for a new producer to replace Steve Levine. A drawing Arif presented to me in Montreux is still one of my proudest possessions. "Do you think he'd consider working with us?" Jon asked me one day. "Definitely," I said. "Shall I get in touch and ask him?" Whilst on tour and in New York very early in 1983, I popped in to see my regal Turkish friend and aristocratic genius in his penthouse office apartment on Broadway. I was intending to play him the, as yet unreleased, rough mix of 'Karma Chameleon' to see what he thought of it. Due to the track's poppy and catchy chorus and Arif being one of the finest musicians I'd ever met, I suddenly came over all coy about playing such an overtly pop track to the man who had just produced the coolest and hippest record of all time; 'Ain't Nobody' for Chaka Khan (incidentally I was at this session watching in awe as the unfeasibly cool synth bass was laid down. A part I only wish I could say I had created!).

Arif listened to "Karma" intently and motionless, in his black leather swivel chair, facing the window and the Fifth Avenue skyscrapers opposite. He wasn't tapping his fingers or feet or showing any signs of appreciation of the track. Naturally, I feared that, at the very best, he was not overly impressed. But when the track finished playing and after a couple of seconds or so, he slowly turned around in his chair and said; "This song will be a very big hit record all over the world Phil. Well done and thank you for playing it to me. I like it a lot, so original, so fresh." I bounded out on to the Broadway sidewalk into the sunlight, a very happy man indeed.

Before their divorce, Ann and I had only seen Roy and Alison a few times since the glory years. Once whilst staying with our boys Jack and Gus at Frank Musker's tree house in Laurel Canyon in 1987, where sadly, a little higher up the canyon at Roy and Alison's mansion in the sky, it seemed obvious that our two, still very young, friends seemed to be tearing themselves apart. Sadly they seemed to be in the none too hidden throes of a Bonfire of the Vanities style meltdown of their Hollywood lifestyle, marriage and finances. There were tales allegedly involving gangsters, drugs and Hollywood actors, strung out on the bleeding edge that were worthy of a Hunter S. Thompson sequel. As Roy described events, however, that period looking back was the calm before the storm of what their fragile lives would learn to endure and somehow have to find a way back from.

Thankfully now he's as fully recovered and blessed as he could ever have hoped to be. His beloved band back together successfully touring the world. I was relieved that a fellow music traveller, after so many rumours of heartache, catastrophe and dissolution over the years, he had clearly worked his ass off to make it back from the dark side. Although undeniably scarred from such a challenging journey, Roy had made peace with his family and come to terms with his previous life, by bringing the best aspects along with him into the present. With his new American partner, Georgie, on his arm, planning their wedding in California and both looking on top of the world, Roy was back in business and in amazingly good form again.

Chapter 25
Rubber Meets The Road

We touched down in America on an ancient Cathay Pacific 747, resprayed in Virgin Atlantic red and held together, as far as one could see, with only gaffer tape, pretty stewardesses and Branson's toothy smile. The aeroplane, the first in his new airline venture's fleet had been purchased, as he would tell me himself in later years, entirely on the proceeds of Culture Club's newfound success.

Once on the sidewalk at JFK Airport, we got our first initiation, as Rob Reiner, director of *Spinal Tap* might have put it, into, "the sights, sounds... and smells of a hard working rock band on the road." Or thousands of them, more like! An all brown, all American tour bus, straight out of the Wild West was there waiting for us. Similar to the plane we had just disembarked from, the old crate must have knocked up as many, if not, even more, miles. Helen looked aghast at the prospect of what was, for her, a deeply undignified mode of transport. George was similarly unimpressed at the gallery of graphic photographs of naked women all over the interior. At first sight, the vehicle appeared to be a travelling temple, devoted to wild, heterosexual excess. George, looking as though he might vomit at any second, berated the band's manager, Tony Gordon, who attempted, unconvincingly, to reassure him on the many advantages of bussing. But the young singing star, embarking on his first major tour of America, was not impressed and remained sullen and glum; for a while anyway.

Tony meanwhile, anxiously clucking around like a crestfallen mother hen, had more luck with Roy and Mikey, who looked absolutely made up at visions of the implied adventures ahead. For them and similar to many young British bands arriving in the USA for their first-ever tour, having transport like this was a Rock 'n' Roll laddish dream made real. Proof, if proof were ever needed that they were now on their way to really 'making it'. "Wor, look at this Mikey," chuckled Roy, dazzled by the array of sensationally erotic posters and a cornucopia of overflowing drinks and food in the lounge area. "If this is America, BRING IT ON!" said Mikey, boggle-eyed at the amount and variety of VHS movies and endless porn on tap.

George obviously had a different kind of rock 'n' roll experience in mind, and Jon, as ever, torn between, being one of the lads and George's more sensible, caring and on-the-road partner, exhibited something between the two extremes depending on the company.

Tony had sold the idea of travelling by bus to the band on the pretext that, "It was the best way to really see America boys." Whereas in reality, the tinted windows were so dark it turned daytime into night, making it hardly possible to see outside at all. "Everything looks like Shepherds Bush from in here," George complained bitterly, as we drove down Fifth Avenue in Manhattan. It began to dawn on everyone that saving money was, as ever, the most likely rationale behind the choice of transportation and not, after all, a tourist excursion, thoughtfully provided by management. We were a big party to get from A to Z, via Kalamazoo however and on paper, until the stage of being able to jump on and off private planes, where rubber meets the road really was the only way to do America.

I quite liked my little onboard billet, and it had to be said that there was still a romantic Jack Kerouac allure to the on the road lifestyle of a touring musician. Every day a different town, free as a bird, suitcase and guitar in hand etc. Except that after only a few days of cheek by jowl proximity with one's colleagues, the experience began to pall and frankly... smell. In the end, I arrived at the conclusion that this mode of transport was only endurable when out of one's brain on drugs, mayhem and depravity but that it made no sense at all on crisps, lemonade and cheese sandwiches.

Long Island, Passaic New Jersey, Washington, Philadelphia; we soon settled into the dates, which were flashing by and apart from one or two hiccups and sound problems the shows were a roaring success. In contrast to Sailor, who I'd toured with on this side of the pond previously, America seemed to love the sound and music of Culture Club, which was more of a natural fit with US audiences.

After initial hesitation about George in conservative America; after all the record company didn't even put his picture on the record sleeve for fear of alienating the US audience, who after all, had never seen or heard anything like Boy George, were soon, like everywhere else in the world, eating out of his hand. Later on in the tour or tours, we were driving through endlessly flat and torpid Indiana, in what George called "Dralon on wheels". This was the very same vehicle that from Led Zeppelin days onward had seen more glandular action, alcoholic consumption and drug taking than the fall of Rome. These days, however, the New Romantic, gender-bending 1980's, George's stringently applied, Mary Whitehouse regime of no weed, whiskey, porno or groupies had converted our anticipated mothership of debauchery into a travelling oasis of puritanical zeal. Still a few years before his enthusiastic conversion to substance abuse and hedonism that might have put Caligula to shame, in Culture Club's early touring days, it was more like being on the road with Mary Poppins.

The sight of an exotic sign outside a depression era, white clapperboard building, half way across Indiana advertising itself as the "Indianapolis Speedway Church Of The Nazarene", conjured up startling gothic imagery of the faded American dream which perked up the travel-weary spirits somewhat. After another long day on the road, we were looking forward to our evening show at Indianapolis. Breaking the tedious journeys through the endless mid-western flatlands; a few hours of nightly relief cavorting around on stage under the bright lights in front of adoring fans was a most welcome diversion. Especially now the band had become such a well-oiled entertainment machine. 'Culture Club Mania' was now well beyond having established itself and George was loving the fact that he was now a huge international star who could do more or less what he liked. I am not sure his long-suffering tour manager Gary Lee would have agreed. Particularly when Jon and George weren't getting on. But when they were and on shining form, the two of them were a delight to be around.

Post-gig banquets back at the hotel, in particular, were amusing and lively affairs if you were invited, which I was with increasing regularity. I soon christened such nightly gatherings as 'The Bear Pit'. To thrust and parry against the barrage of the band's sparkling wit when in full flight, especially after a great gig, was an endurance test of verbal skill and resolve. You had to give as good as you got, especially with Jon and George. Lose your footing for an instant, betray weakness, or the mere whiff of insecurity and the skin would be mercilessly ripped off your back; all in good fun of course. That is unless things veered off the road and turned sour unexpectedly, which could happen occasionally. Unsurprising I suppose, what with the spikey, alpha-personalities involved. But on the whole, the evenings were often boisterous and exhilarating interludes of gossip and repartee. Bets and jousting and taking of piss were de rigueur, all extremely convivial. That is if you could hold your ground, keep your wits about you and above all, be entertaining. Besides, by now I'd been around the guys for some time on these tours and although there were lines of demarcation, I'd got to know them well.

The early, self-conscious and polite meeting before they'd secured a record deal, back when I was the big cheese of Sailor, deeming to drive in from my mansion and play on their first album, now seemed ages away. In a much shorter period, their phenomenal success had already eclipsed anything I'd previously been involved with so it was deeply gratifying to see four young musicians I'd grown extremely fond of achieving greatness and coming of age. Was I proud of them? I think I was.

Mikey always seemed to be more easygoing and elegant, counter to the other three, full-on characters, invariably adding a gentle warmth and humour to the occasion. After all, he had been the one with the easygoing charm to walk up to George in a club in London and ask if he wanted to join a band. On a good night, therefore, the chemistry of what makes something as original, special and successful as Culture Club was there for all to see. On a bad one, it was something else!

The morning after the sell-out show at Indianapolis, still high on the adrenaline of the performance, the band and travelling party were desperately late leaving the hotel in order to catch the one remaining flight that day to Los Angeles where we were to perform another sold out show. Gary was frantically rushing around the hotel lobby like a demented bat, pleading with everyone to get a move on. "We're going to miss the plane and there's no other way we can get there!" said the poor guy; red in the face and perspiring like a pig in a bacon factory. Shocking to admit I know, but ask any touring musician; a 'guilty pleasure' on long tours like this, punctuated only by an hour or so every night of frantic 'hoo-hah' under the hot lights, was the schadenfreude of seeing one's tour manager in obvious distress and poor Gary was rushing around as if he was about to have a coronary. "We've got forty-five minutes before the plane leaves guys, and... and, where's George? Oh my god, has anyone seen George?" Somewhere behind the tour manager's hysterical eyes, you could smell the fear; part of him was dying inside, poor chap.

Roy and Alison, Jon and even Mikey had made it down to the lobby and, 'the sessions', preferring the carrot to Gary's 'schtick' were shuffling around, all packed, present and correct. Grainger mumbled something in 'RAF-speak'. Jon meanwhile, exclaimed that George might still be in bed. Gary was now turning an even deeper shade of purple and almost exploded. In his befuddled brain the whole tour, and therefore his job was hanging by a thread; with a look of blind horror, he snatched at the reception desk phone, "Put me through to Geor... er, Ed Beringer please... George, is that you? Please mate, where the fuck a... what? No, George, you MUST get down here right away, NOW!" He was losing it! "We've got a convoy of police outriders to hold back the traffic on the way to the airport - What? No, I've got the Mayor of Indianapolis on the other line, George. PLEASE, the plane is leaving in thirty minutes and we should have left the hotel an hour ago. Tony will fire me over this!" After having slammed the phone down, our clearly overwrought tour manager, on the edge of a nervous breakdown, decided to shepherd everyone on to the bus to save time. As I was in his line of vision and considered as one of the more responsible members of the rabble (God knows why!) I got delegated to go up to George's room and without fail to bring him down to the lobby immediately. Extra per diems were alluded to if my mission was successful.

Sensing the urgency of the situation and imagining the passengers already boarding the plane several miles away, jumping out of the elevator, I ran down the corridor towards George's room and loudly knocked on the door. George's American assistant Bonnie came to the door and with absolutely no degree of urgency whatsoever, was languidly dabbling around getting a few of George's many things together v-e-r-y s-l-o-w-l-y. His lounge looked like the aftermath of a disco orgy in a hospital cafeteria, with exhausted food trolleys, half-eaten plates of lobster, fag ends in boiled eggs, powder puffs, teddy bears, hair-pieces and extravagant stage clothing draped over chairs, beds, everywhere!

Meanwhile still in the lounge, I could hear George from the bedroom, "I vant to be alone, tell zem to go away!" George vamped in a Dietrich persona this time, chuckling at the rebellious fun of it all. As usual, he was Queen of all he surveyed, which, today, was high up in the penthouse suite with a commanding view over the entire city. It was a beautiful day and he was sitting up in bed, still in his bathrobe, casually doing his makeup. He was also sipping tea and looking very, very pleased with himself. "Hi Phil, what's wrong with Gary?" George enquired, mischievously, and then whispering conspiratorially, "He always seems so stressed!" "I love being a star!" he went on, "I feel like Joan Collins on steroids. I can keep EVERYBODY waiting darling!" he cackled, completely disconnected from the mayhem and heart failure going on downstairs with police outriders waiting, concerned mayors collaborating, tour managers defibrillating, and airline passengers ruminating. One could imagine them wondering why the fuck they weren't being allowed to leave Indianapolis until an Irish transvestite had bothered to apply his makeup and even got out of bed. It was perverse of course, but George's banter inviting collusion in his delightful game of utter indifference, was, as usual, irresistibly funny. Suddenly I realised I'd been sent up at least five minutes earlier with strict instructions to bring him down to the hotel lobby immediately, otherwise the world as we knew it would come to an end; certainly not to laugh at his jokes and be mesmerised and beguiled as usual by his larger-than-life, fearless personality.

While Boy George was in full flow the telephone on the bedside table suddenly rang again. Momentarily placing the amusing conversation on hold all eyes stared at the cause of the intrusion for a second or two. One could feel the instrument vibrating with the concentrated stress and angst of the person at the end of the line, at the end of their tether and about to have a stroke. The world, it appeared, in this case, (represented by the shrill ring of the telephone), was urgently waiting for Boy George.

He looked across at Bonnie and I. Beaming with delight he picked up the receiver and in his most breathy Marilyn Monroe voice said; "Fuck off!" and delicately placed the receiver back in its holder.

I'll never know how Gary survived his stressful ordeal but in the end, as usual, he performed a minor miracle. This is why he had the job I guess. But without the aid of the police riders and the clout of the Mayor of Indianapolis, who'd ordered the bikers to escort us direct to the aircraft's steps, I doubt if we ever would have made the flight. But that's the kind of thing that happens when you are playing in a band with a real, bona fide authentic worldwide star.

***

A few nights earlier, or could have been later (one never knew even at the time!) and we were playing in Cleveland; a town Randy Newman made famous in 'Burn On - City of Light, City of Magic' - An ugly industrial conurbation that was probably America's closest equivalent to Birmingham in England. Supporting us on the show that night was The Eurythmics. We'd been on the road endlessly, it seemed and driving thousands of miles across mid- America in our smelly old wagon, so it was a delight to meet and spend time with, some other Brits. I'd known Annie Lennox since the seventies when she and Dave Stewart were in The Tourists and we reminisced about the days when Sailor and their band rehearsed at Alistair Crawford's studio in Hendon. Ten years on and we were in a cavernous, downtown Cleveland bar, one of those places open to the general public but also adjoining the hotel, where both bands were staying. Later, when The Eurythmics were performing their show, the monitoring was so quiet you could hear a pin drop on stage. But the sound out front? Wow! It was spectacularly loud and unbelievably good. I grabbed Jon from the dressing room and got him to come and check it out, he was similarly impressed. We watched nearly all of their show side-stage then went off to prepare for Culture Club's headline spot.

After the show, festivities resumed with Annie and Dave back at the hotel. I got a round in and as it was deafening in the packed bar, shouted across to the barman, "Stick it on my tab, would you? Marty Parducci, room 1809."

Annie was just as I remembered her from the Hendon days, a humble soft-spoken and deeply compassionate lady from Aberdeen. She and George were getting on famously. Dave Stewart at this stage of the evening was planning a controversial guest appearance at Culture Club's forthcoming Wembley show, dressed in a caterpillar suit! I found him to be a delightfully surreal character but, as I say, there was a lot of drink involved! I wasn't feeling too great, and with Dave becoming more and more bizarre as the evening and the drinking wore on, I cried off and went to bed around midnight, although the party apparently still rocked until the early hours.

Checking out of the hotel next morning, however, I came in for quite a shock. "Mr Parducci? Er, sir, your extras bill in the bar last night comes to... er, eleven thousand, seven hundred and eighty five dollars, will you be paying by cash or card?" he smiled pleasantly. I was stunned but the check out assistant's demeanour was still beaming in that, "Have a nice day" manner that Americans in the service industry affect with cold precision. I nearly fainted and came out in a cold sweat. "Can I see that?" I asked feebly, gasping for air. There were reams of tabs from the adjoining bar next door, all of them clearly indicating "Marty Parducci, room 1809" with hundreds of different signatures.

Gary Lee came over to see what the fuss was about and for once I was glad to see him. "Spot of bother Phil?" he enquired. He'd obviously seen this kind of thing many times before. "Phil?" remarked the hotel receptionist archly, "His name's Marty isn't it?" Gary and I looked at each other momentarily, but both thought better of offering an explanation. "I don't have eleven bucks, let alone eleven thousand," I pleaded to Gary, trying to look doleful. "Some of those bastards last night must have overheard me giving my room number to the bartender". Apparently, the joke of the evening and the bill was on me, or at least Marty Parducci, my profligate and pissed Sicilian cousin.

After I'd gone to bed, my name and number got passed around the bar and hundreds of people must have been in there last night; "Stick it on Marty's tab, ROOM EIGHTEEN O NINE!" laughing merrily. Driving away from Cleveland, for once I was comforted and relieved to be back in the dowdy confines of the acrid and ancient charabanc. I don't know to this day if Gary picked up the tab, but I certainly didn't!

I woke up at 10am the morning after my birthday feeling low. After another long day of travelling, on our way to Detroit, Michigan, I'd felt an ominous cold coming on. But a sinking feeling in the pit of my stomach told me this was much more than a regular sniffle, it was full-on flu and my temperature was roaring off the scale. Some of my band mates had planned a bit of a knees-up after the previous gig, but I felt so bad I had to bale and get an early night. We had another huge show the next evening so I really needed to hunker down, go to bed early and get better. Sick notes, when twenty thousand people had bought tickets to see your show are never an option in our business. As a musician, the only thing you had to rely on in this scenario was Doctor Gig.

I was also seriously missing Ann and my family and friends, which is what long tours like this do to you, especially when you are under the weather, under pressure and so far from home. Yes, it can be glamorous and exciting, enviable even, but often more in the eye of the beholder than in reality. Sometimes all you really want to do is to curl up on the sofa with those you love. Especially on birthdays or other family and social occasions - but they are all thousands of miles away. This is what the touring musician craves for and the downside of playing music for a living. Not being there and missing those important milestones in people's lives; your partner's, kids' and friends' special celebrations, is something that can never be put back in the bottle. But, hey, you can't have it all. Where would you put it?

Playing music you love every night all over the world is a privilege and is both exhilarating and rewarding, but homesickness and a weird kind of separateness is the curse and cost that every musician learns to live with. "How are you sweetheart?" Ann said when I finally managed to get through on the hotel phone by my bed. "Happy Birthday for yesterday, sorry we couldn't speak, anyway, are you having a lovely time and are they making a big fat fuss of you?" She sounded so far away, morning here, night time there and my emotions were heightened even more by feeling sick and vulnerable. Also, we hadn't been able to speak on the actual day of my birthday. So frankly, I was feeling very sorry for myself. Before mobile phones and 24/7 communication it was almost always impossible to call home from Stateside. Even if you could afford the extortionate hotel charges, the time difference was also a major problem.

Suddenly in the middle of the conversation, there was an urgent banging on the hotel door. "Hang on sweetheart, I'm going to have to call you back I'm afraid, somebody wants me". Whoever was at the door had obviously chosen to ignore the, "Shhh, I'm still sleeping idiot!" sign I'd carefully placed on the handle the night before. I looked through the tiny security glass and saw the distorted, fish-eye lens view of Gary Lee's face up close. It was not a pretty sight. Gary was my nemesis, my tour manager, persecutor, per diem dispenser and life-support machine all rolled into one. He was perspiring and again, looked very stressed. "God Gary, I feel like shit, I was trying to sleep it off, what the hell do you want mate?" I croaked, coughing and sneezing to oblivion "It's a bit early for the sound check isn't it?" "Your keyboards haven't arrived for the show tonight Phil", he said matter-of-factly, "none of your gear made the flight and there isn't another one until Monday!" "Oh Jesus! What about the gig tonight then?"

This was a keyboard player's worst nightmare. We were in Detroit about to play at the giant Cobo Hall in front of twenty thousand people; it was a Sunday so it would be difficult to hire replacement gear in time. We were in the city of Tamla Motown but Detroit was certainly not New York or L.A., where you could hire anything at any time around the clock. Besides, my Culture Club sounds were unique and which I'd painstakingly customised to suit all of the songs. This was long before the time you could simply plug in and replace everything from a tiny memory card. "Surely we'll be able to find something," I said out of desperation, my head slowly kicking into gear in spite of how I terrible I felt. "We've already tried all the companies and stores in Detroit," Gary answered. "I'm ahead of you there but absolutely nothing is open until tomorrow. I promise you... er, just a minute. What's that little keyboard you've got there Phil?" On the desk, in my bedroom, there was a tiny portable piano. My heart sank again, "Don't be daft Gary, that's Jack's, it's my son's toy keyboard" I explained. "I brought it out on tour just to write songs with. We got it from Woolworths and it only has about five sounds anyway. Look, no Gary, I couldn't possibly play that in front of..." "Wait a second Phil." Gary interrupted having suddenly perked up, "I'll talk to the guys. We may have no choice at the end of the day." (I've always hated that expression!)

I told him it all felt like a bad dream and that I was going back to bed. Whatever happened, I didn't think I'd be able to do the show later if I felt like this. I was actually starting to hallucinate. Gary said he'd get a doctor to check me out and then was going off to talk to the band. They didn't even wake me up for the soundcheck, which was considerate I guess, so I slept right through until an hour before show time when Gary reappeared. "Look, it's going to be okay Phil, we've got one of the best sound engineers in America and they've mic'd it up and put the sound through all kinds of magic devices," Gary tried to assure me. "It's going to be brilliant, trust me!" I didn't, but what else could I do? I simply had no choice in the matter.

Later, just before show time at the giant Cobo Arena, Tony came over looking terribly nervous. God knows how many millions of dollars were at stake tonight and if a few of Phil Pickett's keyboards were locked away in an airport baggage area hundreds of miles away that certainly wasn't going to spoil the party was it? Except for me! But whilst trying to smile and reassure me that "everything was going to be GREAT!" his eyes betrayed a feeling of huge doubt and concern, forming a strangely conflicted grimace. "Tony, does the band actually know about this?" I asked. But instead of answering he mumbled something inaudible as the lights were going down, and with the crowd roaring, simultaneously pushed me out onto the vast stage, noticing that the rest of the band had already gone on.

With my head throbbing and clothes already soaking wet with fever, I walked out alone into the spotlights, I think that, without a doubt, this was the worst night of my thirty seven-year old life. Twenty thousand roaring fans had paid very hard-earned money to hear Culture Club and I'd been asked to entertain them on a keyboard that had cost thirty-nine quid in Woolworths. It looked completely ridiculous, like a joke even, only smaller. The miniature plastic instrument was dwarfed by professional banks of expensive condenser microphones on their stands all pointing towards the toy's laughable speakers on the top of the unit.

Earlier the hotel doctor had informed me that I was running a temperature of 103, but referring to my earlier comments, there was no question whatsoever of pulling the gig. They didn't even have to ask me in fact and an old familiar showbiz adage no doubt comes to mind. I have never felt so exposed and naked up there on a stage; being in front of all of those thousands of people, but having no choice other than to play my son's toy piano, was even beyond my fabled and renowned, "jolly hockey sticks - let's get the job done" mentality. Like Tom Cruise's desperate last-ditch speech in Jerry Maguire, this was a full, up-at-dawn, pride-swallowing siege of professional humiliation and every second I prayed that a giant hole would appear in the earth's crust so I could disappear and never come out again.

At least, I was sure the band would appreciate the hell I was putting myself through on their behalf in order for Culture Club to have a show at all. Wouldn't they? Surely they wouldn't think for a minute that it was my fault the airline had lost my keyboards and that not one music store was open in Detroit on a Sunday? By now though, gallons of sweat were pouring off my body as the fever ran riot. At the end of the ordeal, George, by now the consummate frontman and never giving any impression or outward sign of irritation or, for that matter, there was anything remotely wrong with the performance at all, pleasantly skipped over in my direction. What's this? Was he coming to praise me for my fortitude and bravery under fire perhaps? Leaning over my tiny keyboard with his back to the audience with a rictus, professional smile said; "Your keyboards sound like shit!"

Reunited with my equipment for the next gig and the rest of the tour, the transcontinental, travelling circus of Culture Club ploughed on. City to city, arena to arena, as the band's reputation grew around the world. You may have heard, many times, how that being up on stage, playing to such vast stadium audiences night after night begins to feel impersonal and detached for the musicians. Especially when the stages were, by now, so large; one's nearest band mate could often be twenty metres away. Up on your riser, in your own little private world of keyboards entirely insulated from everyone else in the band, except for being audibly connected through a monitor speaker, in all other ways, it was easy to become disconnected.

Mistake Number Three

In the end, most of my memories of the hundreds of shows I performed with Culture Club all merge into one glorious smile of funky, soulful satisfaction and after this many years, it's only the exceptionally good, the bad and the downright ugly that stand out. There were one or two in the latter category, plus some that were hilarious. Like the night in 1984 when we were playing the first of three sold out shows in my home town of Birmingham at the cavernous NEC Indoor Stadium.

The strains of constant touring were beginning to take their toll on the quartet and certainly, as things turned out, this gig qualified in spades. For some reason, only known to George, he'd invited a gaggle of the band's most ardent female fans to come on stage and dance during the performance. Controversially as things turned out, he chose not to inform his band mates prior to the show. He simply told the girls to come on stage during a song called 'Mistake Number Three', the current single from the third album, *Waking Up With The House On Fire* and artistically interact with him and the band during the performance. What could possibly go wrong?

The girls, it had to be said, were all shapes, but mainly quite large sizes, and had been fitted into flamboyantly designed white wedding dresses, many with white veils and long chiffon trains. The eye-watering expense of these creations, all paid for from the band's account, was also, it transpired, another small detail George had omitted to mention. His own white dress, a highly elaborate, and over-the-top, 'Miss Faversham' showstopper which, according to Helen who knew the designer, had allegedly cost nigh on twenty thousand pounds. Enough, she remarked memorably at the time, "to buy a semi-detached house in Leeds!" (Henceforth this outfit would forever be known as "The house in Leeds").

Ron Williams, the lugubrious but extremely droll, ex-RAF trumpet player, was sitting disconsolately in the back of the VW van with its engine still running, in the basement of a Birmingham Hotel. He, like the rest of us, had been kept waiting for George's arrival for nearly an hour. "Are you okay Ron?" I enquired, "No I'm not Phil, thanks. Apparently, I'm being kept waiting, as I have been on every other night of this fucking tour, for a man who wears a dress to decide whether he eventually wants to join us so I can make a living!"

Most of my family and friends from Birmingham were in the audience that night, so I too shared the sense of shock and embarrassment with Jon, Roy and Mikey (outrage in Roy's case!), when the bizarre apparitions of these ungainly, intensely self-conscious, ladies traipsed on stage and aimlessly started wandering about as we played. None of them seemed to have any idea whatsoever of what they were meant to do after they'd come on stage. If George had given them any directions and cues, then the poor creatures had obviously forgotten whatever it was they were supposed to do. Over in the wings, meanwhile, the more nervous of the hapless ensemble had to be pushed out on stage by the road crew in the manner of psychotic and bewildered wind-up toys. I started to see the funny side of it now, hilarious even, but we couldn't laugh, especially as the song, not, it has to be said, one of George's most memorable, was serious, moody and dramatic.

> *And why is my love such a struggle with life*
> *You can't bystand all of the people*
> *Stand them on their own*
> *They will fall to pieces*
> *So we watch them grow,*
> *Make mistake number three*

© Culture Club. Reproduced by kind permission of EMI Music Publishing Ltd.

He could say that again! George sang on, oblivious to the fact that the brass players and by now, a growing number of the audiences' shoulders were shaking. What the actual fuck was going on here? By now sensing a theatrical disaster unfolding, George determinedly took the ringleader fan by the hand as if to intimate a pre-planned routine, but even then she went the wrong way, making an already doomed dance move collapse into farce. Roy, out in front of me, played the stage piano on this song, as he always did, but, by now, was fuming with steam coming out of his ears. At the end of the song, many of the audience thought it was a joke and were openly laughing, while the poor, exploited young women just stood there in their white taffeta creations like startled rabbits, mesmerised by the lights and applause.

My friends and close family all came to the show but, due to what sounded like the mother of all arguments going on in the band's dressing room, I thought better of taking them to meet everyone this time, so we retired to 'the sessions' green room for our celebrations that night.

Leaving Brum and on our way to London, for the first of five sell-out shows at Wembley Arena, the last of this year, I was looking forward to spending time with my family over Christmas. What another breathtaking year 1984 had been! On the coach Gary Lee tapped me on the shoulder, he was smiling, "Do they know it's Christmas Phil?" he said looking pleased with himself, "What on earth are you talking about Gary? Does who know it's Christmas?" "You know," he said, this time more emphatically; "Do They Know It's Christmas,' Bob Geldof's charity record!"

I'd been on the road for months and hadn't got a clue what he was talking about. I very rarely listened to the radio or watched telly when on tour as usually, I preferred to read. "Well you better learn it quick, you're playing it tonight; with Elton John, George Michael, Bob Geldof and Paul Young! They're joining George on stage tonight!" he said chuckling while passing me a cassette of the track. "You can do it mate, I've every faith," he said. Utterly horrified I almost threw up on the spot. I was already nervous about playing Wembley, who wouldn't be? But this was just the end. Practically the first half of the song was just keyboards and I'd be backing the biggest stars in the world playing a song I'd only just learned - and in front of twelve thousand people! Beam me up Scotty, I thought. I spent every second available with my headphones on. Right up to the sound check in fact, playing the tape over and over again. Then, after our regular sound check, I only had three minutes to have one run through before the crowds came in to make sure it was okay.

The one and only time I ever met George Michael was just as we were about to go on stage for our main set. He was very sweet and seemed to sense my apprehension. "Good luck, you'll be fine," he said, "I only heard it today for the first time though," I told him. Elton came on, followed by Geldof, who, as usual, went up to the mic, truly the man of pith and moment. Bob had organised the massive international charity effort and was, as ever, extremely convincing and clearly owned the gift of the gab. Despite my nerves, I'm proud to say it went exceptionally well and the audience reaction at the end of the show was astonishing. George Michael came over and said; "See, you had it nailed!" It was one of the best concerts of my career and I was very proud and knackered! Ann was there for the show and had come to pick me up in our brand new Merc convertible, she'd been allowed to park it backstage amongst Elton's and George Michael's limos. We were both made up!

"Happy Christmas", she said as we whisked past the security gates at Wembley on our way back to our new home at 44 Teddington Park, crossing the bridge over the Thames at Richmond and past the iconic Odeon Cinema. The three films advertised on the illuminated hoarding outside the theatre were *Electric Dreams*, *The Lost Boys* and *Top Secret* - and I had a song in each movie! (On *The Lost Boys* movie, I co-wrote the tune with one of my oldest friends, Scottish singer songwriter, B.A. Robertson, who I'd known from my earliest days at E.H. Morris. Both of us were huge fans of Ace. So for the demo, we hired their ex-vocalist Paul Carrack who in the early eighties was a little down on his luck and out of a job. Playing the song to B.A's publishers, Hit & Run Music, Mike Rutherford happened to be passing by, overheard our tune, Paul's amazing voice and popped his head round the door. "Who the hell's that"? The Genesis guitarist inquired enthusiastically. In very short order, Paul was contracted by Mike as one of the lead singers for The Mechanics, and the 'hist' as they say, is restory!)

But as far as 1984 had gone, far from Orwell's grim predictions, it had been an amazing tour, an unforgettable night and a very good year.

I was sad, though none too surprised, to find out Helen had decided to finally take her leave of the worldwide juggernaut that Culture Club had now become. We had shared so many fantastic adventures, career highs and incredibly funny moments, as the principal, creative adjutants in helping the guys achieve the distinctive sound of Culture Club. And in my case, having become part of the writing team, I suppose we were considered to have played a more fundamental role in the group than that of purely hired-gun session players and singers.

From the very earliest days, when it was just us up there with the four of them, playing small rooms and clubs through to selling out the largest stadiums in every part of the world, two characters, who could not have been more diversely opposite politically, generationally, socially and musically, got on like the house on fire we helped create. I was also very proud to have written for Helen's first and only album, a song called 'Forbidden Fruit', also with B.A. Robertson. Helen, whose resignation was accepted, extremely reluctantly by George, who, in turn, had begged her not to leave. She was eventually replaced, first by British session singer Ruby Turner, then finally by American soul diva, Jocelyn Brown. Ruby, whilst not in Helen's vocal class, was a delightful Brummie lady with an enormous voice and a bubbly personality. Off to America, again, for yet another tour, she sat next to me at the pointy end of the plane, just as we were about to take off from Heathrow. I held her hand tightly, as she was shaking like a leaf, clearly terrified. Ruby, bless her, looked as if she might pass out at any minute, so I called the stewardess for some water. "Are you okay?" I asked her as the engines roared into full throttle, "No Phil, I'm not mate!" She said nervously, in her broad Perry Barr accent, "I've never been on an aeroplane in my life!"

Whether it was fear of flying or not (we certainly did a lot of it!), sometime later, replacing Ruby was American Soul Diva, Jocelyn Brown. Jocelyn had already enjoyed considerable worldwide success in the clubs with her hit, 'Somebody Else's Guy', a song that became part of Culture Club's live repertoire during the time she spent with us. A wonderful lanky American guy named Wendell Morrison, with a rich golden brown baritone voice, also joined the band's line-up at that time. They were an outrageously hilarious duo and we kept each other in hysterics most of the time.

It was this with this line-up that we set off together again, as always from good old Hammersmith Odeon for, what would turn out to be, my last tour with the band. I guess, looking back, especially with what had been going on lately, and what I was about to find out; the writing was already on the wall.

The first stop was Israel. Jon and I walked around Jerusalem together after the first show on 22nd July 1985, on open-air gig at Hayarkon Park, Tel Aviv. It was so stiflingly hot that my keyboards were covered in silver foil during the day, to prevent the plastic keys from melting. After the show, we were informed that thirty-five thousand people had come to see the spectacle, one percent of the entire population of Israel. In spite of the reaction, George seemed distracted and not his usual self at all. For instance, it was the first time I'd seen him deliberately miss a costume change, he seemed distracted during the whole performance; "What's wrong with him Mikey?" I asked. "Have they fallen out again? He seems to have lost his sparkle and wasn't on it tonight at all". I put it down to the extreme heat but the unmistakable and for Culture Club, the unprecedented smell of cannabis was lingering in the air backstage. "George has been spending a lot of time in New York, hanging out with a really dodgy crowd," Mikey told me with a concerned and resigned look. "We think he's doing drugs a lot more than he is letting on." "Are you sure? He's always been so anti that kind of thing," I said. "He didn't bother with the costume change tonight though, and that's a first."

Jon, meanwhile, seemed totally relaxed and at home in Israel and I was surprised at the sheer amount of knowledge regarding the history, people and politics he possessed of a land he obviously understood and knew well. Therefore he was the best guide to have. In fact, whenever there was an art gallery, like the Prado in Madrid, or a cathedral, such as the Sagrada Familia in Barcelona, indeed any culturally important or interesting places or architecture to see in the many parts of the world we visited, never being able to find any other willing takers within the band, more often than not, Jon came knocking on my door. These were usually always calm and enjoyable interludes, away from the constant, ongoing, hysterical drama of Culture Club; revealing a more serious and intellectual side of Jon's complex nature. I'm pretty sure he enjoyed these arty excursions as much as I did, being, as they were, a few hours respite being a 'normal' person and a chance to break free of being a pop star in one of the biggest bands in the world.

We went to the Wailing Wall, walked the Via Dolorosa and suddenly came across the Garden of Gethsemane, the holy place where Jesus spent the last night talking to his disciples prior to being crucified. Sitting under an ancient olive tree, as if in a dream, Tina Turner's iconic hit, 'What's Love Got To Do With It', written and produced by one of my oldest friends, Terry Britten, came blasting out of a passing beat box. The bizarre irony of such a contrasting juxtaposition of time and place was not lost on me. Especially as I'd played keyboards on the original demo (which, not many people know was a tune first recorded by Bucks Fizz).

A few days later after Jerusalem, we flew into the boiling cauldron that was Athens on a specially chartered 707. We were topping the bill with other UK bands, The Cure, The Stranglers and Depeche Mode. It wasn't just the intense heat, but also burning revolution in the air in Greece's smouldering capital city and the atmosphere was febrile. All over the city, there were riots going on and cars being torched. The Greeks were clearly not happy bunnies. Arriving later at the Panathinaiko Stadium, there was chaos everywhere as thousands of hot, angry and obviously penniless Greeks were storming the entrances trying to get in for free. Blood on the streets, and even inside the event was flowing, as activists were immensely cheesed off about paying 50p to see all of these acts. That's anarchy for you!

On making a beeline for one of the Artistes caravans that had been parked in a circle like Wild West covered wagons. I was trying to get out of the way of stones and debris raining down into the VIP area from the hostile hoards outside. Just about to step in one of them for safety, Micky Boddy, one of our knights of the road offered some sage but terrifying advice. "Whatever you do Phil, don't go near the caravans if I were you, last year they were the first things to get rolled over when the bastards stormed the security fence."

Tony was deep in discussions with the organisers, who were desperately trying to reassure him that it would be safe for us to go on. "I don't think we should do it guys, it's far too dangerous," he came over to tell us, although we were all side stage and ready to play. Although George was obviously concerned, after all, he was the one upfront, and could see the whites of their eyes; he still thought we should go on. After the terrible reviews in Israel, if we were to baulk at such a massive show in Greece, the press back home would murder us. "The audience might too!" Mikey said. So reluctantly we went on stage, in a continuing hail of bottles, stones and drinks cans, some of them even full. There had been no time for a soundcheck, so when I climbed up on my keyboard riser, which, at three metres, was the highest on which I'd ever performed, I felt doubly exposed, as there was nothing to hide behind. True to form but on this occasion hot, bothered and extremely vulnerable, George verbally let rip on the audience, leading from the front as usual, and confronted the enemy on equal terms. "I thought you Greeks invented homosexuality," he berated the 60,000 strong crowd who were jeering. We were in full view of the majestic crumbling Parthenon, on a distant hilltop overlooking Athens. "So why are you throwing stones? Fucking wankers!" He was very angry. Many of the crowd were genuine fans, however, and loving the show but confused at George's language against a nasty and persistent minority who were out to cause mayhem.

Half way through 'Victims' (appropriately enough in retrospect), very soon after Jon's, Ringo Starr-like dramatic drum fill entry, a stone caught me full on the forehead making me topple back off my towering riser and landing a good ten feet down on my back and out cold. The show came to an abrupt halt, mid-song; as everyone came over see if I was okay, including Tony who looked like he was about to expire. "That's it Tony, enough, let's go!" I heard George shouting while I was coming round. Luckily it must have been only a few seconds and I was back on my feet again. Although still dizzy and concussed, I was hugely relieved that the gig had been cancelled and that the terrifying ordeal was now over.

Later that night, on the eve of flying to Japan, one of the most bizarre and surreal events of my entire touring career took place. Not for the first time, George, feeling sorry for me and for what had happened, called my room to invite me for a little soiree in Roy and Alison's room to chill out a little after the utter madness of the day. After the party, around 2 am and realising we had an early flight to Tokyo first thing, I left with George to walk back to our rooms down a very long corridor. By now, seriously refreshed on champagne and whatever else was going on, plus tired and emotional from a day I'll never forget, I suddenly thought I was seeing things and stopped in my tracks. "What's the matter with you?" George asked, understandably; my face had gone as white as a sheet as I looked at the figure still fifty metres down the corridor heading towards us. "That's my Mum", I said, "What the hell's she doing here?" I thought the whole thing was a dream again. Unbeknown to me, or anyone come to that, Eileen had been on her way to a Greek island to "Bloody well get away from it all darling" and had flown out from London on the same plane as Depeche Mode. Bold as brass and true to form (probably why she always got on so well with George!) she waltzed over to Dave Gahan in the baggage area and heard that we were playing at the same concert with Depeche Mode in Athens, "They offered me a ride in their tour bus darling, and here I am!"

What a night it turned out to be. We stayed up all night chatting, drinking, her fussing over the lump on her son's battered head. Tearfully we said our goodbyes in the morning when I left her there at 7 am to fly to Tokyo. (B.A. Robertson, to whom I referred earlier, was not quite as sympathetic to my plight as I might have hoped. Having read about the episode, which was all over the press back home, he forwarded an urgent telegram to my hotel in Athens which read; "Congratulations are in order Phil Pickett; must have been the closest encounter with heavy rock in your career to date! Get well soon, love B.A").

Chapter 26
Karma Nirvana

"What we need on this track is one of your classic Sailor synth bass lines, Phil," said Steve Levine, giving me some guidance on my arrival at Red Bus, just off the Edgware Road in London. The recording studios booked to complete Culture Club's second album, *Colour By Numbers* soon became the band's impromptu London base of operations. Running the gauntlet of the growing gaggle of George clones outside Red Bus every day was now a regular occurrence and whether straights, outrageously-dressed space monkeys, or punky, pierced Goth-like drones, despite their often blood-curdling appearance, these softly-spoken beings were always strangely respectful, sweet and extremely polite. "Is George coming in today Phil? What time will he here be here? Can you give him this?" 'This' was often a letter, a card, some flowers, a teddy bear with dreadlocks, ribbons and a rabbi's hat. The country was immersed in the critical and uncertain period during the Falklands War when a successful outcome was still far from assured. On the front page of the *Sun* newspaper, Margaret Thatcher was pictured wearing khaki clothing and a Grace Kelly-styled headscarf at the controls of a tank. I was struck by the power of the shot and, more generally, the clout that a visual image often conveys over that of mere words.

Steve had asked me especially, to arrive at the studio early and help prepare an instrumental bed for one of the songs he intended to cut that day; 'Church Of The Poison Mind'. Although I'd always previously used ARP 2600 synth for Sailor bass parts, Steve had rigged up a brilliant sounding Moog keyboard bass on this occasion. His brief was to go for a Motown feel, so I programmed an 8-bar classic, four-on-the-floor, bass drum loop on Steve's Linn Drum machine. A snare drum pattern, recalling the Four Tops' 'Reach Out I'll Be There' was then added to make up the rhythm template on which to overdub the bass and other parts.

The tempo we arrived at felt great, just a little up on Roy Orbison's 'Pretty Woman'. With an American soulful and bluesy feel, this kind of music was right up my street, having grown up on Tamla Motown. Thanks to the very early Beatles recordings and the moptops enthusiasm for Tamla, the sound of Detroit was always the coolest and hippest thing on the block. I'd been starved of playing the kind of music I loved in Sailor, so I relished playing in this style and all of the parts came naturally. Steve was very enthusiastic all the while egging me on: "Great, now how about adding some Hammond?

I've already rigged it all up through the Leslie". The classic trademark sound of the Hammond coming from the rapidly spinning horns inside the Leslie's polished wooden cabinet, the size of a small wardrobe, was already sounding spine-tinglingly good and a 200% improvement on any ersatz synth copy. He then asked if I could come up with an intro so I laid down the now familiar Moog bass and Hammond organ 8-bar motif, prior to the harmonica intro, which would be added on a few days later by Judd Lander. George had asked me if I knew any good players and without hesitation suggested Judd; a charming, wacky and extremely talented Liverpudlian promo guy, who'd worked for Sailor at CBS Records.

With pop music, when things are that easy and simple in the studio it usually means they're good. Right now I was in, the zone, being given free rein by my producer to play around with the track, just as we had with many other projects Steve and I had successfully collaborated on prior to Culture Club. He seemed pleased with the results we were getting; he always knew exactly what he wanted. "It's perfect Phil, we'll replace the Linn with real drums as soon as Jon gets in, but the song also needs a middle-eight section. Can you come up with something?" Being on a roll, it only took as long as it takes to play eight bars of a descending gospel-like chord sequence and a suggested top line melody over the entire section (which, incidentally, ended up being played on brass). "Don't forget that tune Phil, it sounds great", Steve said. So I sang the idea into my ever-present cassette recorder. A week or so later, Helen and I recorded the multi-tracked, heavenly choir, effect of layered harmony vocals, with the Hammond wailing away in the background. "Fantastic, but the chorus needs a riff or instrumental line, what have you got?" Suddenly, realising we'd almost finished the entire arrangement of the track I asked him what he thought the band would say when they arrived. "Don't worry," Steve said, "They're going to love it, it sounds great."

The many artists and bands I'd worked on with Steve prior to these boys, I now realised was merely an apprenticeship. Indeed, young Mr Levine was himself apprentice second engineer at CBS Studios at Whitfield Street when I was recording the Sailor albums. Now I realised that all of that experience was coming to fruition on Culture Club. By now we had built up a quick-fire working relationship and effectively knew how to communicate arrangement and musical ideas to and from one another.

At this point, George suddenly burst into the control room along with Jon, both of whom were enthusiastically energised by the simplicity and directness of the track that had been laid down in their absence. George was scribbling lyrics into his notebook furiously, deep in thought, while simultaneously dancing to the backing track. Jon meanwhile was itching to get to his drums to replace the Linn drum Steve and I had earlier recorded as a template. With the sudden arrival of Roy and Mikey on the scene, the blistering "Church" that we all now know and love came together in an instant. It sounded like another huge hit record in the making.

Having by this stage, written and recorded songs for years, whilst not wishing to create unnecessary waves, I realised that the contribution I had made to this particular song already crossed well over the line of what would be normally considered merely session playing. Therefore I raised the issue quietly with Steve; "I don't know really," he said, "But if the right moment comes up, why don't you talk to George about it?"

Meanwhile, at sound checks on the frequent tours and shows we were now performing all over the place, George loved trying out Motown songs like 'Private Number', a particular favourite of Jon's and other retro material from the sixties, like Beatles songs, 'You've Lost That Lovin' Feeling', Smokey Robinson's 'Tears Of A Clown' and Marvin Gaye's 'Heard It Through The Grapevine' ("Was Marvin gay?" - a favourite George quip).

Through these sound check experiences, I developed a feel for the keys George liked to sing in, the type of chord progressions and playing style he seemed to like. Mainly they were very simple progressions and in keys which suited his richly unique vocal styling. As the Boy obviously loved sixties & seventies soul, disco and R&B; being older than the band and having grown up in the era these songs came from, most of them were still imprinted in my brain. It meant that, unlike my younger contemporaries in the band, I inevitably knew the chords to the old school tunes he liked, which over time developed into a subtle musical connection, possibly a bridge between very different musical eras. George and I, although we didn't realise it yet, were planting the seeds of an effective writing partnership.

Culture Club's music was now frequently being dubbed, "Blue Eyed Soul", in the media, as George's voice particularly lent itself to those simple, bluesy and gospel styles that the band were leaning towards after the first album. As mentioned, from the first day I'd heard his unique voice at Maison Rouge, George was the epitome of many of the great pop singers, black or white rolled into one. A good example of this was 'Time (Clock Of The Heart)', a new song the band had just written, which we quickly recorded at Red Bus, shortly before driving up the M6 for a show at Keele University. We added the song in our set for the first time and it went down a storm, already sounding like the huge hit record it would soon become. The track also featured the spectacular harmonic dexterity and layered vocals of Helen Terry, joined by yours truly on backing vocals. Having already laid down the main piano arrangement on Red Bus's sumptuous Steinway Grand, at Steve's request, I doubled the piano part with a Fender Rhodes preset on Steve's Yamaha DX7, all the rage back then. Similar to "Church" Steve also asked me to play the Moog bass part in real time.

This fill-in track between albums was thus released as a single in the massively successful aftermath of 'Do You Really Want To Hurt Me'. Three singles had already been released from *Kissing To Be Clever* and with their new album still some time off, nothing else from the first album seemed appropriate. 'Time', however, proved to be a blinder, reaching number 3 in the UK singles chart and selling over 500,000 copies. It reached number 2 in the USA Billboard chart; one up from where its predecessor, 'Do You Really Want To Hurt Me', had peaked. Two top five singles already in the States! Things were looking very rosy indeed. *Allmusic* journalist Stewart Mason later wrote: *"Of all of Culture Club's early hits, 'Time (Clock of the Heart', has probably aged the best. Boy George drops the cryptic self-mythology long enough to deliver a tender, heartfelt lyric on lost love."*

The fact that tracks were now being released almost as soon as we had recorded them at Red Bus and then immediately storming up the charts, was another milestone for me and a tremendously exciting aspect of playing - and of course, now writing for Culture Club. I was on top of the world.

After Keele and many more live shows, we resumed at Red Bus to work on more tracks for Colour By Numbers. Shortly before doing some more work on "Church" at Red Bus, and after my initial chat with Steve, I picked my moment to take George to one side for a quiet word; "You do know that the input I had in helping you to create "Church" constituted a lot more than just playing keyboards don't you George?" I said. The topic was chosen carefully, if a little tentatively, as although confident I was justified in asking the question. George was not a person one took on verbally without being on sure ground. "I mean, I practically came up with the entire chord sequence, riff and middle-eight melody and by rights, I think I deserve a piece of that song."

He looked surprised, taken aback even; "Look, Phil, it's tricky okay," he said none too comfortably. "I'm aware that what you did was great and a real contribution, but the band have a very strict policy on who is involved in the writing. It's about politics. You know how it is in bands!" I certainly did. At least I felt he appreciated what I was saying and that I had a point, in spite of how outwardly outrageous and formidable George could be, in many ways, he was quite noble and moral when it came to issues like this. I got the feeling that if it had been down to him, he wouldn't have minded sharing some of the action. After talking it over some more, he came up with a solution he hoped would keep his band, and me happy. "Look, I'll write the next one that comes along with you okay? We will write one together I promise and I'll let Roy, Jon and Mikey know. But not "Church" Phil, we have to leave that as it is for now, is that okay with you?" "Alright George", I said and although a little disappointed, I took his point and was content with a promise of future writing. "I know how it is, believe me, George, I love working with you guys and anyway I don't want to be seen to rock the boat."

Very soon after I found out that George was true to his word. At a rehearsal at Nomis in Shepherds Bush, it was obvious he'd already bent everybody's ear and prepared the ground for me to contribute some ideas. We were working on a track called 'It's America', the lyrics of which he'd written after the band's first New York appearance at The Palladium. Although the show was an anti-climax, with George appearing to be uncomfortable with the crowd, it was still his first visit to America and he was clearly exhilarated by the experience. Already dealt with at length in another chapter, the song famously evolved into 'It's A Miracle', which in short order, eventually became a US and UK top 5 hit, a worldwide radio smash. 'Miracle' was, in fact, the first song I was credited as having co-written with Culture Club.

A day soon followed again at Nomis: a bright, serendipitous day that for many reasons I shall never forget. It was the day that George presented the initial seed idea for 'Karma Chameleon' to the rest of the band and to me during some rehearsals. His innocent enthusiasm at presenting an idea he obviously loved was at once crushed from a great height with much scorn and open derision all round, but particularly from Roy. I couldn't believe it, I was witnessing the very rare sight of a crestfallen George (even though he tried to hide it) and for once I actually felt quite sorry for him. It was like seeing a beautiful delicate butterfly being torn apart by a pit bull. After all, as the lead vocalist of Culture Club, he was only trying to sell an idea he loved to his own band. "It's a fucking nursery rhyme George, come on man, we can't do that!" Roy said laughing mirthlessly. "What's karma supposed to mean anyway?"

He was adamant that the song wouldn't be suitable for Culture Club; the main reason being, I ascertained, was that the melody and lyric of the snippet George had managed to present sounded far too lightweight. Jon was less cruel and at least tried to articulate a more measured response, no doubt taking on board his lover's feelings. I imagined that having shared each other's more intimate hopes and dreams within their fiery but also often tender relationship, he may have appreciated what a delicate procedure it can sometimes be when an individual presents the fragile seed of a basic idea to his musical accomplices for the first time. Then again part of the charm of Culture Club was that they were an outspoken bunch of individuals, often brutally so and I suppose George may just have been getting a taste of his own medicine. "It is a bit poppy George, why don't we work on the other ideas instead?" Jon said reasonably. In fairness, the way Roy was interpreting George's idea on guitar, although clearly taking the piss and hoping it would all go away, was by playing simple major chords, C, G, C, G, C, as one might in say, 'The Wheels On The Bus Go Round And Round'. But Roy's approach only made the song even more childish, innocent and predictable.

If George was upset he wasn't letting it show which, having got to know them well by this stage, surprised me. Normally he would have demolished all opposition, verbal and otherwise. No stone or sensibility left unturned with a devastating quip or withering look. But band politics are band politics the world over, and in these early years at least, Culture Club was still a fragile, if not occasionally vexatious, democracy, of sorts!

Not knowing what would happen next but not letting on either, it dawned on me that by changing the chords and descending from the major key into a minor, more in the style of classic gospel and blues transition, say like Ray Charles in 'Georgia On My Mind', the song could still have huge possibilities. Privately, I was stunned at what I thought could easily be turned into a hit song being turned down, lock stock and barrel, and even more so, that his band mates didn't have the wit or wisdom to see it at all. Knowing by now the various sensitivities involved, under the circumstances, I thought it best to keep my opinion to myself and keep my powder dry. It was a very good idea in retrospect, as on a break, clearly not having given up on the tune, despite the band's negative reaction, George again took me to one side. "What do you think of it, Phil? Will you write it with me?" Impishly George then added in his camp voice, "Fuck Roy, if he doesn't like the song, we'll keep his royalties!" I almost bit his arm off. Not about the royalties necessarily, but certainly the song. I could instantly hear how it could all be put together. "I'd love to write it with you George," I said, not really believing my luck. I was so confident we could expand and develop his initial idea into something truly great. "Do you think the title will make any sense to anyone though. Should we change it?" He asked me, obviously having had the wind out knocked out of his normally billowing and confident, sails by the others. "No, not at all", I said, "That's what I really love about it. Who would ever have thought of calling a song 'Karma Chameleon'?"

It was pure genius from someone at the top of his game. I couldn't understand why the band seemed to loathe it so much but I relished the opportunity I'd been presented with on a big golden plate. Having only really turned up for a rehearsal, I was now apparently writing a hit song, one-on-one, with Boy George! How good was that? I don't know where it came from but I had a very strong sense that the experiences I'd gained over many years of trials and tribulations in music were about to come to fruition in a moment I intended to grab with both hands, and that everything I'd done, or been involved with up to this point, had somehow prepared me.

A title can often be a vital component in the success of a song, and which, for many writers, is beyond doubt the most important ingredient. But 'Karma Chameleon', even though George hadn't a clue what it meant, for some reason had an uncommonly strong resonance for me. It was like something out of a dream; not necessarily understood, but overlaid with an unconscious hidden meaning. There was also a strong connection to the spiritual leanings I'd had towards TM and the Maharishi, where the term and reality of Karma was referred to constantly. I explained the concept a little to George who, in any event, had always seemed inquisitive about my going off to meditate backstage or in hotels; why I did it and what the benefits were. George's own spiritual journey; exploring the rich timeless philosophies of the Hare Krishna movement and Buddhism was still some way off in the future. Maybe this had something to do with it? I'll never know. But as far as I was concerned, I'd had so many jobs, so many different adventures and occupations, lived all over the world, pillar-to-post most of my life, and this song, out of all the others I'd either written myself or helped create, seemed to fit me like a glove for some reason.

From losing my father when very young I'd always been subject to frequent, dramatic and sudden changes of fortune, fame, pomp and circumstance. Finding myself in Culture Club and now becoming part of their DNA by writing such a game-changing song with George was just another example. How on earth did this actually happen? How come a twenty-two year old androgynous, New Romantic, gay pop icon and me, a 36-year-old ex-Sailor ended up in the same tiny, cramped room in Shepherds Bush, writing a song called 'Karma Chameleon'? Life is like a dream sometimes. Perhaps this is one! I digress.

We managed to find a small rehearsal room just down the corridor from the main studio which thankfully was unoccupied. There was even an old upright piano in the corner so this was surely meant to be. I always took a small cassette player everywhere in those days for snippets of song ideas and in order to recall arrangements during rehearsals. I learned over time that when writing with George it became absolutely vital never to miss the first thing he sang; by hopefully capturing it all on tape as often he would never repeat anything in quite the same way twice.

My previous experiences in music also made me recognise that George back then, was in the zone of that rarified and extraordinary creative phase that many important artists, such as the Beatles or Dylan were going through when they seemed somehow inexplicably tuned-in to the ears of the world. This was the time they were clearly inhabited by a creative spirit, where practically everything they came out with mattered. Somehow you knew the altered state might not last forever so it was vital to catch the ideas like a butterfly in a net. Another reason the recorder came in handy was George's boredom factor! He tended to get restless very quickly; especially with the amount of time it took to get everything sounding right. Losing patience, he would abruptly depart the proceedings, leaving you alone with the various ideas he had scattered into the ether like confetti on the wind. Sleuth-like, one could then rearrange and reassemble them into songs at one's leisure; presenting them back to him later as completed arranged works. "Did I write that bit?" "Yes, you did George" "Oh, okay!"

When I showed George the descending chords I had in mind for the chorus, he loved the sound of it, as by going to the minor chords on the second and third positions somehow made the simple melody sound more profound, even with a tinge of soulful melancholy. The simpler and naive nursery rhyme equivalent major chords of C-G-C major then seemed to work well on the verses in contrast;

> *Desert loving in your eyes, all the way*
> *If I listen to your lies would you say?*

Again the opening 8-bar verse lyric was clearly written about Jon, but then I played some different chords and suggested a melody line for a bridge or step, the section where George sings;

> *I'm a man without conviction,*
> *I'm a man who doesn't know*
> *How to sell a contradiction,*
> *You come and go, you come and go...*
> © Culture Club, Phil Pickett. Reproduced with kind permission of
> EMI Music Publishers and Imagem Music Publishers.

As in "Church", everything seemed to happen instantaneously and naturally with the song almost writing itself on the pure energised fuel of enthusiasm and the simplest possible chord motifs. These are moments every songwriter lives for when all the contrasting moments of one's life and experience effortlessly merge in a pure blast of unselfconscious creativity. I realised I'd probably spent a good part of the first twenty years of my musical life mainly in toil, struggle and rejection, in preparation for this magical twenty minutes, when a song of this quality and instant appeal was coming to fruition before our eyes and ears. Out of the blue, we had a verse, a bridge and a fantastic chorus, but somehow an extra idiot proof ingredient was still missing. By this time, however, only about fifteen minutes into the writing session, we were belting the song out around the piano as if it was already a massive hit. But then a second bridge, or what I suppose was more of a classic middle-eight, appeared out of thin air when I tried the descending chords from the second position, not the dominant key, as in the chorus. It could have been a mistake, it probably was, but as happy accidents sometimes prove, in the realms of the unconscious, anything, yes absolutely anything is possible. In our case, it opened another magic door. George leapt on the melodic idea I'd suggested from this new chord progression, refining and improving the tune to suit his range. As if by magic, as I recall, he came up with the following genius line immediately;

> *Every day is like survival, you're my lover, not my rival*

Like some crazed idiot on speed, I echoed his hooky line on "survival" (the bit that Helen eventually performed on the recording and made her own) which refused to go away and we instantly felt as if it 'belonged' to the song. It was so good we tried it again - the same melody line and chords. But on the next four bars, I suggested George write a different rhyming couplet. But in classic Tin Pan Alley style, as only a hit songwriter gets a feel for, Boy George wasn't having any of it! "No, let's just repeat the same line again Phil, it's another hook! He was right; it was another massive earworm, a better bridge than the first, and the icing on an already over laden and delicious cake! George, already a seasoned pro in the art of songwriting, had simply nailed it; just repeat the same line again, bloody obvious!

That was it. Twenty or so minutes from start to finish and I knew beyond doubt in my heart that even in the most basic round the piano, down the pub scenario, the tune was a biggie. Fired up and preparing to represent the completed song, we went back into the main band room to the others. George was full of it this time, with an attitude that screamed; "So there munchkins!" as we had now transformed a very sketchy and minimal basic idea into a real song with all of the arrangement, lyrics, chords and internal architecture working a treat; we thought so anyway.

There was still a certain amount of resistance in the room, but George was now more bullish, on firmer ground and knew that in spite of what anyone felt or said, he knew we had written a hit song. At first, I was a little sensitive to the brand new situation of having written with George on my own, so was reticent about appearing too triumphant. But on the inside I was glowing, knowing that the song could easily wipe its face and tie its own bootstraps in any company.

Roy was climbing down just a little but still damning our creation with faint praise, "Yeh, it sounds better I suppose, but it'll never be a single." Jon positively, and in my view at the time, quite brilliantly kicked everything into touch by suggesting a rockabilly setting for the rhythm, which immediately made the tune sound even more unique and catchy at the same time. The bubblegum factor was still worrying Mikey and Roy. But all credit to them (although George was already recommending taking all credit off them in mine and his favour!) as everyone began to respond more positively to the idea, even though Roy was still smarting over some of the lyrics.

"We need a good rockabilly intro" Jon suggested, so I presented an idea stolen from one of my own songs, a rockabilly track I'd written for the movie, Top Secret sung by Val Kilmer. At the time I was convinced the song had ended up on the cutting room floor, so didn't think it would matter too much.

"That's great Phil" Jon said and the band immediately leapt on the idea. Roy in particular, as it featured a twangy, Duane Eddy, guitar riff, repeated twice before the main intro stormed in, which would eventually feature harmonica, again played by Judd Lander. After a while the intro seemed inseparable from "Karma" and was so distinctive and catchy, it was a perfect fit.

As I'd confronted George over a possible share of the 'Church Of The Poison Mind' copyright, Jon and George now took me to one side to have a little chat, over the royalty distribution for "Karma". "As George explained Phil", Jon said 'we share everything equally on the songwriting', so even though you may have technically written "Karma" with George, we still need to split the royalties with everyone in the band, okay?" He explained further; "Therefore that's five ways, so 20% each". They both looked at me questioningly, I suppose hoping I wouldn't complain. The way I looked at it was that I was now much more closely associated than Helen or any of the other fringe members of the band and was loving my role as the keyboard player and backing vocalist in Culture Club. I was helping to fundamentally shape their musical arrangements and was already receiving a very healthy salary for my live work, sessions and TV shows. The cachet of working with one of the most exciting and successful bands on the planet was also priceless. Besides, I had now been invited into the inner circle of trust of a group that had already achieved massive success all over the world and which was still on a huge upward surge. There is a surfing term that came to mind; catching a wave and I was definitely all over it. "I'm more than happy with that guys, seriously, it's fine with me" I said it and meant it, we shook hands on the agreement. Jon, being the business head of the group, looked very pleased and also slightly relieved, "Thanks, Phil, it really is a great song, well done."

My experiences in the music business had proved that collaboration with teams is the key factor in the longevity of true success and that in an already difficult business, it was far more important that harmony prevail as much as possible. After all, it was the entire unit that prospered and worked their asses off for every dime the band earned. I now knew that I would be earning exactly the same as George from a song that I'd helped him create. Despite that, I was not obliged to arrive in Japan five days earlier than the rest of the band, fully made-up after a twelve-hour flight, and then take part in days and days of endless interviews and photo calls - even before the first note of music was played! Life was very good.

***

On the *Top Secret* movie mentioned earlier directed by the Zucker brothers, the musical director was Bruce Welch from the Shadows, these days my mate in the SODS. Val Kilmer was playing the lead role. "I know he's a big star an' all, but can he sing?" I asked Bruce at Pinewood Studios. "No, of course not. And your point is?" In other words, when has that ever been a problem in our business? The producers were after something with an early-Elvis feel so I wrote the tune and lyrics for 'How Silly Can You Get'. It was inspired by arriving home at dawn in Ham one day after an all-night gig with Sailor at Oxford University, but "me darling woman" had forgotten to leave the key out for me!

Paramount Pictures had demanded all of the publishing on the song but hadn't yet committed to use it in the movie. Warner Bros, my publishers were acting as go- betweens. Rob Dickens at Warners called me; "We asked for five thousand dollars on your behalf Phil but Paramount is playing hardball and saying they're only going to pay you two," he said. "Anyway, they also told me they haven't made their minds up on the song yet, you know the usual stuff, 'they can get Phil Collins blah blah', anyway, can you come up and meet with their legal people next week and we'll try and get something sorted out?" "Sure thing," I said, "I'm in no position to bargain with them, so I guess I'll just have to take what they're offering."

The following week on the train going up to London for the meeting, I happened to bump into Paul Boross, a budding comedian, one-time tennis partner, and bit-part actor, who I'd met through Henry Marsh, Paul's ex-guitar teacher at Holmbush Road. "Wow Phil, how are you? Haven't seen you in a while mate..." The usual conversation; then I asked him what he'd been up to lately, "Oh, you know, this and that, film extra work mainly. In fact, I've just been working on a movie by the same directors that did the *Airplane!* movie. It's called *Top Secret* with Omar Sharif and Val Kilmer. "Get away!" I said, almost falling over in astonishment. "I wrote a song for that film, in fact, I'm just going up to meet the Paramount lawyers to talk about it. But I'm not even sure at this stage if it's even in the movie." "What's the song called Phil?" Paul asked. When I told him his face lit up, "Bloody hell mate, it's the biggest scene in the picture! We spent three days over at the Odeon Cinema in Staines shooting that one scene. In fact, I heard they spent half the film's total budget on it." "'How Silly Can You Get!' right?" "That's the one, well-done mate, brilliant!"

I walked up Berners Street to the Paramount meeting at Warners with renewed vigour and a definite spring in my step but didn't let on at all what I'd just been told; knowledge truly being power in any business. Thanks to Paul, for once I had one up. In fact, in this case, several up in this cutthroat, snake-pit industry of ours. "Well Phil," the lawyer drawled, "the directors are not even sure they're gonna use your song yet but are prepared to make an initial offer of two thousand dollars." "That's nice of them," I remarked, "but no thanks, I'm afraid it's nowhere near enough" and got up as if to leave the room. "Wait a second Phil, they might not even use your song in the movie at all." "Fine, you have my number," I said. "By the way, I want twenty-five thousand!"

Rob still didn't know what was going on but called me as soon as I got back home. "What in God's name did you say to them Phil?" he said clearly perplexed. "Paramount just sent a payment of twenty-five thousand dollars!"

***

In and around the work for Culture Club in '82 and '83, George and I also began to hit it off working together very effectively on a number of writing projects separate from the band. One of the songs we were invited to co-write by Virgin Music Publishers, was for a forthcoming Virgin movie called *Electric Dreams*. The story was of an artificially intelligent PC and its human owner finding each other in a romantic rivalry over an extremely pretty girl.

The subsequent movie went on to be a huge success as it was based on the then brand new phenomena of home PCs. Looking back, corny as hell like most zeitgeist movies, but another great opportunity. George and Roy had already composed two songs for the film, but the former seemed to bitterly resent the fact that he still had to split the song four ways and include Mikey and Jon too, even though they'd had nothing to do with it.

Not knowing at the time that Phil Oakey of Human League had composed 'Together In Electric Dreams' for the movie, I asked George what he thought about calling our song 'Electric Dreams'. "Yes, okay, good idea and we'll split this one two ways only, 50/50." He seemed to delight in telling me and I wasn't arguing. George said they'd got someone called P.P. Arnold to put the lead vocal on. "Have you heard of her?" he asked me. "Heard of her?" I exclaimed, "I did loads of session work with Pat (also with Sue and Sunny and Madeleine Bell), in the early seventies." I was thrilled. P. P was a lovely person and an unbelievable singer. Plus, as I'd worked with her so many times, I knew the exact key to write the song in. It couldn't have been better.

One of the hippest guys on the block at that time was producer Don Was, who'd flown in especially from L.A. to cut the track together with a star-studded array of musicians, including the amazing rock guitarist Pete Frampton. He played like the true guitar legend he undoubtedly was and couldn't have been a nicer or more humble guy to work with. George and I were blown away by how good it was sounding and eventually ended up with the producers using our track, 'Electric Dreams' as the closing credits song.

For the official studio playback, Ann came to join me up in town and we sat around chatting with the band in the upstairs studio at Trevor Horn's Sarm West Studio. Pat Arnold and everyone else had gone and I can't remember why, but we hung around awhile afterwards, during which time a call came through to the control room for George. Whoever it was, George slammed the phone down but not before telling whoever had made the call to "fuck off wanker".

The caller was one of the members of a new band that Trevor Horn was producing called Frankie Goes To Hollywood, who were recording downstairs. Judging by the extremely aggressive tone and homophobic content of the call, they obviously considered themselves rivals or at least pretenders to the Culture Club throne. "He called me a 'dirty bent cunt' Jon, I can't believe it!" George said. I couldn't tell if he was angry or vaguely amused. "I thought they were gay anyway!" he quipped sourly.

Jon assured George emphatically that FGTH were just a bunch of ignorant idiots with very little talent. The mood in the control room, previously euphoric, from listening to 'Electric Dreams' played mega-loud on Trevor Horn's incredible speaker system, immediately turned tense. They kept calling back and George was getting more distressed at the homophobic and insulting abuse aimed at him personally. "I'm not having it Jon", said George ominously, when his partner tried to calm things down. "Take no notice George, they're just losers," Jon said. George suddenly smiled as if a brain wave had occurred; dialling a number from his little black book, he waited for an answer. The rest of us looked over at him questioningly while the room when quiet. Who was he calling? "Stuart, is that you?" George said, "We've got some bother over here at Sarm West, Yeh, Trevor Horn's place, can you bring some people?" On the word people he shot a mischievous look at the rest of us.

Stuart Page often worked with George as a security minder and as an ex-policeman knew some extremely mean-looking people. Putting the phone down, George chuckled at the prospect. "So what! I'm a pop star and this is what pop stars do! I don't have to take shit from people, I can have them beaten up!" he said in his campest 'Marilyn' voice. "Or at least roughed up a bit. I'm a star now, I can afford it!" Although George clearly thought the whole thing hilarious, Jon and Roy looked nervous. What started as farce was turning into a bad Guy Ritchie movie.

Only a few moments later it seemed, Stuart quietly entered the control room with three other, smartly dressed thugs the size of gorillas and as hard as nails. "Where are they George?" one of them said, almost casually and quietly, somehow making them seem even more menacing. The evil quartet disappeared as quietly as they'd entered and we imagined all kinds of mayhem going on in the studio below, with heads being nailed to coffee tables and ears turned into cauliflowers.

But only five or so minutes later Stuart returned, accompanied by three, very sheepish looking 'Frankies' determined for some reason (not entirely unconnected with quite liking the use of their fingers) to impress upon George how they hadn't "meant it" and how "sad" they were to have given the wrong impression. "We were only havin' a laff George, honest, just a 'birra fun' mate, you know how it is", said the one whose face was covered in spots. Suddenly it appeared that Culture Club and Frankie Goes To Hollywood, two of the biggest bands of the 1980's, were not 'Two Tribes' going to war at all. They were, in fact, the very best of friends all of a sudden!

Chapter 27
Cold Shoulder Nightmare

I t was in early 1983 when Johnny Stirling called, just as I was about to go off on a balls-to-the-wall, coast-to-coast, six-week tour of America with Culture Club. My case was packed and my keyboards and gear had been picked up that morning and sent off to Culture Club's lockup to be flown out next day from Heathrow. I was buoyant, full of the joys of spring and looking forward to another sell-out tour. This time with the massive bonus of having written a couple of blinders with a band that looked like they were going to take over the world. However, Johnny, my friend and music publisher at Pendulum sounded tense and not his usual self. "Phil, I thought you told me you'd agreed, with George and the band, that you were getting 20% of 'It's A Miracle' and 'Karma Chameleon'?" "Yes," I said, although surprised to be asked. "I shook hands with Jon and George on 20%. No possible doubt about that, why do you ask?" "I think we may have a problem, Phil. Steve Lewis, Head of Virgin publishing just called me and was very rude. He told me that they had decided to now only pay you 10% and frankly you should think yourself lucky with that!"

My heart sank. Surely this couldn't be true? There was treachery afoot and I was going to have to fight my corner hard; something inside me knew these songs would be life-changers, one in particular so it was well worth fighting for. "That's bollocks, Johnny. They faithfully agreed, we all shook hands on it. I can't believe George would do this, Jon perhaps, but not George; we wrote "Karma" together, just the two of us." I was trying to contain myself; "I bet fucking Tony Gordon has put them up to this." "What a drag Phil. I'm so sorry, why does the bloody music business always have to be this way?" he said wearily. "You're going to have to be very careful if you want to maintain your position within the band though. But when they release "Karma" it's bound to be a huge hit so probably worth a bit of the old argy bargy!"

I was not cheered by Johnny's attempt to lighten the mood but resolved to call Jon immediately and try to sort things out without losing my rag. I knew Culture Club's forthcoming tour of America was make-or-break for the band and everything was riding on it. Instinctively, therefore I also knew my only ace card was that it was far too late in the day to replace me in the line-up. Calling Skirmish, my appropriately named keyboard roadie, I told him to go immediately to Culture Club's lock-up at John Henry's in Kings Cross and remove all of my equipment and instruments. It was a risky move but hoped a symbolic gesture like that would send all the right signals and prove my resolve. As soon as I put the phone down on Skirmish, it rang again. My heart sank as this time it was Jon Moss. "Look, Phil, I know we agreed on this mate, but Virgin just isn't having it and Tony has also put his foot down, there's nothing we can do..." Jon wasn't even coming up for air... "They've advised that it might be better for you if you accept 10% or you could end up with nothing. I'm just saying." "That's just not going to happen, Jon," I said firmly, but my voice was shaking. After a few choice expletives I'd probably come to regret, I left him in no doubt that I'd be calling my lawyer and for good measure that I definitely wouldn't be going on tour with the band in two days time unless my agreed royalty share was reinstated.

It was a high-risk strategy but I was in a desperate fix. The imminent tour gave me leverage, at least I prayed it did, and anyway it was the only chance I had. "We shook hands on this Jon, I can't believe you would go back on your word so quickly," I said, furiously. George who I hadn't realised had been next to Jon all the while, then came on the line. He sounded upset, especially so, as his friend was shaken to the core by the heated exchange between us. "What did Jon expect George?" I said, "I'm sorry, but you and I agreed this in good faith. What on earth have Virgin and Tony now got to do with it?" "Look, Phil, I think you should come up to town, we must meet up and sort this out today," he said dolefully, "we're supposed to be going on tour the day after tomorrow."

Deep in thought all the way up to London, I arrived at Tony Gordon's office a couple of hours later with Jon and George already there, but no Tony or the others, just Tony's secretary. The atmosphere was dark in TG's tiny airless basement office in Grosvenor Street, Mayfair. I tried to appeal to what I hoped was the more noble and trustworthy side of their natures, "Look we had a deal didn't we?" I said, "We shook hands and I agreed to share my royalties equally with everyone as you'd asked, no problem. So what went wrong?"

George passionately maintained that the decision to go back on their word was forced upon them by their music publisher due to the band's contractual situation but this time I wasn't having any of it. "Look, George, ten per cent may not seem like a lot to argue and fall out over but it will literally halve my income over the song's lifetime, I simply can't afford to back down on this, we wrote it together fair and square." Although I could see George was weakening and possibly willing to acquiesce, Jon was still making a vain attempt to hold on to the narrative, namely that it wasn't personal and had nothing to do with the band, but was merely a management and publishing stitch-up. "Well let's unstitch it then", I said, adding that it was contemptible to pretend we couldn't agree, the three of us, there and then in that room; my share should be honoured and not effectively demolished on a publisher's whim. The atmosphere in the room would have blunted a sharp knife. "Look, guys, I'm really sorry, but I can't go on the tour unless you put it back to what it was and instruct Virgin and

Tony accordingly."

Most musicians in my not exactly secure position may well have backed down and accepted the crumbs being offered from those who clearly held the upper hand. I knew I was on very thin ice, up against industry Goliaths far richer and more resourceful than I. Furthermore, I knew that to lose this gig would be devastating on so many levels; friendship, livelihood, relevance, not to mention professional esteem. But after all the false-starts and false dawns of a lively but chequered career to date, I knew that "Karma" was my destiny, my big break and that it would probably change my life for better and forever. I simply couldn't stand by knowing that all income from that copyright would effectively be halved. In the end and driven by George's urging and my admittedly pain-in-the-ass tenacity, resistance suddenly caved in. "Okay Phil, I'll call Steve at Virgin and order them to put it back to twenty per cent", Jon said finally with an air of injured resignation. "Thank you for that Jon," I said, relieved but still pissed off they'd put me through the mill; "I'm going to need it all in writing from Virgin's legal department before I leave today though" I insisted. "I just don't trust them now." "Okay, we'll do it", Jon said, picking up the phone to Virgin, while George stared vacantly out of the window. On paper, I was home and dry, having prevailed but on the ground, I could see that things were a million miles short of okay.

Heading off for a six-week marathon tour, no one in the band spoke to me at the airport. Even the normally cheery sessions and crew were frosty and arms-length, giving me short shrift. The word had obviously filtered down that Phil Pickett was a difficult bastard or knowing them, probably something worse. Whether I was too overwrought from the emotional confrontation with George and Jon and therefore paranoid I'll never know, but what was plain to see was that George, Jon, Roy and even Mikey were avoiding all eye contact. I'd blown it big time but now had to see it out and stick to my guns even though the whole thing could well turn out to be a pyrrhic victory.

In the days before constant communication, text messaging and mobile phones there was only the stupidly-expensive rip-off hotel phone when you desperately needed to call home. Even so, I was feeling so low about everything I was calling Ann at every opportunity; "I'm only here because they couldn't sack me and get someone else," I said, feeling sorry for myself. "I think I've really blown it this time."

"Don't worry, just hang on in there", she said, trying to calm me down, but having great difficulty; "This has Jon Moss's and Tony Gordon's finger prints all over it, the sods!" she said, clearly recalling my face the day I received the call from Johnny. "Just stand your ground sweetheart, it'll be worth it in the long run, wait and see. Even if they're not showing it right now, they'll respect you in the end". "I'm really not sure about that," I said, strung out on desolation row, five thousand miles away from home in one of the countless, identically beige motel rooms in the vastness of the American Midwest. I was more lonely and depressed than I'd ever been. Was my principled stand really worth all this?

Around a week or so into the tour I was still feeling the chill winds of the emotional embargo from all quarters. Then one day on the way to Philly, hiding away in my cramped sleeping compartment on the bus I suddenly had a Eureka moment. What if anyone, I thought, right or wrong, had spoken to Ann as I had to Jon and humiliated her like that? I'd have staunchly defended her to the very end. I realised I had been relating to George and Jon as a couple of guys in the band but not as an actual couple. Of course George would find the robust and dismissive way I had spoken to Jon completely unforgivable.

Peaceful and mild most of the time, a calmer chameleon indeed, but when riled you could take the boy out of Birmingham but not the Brummy out of the boy! And boy, my blood had been up with Jon! I'd insulted George's lover to his face and even though the two of them routinely took part in vicious and toxic humdingers between themselves it was obvious they loved each other with a dark passion. Jon was George's muse and each and every song was about him, therefore George was never going to forgive me unless I conspicuously climbed down and apologised to Jon. Preferably in front of him otherwise the rest of the tour would be more of the same cold shoulder nightmare.

In Philadelphia, getting ready for our show next day, luckily we had the afternoon and evening off and I now knew exactly what had to be done. Gary Lee our irrepressibly jolly and often infuriating tour manager supplied the rooming list upon request. Due to the persistence of Culture Club's growing lunatic legions of US fans who seemed, even years before the Internet, capable of locating precisely which hotel and in which rooms the band were staying with ease; all band personnel had been given tour name aliases to throw the insatiable buggers off the scent.

For reasons only known to Gary and US Travel Agent Jim Rodman (although we would find out at the end of the tour were based on California vineyards!), George's hotel name was Ed Beringer and mine, Marty Parducci, my Italian alter-ego. Confident I would find George and Jon together, having not long checked in, I found the right floor and timidly knocked on "Ed's" door. George opened it, obviously unhappy to see me, but turning to walk back inside, somehow I got the feeling he had been expecting me. "Is Jon there?" I said, "I'd like to speak to him if possible". Jon dutifully appeared from another room in the suite, drying his hair in a white bathrobe. There was a pregnant silence. "Look, Jon, can we have a chat?" I said nervously, still in the hallway, "I feel I must apologise for what I said back in London, I was wrong to say some of those things. However justified I may have felt at the time, honestly, mate, I am very, very sorry, it was completely out of order."

Jon's initially rigid stance appeared to soften a little. "Yeh look come in Phil, sit down. Thank you by the way". George made some tea while Jon and I proceeded to have a quiet and more measured chat on the sofa, about how and why things happened the way they did. Although their stance was still cool and formal, at the end of our impromptu meeting I knew I'd done the right thing by exhibiting such remorse. Business-wise I'd already got what I wanted, but on a personal level, it would still be a matter of time before I found out if I'd be accepted again in quite the same way.

Back in my hotel room, I must have fallen asleep out of the sheer emotional exhaustion of the hellish two weeks; so when the phone went off, by my bed, I couldn't for the life of me remember where, or even who I was for a second. "Phil, come up to Billy's room on the tenth floor." It was a very bubbly and excited George, "We're having a 'Welcome back Phil' party and you're invited!"

Everyone in the band was there, Helen and all 'the sessions', cheering me into the room with food, champagne on ice and music playing. There was even a 'Welcome Back Phil' cake George had somehow managed to arrange, although from God knows where at that time of night. I was so relieved the storm had passed and could now start to enjoy the tour. In spite of the occasional local difficulties in working with such a young band of remarkably vibrant and sparkling characters, I realised that Culture Club was indeed a family of sorts, albeit highly unconventional and that its members were becoming very important to me. Over and above the obvious professional opportunity, I realised I cared about these people. It's easy to take for granted how we all need the love, friendship and acceptance of our compatriots and fellow travellers, no matter what. It had been a hideous couple of weeks but finally, blissful, peace of mind reigned again. "Thank God that's over," said Helen, beaming. "I got the gist of it, but it all sounded very unpleasant, the troops were confused coz no one knew how to react!"

In any event, a good old 'knees-up' was well overdue this far into the tour, so, if anything, the release of the tension that my situation had provided only added to the sense of occasion of our impromptu gathering. Billy Button, George's gofer & driver, bizarrely having dressed up in one of George's outfits, was going around as the Maitre-d, regularly filling everyone's glass. As the evening wore on, the celebration became more *Famous Five* than *Spinal Tap* with team piggyback races now taking place around the vast, ancient, corridors of the 1930s Loews Hotel. These hilarious goings-on frequently culminated in collapsed heaps of inebriated people laughing their heads off like school children in a playground. That is until around 3 am when the fun and games were abruptly terminated by angry hotel staff, understandably due to complaints from the other hotel guests.

Arriving in New York for the second time after the triumphant success, against all the odds of 'Do You Really Want To Hurt Me' the city, indifferent, but mildly inquisitive last time round, now appeared to be at Culture Club's feet. In spite of the new celebrity, however, Mikey, Roy, Alison, Helen and I, having been invited to an incredibly exclusive and swanky uptown party in the band's honour with people like De Niro and Madonna in attendance, found ourselves outside on the sidewalk being denied entry by security flunkies.

Even laid back Mikey, who never lost his rag about anything, was rattled but, somehow, still appreciated the irony of the situation with typical self-deprecating humour, "Who am I?" Mikey said with mock outrage, "I am in Culture Club for heaven's sake! It's my band, I'm the bloody bass player!" he protested vainly but as ever good-naturedly to the security guys on the door. At the same time, we were being jostled by a swathe of hangers-on trying to get his and Roy's autographs. Similarly, Roy was amused although Alison not so. She found it totally humiliating to be out on the street with the plebs trying to get into the band's own party. In the end, Tony Gordon came to our rescue and got us all in but not without an irate artist's ear-bending from Roy, a show of strength to protect his wife's feelings. As a true force of nature that almost rivalled George's, Alison was more than capable of standing her own ground though. "Fucking hell Tony, Roy and Mikey are in this band too, not just Jon and George! What's going on here?" the lead guitarist's wife complained bitterly.

Earlier that evening we'd been playing to a sell-out crowd at the world-renowned Radio City Music Hall, where to my stupefying dread, not ten yards away from my keyboards at the side of the stage and watching the entire show was my greatest musical hero, Steve Winwood. As a faithful Brummie music fan, I'd gone to watch Steve in awe countless times at Birmingham Town Hall or the Speakeasy Club, both of us not long out of school. Warm memories of my musical hinterland all came flooding back. Back then I simply couldn't believe someone from my own town and my own age could play and sing like he did.

My hands suddenly turned into frozen jelly, hopelessly and self-consciously dabbling away at the keyboards in clear view of my fellow Midlands idol who, tables turned, was now closely observing me on stage. A little later, now at the swish post-gig party in New York, I was mesmerised in his company and we chatted about those early Brum days when he was the shining star of the Spencer Davies Group. To this day they were, for me, one of the very best groups of the sixties era. Quiet, shy and softly spoken, Steve's prodigious talent when still not much more than a deferential and mild-mannered schoolboy was unfathomable to me then. Still was. How could anyone sound or play like that at any age, let alone sixteen? A few years later when we became friends and neighbours in Gloucestershire, Ann and I got to know him a lot better but here in New York I was still agog. As it happened, he really liked Culture Club's show, particularly George's voice

Flight Lieutenant Phil Pickett Senior at the Streatham Locarno, 1943.

With my late Father, taken by my late Mother in Bulawayo, Southern Rhodesia 1949.

Right, top: Mel Tormé with my Mother Eileen modelling the 'Velvet Fog' hairstyle, 1954.

Right: The late Philip Sutton.

Left: Dave Peters, the late Paddy Maguire, Pam Hirsch & myself in Sutton Coldfield circa 1964. (*Pam Hirsch*)

Above: Kajanus Pickett 1971.

Below: Sailor on stage at the Victoria Palace Theatre, 1975.

With Ann in Golant, Cornwall, 1977.

Gavin David, Henry Marsh, James William Guercio, me and Ginny David at
Caribou Ranch recording Sailor's *Dressed For Drowning* album, 1979.

The first Culture Club US Tour Party in front of
our "Dralon Wheels" tour bus, Washington D.C.

Above: Jon & George having fun in Brighton during the 1982 UK Tour 1982.

Right: George backstage ironing my stage clothes at Heaven, London, 1982.

With Helen Terry and Terry Bailey on the second UK Tour 1982. *(Rob Pruess)*

With Mikey and Jon during the UK Tour, 1982 *(Rob Pruess)*

Left: Jon, Boy George and Terry Bailey on the first UK Tour 1982 - Tears Tours & Tantrums. *(Andre Csillag)*

Right: Album shot for *Colour By Numbers*. *(Jamie Morgan)*

At Denver Airport 1983.

All dressed up with
somewhere to go - the stage!
(Andre Csillag)

With Roy & Alison Hay during the "Niagara Incident" 1984.

With Gary Lee, my son Jack and Ann at the NEC, Birmingham, 1984.
(Andre Csillag)

"Alone" at Wembley 1984 with Elton John, George Michael, Paul Young, Bob Geldof, Midge Ure & Boy George.
(Andre Csillag)

On guitar for a change with Boy George at Wembley 1985. *(Andre Csillag)*

With Paul McCartney & Duane Eddy, plus Charlie Morgan & Nick Glennie-Smith at The Mill 1988. *(Courtesy of Charlie Morgan)*

With Henry Marsh at the Shaftesbury Theatre on the opening night of our musical *Casper*, 1999.

Sailor's *Full Monty* dance routine with choreography by Dee Dee Wilde. Sailor's second innings 1993-2013. *(Katrin Wagner)*

Olufemi Sanyaolu a.k.a. "Keziah Jones" in 1990. Keziah was my first foray into management. We split in the nineties but are back working together again now.

My three sons, Jack, Harry & Gus in Sussex 2012.

and was complimentary about the band and its music. He was also impressed as I recall with the fact that a group from England were topping the charts on both sides of the Atlantic, an exceptionally rare feat that not many artists achieve.

Suddenly from across the room, I heard the distinctive voice of someone I instantly recognised, Susan Blond. "Oh my Gawwd, Phil, I can't believe you are in Culture Club with Boy George!" she shrieked. Susan was CBS's head of press, who I'd first met in New York with Sailor. We'd always hit it off a treat and at one time the Manhattan socialite, like fish out of water, incongruously showed up in our sleepy Cornish village and stayed at our house. Looking her usual self, a beautiful porcelain angel, head to foot in *Chanel*, but with a voice like a Brooklyn Docker, the ex-Warhol movie actress was the Queen of New York's social whirl as well as Culture Club's press agent. Work always came first though. "Phil, you gotta come and meet Ron he wants to put you guys on at the Garden!" Ron Delsner the promoter who owned and operated the legendary Madison Square Garden, New York's most prestigious venue, had been trying to beat a path to George at Culture Club's after-show party but with Susan's introduction took me to one side instead.

"Would you guys come and play the Garden?" he asked me, after some preliminary chitchat. "Bloody right, I'm sure we would," I said, "but I'm just the keyboard player, shall I introduce you to Tony, the band's manager?" "Phil, tell you what, why don't you ask them to come and meet me for a late dinner at this place?" Ron said, proffering a card on which he'd scribbled the address. "It's one of the best restaurants in town, especially after midnight; Andy Warhol is joining us later and very much wants to meet Boy George."

This was all getting way above my pay grade but somehow, after mentioning it to Tony, I was invited to tag along with Susan and the rest of them to meet yet another iconic figure through my growing association with this band of upstarts and ex-squat-dwellers! We got to the place around 1 am and Andy arrived shortly after timidly shaking everyone's hand. The famous artist's handshake felt like cold, moist plasticine; very creepy and I have to say, not at all pleasant. His complexion was like cardboard and his face, expressionless, not giving anything away. I suppose it would have been considered, by many to be the beating heart and epicentre of the success/fashion zeitgeist of eighties New York, but in reality, there was nothing going on either on the surface or underneath it as far as I could see; maybe I was missing something.

George, bless him, already by now a huge star all over the world could still be delightfully gauche at times. Over dinner, for instance, having been asked by Delsner if he'd like to "come over and play the Garden sometime," George answered peevishly, "I'm not playing in anyone's fucking garden!" This raised an embarrassed and slightly nervous titter from the über-cool throng around the table, covering the gaffe, as one might with an ill-timed joke. But George, as unpredictable as ever, was still looking quite put out. "No George, he's talking about Madison Square Garden!" I whispered in his ear affecting an air of jocular empathy and bonhomie, "Why didn't he say so then?" George said looking back towards Ron, now smiling. "Of course we would wouldn't we?" he said, looking around the table for support. "I'll play anywhere if they pay me!"

The charmingly naïve spectacle contained echoes of the Richard Branson incident at the Lyceum in 1982. We nodded affirmatively and indeed the following year would sell out four nights at New York's vast and most celebrated venue. George and Andy meanwhile were parrying opinions, while guardedly making polite conversation about a friend of Andy's, Keith Haring, another famous artist supposed to be joining the party later.

George, the new kid in town, seemed animated by the exchanges, while Andy appeared cool and strangely vacant. In his shop-dummy wig and strange discombobulated eyebrows, Warhol seemed every bit as other-worldly and disengaged as one might have expected, but I also detected a faint look of lofty disdain towards the latest young parvenue contender sitting opposite him; the new star on the block, who the iconic artist had manifestly come to peruse at closer quarters. After thirty minutes or so, however, possibly tiring of the company and on his way to something more intellectually amusing, made his excuses and suddenly got up to leave. We departed shortly afterwards and like a strange exotic fish, Andy Warhol cut a rather forlorn figure sloping off down the deserted street at two in the morning. For all we knew, to some wild party or other. Or he might just as well have been going back to an empty apartment block on his own for beans on toast, who could say?

Chapter 28
Quincy

At the end of the recording sessions for Culture Club's second album, *Colour By Numbers*, a record which would prove to be the colossus of their career by a huge margin, an impromptu listening party was arranged by Steve Levine at Red Bus Studios in celebration of having finished the mixes. Driving into town on the Westway in my old bullet grey Daimler in the distance, looking south, I could see the RAF flypast down the Mall over Buckingham Palace, a state celebration of having seen off the Argies in the Falklands War.

Arriving at Red Bus, back in the music world, I could see that Steve was very proud of his mixes, and for the super-positive character, the man invariably was, even more confident than usual. There was a smell of all-round victory in the air. Itching to play the finished masters to the band the accomplished young producer I'd known since Sailor days was bursting with pride and grinning like a Cheshire cat as this was a very big moment for him too.

Much to everyone's chagrin however, George instantly put backs up by inviting Red Bus's tea lady to take part in the playback proceedings, having just clanked her way with trolley and urn into the studio's small control room. George's natural openhearted inclusiveness to all and sundry could at times be a little too much for his group to handle. The large friendly woman in her white catering overall cut an unlikely but imposing figure sitting incongruously on the corner of the studio's plush leather sofa, one hand warily resting on her trolley, a touchstone of security perhaps in this strange new transsexual pop star landscape. As Culture Club was considered one of the coolest and hippest bands in the known universe at this point, George's invitation to an ordinary member of the public to take part in such a professionally important and intimate occasion might well have astonished some. Too polite to show her the door and anyway, wary of George's likely reaction, passive aggressive looks were exchanged while communal cages were rattled.

The other band members seemed even more peeved when the woman started to give enthusiastic vent to her preferences by picking out "Karma" as the big hit of the album. The band's body language spoke volumes; "Ooh, it's lovely that song" she said, warmly, undeterred. "That's the one everyone will like, I can hear it on the radio now" she went on. "It's like *Juke Box Jury* this!" the tea lady said smiling comfortingly around the room, referring to the popular sixties BBC TV programme hosted by ultra-posh David Jacobs.

Sensing a mild frisson of discontent from certain band members, however, she quickly adjoined; "They're all lovely though, very good, very professional too! Anyway, well-done boys!" she said looking over to George for encouragement. "Shall we all have a nice cup of tea now?"

Somehow the event didn't turn out to be exactly what the participants had in mind for the official playback of their shiny new studio album. Finally, when the tea lady had departed along with her catering unit, an altercation ensued; "Why did you ask her to take part, George?" Roy questioned earnestly, as ever frustrated with George's unpredictability. "What the fuck does she know? It's our band and it shouldn't be up to complete strangers to pick out singles, I can't believe you sometimes!"

George meanwhile was unabashed. "You're wrong Roy, these are exactly the kind of people that listen to the radio, not your club types, musos and A&R men" he explained imperiously. "Regular punters, normal people. I'm far more interested in their opinions. Who gives a shit what labels and A&R departments think anyway? They don't buy records!" As usual, as soon as the thought had arrived in George's mind it came right out of his mouth and was delivered with insouciant precision. You had to admit he had a point though. In any event, the band and producer's carefully discussed plans of what should and shouldn't be released; when, and in which order etc were rudely cast asunder by the label and publishers as soon as they heard the album.

Literally, from the tea lady to Virgin A&R and promo departments, the BBC and every radio station in the country the verdict was unanimous. After the current single, 'Church Of The Poison Mind' already doing well, "Karma" was to be the next single, no contest. I was beyond thrilled as, already having 'It's A Miracle' under my belt, I'd now co-written two songs on the *Colour By Numbers* album and played a significant role in the completion of the aforementioned "Church", all of which would become major hit records the world over and a mainstay of Culture Club's live shows to the present day.

On 5th September 1983, our eighth Wedding Anniversary, 'Karma Chameleon' was released with great fanfare by Virgin Records. One week later the record immediately entered the UK chart at number three and a week after that, "Karma" replaced UB40's 'Red Red Wine' at the coveted number one spot. (Although not 'gold', as in "red gold and green", this was the best anniversary present one could have ever wished for. Eighth Anniversaries are traditionally celebrated with gifts of bronze, created by combining two different metals, copper and tin to make something stronger and even more beautiful!)

"Karma" meanwhile, seemed to go straight for the nation's jugular and was being played on heavy rotation around the clock on each and every radio station, large and small, local and national going on to hold its position at the top of the UK charts for a sensational six weeks! Quickly selling over a million copies the song joined the elite and exclusive '123 club', one hundred and twenty-three being the number of artists in the UK whose sales exceeded a million singles in sixty years since the Official Singles Chart began. Pinching myself daily, hourly almost, none of it seemed real. That is, until the day I heard "Karma" blasting out of the radio in my old Daimler driving across Richmond Bridge on my way back home. It was something I'd worked so hard to achieve as a writer and had always prayed for the day that my dream would come true. In that moment, one to savour, nothing could take the feeling away. I'd done it. I was back on the block with a vengeance! Or rather, we were.

Ann and I with Jack, by then aged seven; and now with our three-year-old Augustus ('Gus'), born in Kingston during the long, hot lazy summer of '81, were still living at 39 Lock Road near Ham Common in Richmond. It was from here after Sailor had folded effectively twice and numerous associated professional trials and tribulations in between, that we had re-launched our lives and were well on our way again. This time though through star-crossed good fortune and being in the right place at the right time, I'd somehow managed to play a major part in what had every sign of becoming a massive hit record. Not just here but all over the world.

We had sailed the family ship through some deeply unsettled weather of late, although the kids were probably too young to appreciate some of the hairier moments. Like our Cornish house losing two-thirds of its value overnight, Ann losing her beloved father Bob Sinsheimer on the eve of moving back to London and me, with all my career comings and goings one might have assumed our little boys would have picked up on their parents' insecurity at times. Therefore in my heart of hearts, I knew this unplanned and unexpected triumph out of the blue was a joint effort and in a very real sense a celebration to share... and celebrate we certainly did!

I was an only child who, for so many years, was convinced that a pillar to post, transient and nomadic existence, a half-orphaned little boy tagging along with his mercurial artistic mother Eileen, rich one minute, poor the next, was normal and run-of-the-mill. It was, of course, anything but. Falling in love with Ann, meeting her folks, dinner on the table at 6 and cosy fireside normality might sound prosaically calm and predictable but in fact, it was the elixir my soul was crying out for. A soothing contrast to the roulette wheel of my former existence. Now, having my own cherished family set-up finally gave me the stability and peace I'd unconsciously craved for all of my life. At last, I was a calmer chameleon!

Nothing quite prepares you for the non-stop euphoria of hearing your record at number one everywhere you go. In shops, in the car, round at friends houses and constantly on the radio and television; even at football matches. One day I took Jack, 7, to see his first ever football game; it was Queens Park Rangers at Loftus Road playing at home against Aston Villa.

Upon scoring the winning goal, the packed to the rafters home crowd spontaneously burst into song; "Come-a, come-a, come-a, come-a, come-a, come on the blues" rang out across the West London stadium and nothing had prepared either of us for the astonishing power of hearing thousands and thousands of voices unexpectedly belting out our song.

Their spontaneous joyful rendition of "Karma" was ear-splittingly loud and haphazardly irreverent but never more moving. Little Jack beamed with pride all the way home.

***

The song was surpassing all expectations week after ecstatic week. The all-pervading jaunty pop juggernaut resolutely stayed on at number one, seeing off all-comers with ease and selling in tens of thousands every day. Thursdays were champagne nights over at our house and every one of those six weeks we enjoyed a Top Of The Pops house party. Just at the point my weekly embarrassment of riches was becoming too much and dare I say, almost irritating, "Karma" suddenly slipped all the way down to number three. Billy Joel's 'Uptown Girl' knocked us off the top spot and it was like; "Oh my God, that's heartbreaking!" Even though one knew it simply couldn't stay up there forever, defying reality and gravity, an unreasonable black dog depression immediately replaced the jubilation of the previous six weeks. What strange creatures human beings are; we fully expect, indeed even feel entitled to the most superlative thing that could ever happen to last indefinitely, then when things change, we immediately cry! Nothing remotely compares, however, with having the biggest hit record on the planet.

Culture Club were already one of the hottest acts in the UK, with growing promise internationally, but 'Karma Chameleon', over and above all their other songs, rocketed the band into glittering orbit as world-wide megastars who could do no wrong. From the day the song was written I knew it couldn't fail, but the immediacy, speed and sheer scale of this six times platinum success was way off the scale and by a huge margin quickly exceeded mine and everyone's wildest dreams and expectations.

In the weeks and months to come, riding high on the best possible news from all over the world as "Karma" was eventually released everywhere, it was remarkable to experience the arm-pinching reality I had dared to hope and pray for. As my friend and mentor Arif Mardin had confidently predicted, music-loving public the whole world over were buying our record in their millions. Sounding unique and fresh, the record, let's not forget Steve's incredible production, hit a nerve and a sweet spot that the radio found addictive. The pleasure a songwriter has when that happens is indescribable and for this writer although having come close a few times and thwarted many, the sweet smell of success was at last, overpowering.

The day "Karma" hit number one in the UK, week ending 24th September

1983 my band mates and I again met at the Hammersmith Odeon to set off on yet another UK tour. Similar to the first time around when experiencing their first number one record, the mood in the band seemed, if anything, even more fractious and divided. After having achieved such astonishing success in a relatively short time it was as if all the excitement, emotion, hysteria, never-ending promotional activity, photo sessions and endless interviews around-the-clock, culminating in the sheer scale of this new massive hit had brought with it a whole new world of excessive demands on their time and energies. A million watt laser-beam of frenzied worldwide attention was honing in on them and of course on one of them in particular, Boy George.

***

George and Jon's combined worlds, meanwhile were colliding hourly, daily and weekly with the amount of time they were now obliged to spend together throwing coal into the burning furnace of an international music career now at full blast. For two vastly different personalities from contrasting backgrounds; George from a large and uncouth fighting Irish working-class family, and Jon the privileged adopted son of North London Jewish manufacturing millionaires; the demands of presenting the kind of united front the media and their fans expected was increasingly taking its toll on theirs, and everyone's nerves.

George and Jon were two of the most charged, charismatic and dogmatically wilful people I'd ever met. One with sultry movie star good looks, an avid heterosexual with an eye for the London ladies, who appeared to be nowhere near coming to terms with simultaneously being in a passionate homosexual relationship with the other; a force-of-nature, physically imposing, opinionated, Irish transvestite prone to biblical green-eyed jealous rages. Whilst fulfilling every professional dream in spades, the two of them seemed to be finding it hard to come to terms with not just their own demons, but at the (still) secret doomed relationship that lay at the heart of Culture Club.

The two stars around which the band's planetary universe and empire orbited, were highly unstable and battling it out mentally, professionally, spiritually - and physically throughout the duration of the group's success. The insatiable attention of the whole world was, by now, shining a concentrated beam of light on their vastly different lives, personalities and backgrounds, which seemed from the outside, far too much for their young souls to cope with. In particular, the tensions, even more than usual, were now out on full display; neither of them attempting to keep the poisonous vitriol under wraps. Some of their playing to the gallery interactions recalled the grisly acrimonious exhibitionism and brinkmanship of Elizabeth Taylor and Richard Burton in their movie, *Who's Afraid Of Virginia Woolf.*

Everyone was wary of George especially when he was in that sullen, aggressive mood, but not Jon apparently. He seemed to know all of the pressure points and emotional buttons to press and applied them with a combination of ruthless efficiency and reckless abandon, and at every opportunity. Not many of Jon's spiteful put-downs missed their mark but seemed to be lapped up with masochistic fervour by his drama queen on steroids lover. Out of the limelight of instant decisions, opinions and vital professional interactions, there were, one would have assumed no doubt serene private and affectionate moments. In retrospect, apart from a few notable exceptions, it was all work, work, work and therefore was never too long before one sensed the darkness and destructiveness reappearing. The vulnerable expressions of angst behind Roy and Mikey's eyes whilst desperately trying to hold everything together as this behaviour went on, spoke volumes. All tours at this level and the early stages of an artist's career are vital, the major aspect of which is to keep morale high within the band.

In a rare, unguarded moment on the second night of the tour, after George and Jon had left the dressing room to argue, even the normally polite and affable Mikey let rip; "I bet Duran Duran don't have to put up with this fucking nonsense night after night!" Mikey being incensed that things had to be like this at all in a band. "They could be having so much fun," the poor bassist went on, now at the end of his tether. "We all could! But they make everything so bloody difficult - for themselves and everyone else!"

Talking things over at breakfast after the first night of this latest new tour, Helen and I recognised that the whole shebang might go up in smoke at any minute, but even then we didn't realise how close to the truth that premonition was.

On the tour bus again, making our way to Sheffield for another sold-out show, all of the pent-up venom of the last few days and weeks boiled over into a furious no-holds-barred punch-up; George and Jon going at each other like tomcats in a sack. Everything went batshit crazy at least momentarily (why was it always Sheffield I wondered).

As a veteran of numerous worldwide tours and an expert in grabbing a few stolen moments of kip wherever I could at any time of the day or night, Helen shook my shoulder to wake me up and tell me the news; "Jon's broken his hand, it's really bad this time. No honestly, the tour's off!" she said as quietly as she could. "We mustn't tell anyone apparently, they've had to bribe the driver to say that Jon fell over when the coach braked, or some other bullshit, I don't know." "Can't say I'm surprised," I said, "they've been going at it hammer and tongue all bloody day!" "All bloody year, more like!" Helen retorted. Jon had apparently aimed a hard punch to George's face after a bitter row; George had insulted Jon, but had apparently ducked out of the way just in time, Jon's fist smashing into the window instead. I mused on George's dad, ex-boxer Jerry, that his techniques over the years must have subliminally rubbed off on his effeminate, but extremely tough street kid.

Like any father no doubt he would have taught his son the best way to avoid getting punched by school bullies. In that blind moment of Jon's rage had George ducked and weaved like Muhammed Ali? Somehow Tony Gordon - the manager's apoplectic concern on full display, managed to keep the incident out of the papers and the media and fans duped. A few weeks later, however, the tour was underway again as if nothing had happened, George and Jon having seemingly patched things up; at least for the time being.

***

At Gatwick Airport we were now about to board the plane for Culture Club's major headline tour of America and the excitement that was in the air was palpable. The aircraft, an ex-Cathay Pacific jumbo jet, was so old it had pieces of gaffer tape holding bits onto the wings. The crate looked as if it had already flown the equivalent of Earth to Mars and back five times. Its proud new owner was Richard Branson and this was the very first aircraft he'd purchased in a new venture he was planning to call Virgin Atlantic Airlines.

The student-like entrepreneur in his familiar scruffy gardening sweater looked distinctly hot under the collar as the ancient aircraft was apparently still waiting for a vital part of kit before it, and therefore we, could take off. While all this was going on, the Culture Club travelling party patiently waited on the tarmac shuffling about at the foot of the aircraft's steps. Richard looked extremely agitated and was anxiously talking to someone on one of the first mobile phones I'd seen. It was the size of a half brick and appeared to be glued to the side of the mogul's head. "He's talking to Coutt's Bank apparently", whispered Steve Grainger, our sax player with the driest sense of humour I had ever known. "He's after an overdraft so he can buy the part. Maybe he can ask for one for me too".

Years later when Ann and I were living near Oxford, Branson invited us to a cricket match at his house. When reminding him of this incident he told me he'd actually bought the ageing plane with the proceeds of 'Karma Chameleon'. "I never got to thank you for the part you played in that song Phil!" he said generously. "I'm just glad it took off at all!" I said. At tea, Branson recounted this story to the two teams for that day's game and to the opposing captain Bob Ayling, an Aussie and the managing director of his major rival, British Airways, so had no reason to doubt the tale was true. (Incidentally, I bowled him out in the first innings and caught him at slips in the second, so Ann scolded me on the way home. "What did you do that for? He'll never invite us again!")

It was March 28th 1984 and we were already midway across the Atlantic Ocean on our way to start the triumphant *Kiss Across The Ocean Tour* of Canada and America kicking off in Montreal. The prominent local radio station, no doubt wound up by the local promoters to capitalise on the phenomenal North American success of the band was broadcasting on the hour, exactly where Culture Club and Boy George now were with frequent updates on the band's ETA in Canada. The tumultuous scenes upon our landing at Montreal's Miracle airport were reminiscent of many I'd seen in grainy back and white movies of The Beatles arriving at various airports throughout the world a couple of decades earlier, always attended by thousands of adoring fans screaming their heads off from the airport's observation areas.

Helen and I got fairly refreshed on the way over in business class, the band almost always being up at the front in First. As sessioneers the world over, a scheming private chat was taking place about wages and conditions. However, we certainly couldn't complain about the hotels anymore, which were a million miles away from Dai and his "best one yet" hovels only a couple of years previously. Also, we were now regularly booked in business class, even toff class sometimes, which was a cut above most bands. Culture Club as an organisation certainly had its flaws but they were usually very generous in that respect. I sympathised with Helen's position in the band however, as her incredible powerhouse voice was such an integral part of the records and live shows, which in my view and many others', was well in excess of most backing vocalists' contributions.

We knew we'd have a couple of days off after our arrival in Montreal while the band were doing TV shows and interviews so sat back and enjoyed a couple more large ones. "George suggested to the others that they should pay me more but Jon and Roy and that bastard Tony Gordon adamantly refused," said Helen with a shrug. "Anyway, I'm not sure I can do this much longer, I find touring unsettling and it disrupts my life." I thought the band could be missing a trick by not recognising Helen's unique musical gifts properly and that she deserved more recognition as an integral part of the Culture Club sound. But it certainly wasn't my business to interfere. Besides, the elephant in the room was that I was now earning a small fortune from songwriting royalties, plus the performance income from the shows alone was already dwarfing my gig fees. The truth was I'd have happily come along for the ride and waived the fee, but thankfully no one ever asked!

Although I sympathised with Helen's position, sadly it was the same as many touring musicians and singers found themselves in; namely working your ass off while witnessing vast disparities in wealth between you and the band and the consequent lack of security. These were the Thatcher 'loadsamoney' years, however, one of the attributes being that it was every man and woman for themselves. Right or wrong, I felt that being too free with the exact details of my late and extremely welcome good fortune would have either been misunderstood or even worse, seemed like rubbing it in. I knew full well that my luck by being in the right place at the right time when co-writing "Karma" and "Miracle" had known no bounds.

Somewhere over the other-worldly, icy wastes of Greenland, Gary interrupted our works-do to tell us and the other 'sessions', that the Montreal airport authorities were having trouble containing thousands of hysterical fans and that we were to stick together like glue upon arrival. He wasn't sure how much security if any, there would be upon our arrival.

In a highly unprecedented situation, the pilot and Montreal ATC had been discussing the band's arrival while George and Jon were up on the flight deck. Practically the entire city was tuning into radio reports on the hour. Nothing Gary had said could have prepared him or any of us for the sheer insanity of the situation as we touched down in Montreal and we got our first glimpse from the plane of the mayhem to come.

Shrieking fans in their thousands could be seen hanging over the balconies of the observation areas and we prayed we'd be plucked by security from the steps of the aircraft and whisked off to a private area under the circumstances. But no such luck! With all of our bags and instruments and only hapless tour manager Gary Lee to assist along with a clearly terrified and perspiring Tony Gordon and Billy Button standing between us and utter oblivion. Thousands of swarming fans were not only outside but also throughout the arrivals hall.

To add to what was a genuine and growing feeling of danger and harm, almost immediately we were separated; the band and main party ahead being pulled to bits, whilst shepherded to the cars and vehicles outside, leaving the rest of us at the rear desperately trying to fight our way through the tearful screaming throng. "Bloody hell Phil this is madness!" said Steve Grainger, sax case on his back and a look of fear in his bloodshot eyes. He then appeared to be jostled off by the crowd in a different direction to Ron, Helen and I, who had managed somehow to stay together. "Over here mate, by the door," I shouted, trying to pull Steve by his arm. Luckily the American travel agent and friend of the band, Jim Rodman, came back for us and guided our party of sessions and crewmembers to a waiting black VW bus. Once packed inside like fretting sardines, the situation soon became scarily claustrophobic as hundreds of delirious, tearful fans were literally all over the bus banging on the windows and doors, a genuinely terrifying experience. Suddenly, the roof of the VW started caving in with the pressure of the more persistent fans who had climbed on top of the van. Jim opened the opposite door yelling, "Everybody out, come on people, go, go, GO!"

Whoever had been up there then ran off, giving us a brief respite to climb onto the bigger bus that band and management had boarded. Once safely inside and freed from the madness, we could all breath again. On reflection, I suppose we were all quietly buoyed by the adrenaline and excitement of being part of a band that was producing this kind of mania worldwide, a situation that was the ultimate dream of many professional musicians.

Having arrived in Montreal, similar to all of the other countries and continents we visited with Culture Club, we knew we'd have at least two or even three days enjoying ourselves doing very little except drinking, having a laugh and perhaps a spot of sightseeing, until called for the soundcheck on the day of the show. The reason for these mini-vacations was that George, Roy, Jon and Mikey on arrival in any new country would inevitably be whisked off by the record label to do their duties as true global pop stars and take part in never-ending interviews, photo sessions and PAs. Although it was enviable to a certain extent, having already been in my own pop band during the previous decade, I knew which I preferred!

Other than just liking having us around (understandable of course!), another reason for our paid holidays was probably just another sinister management ruse to save money. By keeping us all in one travelling party (and we had more than a few of those!), even if management was obliged to pay us for a few more travel days, due to the group-rate hotel and flight deals they'd still be saving money. But as I say, no one was complaining!

Things were still not looking, or sounding, very good between Jon and George and some initial skirmishing which had been in evidence after the previous gig was now in full force. The band, briefly in tourist excursion mode the day after our show at Buffalo's Memorial Auditorium, had requested a visit to the iconic Niagara Falls, usually, a location that represented blissful marital harmony and hopes for future happiness. Not on this day, however.

In the damp misty air surrounding the falls the exact opposite appeared to be the case and a huge fight broke out between... yes, you guessed it, Jon and George, just as we were pulling up opposite the famous tourist attraction. Tour Manager Gary Lee hastily requested the rest of the party's instant disembarkation from the bus, which was now shaking violently from side to side from the nasty fight going on.

We couldn't help laughing at the reactions of perplexed American tourists scuttling by who'd never heard anything quite like it. Accompanied by bitching and screaming that sounded more like a pair of hysterical but extremely aggressive baboons, anyone could have been forgiven for believing we were nowhere near Niagara - but up the Zambezi River in darkest Africa and the Victoria Falls!

A proper rumble in the jungle was going on but a photo of Roy, Alison and I overlooking the spectacular waterfalls shows that by this stage, although rightly concerned something might get broken again and the tour cancelled, we'd all grown wearily accustomed to the grim, hot-headed soap opera that, "The Jon and George Show" had become. Having achieved the glittering success and worldwide acceptance most bands would die for, it was immensely sad when things were like this; to realise that they were not allowing themselves or each other to enjoy the journey and that even once-in-a-lifetime sights and experiences such as Niagara, were washed away in self-absorbed misery.

Decades later as George reflected in his book *Take It Like A Man* - "I worried so much about failure, I often forgot to enjoy what was happening."

***

Taking a couple of days off, I flew into Los Angeles a little earlier than strictly required for my Culture Club shows. Joe Cocker, one of my favourite singers who I'd once saved up to see at Mother's in Erdington was about to record one of my songs in Hollywood. Joe's producer Stewart Levine (unrelated to Steve) had invited me along to Joe's vocal session while they were cutting my tune and of course I jumped at the chance to take part. (A few years later, my relationship with Stewart would come to the fore and become key with another artist, Keziah Jones, an amazingly funky blues guitarist I first saw playing in a London street, but read on).

A couple of months earlier, I'd played the song, called 'Threw It Away', (a tune I'd penned with Pauline Black from The Selector) to Warner Publishing's London MD, Rob Dickens. As I didn't yet have a demo of the song, he got me to play it on the upright piano in his office. He was crazy about the tune. In true Tin Pan Alley old-school style, after a seriously liquid three-hour lunch, Dickens got highly-regarded US producer Stewart Levine on the phone down in Muscle Shoals Studios in Alabama. Holding the phone up towards me at the piano, he said, "Play it to Stewart, go on Phil, play it again!"

"Love it! It's fantastic!" I heard Levine shouting down the crackly line, "We'll cut it tonight with the Muscle Shoals rhythm section!" These guys were among the most famous players in the world and very highly respected.

So months later, here I was in L.A where they were finally laying down the vocal part with Joe Cocker. "Nice tune, I hope I do it justice for you Phil," Joe said humbly while putting his headphones on. Cocker, the ex-Sheffield plumber had already made impressive inroads on a crate of Newcastle Brown Ale which Levine had thoughtfully arranged for his iconic, but at that time, fragile singing star. Slight, with dishevelled appearance and demeanour and in total contrast with the power of his voice, Joe blew me away and nailed it practically first take, the lyric seeming to fit his vocal styling like a glove;

> *I'm not a pauper or a millionaire*
> *Done all my living on a song and a prayer*
> *I played to win and took the lion's share so sweetly.*
> *Memories of friends upon my wall*
> *When I met you I thought that I had it all*
> *Too young to understand the mighty fall so easy*
>
> *Still, I threw it away*
> *Just when I had it*

I threw it away
Just when I held it,
I threw it away
That precious feeling
I threw it away, just when I really cared.

Revered guitarist and songwriter Richard Thompson, who I'd also seen a number of times at Mother's, was also someone I knew from the Sound Techniques days in Chelsea when working with Tony Cox on various projects. Richard was recording in the next studio and decided to pop his head round the door; "What are you doing here Phil?" he enquired amiably. He seemed surprised and impressed that I was not only part of Culture Club and its huge success story, but also was having one of my tunes recorded with the mighty Cocker. "You've been busy since we last met!" he said. After the session and now back out on the street at 1 am, I strode along star-studded Hollywood Boulevard, my head still spinning around at Joe's amazing vocal and full of the dreams and possibilities of the moment. I'd got my song recorded with someone I'd loved since the first day I'd heard his voice when just a teenager in Brum after he'd got his break recording a cover of the Beatles' classic 'With A Little Help From My Friends'.

It felt like yet another significant benchmark in my career. However, like many that get away, unfortunately, the record didn't go on to be a hit. But just to be working at this level with a seat at the table, my hat in the ring. was a massive privilege and a huge and timely boost to my growing confidence as a songwriter.

Around the time of 'Threw It Away,' I co-wrote another tune with my lovely songwriting neighbour in Ham, Florrie Palmer.

She'd written some huge songs for Sheena Easton including 'Modern Girl' and '9 to 5 (Morning Train)'. Having had my own song; 'Don't Send Flowers' recorded on Sheena's first album, Florrie and I met and got on famously at a record biz party at The Ritz to celebrate Sheena's number one platinum album *Take My Time*. Our joint effort, the first we'd written together, was called 'The Real Me' and Quincy Jones, legend and mega-producer of Michael Jackson had personally picked it out to record with Donna Summer.

Florrie, her late husband Martin Revely, Ann and I spent many a happy hour in our local pub in Ham planning how we would spend the money, presenting each other with tasteful cushion designs for our eventual Monaco yachts! It was not meant to be however as Donna endured some kind of religious conversion suddenly taking umbrage at some of Florrie's lyrics. Yet again the songwriter's curse had struck; "Never final 'til it's vinyl". (The eventual title of Florrie's book!) Therefore on this occasion, sadly although cushions had been purchased, the yachts would have to wait!

Lost in the mists of time, an ancient artefact once known as a telegram eventually arrived at my house in Ham from Quincy himself, berating his artist for passing up on such an obviously massive hit. The crumpled missive also contained an invitation to call him "anytime I was in L.A." so I wondered if he would actually remember me, or even find the time to see me now I was there. With "Karma" now racing up the US charts and favourably looking to repeat the same kind of magical success it was enjoying elsewhere, plus, as I was playing in L.A. with the band in just a few days time at the Greek Theatre, I felt on a roll. "So why not call him?" I thought.

"Mr Jones is available Phil," Ed Eckstein his assistant said. Ed, I would later learn was the son of my mother Eileen's all-time favourite singer, Billy Eckstein. Billy's music and rich mellifluous voice in songs like 'Passing Strangers' was part of the soundtrack to my early life in and around West Bromwich and Birmingham in the early fifties. "Can you swing by the office in Beverley Boulevard around 10 am tomorrow Phil? He has a very busy day lined up but would love to meet with you if at all possible.

"Wow, something in me hadn't felt it would be this easy to meet the great man himself.

***

The following day, parking a couple of blocks away, nervous and a little early for my appointment, I waited outside Quincy's office with trepidation. Hell, I was tense, but what was I doing here in the first place? I shouldn't have been apprehensive at all however, Quincy was the personification of quiet charm, graciousness and generosity of spirit; proving, yet again that those truly at the top of their game were almost always genuine and self-effacing individuals. Unlike the many grasping pretenders, snakes and wannabes further down the food chain. "Boy, I loved that song Phil, 'The Real Me', total class. It was such a shame I couldn't get Donna to sing the lyric," he said thoughtfully. "She'd had some kind of problem with it due to her beliefs or some such nonsense, but it was a hit song from the get-go man! You're a great writer."

Compliments like that from someone such as the mighty 'Q' I could handle any day of the week! "Anyway, talking of hit songs, how is 'Karma Chameleon' doing? That's a great record man", he said. I said as far as I knew it was moving rapidly up the American charts, which was intense, especially as we were touring the States. But that I wouldn't know until the next day when the new Billboard chart was published how well it was doing or whether it had slipped back down. Our hopes were high though and fingers, toes and everything else was crossed. Quincy flashed me a knowing look and a warm smile, "I have a mole at Billboard," he said enticingly with a twinkle in his eye. "Shall I call him? We might be able to find out for you!" This was all just too good to be true! 'Q' himself was calling Billboard on my behalf and I could instinctively feel another musical milestone on its way, in a big golden package. Still sitting behind his vast mahogany desk, glasses on, he picked up the receiver and carefully dialled the number; "Uh huh, okay," he said to the person on the other end of the line, while all the time looking over at me and smiling.

"Thank you. Yep, I have the writer of the song here in my office and he'll be very, very pleased I am sure" Then, covering the mouthpiece with his other hand and with a beaming smile said the words which will be forever imprinted on my soul; "Congratulations Phil, 'Karma Chameleon' is Number One in the USA!"

***

We stayed conversing in his office for well over my allotted time of an hour, talking about music, recording and the art and importance of songwriting in the general scheme of things. He played me some recent songs he liked, including a brand new Michael Jackson cut that no one had heard yet, and also told me all about a movie he was producing called *The Color Purple*.

Asking me how I got into music in the first place, Quincy seemed particularly interested in my story about meeting Duke Ellington, the music legend who was apparently also his greatest influence. The inspiration gained from spending time with Quincy Jones and absorbing the quiet gentility of a musical genius at that level was priceless and immeasurable. I pinched myself again; the very familiar thought of "Why is this happening to me?" occurred yet again.

Breaking the spell, a nervous Ed popped his head around the door interrupting the lazy flow of rambling dialogue and by now, the dream-like blissful state I was in, spending time with someone who seemed to have all the time in the world for me. "Phil Collins and Tony are still waiting outside Q, you've gone twenty minutes over and they're getting mighty restless," his boss said anxiously. I'd never met Phil, but I knew Tony Smith, the ex-roadie and giant bear of a man, now manager of Genesis, who was definitely not someone who could be kept waiting. They looked none too happy as we came out into the reception area, but Quincy was relaxed and unabashed about having kept them hanging around; he was Quincy Jones after all. "I'm just seeing Phil out guys, I'll be right back," he said and then he walked me down the stairs to the glass doors, barely keeping the blistering furnace of L.A.'s midday heat on the outside of his imposing, super-cool, two-storey, office building.

Naturally, thinking he would quickly turn around and go back inside to his next meeting, surprisingly, he stepped outside into the heat and asked where my car was. "Oh it's a block or two down the road, don't worry Quincy, I'll be fine," I said, also anxious about the two waiting VIP's upstairs. But he was now accompanying me down the road and carrying on the conversation with one hand on my shoulder! I couldn't believe what was happening. Was he actually going to walk all the way to my car? We carried on talking as we walked; "Songs are the most important thing Phil, the basis of our whole business and it's always a real privilege to meet writers, they're the lifeblood of our industry," he said, "I just know you're going to have a great career in music, this is your time man, so please come back and see me anytime you're in L.A".

It's a cliché of course but by this time I was floating on air, even though it was currently so hot it almost scorched my lungs. The great man even held open my car door, shaking my hand as I got in; the painstaking care and genuine interest he afforded me for my time went against all preconceived notions of how the meeting might go. As I drove off I saw him slowly walking the two blocks back to his office in my rear view mirror, surely, by now, to a disgruntled and tetchy Smith and Collins. So far, it was as unforgettable as mornings go.

***

Back at the Beverley Comstock Hotel, Boy George, on his way out to a photo session looked surprised when I told him the news, not at the chart position; they also already knew in advance too, but that Quincy Jones had personally informed me, Phil Pickett, their keyboard player. "How do you know him? George said looking completely baffled. I could tell from his reaction that even he was impressed.

Still addled with jet lag, I'd been avidly reading Norman Mailer's book on Marilyn Monroe and around 5 am I suddenly realised from the description that she must have been buried quite close to the Beverly Comstock Hotel where I was staying. Musing on the vicissitudes of transient fame and fortune and also George's apparent fascination with Marilyn's iconic femininity, voice and reputation, as I really couldn't sleep, I found myself walking the deserted streets of Beverley Hills looking for her. Finally, after a few blind alleys and just as the burning L.A sun was making its presence felt on another new day, I came upon a tiny and unassuming cemetery of vaulted white catacombs behind a couple of opulent but nondescript apartment blocks. A little more searching, and suddenly there she was, her final resting place halfway up a wall, bless her; 'Marilyn Monroe 1926-1962' her unassuming plaque read. She was buried just a few yards away from a very busy six-lane highway.

Later that day, whilst sunbathing around the pool back at the Comstock and seeing George on his way out this time to take part in Culture Club's *A-Team* TV appearance, I thought he might be interested. "Would you like to come with me, when you have some time, it's only up the road," I said encouragingly. "I'll show you where she is." "No thanks," he said archly, looking at me as if I was off my head. "Why on earth would I want to do that? She's dead!" I realised, of course, that it was her look, provenance and fame and its acquisition, not the star's actualité that had bewitched and beguiled the young George O'Dowd as a young boy growing up. "Anyway cover yourself up, you look... hideous!" George said, as ever poking fun in his breathy 'Marilyn' voice.

***

Colour By Numbers was scorching up the album charts everywhere, on its way to going six times over platinum and selling over six million copies; while "Karma" topped the American charts for a consecutive three weeks, another notch on the gun that meant that Culture Club had now joined the incredibly rare and select band of artists who'd simultaneously topped the chart on both sides of the Atlantic.

The success of "Karma" and of our album in America, meanwhile, guaranteed the band their prestigious Grammy Award as 'Best Newcomer' and, back in their home country, Culture Club was congratulated on the floor of the House Of Commons; "...on their success at the Grammys and (this House) acknowledges the enormous pleasure they bring to millions of people around the world and the exports they and their industry achieve for the United Kingdom."

Sir Richard Branson in his book *Losing My Virginity* states that 'Karma Chameleon' "became number one in every country in the world that had a chart".

On the cover of Newsweek, with a big picture of George and Annie Lennox, the headline read *Britain Rocks America Again. From the Beatles to Boy George and Beyond.*

"Thank you America," George's Grammy acceptance speech began promisingly our eyes and everyone's glued to the screen, before catastrophically veering off the highway by taking an ominous left-hand turn; "You have taste, style... and you know a good drag queen when you see one!"

Whoops! Oh dear, there it was; a moment that was pure George, full of reckless, camp frivolity and hubris. A few seconds which Tony Gordon and Jon Moss evidently, for once, had been unable to curtail the natural effervescence and outrageousness of the band's lead singer. It was as if someone had farted at the Coronation.

All over America false teeth and coffee was spat out again and feathers distinctly ruffled in a deeply conservative nation which again, as Winston Churchill once famously noted, were "two countries divided by the same language." Our dear American cousins were not happy. This wasn't England, where from the bawdy era of Music Hall Theatre, gay entertainers, their jokes and innuendos were meat and two veg to the Brits. We had grown up with it, but in big, bold, country and western, bible bashing, USA they did not like it one little bit. From this moment on the watershed, fulcrum, turning point, call it what you will, things started to go adrift. At first imperceptibly and then in the end like a mighty crashing wave.

***

Much later on in the year, with yet another North American tour under our belts, exhausted after a hard year's touring and looking forward to spending Christmas with our families, we finally completed an almost unheard of four sold-out nights at Ron Delsener's famous New York venue, Madison Square Garden.

It seemed that only a short while ago I had sat between George and Andy Warhol in a Manhattan restaurant, where, even though we managed to laugh it off, George irately told Delsener he wasn't, "going to play in anyone's fucking garden!" In my mind, those four tumultuous and spectacular concerts represented the zenith of the Culture Club years and where that incarnation of the band probably played at its very best.

Having partied heavily the previous evening at the Mayflower Hotel I'd overslept and therefore was very late for my flight home to London. I'd missed the 'sessions' bus and as there were no more gigs on the tour with everyone in a desperate hurry to get home, I realised it was 'every man for himself' and I'd been left to make my own arrangements.

I dashed out of the hotel and took a cab to the airport bumping into George on the sidewalk at JFK who was just arriving in his limo. "Hi Phil, are you on Concorde?" he said smiling, looking as fresh as a daisy. "No, I don't think so George, I'm in business on the British Airways 'red-eye'." "Bollocks to that!" George said dismissively, "Come on, I'll get you on Concorde with us. The BA front-of-house woman likes me!" I had been a huge aeroplane buff all of my life and was terribly excited about the possibility, but still didn't really believe that with my ticket they'd let me on. "This is Phil Pickett our keyboard player who co-wrote 'Karma Chameleon'." George addressed the BA Concorde concierge lady demurely on his best behaviour; "I'd like him to fly with us if possible - can you upgrade his ticket?" "Of course I can George, that's my favourite song of all time!" she said. "Come this way, Phil".

I climbed aboard the beautiful slender aircraft almost shaking with anticipation and pride. My first thought, strangely enough, was of all the shattered greenhouses Concorde had caused while rocketing to America over the Fowey River where we lived all those years ago. The second thought was how tiny the aircraft was: Seats only four abreast and windows no bigger than saucers. This miracle of engineering and British/French ingenuity was basically a rocket with a few seats on top. I was so excited I could hardly breath. Once ticket formalities had been taken care of I was shown to a window seat. George and everyone must have gone on earlier so presumably were at the back of the plane, so I couldn't immediately make contact with the group. George had said that Lol Creme and Kevin Godley, who were planning the shoot for the 'Victims' video, were also onboard and were fully intending to have a little party at the back of the plane. "When you're settled in, come on back," George said.

The stewardess showed me to an inside seat by the window. The aisle seat was occupied by a very distinguished aristocratic gentleman who I later recognised as being the Duke of Kent. Buckling up next to royalty, we taxied out to the runway and once again was astonished at how relatively flimsy, bumpy and awkward this small and sleek flying machine seemed to be while on the ground. But in the air, good grief, it was an entirely different story. Now at the end of the runway, the engines were pushed up to full thrust and the noise they made and the sheer power one felt vibrating throughout your body and pushing into your back was like nothing I've ever experienced before or since. So much so in fact that I could hardly contain my emotions: I just wanted to punch the air! Looking to my left, to perhaps share this moment of unbridled joy with someone, anyone, my eyes met with a non-plussed regal stare. No matter, the angle of climb and the speed while lifting from the ground was completely overwhelming and way, way beyond the most exhilarating theme park rides I'd ever been on. As the speedbird punched through the clouds at an almost vertical angle I thought of my father and how proud he would have been to see me aboard an aircraft like this.

After about twenty minutes, eleven miles above sea level and now practically in space, I was transfixed by yet another experience of a lifetime. George, meanwhile, had ventured from the back of Concorde to come looking for me and wafting a pungent aroma of exotic perfume while leaning across the clearly horrified and perplexed Duke, said enthusiastically, "Come on Phil, we're having a party at the back of the plane with Kevin and Lol, why don't you come and join us?" But seeing the look of seething royal disdain on the Duke's face added, "Don't stay up here with these... POOFS!" Climbing over the clearly appalled aristocrat, I followed George and joined the riotous party going on at the back of the plane where everyone, including the cabin crew, was tucking into caviar and champagne with gusto. The fun and inter-band conviviality went on non-stop until we landed at Heathrow, which to my utter astonishment was only three hours later, just in time, in fact, for breakfast.

In due course, I would repeat the experience of flying Concorde again a couple times, visiting the cockpit on one memorable occasion, but nothing will ever come close to the first, unforgettable experience of flying on such a remarkable machine, now sadly gone.

***

An increasingly bizarre aspect of being the keyboard player in "the most famous band in the world" in that brief but tumultuous period post the worldwide triumph of "Karma" was that you never knew who you were going to bump into when coming off stage. Wherever we played in the world, the most famous celebrities who happened to be in that city and who weren't working that evening would more often than not be found backstage at our gigs to greet, congratulate and often party with George and the band after our shows. I already mentioned my idol Steve Winwood but among many others were such diverse and random stars as Torville and Dean in Sydney; Debbie Harry in Long Island; Sting in L.A a couple of times and Yoko Ono and John McEnroe back in New York.

John was a big music fan who came to several Culture Club shows, once returning the favour by inviting us to see him and his band play in a tiny club in L.A. Although we had a great night watching him and his band play, next morning's verdict was that he'd probably been wise to stick with tennis! Julian Lennon also came to quite a few of our shows (in fact, was backstage at the Hollywood Bowl show Ann and I attended in 2016). After once playing piano for him at a surprise birthday party in his honour, over the years we became good friends. The most enthralling evening for me as a stage-struck brummie kid, however, was when Ann and I were once invited out, post-show to a dinner at the Groucho Club. Quite randomly among large table of actors and musicians, Geraldine James, having just played Portia to Dustin Hoffman's Shylock in the West End production of *Merchant of Venice* and whose party it was, placed Ann and I on either side of Dustin; now, as he was then, true Hollywood royalty.

Although one of the biggest stars in the world, Dustin was also one of the most charming, modest and self-effacing humans either of us had ever met. Not only did we both immediately warm to the man but actually I believe, fell in love with him there and then! All he wanted to talk about, genuinely, was music, music, music; how it worked, how you wrote a song, what it was like to have a hit, etc. Every time you tried to steer him on to *Rain Man*, *Midnight Cowboy* or acting in general he just said; "Yeh, but anyone can do that. But playing and writing music? Wow, that's really something!" At around 2 am he quietly got up, put his mac on, bid us farewell and carrying two little plastic grocery bags, walked up Dean Street on his own into the night and hailed a passing cab. That was it. A perfect evening.

Most memorably and possibly for all the wrong reasons, was once backstage at the Greek Theatre in Los Angeles, the band experienced a very bizarre encounter with the late, great, Michael Jackson. The 'Thriller' star had come to see Culture Club in a highly elaborate Howard Hughes-type disguise, consisting of a false beard, dark glasses and a big floppy hat. Not only that, but one of his minders was pushing the great MJ around the backstage area in a wheelchair! Even odder was that while this eccentrically elaborate charade was going on, Michael nevertheless had decided to wear a tour jacket with The Jacksons emblazoned across his back. Work that one out!

***

Through my friend Judd Lander, part-time magician, harmonica and bagpipe-playing promo man, I got a chance to submit a piece of music for the official ITV Olympic Games theme in 1984. Going up against the best media writers and composers for TV and film music in the country, out of hundreds of submissions, I was thrilled to hear that my song, 'Destiny' had 'made the cut' and was awarded the commission just a few weeks before going off on tour in Australia with Culture Club.

As they were intending to play the theme every night on ITV's News At Ten as well as on rotation throughout the competition, the producers were looking for something powerful and dynamic. So with a full orchestral score that I'd arranged for a section of the LSO, I thought I'd book one of the loudest and hardest drummers of all time, an old mate from my early Birmingham days and at various times, the drummer for Jeff Beck, Rainbow and Black Sabbath; Mr Cozy Powell.

We'd fallen out around ten years earlier after he ran off with an old flame, but over the years we had competed in several Brum bands after leaving college, so I suppose there had always been a frisson of healthy professional rivalry between us. But as we'd both subsequently done rather well in our careers, all that silverback gorilla stuff was quickly brushed over and forgotten. "Hello mate," Cozy said in his famous Cirencester brogue, "Yeh, I'd love to Phil, see you next week then, "Destiny' it is then!"

Tragically, a few years after the session, Cozy was killed in a serious car accident while driving home to Gloucestershire on the M4, but the sight and the sound of him thrashing his drums to pieces in amongst all those fine classical musicians is an enduring memory I shall always have of the late, awesomely great, Cozy Powell.

Chapter 29
Waking Up With the House on Fire

C oming off an album as inspired and globally successful as *Colour By Numbers* and approaching the vital third album is a challenge for many recording artists and which I'd already experienced with Sailor. Although nowhere remotely near the vast worldwide sales of *Colour By Numbers*, Sailor's second album, *Trouble* nevertheless went gold and silver in many countries around the world, although the band ran out of creative steam by the time of its *Third Step* album.

Naturally I guess as I'd already successfully contributed on Culture Club's first and even more so, their second album, having co-written two of the biggest hits, I assumed the telephone might be ringing off the hook inviting me back into the fold to work on the new record, but on the contrary. The phone fell strangely silent.

I'd heard rumours mainly through Helen, who as usual knew more about the inside track, that an impenetrable creative regime had been established between Roy Hay and producer Steve Levine. With their shiny, new state-of-the-art, expensive digital toys, combined with the ruthless efficiency of schoolboy boffins, they had all but taken over the creative processes and direction on this new and very important record. "What does George think about that?" I asked her. "He's not too happy, but as you know, is not as musical in the same way Roy is. Anyway, he and Steve seem to have an iron grip on the songs and arrangements and they're the only ones who know which buttons to press!"

I assumed, correctly as things turned out. Now Roy was more in the driving seat on this record he probably wouldn't need me around. "What about the songs though?" I said. "Those machines are great servants but they can't write hits can they?" "Give them enough rope I suppose; they'll learn!" Helen said philosophically. Even so, I was surprised if it were indeed true that George had given way so compliantly to Roy and Steve's direction.

When the results of these collaborations began to filter through I was struck, as was everyone else at how leaden and laboured the production sounded in contrast to the audio transparency and lightness of touch of *Colour By Numbers*. Those songs, like "Karma", "Church" "Black Money" and "Miracle" had been written from the keyboards and guitars with real musicians belting out spontaneous ideas with soul and commitment. The lesson learned, as always I guess, was that machines and fancy equipment don't write songs; living, breathing and bleeding humans do. Although I suppose, sour grapes to a certain extent as I had been clearly sidelined on this record, where were the hits? Why did it all sound so stodgy and plodding?

In *Smash Hits* magazine, reviewer Tom Hibbert stated that the album was "a disaster of mediocrity" and that most of the tracks were "a characterless stodge of bland, blue-eyed soul, slouching rhythms, pedestrian horns and nonchalant vocals." Tell us what you really think Tom!

Allmusic's Lindsay Planer later noted that "overexposure in the media, the ever-changing tides and trends of pop music and, quite frankly, a less than laudable collection of songs resulted in the album receiving a less than enthusiastic response." *Waking Up With The House On Fire* had more than a whiff of the midnight oil about it and in the end, a testament to over-promoted self-belief, ego and youthful folly. Never mind, there was always tomorrow and still plenty of gigs in the book. Plus the folding stuff was heading my way in embarrassingly large amounts from the successes of the previous album. In addition, Culture Club was paying me a princely retainer for my live work so there really wasn't anything to complain about.

During one of the rehearsals, Jon mentioned privately they might be looking around for a new producer for the next album. It was a sensitive subject due to the perceived failure of the third album. But the feeling was that Steve had perhaps run his course and it was time to move on with someone new. "Have you thought of Arif Mardin?" I suggested. I told Jon and George about the amazing records he'd produced for Aretha Franklyn, Roberta Flack and Chaka Khan, all the way through to Queen and the Bee Gees' *Saturday Night Fever* collaborations.

Arif's diamond relevance to pop was still currently powering ahead in the eighties, having played a fundamental role in creating the era-defining sound of Scritti Politti, possibly the hippest new band around at that time. "Do you know him?" Jon enquired, "Yes, I worked with him on some stuff I wrote for Dollar with Simon Darlow plus a few other things. Do you want me to ask him for you?" Having played Culture Club's music to Arif previously in New York I knew he was very complimentary about the sound and in particular, George's voice. I felt confident he would be interested, that is if he had the time available.

"I would love to do this record Phil, thank you," the old master said when I finally managed to get through to him at his office at Atlantic Records in New York, "but would prefer to do it in Switzerland, in Montreux, in fact, at Queen's studio." A few days later George called to invite me to the writing and rehearsal sessions in Brixton for work on the new album, *From Luxury To Heartache*, a providential title if ever I'd heard one. "That's great George, thanks, I'd love to, but do the others know you've asked me to come?" "No, not right now, but let me worry about that," he said confidently. "Our last record got dreadful reviews so we need to change things this time. It might be tricky at first but will you come tomorrow?" "Of course," I said, but with a sinking feeling knowing I'd have to run the creative gauntlet with the others all over again.

I arrived at the giant rehearsal hanger on a boiling hot day in the summer of 1985. It was part of a fortress-style courtyard complex bang in the middle of Brixton, a dangerous location at the best of times but especially so when you'd turned up in a brand new open-topped Mercedes. I was nervous and apprehensive about seeing them all again. Jon was already at his drums and looked surprised when I breezed in with my keyboards, as was Roy who was barely polite. "Hello Phil, what are you doing here?" he asked archly. "George asked me to come", I said. This was an embarrassing moment. Mikey as ever was gracious and came over smiling, "Good to see you, Phil. How are Ann and the boys?" he enquired, as ever the perfect gentleman. Roy insisted on a little private chat with the others meanwhile and went off to an adjoining room.

As George had previously predicted, it was indeed tricky and as voices were raised I could hear them clearly in the next room. "Why did you invite Phil again George?" Roy said, "You could have mentioned it, man!" He wasn't happy but I suppose he had a point. Reacting to the local difficulty I decided to go outside for some air, as I didn't particularly want to hear any more. They'd have to make up their own minds whether I stayed or not, but in his tone, I could hear that George was determined to have his way. Mikey, the soothing interlocutor came outside to join me in the heat. He was sympathetic and confided that in his opinion they certainly needed a bit of outside help this time. "The last record wasn't good man, Roy and Steve had too much say and we need to open things out again this time. Don't worry though" he consoled, "Roy and Jon are headstrong but they'll come round." After ten minutes or so I could hear Jon bashing around on his drums again, so, biting the bullet, decided to go back into the bear pit a second time. Whatever had gone down earlier seemed to have calmed things down and although at first undeniably tense, we began to exchange ideas, chord progressions and arrangements. Together we thus began work on all of the new songs for what would be their last eighties record, *From Luxury To Heartache.*

No one referred to my presence and participation again but it looked as if I was now co-writing all the songs on Culture Club's fourth album. What a turn of events!

Already having anticipated a creative role after the initial hurdles, I'd been working on a few ideas; one of them inspired by a killer track by Ace called 'How Long', sung by Paul Carrack who, through BA and me, had landed the Mike and the Mechanics gig. I was pleased with the chord progression for which George immediately created a moody and atmospheric top line melody. At the end of the first day, we'd outlined a few promising ideas, including 'God Thank You Woman' and the Ace-inspired 'Move Like A Spider' (which later 'morphed' into 'Move Away'). Once all the usual shenanigans were out of the way everyone seemed happy again, at least on the surface. It was yet another lesson in not taking things too personally and just getting on with it.

The lyric change on 'Move Like A Spider' took place a few weeks later at Commodore Studios in Holland. Something was going on with George and I couldn't put my finger on it. But it just didn't feel right. Also as Helen was sadly no longer part of the Culture Club (although she would go on to have a cameo role on *From Luxury To Heartache*) the major source of my intelligence and point of contact had disappeared along with her departure. I didn't realise therefore until later on that the location of the studio out in the wilds of Holland near the German border, was booked deliberately in order to get George as far away as possible from his more druggy acquaintances and London dealers. In every other respect, it could not have been a more uninspiring place in which to create music. But the realisation that George was now doing drugs came as a huge and unpleasant surprise.

Taking a break for dinner, the rest of the crew went out to a restaurant leaving George and me on our own with the studio engineer. George had been having some thoughts on the lyric and wanted to see if he could get a lead vocal down. Sweating profusely in what I, as ever innocently assumed was purely attributable to the heat, he soldiered on wanting to get it out of the way before the band returned. "While you're at it George, can you change the words in the chorus a little?" I asked hesitantly, as he was definitely not his usual bubbly self; "Fuck off Phil, why?" he said bluntly. "I'm not sure that "Move, move, move, like a spider", conjures up the best image to have in a chorus, that's all. I don't know, people generally hate spiders though. Can't you think of something else?"

He harrumphed!

I was skating on much thinner ice than I would have ever known at the time, but I suppose I was harking back to his instant breezy compliance when, turning on a sixpence, he changed "It's America" to 'It's a Miracle' and the days when getting him to change things was never a problem. After a few seconds thought he said, "Okay, send me the track again", suddenly accepting my suggestion. I was relieved. He then did something that to this day made me realise what George's creative genius was all about. In one take he performed the entire vocal and spontaneously wrote the lyric that would end up as the actual, finished recording of 'Move Away' that would end up being produced by Arif Mardin a few months later. Without any pre-written lyrics on bits of paper, and whether high' or not, George sang the song from beginning to end, creating the lyrics out of thin air as he went along. The Dutch sound engineer and I looked at each other both blown away as were the rest of the band on returning from the restaurant an hour or so later.

A few months later, by now working in Switzerland with Arif, emotionally George was hanging on by the barest thread with Jon and was clearly out of his mind with a serious drug habit in full flow. Consequently, he seemed incapable of performing the song with anything like the depth, tunefulness and sensitivity of the Dutch demo. In the end, I suggested to Arif that we perhaps fly in George's original performance on to our new Montreux version of the backing track.

***

Arriving at the house that had been rented for my family on a Swiss mountainside to begin recording, Ann and the boys were exhausted after the long drive through France. It was in the dead of night when we arrived, so we all crashed out. To the kids' horror, looking out of the window of the creepy Gothic mansion the next morning, they realised we'd been asleep all night in the middle of a sprawling Swiss graveyard. This felt ominous right from the start, but at the time I didn't know why (or more likely didn't want to!)

For all kinds of reasons, financial, emotional and cultural, the four individual members of Culture Club were now living in different countries, continents and time zones pursuing their various enthusiasms and tax schemes individually. In effect, and out of perceived necessity, they'd become separated by the success they'd created together. What accountants and managers never seem to realise back then with their clever schemes, was that by separating and isolating the very individuals who had created the success in the first place, they were killing the golden goose. In Culture Club's case, the most damaging aspect of this particular regime was that it set George free to go off under the radar and exploit his huge celebrity, wealth and indulgences with wild abandon. And the 'Boy' was never known for doing anything by halves! Already underway, therefore, was the most damaging, disjointed and dysfunctional period for George, and thus his band. Looking back, clearly the 'fin de siecle', or end game of Culture Club's eighties reign. In many ways, it would be curtains for me too although I didn't know it yet.

George and Jon's relationship, as my dear Gran might have put it was, "all over bar the shouting", although in their case, shouting seemed to have been from the outset, the all-pervading backdrop to their entire affair. In what would become painfully apparent to the world in the months to come and as had been privately predicted from the beginning, George and Jon's final bust up and in particular, the former's growing dependence on industrial supplies of non-prescribed drugs, signalled the coming end of the group, at least for many painful years to come.

Although Arif was supremely patient and non-judgemental about George's increasingly erratic behaviour, it was difficult to see how we could ever finish the record. For one thing, George kept disappearing off to London as, in his own words; "The only thing you could score in Montreux was cheese!" There were some fabulous moments with Arif in Switzerland however, even though one felt the earth imperceptibly shifting and doubts growing as to how the band could possibly go on working together after this experience. In addition the strange labyrinthine set-up of Queen's Mountain Studios; small windowless rooms connected to vast gambling casino halls, only available on certain days for recording, all added to a peculiar disconnected and claustrophobic atmosphere and a stifling cloak over the entire recording project.

George's transvestite friends along with some other very dubious characters kept turning up at all hours of the day and night in the otherwise buttoned-down, straight-laced Swiss town, providing a seedy contrast to its more regular, chocolate, cuckoo-clock affluence. As I was now co-writing all of the songs for Culture Club and thus playing more of a central role in the overall recording project, in retrospect I must have been living more in hope and denial about just how dysfunctional and out of control everything was becoming under the surface. As the band now seemed to be coming and going most of the time, now living with their families in different parts of the world, my position within the organisation (if one could call it that by this stage), seemed to have unwittingly grown into that of a de facto production supervisor and go-between. Arif nicknamed me 'Herr Kapellmeister' (The Choirmaster) and as he was about to leave for New York, presented me with a picture he'd painted as a gift to celebrate the end of the *From Luxury To Heartache* sessions at Mountain Studios. It still hangs on my wall and is one of my most revered possessions.

'Move Away' was immediately picked out as the first single and universally considered a welcome return to form after the perceived creative failures of the previous album. The record, with the vocal I'd recorded with George in Holland, began climbing up the charts all over the world, up to number 7 in the UK and 12 in America, and was still picking up steam, great reviews and airplay.

In spite of the many rumblings of discontent, relationship breakdowns, division within the band and George's newly discovered obsession with hard drugs, together we had created, what we all felt was a very fine album under the circumstances.

Driving at speed along the tree-lined, sunlit roads of France back to England, I thought I was sitting pretty; pension fund and kids' school fees assured, stock and property portfolios moving upward and a writing share on almost all of the songs on Culture Club's new album.

What was there not to feel good about?

Chapter 30
The Cutter

Things couldn't really have been any better throughout 1985. I was touring with the biggest band on the planet and by now, co-writing some of their biggest hits. The success of our US tour was being followed by ITV's News at Ten practically every night as Culture Club took America and the world by storm. Back in England, my kids were allowed to stay up if we were on TV that night. Ann, the boys and I had not long moved into a beautiful five bedroom dream house at 44 Teddington Park not long after I'd signed an eye-watering publishing contract with Warner Brothers. Only a few weeks earlier I'd been on tour in the USA, where Quincy Jones had personally informed me that "Karma" was Number 1 in America. My timing in the music business hadn't always been that great, but this time I knew I'd hit the jackpot with all my ducks in a beautiful row.

As I sat down with my lawyer in the Warners office in London to negotiate the deal, "Karma" had been Number 1 in America for three weeks and also in practically every other country in the world. Johnny Stirling, my friend and publisher at Pendulum Music, not only on the strength and timing of "Karma's" huge success but also his exceptional existing catalogue, had now sold his company to Warners. Luckily for me, he had also been made its joint managing director. "Name a figure Phil, let's just get it done, shall we? Then let's go and have some lunch!" Johnny said smiling broadly while slapping the Warners chequebook on his desk. Brandishing a stylish, exclusive, fountain pen (as Johnny's ancestral home was Stirling Castle in Scotland, no doubt a priceless heirloom), he proceeded to write out a princely cheque.

A few days later, my accountant, Richard Rosenberg rang. He asked me if I was sitting down and then quietly informed me (although he knew me better!) that if diligent and careful I would never have to trouble myself about financial matters ever again. "Congratulations Phil, I know it hasn't always been easy for you but you really deserve this. Well done and bloody well done to Ann too!" I was gobsmacked and indeed, did have to sit down for a while. I'd finally "made a million" from a perilous and often challenging industry and from doing something I loved. I felt like a very lucky man!

Richard had seen so many of my ups and downs since the Sailor days and had stuck with me like glue through thick, thin and no doubt, many unpaid bills. I was just coming up to forty and if I'd ever had time to think along the way, would never have believed I could have entertained such a secret quixotic ambition for one minute having left school with drab expectations and even worse qualifications. Universities wouldn't have touched me with a barge pole!

'Uncle Phil', the late Philip Sutton and my mother's secret 'L'amour' always said that if music didn't work out, I could always go back to baking bread. I can still hear his wise and supportive words; "If you get stuck Philip, there'll always be plenty of dough in this game!" So for a pillar-to-post Brummie lad without a dad to have come this far as a direct result of my musical adventures since arriving in London fifteen years earlier was a humbling experience of deep and enduring gratitude which I admit here for the first time, moved me to tears.

For most of my life money always seemed tight. Now finally we had some breathing space and could have a bit of fun without worrying all the time (not that we ever did much of that, even when living like church mice!) We now had the dream house, a detached beauty which had featured on the front cover of a *Homes & Gardens* magazine, lovely convertible cars on the drive and our boys, Gus and Jack in excellent private schools. Our friends were superbly supportive and enjoyed sharing in this exciting new adventure almost as much as we did.

Observing our changing fortunes they had known all too well how hard it had been to get here. Inevitably I suppose there are always one or two who fall by the wayside, finding it a little harder to come to terms with the conspicuous success of a friend; understandable I guess. After all, you want your mates to do well, but that friggin' well?

Offers of work were now coming in left, right and centre, so it was looking like I'd soon need my own studio. I was still on tour with Culture Club most of the time so how was it going to be possible to find the time to do that? On the eve of yet another jaunt to Australia, the Far East and wherever else my employers decided to go next, Ann took me along to view a charming, but completely dilapidated, ruin of a 19th-century coach house she'd found just opposite Mark Bolan's old house in Kings Road, East Sheen.

The place was all but falling down with an overgrown walled garden at the front of the property which might just as well have been the movie set for *Day Of The Triffids*! The tumbledown hovel was basically a two up one down garage building which had been used as a sculptor's studio since the First World War. This was a good thing as we would presumably be able to change the official usage of what was already a commercial building; from sculptor's studio to music studio.

But like all wildly eccentric schemes and ideas, such a project would also have been very time-consuming and tricky to get the i's dotted, t's crossed and everything sorted. Not that this would normally put off two cock-eyed optimists, but I was about to go off on tour again the very next morning so we really had no time.

Pity, as in spite of the mess the place seemed perfect for requirements and didn't think it would hang around too long in that area, and at that price. Never mind, duty called, I had to go and anyway, we'd probably find other places. On the one or two quiet moments that I did have to myself whilst on tour though, a feeling inside told me I might have missed out on an exciting opportunity; but then again thought of my songwriter mate, Terry Britten and his Ozzie-philosophical words on this kind of stuff; "Don't worry mate, if it ain't for ya, it'll go by ya!" On one of my calls home to Ann late one night, three weeks into the long tour, from a far away time zone, I expressed regret at missing the chance. "Do you think it might have gone?" I asked her forlornly, "Yes, I think it has darling. Someone put in an offer apparently and their arm nearly got bitten off!"

On my return to England a few weeks later at the end of Culture Club's tour, Ann's smile was even wider than usual when she came to meet me at Heathrow. So much so I kept asking her what was going on; "Where are we going?" I said, "We don't usually come home this way." "Wait and see", she said teasingly, "Don't be so impatient, anyway, you don't have to know everything." But at what should have been the turning to our home, she carried on, all the way, in fact, to Kings Road in East Sheen. While pulling up outside the old coach house gates, Ann handed me some keys.

"There you are, it's all yours!" she said proudly beaming like an angel. "What!" I was speechless and completely blown away. She'd only gone ahead and bought it while I was away!

Along with my fortieth surprise birthday when I'd turned up to a house full of my favourite people bursting out of cupboards at Teddington Park, this was one of the best surprises of my life. I was overjoyed at the possibilities of having a place like this and although there was a huge amount of work to be done, you kind of know in your bones when something you really want lands in your lap and it feels right.

So many songs would be written there and so many great artists would be associated with this little building; revealing vignettes, glimpses and short stories featured in this book were all inspired by that little creative bolthole. Take That, Robbie Williams, Culture Club, Sir Paul McCartney, Brian Kennedy, Toyah, Malcolm McLaren, Labi Siffre, Terence Trent D'Arby, Sailor and AC/DC to name but a few, in what we now look back on as the Golden Age of Pop music; the barnstorming, hit-making, gender-bending eighties.

Post-Culture Club and moving on from the late eighties, The Cutter, as my new studio was now named, was not just a private song sanctuary where I could write music to my heart's content, but also with other accomplished and brilliant songwriters such as Albert Hammond, Frank Musker, Jon Lind, Terry Britten, Toyah and others. The studio also became a private retreat for other producers and bands to rent when I was away or taking part in recording projects and sessions elsewhere.

Rising star producer Spike Stent who pre-produced many artists including

Terence Trent D'Arby often worked at The Cutter, and also legendary US producer and dear chum, the late Phil Ramone, through whom I ended up meeting and working with Paul McCartney. Malcolm and Angus Young of AC/DC also started regularly booking the little studio bang under Heathrow's flight path.

The Rapino Brothers, Charlie and Marco were just starting out in London producing in those days and one day Charlie Rapino called and asked if he could bring a new boyband called Take That over to do some vocal work. They'd already had a couple of hits and were all over the media, radio and TV. "Jon Moss told us you were great at vocal arrangements, and as it's not really our thing, would it be okay if we left them with you for a few days?" he explained. "We just don't have the patience!"

Prior to their arrival, Take That's manager, Nigel Martin Smith came over to discuss what he was expecting from the sessions, namely, to push Robbie into more of a front man role for the group. At that time, Gary Barlow, as Charlie explained; "The plump one who plays keyboards and the only songwriter" was singing lead on everything. But most of the girls who came to their shows were going nuts over Robbie. "He doesn't sing too good though and lacks confidence, Phil. Can you help him?" "Sure, send them over," I said. A condition of the booking was that we were to tell absolutely no one the band were coming as fans had been known to storm buildings and create havoc. Everywhere they went there were horrendous problems with security once the word got out.

"Well, there's a girls school just around the corner, so don't worry, we'll be incredibly careful and won't tell a soul!" I assured their manager. All the more surprising and frankly irritating, as when they finally arrived at Kings Road the five young lads pulled up in a black stretch-limo, practically half the length of the street. There were also security beefcakes in black coats running around everywhere with walkie-talkies and earpieces. Several of the suits then conspicuously stood on guard outside the Cutter's gates looking suspiciously up and down the road and muttering into mouthpieces. They may as well have shouted from the rooftops with a megaphone; "OVER HERE EVERYONE, POP STARS IN THE BUILDING, OKAY?" The only thing missing from the tableau was a couple of hovering helicopters above.

The band, impervious to the mayhem around them, all bounded in like young puppies, interested in everything, asking countless questions and immediately nicknaming me "Boss". They were a delightful bunch of young guys, obviously not long out of school, who immediately seemed to appreciate the peace of our old English walled-garden and the private surroundings; a brief respite from the otherwise constant and frenetic madness their lives had recently become.

"I'd love a place like this to write one day Phil", Gary said, cheerily looking in and out of the different rooms and spaces, "It's brilliant mate!" It didn't look as though he'd have to wait that long. Gary was the natural leader of the group, no question and certainly possessed the most honed professionalism - 'chops' if you like of all of them. He was clearly the only real muso and exuded an easygoing authority, especially when he sat down at the piano to play a new composition he'd just written. Wow, the boy could actually play! It was a masterful performance but for the longevity of the band in a fickle teenage market, I could also appreciate why their manager might want the others, particularly Robbie to similarly shine and come to the fore. Especially as he was the one most of the young girls were screaming over at their live shows. "Right then", I said, "Shall we get to work?" "Yes Boss," they said in unison.

"We'll start with Robbie then, come with me mate," I said, guiding him into the vocal booth adjacent to the Cutter's small control room; making sure he was comfortable with the earphones and volume, I attempted to put him at ease in front of Gary and the others. Now that the focus was all on him, he seemed self-conscious and bashful. I sent him the song Charlie and Marco had been working on and although in tune most of the time, Robbie was hesitant looking very nervous, and as Charlie had mentioned, lacking in confidence. His vocal sound was like a caricature of Marti Pellow from Wet, Wet, Wet, obviously not yet having found a real voice of his own. "Is that okay boss?" he said at the end of the take.

There was a little tension in the room initially as Gary, who could sing the phone book with his eyes closed and still sound like, well Gary, was showing Robbie the ropes - what he thought might be the best way to approach the song. Although not on purpose, his words of advice were putting even more pressure on his band mate, who after all at this stage of his career was not used to being in a recording studio at all, an experience many find intimidating at first. I could see it wasn't going to work so I sent Gary scuttling off with the others into the green room upstairs, leaving us on our own in the studio. As Robbie was temporarily busy with me, the rest of the boys, Howard, Mark and Jason now joined by Gary, were busy playing computer games and teaching Jack and Gus some of their dance moves upstairs.

"We're just dancers" Jason Orange confided. "At the auditions, Gary was the only one in the group who could really sing." "And play anything," Mark added. "Yeh, but I can't dance for shit!" Gary interjected, amongst much Mancunian laughter. They really were a lovely bunch of innocent lads at the start of a very bright career and I had a lot of time for them. "Look Robbie," I said, back in the studio now, just the two of us. "You have a great range and can really hold a tune but what we're going to do is find out who the real Robbie Williams is inside of that noddle and bring him out, okay? He's in there somewhere, I promise you." "Yes boss," he said, "let's give it a go mate." He seemed to be more than willing to try anything.

The young Williams was clearly a brilliant mimic who could copy almost anyone in pop, but so far the distinctive power and singular character one could tell he was capable of providing, was teasingly still just over the horizon. We kept plugging away for a couple of hours at least and then continued our work over the next few days. Robbie's stamina and drive to learn, now he was being given his first real chance to come to the fore, was affecting and impressive.

In that situation, when working closely with vocalists, it's more about getting the artist to completely relax and imagine themselves on stage, or in various scenarios in life and above all, connecting with their emotions. For instance, I encouraged Robbie to think of the very best thing that had ever happened to him in his life; to hold onto that thought and then to try a pass of the song with the resulting emotion clearly expressed on his face. Judging by the instant goofy grin however it was quite obvious, not only that he was taking what I'd said very seriously, but that whatever lustful and promiscuous event he was conjuring up to prove my theory had only just taken place the previous evening; "Well perhaps not too literally Robbie", I said as the quick-learning apprentice star from Stoke-on-Trent fell about laughing his head off. Whilst not yet the distinctive signature voice we would all come to know and many of us love, it was as if a light had gone on inside his head and the difference in his vocal sound compared to just a couple of hours before was palpable.

I played his earlier attempts back to him, followed by the most recent and his face lit up again. "Bloody hell boss! Can we try some more tomorrow?" he said calling upstairs to the others to come and have a listen. Over the few precious days they were at the Cutter we made great progress and although I'd happily take credit for helping Robbie discover his unique vocal blueprint, which he undoubtedly managed eventually, it would be pushing things by a huge margin to suggest it was anyone other than Robbie who eventually found what he was looking for, his own signature voice.

In a chance meeting as I was leaving the Groucho Club a few years later, around the time of his massive, co-written hit, 'Angels' he clearly hadn't forgotten his experience at the Cutter. "Hey boss, you were right!" Robbie shouted to me over the hurly-burly of the club's entrance hall, "I found it in the end, didn't I... me voice!" he said proudly, flashing me a huge Robbie grin as the crowd he was with spilt out onto Dean Street. "It was in the old noddle all the time just like you said, mate!"

Labi Siffre

One of my earliest writing assignments now that I was fully operational at Kings Road Sheen was when an industry friend, Bob Grace at China Records suggested I should get together and write a song with one of his artists, Labi

Siffre. I'd always been a huge fan of Labi's voice and his shining integrity as an artist and therefore waited for him to arrive at my studio with a degree of nervous anticipation. 'Something Inside So Strong' as well many other wonderful songs of his was among my favourites and although nervous, I realised how privileged I was to be able to work with such a great songwriter and musician. I recalled the earliest days of my career at E.H Morris with Mickey Clarke in 1969, where, as a budding songwriter I witnessed for myself the reverence shown by BBC producers whenever Labi's name was mentioned.

As usual, as on any special writing assignment, I'd pre-prepared a couple of ideas that inspired me, one of which I was particularly pleased with. The groove had a Marvin Gaye 'Sexual Healing' vibe about it with a Roland 808 reggae-ish beatbox feel. Labi was quiet, self-effacing, charming - but very tired, having driven all the way to London, non-stop from the Brecon Beacons in Wales in his Mini, albeit a very posh and souped-up version. He was reserved too; thoughtful and wasn't really sure if he liked the track at first. "Yes, this is great Phil, your top line's good too. I might change it around a bit though, mind if I take it with me?" "Take it with you?" I said. "You've only just arrived, where are you going then?" "Back home to Wales, I'll have it written by the time I'm home," he said, "I'll fax you the results!" "Wow, okay."

Truthfully at first, I suspected it may have been the ruse of a painfully shy artist just wanting to get the hell away at any cost. Maybe he loathed the track but didn't want to say, the cut of my jib or just hated my brand of coffee. True to his word, however, much later in the early evening I recall, I watched the following lyric slowly tumbling out of my fax machine and tearing it from the machine, was dumbstruck by the power, compassion and sentiment of his words:

LISTEN TO THE VOICES

Old man
Your race is run
You think it's over
It's only begun
A child is born
Who has to face
The world you're leaving,
A dangerous place

Listen to the voices
Crying to be free
Can we be the promise that we promised to be?

Love and understanding
Are better than a war
People just laughing 'cause they've heard it before

Night chills
In 'Plenty Town'
Cardboard hotels
They sleep on the ground
Hard choices
How to respond
Red or rosé
With the Duck à l'orange

Listen To The Voices
So easy to ignore
Choruses of old folk scared to open the door
Living in the shadows
And dying in the cold
Inner city jungle ain't no place to grow old

Helpless
We'll never be
Though justice
Is so hard to see
Kindness, yes
That same old song
But don't stop singing
There's so much strength in kindness. .

Listen to the voices
Crying to be free
Can we be the promise that we promised to be?
Love and understanding
Are better than a war
People just laughing 'cause they've heard it before

© Labi Siffre / Phil Pickett. Reproduced with kind permission of BMG/Chrysalis Music and Imagem Music Publishers.

We finished the demo a few weeks later, after which Labi recorded a more serious and gospel-like version of 'Voices' for his own album in Los Angeles. It was the first track on *So Strong* and was released in 1989. A little later, Jamaican reggae and dancehall musician Junior Reid, the ex-lead Black Uhuru vocalist, covered 'Listen To The Voices' in Kingston, Jamaica where it was a massive hit throughout the Caribbean during the summer of 1996. Reid's version was based more on the reggae-style, voicing and arrangement of my original demo, but in whatever style the song was recorded, 'Listen To The Voices' makes me proud every time I hear it and remains up there among the best songs I have ever written.

***

Whilst staying out in Los Angeles at Frank Musker's wonderful house, built around a redwood tree in Laurel Canyon L.A. in 1988 with my new buddy and writing partner Jon Lind, we enjoyed some legendary times and wrote some terrific songs together, one of which was called, 'More Than A Lifetime'. A few months earlier, I'd come up with a melody in my head whilst walking along the street on my way to seeing Steve Winwood at the Albert Hall near our flat in Queensgate. When I got to L.A., I played the idea to Jon who was incredibly enthusiastic and suggested the title.

The demo of this song, completed with Frank Musker and Elizabeth Lamer's superb backing vocals at Frank's studio in Laurel Canyon, was one of many tunes I played to Simon Fuller several years later when the entrepreneurial genius, turned music publisher came to visit me at my studio in Sheen. This was at a time when most of the big major music publishing houses had stopped offering the kind of deals that a few lucky writers, myself included, had come to rely on as part of their livelihood. Fuller liked the songs and said he'd offer me a deal.

He must have listened to at least thirty demos and works-in-progress and seemed to be able to differentiate and remember each and every one of them with an instant recall that was impressive. "What was that song about the fourth or fifth in you played last week, something to do with life, or lifetime?" he asked when calling me a couple of days later. "That's it", he said, "There's a brilliant artist I manage called Brian Kennedy and the song could be ideal for him."

Fuller called back and said that Brian loved the tune, but ideally would like to change some of the lyrics. All of them in fact! At first, I was taken aback as I knew how much work Jon and I had put into the original and how pleased we were with the finished result.

I told him it might be tricky, thinking more about Jon's likely reaction. "He's had some huge hits like 'Boogie Wonderland' and Madonna's 'Crazy For You'" but I said we'd at least talk it over and come back to him. Jon was a pussycat however and went along with the idea, although he hammered out the business dealings with Fuller very carefully. Brian eventually submitted some superb lyrics for the tune; after all, he had only wanted to personalise the work for himself in order to relate to it better as an artist. When Jon and I heard him sing our track with his new words, we were blown away! What a voice, it was beautiful.

> *Open your eyes*
> *Say what you say and I'll listen*
> *For a while*
> *Where is your smile?*
> *The one that reminds me to whisper*
> *Like a child*
> *How can we stay strong?*
> *Now hope is gone*
>
> *Give me a reason*
> *I can believe in*
> *Help me to be the best I can*
> *Give me a feeling*
> *The love that I'm needing to make me*
> *A better man*
>
> *Will it be there*
> *The taste that reminds me I missed you*
> *All this time?*
> *You know I still care*
> *I'm walking around in a circle*
> *Like I'm blind*
> *Oh it's been so long*
> *But I'm holding on...*

Brian and his producer, Steve Lipson, asked me down to his studio in Willesden to play Hammond organ and mandolin on the eventual master recording. With the Irish singer's glorious vocal on top, 'A Better Man', the first single from Brian's new album shot up to the top of the charts in his native Ireland, staying at Number 1 for many weeks. Visiting Dublin a few months later with Ann for a meeting with Westlife's manager, the highly-strung and often disappearing Louis Walsh, we were treated like royalty by the Irish in every hotel bar, taxi cab and club we entered; Brian Kennedy, already a star was now a national hero.

Spotted by Belfast-born (now fellow SOD), Van Morrison, Brian Kennedy joined Van's renowned Blues and Soul World Tour, performing with many legends of the music industry including, Joni Mitchell, Ray Charles and Bob Dylan. Wider recognition of Brian's exceptional vocal talent came when he was asked by Van to record the soundtrack version of 'Crazy Love' for the film *When A Man Loves a Woman*, based on the huge sixties hit that my old mate Percy Sledge had made famous.

After the incomparable success of the single, Brian's album, also named A Better Man soared to No.1 in the Irish album chart earning quadruple platinum status. He received an Irish Music Industry Award (IRMA) for Best Irish Male Album and a Hot Press/2TV Award for Best Irish Male Artist, all of which Jon and I were immensely proud to have played a part in helping him achieve. I have rarely if ever, met a warmer, more kind and prodigiously talented vocalist in my life than Brian "Voice of an Angel" Kennedy.

In August 2017, just after delivering this book to my publisher, in celebration, Ann and I went up to meet Brian at the Edinburgh Festival to catch him on tour, his voice sounding as glorious as ever. The title of our song, and of his latest tour was even more auspicious as he had just recovered from a bout of cancer.

In 1988 having achieved, or rather Johnny Stirling having achieved on my behalf a rather spectacular publishing deal with MCA Music, the boys, Ann and I were spending so much time out in L.A. at Frank Musker's Laurel Canyon hideout, replete with its own 24-track recording studio that, for all intents and purposes (or "porpoises" as Ann's late dad Bob Sinsheimer used to say, being a Brooklyn man!) we'd practically moved in.

During this period, while trying to become established as a songwriter in L.A., my buddy Jon Lind was similarly staying at our flat in Queensgate with his family and doing the same in London. BA Robertson, my very old friend from E.H Morris days, was also living in L.A. at this time, just up the road as it happened, from Frank in the same Canyon. One morning, prior to a writing session he rang me: "Hey mate, I've been up all night writing a song about my dad" he told me. I was already aware that his father, with whom he'd always had a somewhat challenging relationship had recently died. "I think I'm onto something Phil, will you come up here and give it a listen? I'd be interested to hear what you think." He sat down at the piano and in a faltering and emotional voice sang 'The Living Years' in its entirety. At the end of the song, he turned towards me but I was too moved to speak. "I'm sorry, my voice isn't really up to it this morning, I've been up all night writing the bloody thing!" "I don't care B.A, that's one of the best songs I've ever heard," I said while wiping a warm tear from my eye. "I don't know what to say, but what a sentiment! I don't think anyone's written about that subject before and it's going to affect so many people when they hear it." I congratulated him on having written something that would be heard and celebrated all around the world; BA had truly done his old dad proud.

The following year, back in London after hearing the Genesis guitarist Mike Rutherford speaking on the radio about his song 'The Living Years', a song he'd written in honour of his deceased father and of their relationship, but with no mention of B.A, I was perplexed and called B.A to tell him. "I know Phil, don't ask mate!" he said despondently. "As you well know, if you're a songwriter that's what you have to put up with sometimes to get your song recorded. I ended up with a 50:50 split with the royalties. "Perhaps," I said, "but you wrote that song in its entirety, I heard it for myself on the morning you wrote it."

When back in Hollywood the following year on another writing trip, BA, now a creative director at Disney Pictures, rang me again; 'The Living Years' is bloody number one in America!" he said jubilantly, pleased as punch, as well he might have been. Chris Neil had produced a blinder of a track for Mike and the Mechanics. "And you're coming to my celebration party on Sunset Strip tonight!" It was a riotous and unforgettable night of bun fights, victorious ribaldry, dubious humour and much drink, during which his old mate and fellow countryman, Rod Stewart, got up and gave a speech... "It gives me a modicum of pleasure to congratulate a fellow Scottish git upon having written a half-decent tune for a change, the title of which, er, temporarily escapes me, hang on a minute (much fumbling around with pieces of paper and glasses) ah yes, 'The Living Room'..."

In order to take up the invitation to BA's do, Tim Rice, who had been attending the opening of one of his shows in Las Vegas earlier that evening, had thrown caution to the wind by hiring a private jet to attend the party. The latter stages of BA's do involved those more refreshed singing vulgar rugby songs at the top of their voices, while for some inexplicable reason, encircling the normally exclusive members club with chairs on the top of their heads. That is until we were finally kicked out of the club at 3 am.

The late Phil Ramone, whose wife Karen Kamon had recorded a song of mine called 'Don't Just Stand There, Do Something To Me' arranged to meet me at the Rennaisance Hotel in LA and said he'd like me to write songs with Peter Noone. "He's got his own show on US TV which is huge, still has an amazing voice and is one of the best entertainers I've ever seen".

Although I knew Peter from Herman's Hermits days and appreciated his distinctive vocal style, this was rare praise indeed from the producer of Billy Joel, Paul Simon and Paul McCartney. The tale epitomises for me how the music industry really was, "back in the day" and how wild flights of creative fancy, with no expense spared and in many cases, with no possible hope of recoupment to spoil the fun often happened like this right out of the blue!

At the time we were still living in Strawberry Hill, from where the limo picked me up to go to the Virgin First Class Lounge at London's Heathrow Airport. I told Ann that as far as I knew I'd be back in around 4-5 days but that it would depend on how things were going. My instructions from Phil and the record label were to go to New York, get picked up in one of Ramone's cars at JFK Airport and then taken up to Phil and Karen's mansion in Bedford, upstate New York where I would meet Peter.

I knew the place well as I often stayed with Phil and his family when in New York. "Just come here and chill out with Peter for a few days Phil and we'll get some songs started, you and he are going to get on great, I just know it." Phil had said. When I arrived, however, there had obviously been a sudden change of plan. Peter was, as Phil had assured me, absolutely delightful, charming and very funny and we instantly got on a treat, almost as though we were old friends.

His Northern humour was sublime, to which of course I instantly related. "Look, Phil, I know you've only just walked in the door, but I've just been offered this gig on a brand new ocean liner that's sailing around the Caribbean from Barbados tomorrow, Dionne Warwick and John Denver are on there too and I'm third on the bill," he said. "The thing is," he went on, "I've got a first-class cabin for you too and thought we could just write songs the rest of the time." He made it sound so reasonable, practical almost. "What was there not to like?" I thought. "Besides, I'm only on stage for half an hour a night so we'll have plenty of time," Peter explained. "The thing is," he added, "There's a private jet waiting down at JFK Airport for us, so if you and Phil don't mind, we'll have to get back in the car again and hotfoot it down there!" I looked over at Phil, who also seemed entirely unfazed by the abrupt change of plan as if it was the most normal thing in the world. "Sure, let's do it, it makes total sense," I said, looking at Phil for encouragement and to make sure he really didn't mind. He didn't.

We had a riotous time on the Learjet on the way down to Barbados, whereupon we were whisked off to the harbour and to the waiting, brand new glorious ocean liner on its maiden voyage. My cabin was, in fact, a suite of rooms and thought that so far, all was extremely jolly. Tired from the journey, however, Peter suggested that as he had the first of his three shows that night, he would rest up in his cabin and that we could try some writing either after the show or the next day while sailing to Antigua. Sounds good, I thought and went along that evening to see him perform.

Although technically third on the bill, Peter Noone was, as Phil Ramone had first told me, a totally captivating and extremely funny performer and a real natural up there on stage. He soon had the audiences eating out of his hand and frankly, although Denver and Warwick were excellent, if not a little predictable, (Loved his version of 'Jet Plane' though!) Peter's natural warmth wiped the floor with them. He liked to enjoy himself after a show, however, as I must admit, by reputation, so did I, another thing we seemed to have in common. So over many stories and much genuine hilarity, as the evenings progressed, the potential hit songwriting team of Noone/Pickett became extremely refreshed.

It was the same on the second day, as obviously after the previous night's escapades, both of us this time needed our beauty sleep. By the third day however, without having as much as even looked at a piano, plucked a guitar, or scribbled on a blank sheet of paper, it was looking as if the charts might have to wait a just little longer to be graced by a Noone/Pickett composition - but that one day perhaps a book might be written to tell the tale!

On the fourth day, Peter had to leave to attend another show in California, so like something out of a bad *Carry On* movie and to the consternation and amusement of beach bums and sun-seekers, the two of us were unceremoniously ejected from the ship's nether regions via a rowing boat! We were then obliged to remove our socks and shoes in order to disembark with our suitcases onto the beach, hailed a cab and went to the airport.

At the Waldorf Astoria Hotel in New York sometime later on, due to lack of availability, Peter and I were obliged to share the last available room in New York. This in itself was hilarious as the Concierge was obviously convinced we were a couple of gay limey antique dealers. Needless to say, we did nothing to disavow him of that notion whilst rinsing the minibar and staying up all night telling stories and falling about laughing. I finally arrived home in London six days later not having written a note of music. But I'd had one of the best times of my life in limos, Learjets and ocean liners with my new friend, Peter Noone, a most remarkable man. "Did you write many songs with Peter on your trip", my publisher asked me reasonably upon my return; "No, not that many this time," I said.

***

AC/DC

Malcolm Young from AC/DC called me at The Cutter one day to see if he could come over and take a look at the studio. They were looking for a new place to work in the UK. The group were already, arguably the greatest Rock 'n' Roll band of all time and even at that stage had sold over a hundred and fifty million albums. We had loads to talk about as I'd worked with Mal and Angus's older brother, George, along with his partner Harry Vanda in the very early seventies when a bunch of us were signed to E.H. Morris.

"Yeah, he's always goin' on about his days in London", Mal drawled, in his laconic Ozzie accent, "and the late-sixties when Crosby Stills and Nash formed their band in George's Bayswater flat in Moscow Road," he recalled.

"It's just a bit small here for you guys, that's my only worry," I said, not wanting to put him off, but also not wanting to piss him off, when he eventually realised the place was so small you had to go outside to change your mind. Besides, we'd only really bought it as a writing studio for one, or at the most, a couple of other musicians and writers to work in.

When he, Angus and the others showed up, I was struck at how small they all were; like jockeys, short, skinny and wiry as hell; "We love it mate! It's a beaut," Mal said. "We'll start next week if that's okay Phil". Due to their phenomenal worldwide success and reputation as a band, I suppose I might have expected him to arrive in an opulent limo of some description, darkened windows and the like, but not a bit of it. As I talked him in on our mobile phones, Mal pulled up in an unkempt Jaguar XJ6, which must have been at least twelve years old, rusting wheel arches and a metal coat hanger for an aerial, unostentatious to a fault: Nothing flashy or mindful of status. They didn't need it I guess, they were so far beyond all that and probably the most successful rock band of all time bar the Stones; certainly louder!

Angus and Mal would take days; weeks even to get a riff sounding perfect; debate intricately and endlessly about the amp sound or exact model of guitar or the combinations of either that would deliver the killer rock sound they were after; AC/DC's Holy Grail. I was utterly fascinated by their approach to everything. The two brothers were more like scientists, serious and studious, chasing down the ultimate rock 'n' roll sound to oblivion with silent but deadly determination. Some days they wouldn't show up at all, others for a couple of hours only, but by paying top dollar and then some for the privilege, I wasn't allowed to touch the faders, wires, knobs or anything else in the studio. Fair enough and fine by me. Financially they were dream clients and anyway, by this stage I was getting on with other projects, like Keziah Jones (to which I will return later).

As Eric Clapton was resting during this period, his trusty guitar tech, Alan Rogan, was looking after the AC/DC lads at Sheen. When there was not much for Alan to do, which was quite often, in many ways recalling the same mindset of Spinal Tap, the movie which famously satirised rock 'n' roll bands of a certain era, in AC/DC's case, with money being absolutely no object, Angus and Mal would often invent random things for Rogan to go off and do for them.

With a fag hanging from his lips in time-honoured style, Angus Young said to Alan one day; "Hey mate, I want you to rent a van and go up to Bassett's Licorice Allsorts Factory in Sheffield and get 'em to do an industrial quantity of them little bastard allsorts; you know, the blue ones wi' the little sprinkly blue stuff on 'em." "Yeh, they're our favourites" agreed Mal. Without batting an eyelid or questioning the bizarre and random request whatsoever, Alan took off as if it was the most natural thing in the world to be asked to do. "Sure Angus," he said. "It'll probably take a couple of days though. I'll book a driver and get a hotel up there." "Okay mate, see ya' then," Angus said, casually now preoccupied with tuning his guitar. A few days later Alan proudly returned to Sheen with the enormous consignment of, "the little blue bastards", half a van load of boxes wrapped in all of the proper Liquorice Allsorts packagings. Cost being of no consideration whatsoever, the factory had run a special all-night shift to manufacture AC/DC's unusual order. "Cheers mate, stick it in the shed outside would you, there's not much room in here!" Mal said laughing, but then added, "Oh shit, Alan, I forgot, I should have asked! They make Benson and Hedges ciggies up there too, don't they?" Alan's face dropped, I think he knew where this was going. "Listen, give 'em a call and go up there again okay? Last time they did us a special run of Benson and Hedges Gold but with an additional 20 per cent of nicotine in 'em, do you remember? We got ten thousand didn't we Angus?" "Yeah," Angus recalled, still puffing on one of them.

Weeks and months went by and the guys were slowly taking over the whole building. My office was upstairs next to the green room, and one day, Mal came up to see me; "Listen mate, we love working here and we're getting a great sound, but we're running out of space for the amps downstairs. Mind if I get a carpenter in and build a couple of soundproof boxes for the amps up here in your office?" A team of specialist shop fitters arrived next day and soon my office was completely taken over by huge, immaculately crafted boxes, all wired through to the old Amek Angela desk in the studio downstairs. It amused me no end to realise that some of the most blood-curdling rock 'n' roll the world was ever likely to hear was being produced inches away from where I was making my calls. Also that my sedate, retired and refined neighbours, pruning their roses next door, had no idea that the loudest band on the planet was thrashing out its music only feet away. After nine months or so of AC/DC's rental of the Cutter, the presence of the imposing sound boxes was beginning to take on an air of permanence.

"You live in Aberystwyth?" I asked incredulously as I knew AC/DC's drum roadie, Skum, couldn't drive, "...and the band's storage facility, where they keep all their stage equipment, is at Diss in Norfolk?" I'd observed that this was the entire width of the country and not served by any direct routes. "Yeah", Skum answered as if it was the most normal thing in the world. "That's right, I get a train to London and then hire a driver and van to take me up to Diss, then down to Sheen again with what they need on the van, then travel back home on the train to Aberystwyth," he said cheerfully, wondering what my point was. So just to get an amp or some drums down to the studio in London for the band must have involved around three or four days wages and travelling the breadth of the country, van hire, drivers, fuel, hotels and other expenses.

Genuinely curious, nosey perhaps, I raised the expense and time-consuming impracticality of this arrangement with Mal one morning over a cup of tea; "Why not just get a drum roadie from London who can drive, send him up to Diss and then back again with everything you need? It'd only take a few hours, you'd save about three days and three days-worth of costs that way too," I opined reasonably. Mal stared vacantly into space for a minute or two, unable to comprehend, or even particularly care about logic applied in such a non-rock 'n' roll manner. "Yeah, but Skum's never been able to drive and he lives in Aberystwyth," he explained. "Right," I said.

"How long you think you might be staying here at Sheen?" I asked Mal one morning during one of our lengthy conversations about life and the music biz over coffee. Although it was brilliant having them there, I could hardly ever get in and do my own stuff anymore, "You may as well buy the bloody place off me", I joked without really thinking. After nearly eight years of ownership, I had never thought for a minute about selling The Cutter. On the other hand, most of the gear needed replacing by now after constant use and anyway, the original idea had never been to run a recording studio business, which is what it had now become. "Actually, if you're serious I'd really like to buy it off you mate," Mal said. "As you know, we love this place and have been doing some great work here, it's a brilliant set-up."

Just to get an idea, a local estate agent valued the property at a premium level and our accountant simply added half as much again to the amount, to take account of the equipment, even though it was probably worth nowhere near that figure. He advised Ann and me that if the band really wanted to buy the studio, the price would probably be a minor consideration. Next day I swallowed hard when Mal asked me how much we wanted for the place, then he went into one of his thoughtful silences. "Does that include the microwave and that settee Phil? We really like to have those too." "Of course, I'll even throw in the bloody telly!" I joked although he looked thrilled. "That'd be great, thanks," Mal said while reaching into his back pocket. I thought for an instant he might be about to shoot me for my cheek, but instead, pulled out the AC/DC chequebook and a BiC biro. I was gobsmacked, what on earth was the man doing? "Mal, hang on," I said hopelessly out of my depth. "What about searches, deposits, lawyers and all that kind of stuff?" "Aw, fuck all that!" Mal said chuckling. AC/DC had just bought my studio!

Chapter 31
Bonfire of the Sanities

"There it was, (New York) the Rome, the Paris, the London of the twentieth century, the city of ambition, the dense magnetic rock, the irresistible destination of all those who insist on being where things are happening—and he was among the victors!"
(Tom Wolfe, Bonfire Of The Vanities)

Safely home again at Teddington Park, it wasn't long before snippets of news items on George's growing drug problems were surfacing in the media. At first as a trickle then growing, as most who were around at that time will recall, into a mighty, hope-swallowing career, and in some cases, life-terminating torrent of gloom and destruction. It's hard to recall now the precise order of events as each story seemed to wash over us as yet another wave of bad news rolling in even before the last had subsided. Inside the whirlwind that Boy George and Culture Club were reaping there was a calmer eye of the storm, but events in our family life were similarly unravelling intensely throughout the summer of 1986.

From Ann's and my viewpoint, having not long arrived back in England from Montreux, the fallout was beginning to affect the family profoundly as we were all, in our various ways, inextricably linked, good, bad or ugly to the "karma" fortunes and pratfalls of being a part of the Culture Club family. All was rumour and denial for a while until July 6th, 1986 when the *Daily Mirror*, marshalling all the forces of George's eventual exposure, ran a highly detailed and corroborated story by journalist Nick Ferrari with the headline; *Junkie George has eight weeks to live.*

The newspaper had allegedly offered a bounty of up to £50,000 to anyone who would be prepared to offer unassailable evidence of George's addiction. In a sting, worthy of the classic seventies movie starring Robert Redford and Paul Newman, the unlikely Judas of this sorry affair was David Levine, the younger brother of Culture Club's producer, Steve. Levine was a talented photographer who had shot among many other pictures, the cover for the 'Karma Chameleon' single. In a carefully planned operation, he allegedly tricked George into handing him all the proof he would ever need, under the guise of saving the troubled singer, in which the sneaky exposure certainly played its part. The younger Levine was soon spotted driving around town in a brand new sports car. Steve Levine who had no prior knowledge of the imminent betrayal of his friend was understandably devastated. George later described his nemesis as "the louse that roared", proving that even under intolerable pressure his talent and quest for a quip was undimmed.

Richard Branson then stepped in with great fanfare and very publicly tried to help. It later transpired that Richard had arranged medical and psychiatric supervision at a clinic outside London at the behest of Tony Gordon and George's family. Even though having first, rudely and abruptly brushed off Branson's help, George, at one point was hiding out from the police at Richard's Oxfordshire home. No doubt sincere in wanting to assist his wayward singing star, the record company boss nevertheless appeared to many to be over-egging it on the airwaves. No less than eight questions were tabled in the House of Commons, directly or indirectly related to George's case and its implications for young people.

Even the Home Secretary, Douglas Hurd complained that George's antics were a "most public display of drug disorder" and in no uncertain fashion, put the Police on urgent notice to sort the matter out. After the Levine article, George's younger brother, David, went on television to further expose the truth of George's decline and his family's deep concerns for his life. It was a very painful and public plea for his pop star big brother to come clean and finally seek the help he needed to break his addiction before it was too late. Meanwhile, George's public utterances still indicated insouciant denial, telling the press; "I'm a drag addict, not a drug addict!" but, who years later in his book admitted that at the time he was acting; "Like a blind man on roller blades in a china shop."

But even George couldn't laugh away something of this magnitude and public furore that was already a million miles away from being any kind of joke. The single event that brought it home to us once and for all, however, and quite literally to our own doorstep, was on a fateful day, August 6th, 1986, when a breaking news item interrupted the usual morning programming with the following shocking announcement:

BOY GEORGE'S KEYBOARD PLAYER FOUND DEAD IN CULTURE CLUB SINGER'S HOUSE AFTER SUSPECTED DRUG OVERDOSE

Ann was driving down the Upper Richmond Road when the bulletin came on her radio. In fear and shock, she swerved out of the way and only just avoided crashing into another car. I had been out of town on a session with Phil Ramone the previous evening and was not expected home until that afternoon. Even though it was almost impossible it could have been me, hearing something like this out of the blue on the radio, her mind instantly played tricks. Frantically Ann spent the next half hour trying to make contact, finally managing to get hold of me at the studio where I was working with Phil. Relieved to hear my voice, she told me what she'd just heard on the radio, "Don't worry darling, I'm fine" I said. "I'm so sorry you had such a shock, but I'd better find out what's going on. I'll make a couple of calls and call you back, but please, please don't panic, honestly, I'm okay." After consoling her a little more I said I'd try and get through to Tony Gordon and then make my way home.

Although in its very dark way it was almost predictable, with all of the druggie craziness that had been going on - after all, other friends in George's circle had died recently in similar circumstances - I still couldn't believe what had happened. Finally, having got through to Tony, it turned out to have been George's new musician friend, Michael Rudetsky, an ex-addict and American keyboardist who had been staying at George's house in Hampstead who had tragically taken an overdose. As George had been all over the news, during the previous weeks and throughout the summer, with his all-too-public heroin possession conviction, this latest dreadful misadventure at his house was merely a grim finale of what already been a major rolling news item over several weeks. But would it stop there?

For a few hours at least until Michael's identity and the circumstances had been established beyond doubt, reports merely referred to him as "Boy George's keyboard player". Naturally, I suppose, most people; friends, family and professional buddies assumed it could have been yours truly. Later that day, finally arriving home again, reporters had surrounded our house at Teddington Park. They were pushing and shoving on our doorstep, with cameras going crazy, until the penny dropped that although I had been Culture Club's keyboardist throughout the eighties, they finally accepted I had nothing to do with this story. For days later, however, the more persistent news-sleuths, still hungry for a scoop, hassled and harangued at our door and on the telephone for the inside track. Two of the journalists also offered considerable amounts of cash to Ann and I to 'spill the beans' on what had really been going on behind the scenes with Culture Club all along. "Come on Phil, I was at The Grosvenor in '84 when you got two Ivor Novello's for 'Karma Chameleon'. You must have known what was going on!" the pushier of the two surmised incredulously.

Thirty years on this is the first time I have ever publicly referred to these events, how it affected us all at the time and the outcomes we experienced. Understandably confusion and concern reigned within my family, our friends and even our children's school and their friends. For several days the phone rang, constantly off the hook. Firstly to find out if I was okay but then in short order, to see what was really going on with George and the band. As dreadful as the news of Michael was, the sordid and unspeakable truth was that most felt, even if they didn't say, it seemed to go with the territory. Before these calamitous events, due to many reports surfacing about George's drug dependency and the seamier side of life that accompanied it, and even though 'Move Away' had previously been doing surprisingly well around the world, the constant drip of news about George's problems culminating in Michael's tragic and untimely death was the straw that finally broke the camel's back. Record retailers the world over physically went out and removed our record (my record!) from their shelves, and radio stations stopped playing the song or indeed, any of Culture Club's music overnight. Virgin, had also reached the end of the line in promoting a band which was now clearly damaging their brand. The news was unremittingly grim and this time it really looked like the game was up.

As I'd always flown the flag so passionately and vocally for George and the band, I had to accept that by close association, my reputation, and therefore, prospects, were bound to suffer huge collateral damage. Sadly, it looked like my adventure with Culture Club was all but over.

By 1986, with George's image and Culture Club's music globally omnipresent on MTV and his doomed relationship with Jon Moss on the rocks, George was living in New York surrounded by hustlers, parasites and fellow drug addicts. By accident or design, George was now an Ocean away from Tony and Avi Gordon, Jon and the rest of the band, who were, by now, emotionally or geographically too far away to intervene. Devil-may-care decadence was now running riot in all aspects of the Boy's life. He'd carved himself a place in the universal psyche as he'd always wanted, but where he'd ended up was so far out on the bleeding edge of oblivion that, according to many reports, including in his own book it's a miracle not only that he remembers much of went on at all, but, thankfully, he lived to tell the tale.

In his classic novel, *Bonfire of the Vanities*, described as "the quintessential novel of the eighties", Tom Wolfe created a modern day allegory, a Greek tragedy if you will, set in the rambunctious, seething world of eighties New York excess. Steeped in ego, treachery and entitlement, Wolfe told a nail-biting tale of the self-regarding arrogance and invincibility of his flawed hero, Sheridan McCoy, a Wall Street Master of the Universe and of his subsequent comeuppance and breathtaking fall from grace. His book could just as well have been written about the eighties music business. Like The Beatles, Rolling Stones and The Sex Pistols before them, Culture Club all too briefly became the biggest, most popular and controversial musical group in the world, unleashing, as it always does, or did, the unfathomable all-pervasive forces of nature that world-wide public attention often brings to its rarified recipients. For a quartet of vastly wealthy musicians, still young and in their early twenties with such offbeat and contrasting personalities not to have had their heads turned at the temptations on offer would have also been a miracle. In George's case, the tales of debauchery filtering through the grapevine; that of his Studio 54 lifestyle and wall-to-wall degenerate orgies made Sodom and Gomorrah look like the Teletubbies. Hanging out with dubious drug pushers, hangers on and success junkies (even Madonna!), was clearly taking its toll and control of George's still impressionable young life.

To the Greeks, hubris referred to extreme pride, especially those whose self-esteem and ambition were so great they offended the gods who then conspired to bring them and every aspect and edifice of their life crashing down. Hubris was a character flaw often attributed to the heroes of classical Greek mythology, such as Icarus. But back in Icarus's day they didn't have crack cocaine and Concorde!

At Maison Rouge when even way back then one could clearly see the earliest possibilities of colossal future success in the appeal of George's voice, talent and persona when one of hundreds of squat-dwelling, shoplifting, fare-dodging, music wannabes on Main Street, certain pivotal moments stand out. Like at the very pinnacle of the band's triumphant worldwide reign, that within them contained the seeds of their ultimate dissolution and demise. George's US Grammy's comments for instance, and his ill-advised refusal to appear at Bob Geldof's Live Aid readily come to mind. Corny enough to be a cliché but common enough as a universal truth; where worldwide fame that crosses all boundaries is concerned, "It don't last long honey, four or five years tops!"

After all the hard work and huge expectations of success that in any other situation I might have had every right to expect, all was washed away over that fateful summer in a tidal wave of bad publicity and career disintegration. How prophetic *From Luxury to Heartache* had turned out to be! George; in a *Rolling Stone* interview years later he described the album and its recording as "Art imitating disaster".

I felt not only defeated but ashamed at the seediness of it all and also the terrible waste of life and talent with which I was now seen to have been associated all along. Even writing about this thirty years on is extremely painful. At the same time there was huge concern and anxiety about George for his condition, and as is probably obvious from reading this book, we all cared for George enormously - but could not reach him. In spite of the trials and tribulations, he was and still is a great friend who changed all of our lives for the better.

As things got steadily worse I became more convinced George would not make it. I desperately attempted a number of times to reach out to see if I could help as ever more emotional stories of his deteriorating state were being reported by Branson and various members of his family. When I did manage to track him down, I was hopelessly blindsided by his upbeat attitude to it all. "It's all bollocks Phil, please don't believe everything you read in the press, they're just out to get me. I'm fine honestly," he said. He just wouldn't admit to what was going on. He was either still in hopeless denial or more likely as I suspected, a conniving and convincing master at covering his tracks. In other words, putting on an act like a true dyed-in-the-wool addict. He'd somehow temporarily escaped the confines of his Abercorn Close mews house, now a virtual prison policed by swarms of hungry journalists with arc lights on the building.

Secretly arriving at my studio in Sheen one time, he looked gaunt and tired when we decided we were going to try some writing together. Although I was very happy to see him I was also confused as inexplicably, he seemed his usual boisterous self and in fine form and fettle. "Actually I'm starving," he said, "What's that curry place round the corner called again," "The Taste of Rog", "No George, it's 'Raj'" I said. "We can't go there though," he said. "The press will find out and it will be a fucking disaster; so if I order a takeaway will you go and get it?" He dialled the number from the card next to the phone and as soon as he started placing the order I could hear much Kashmiri chuckling at the other end of the line. "You are Boy George!" exclaimed the voice immediately and exultantly in a heavy Indian accent. Ten minutes later five waiters delivered our order carrying silver platters, cutlery and bone china and with much ostentatious deliberation, served us a meal fit for a Queen.

After the waiters finally disappeared, still I suppose trying to get through to him somehow, anyhow, I told him that my two boys, Jack and Gus had been bullied at their school, Newland House in Twickenham. Kids had been taunting them in the playground, and even their teachers ordered them both to stand up in front of the whole school during Assembly. "Does your Father take drugs?" the Headmaster asked Gus sternly, a little boy of 5 and Jack aged 9. Ann and I complained bitterly to the headmaster and in the end, we had no alternative but to instantly remove them from the school. I felt George's mask slip when he heard the story and he became silent momentarily, his eyes welling up.

Shamelessly, I let it sink in for a while, "Please George, you've really got to stop this, haven't you? Are you going to be okay?" I asked him. He promised that although things had been really bad for a while, he was determined to kick drugs out of his life for good and that he really had "everything under control." Even then I knew this was the classic defensive throw 'em off the scent strategy of a battle-hardened and extremely crafty addict; I didn't believe him for a second but what else could I do?

***

In the end, we decided to make a move up to London to be nearer the boys' new school, St James in Queensgate. And also to make it easier for Ann to get into her new high-flying job at an advertising agency in Chelsea (next door as it happened to Sound Techniques Studios in Church Street where I'd worked in the late sixties). We bought a beautiful and stylish fifth floor duplex apartment in Queensgate, which had belonged to a very old friend from our Cornwall years, Mark Crowdy; these days the successful creator and TV producer of the *Doc Martin* series. It was a penthouse 'to die for' and just a few steps away from The Albert Hall. Not long after moving in Ann's car, a beautiful sky blue VW Convertible, according to the police, was "stolen to order" from the curb outside our building. A few weeks later a fire broke out on a lower floor, forcing us all out on the street in the dead of night with our boys covered in wet towels. Although all was well (if not wet!), in the end, thankfully only minor damage to the property ensued; but we never felt quite the same about the place after that episode. Then to cap it all, two more incidents sealed the deal on Queensgate. Firstly a hurricane of almighty proportions blew some masonry off our roof terrace narrowly missing a vehicle and some pedestrians five floors below. This tumultuous, natural event, christened "The Storm of the Century" was reported by the *Daily Mail* thus; *In the early hours of October 16th, 1987 the infamous storm which battered England and Wales left 18 people dead and caused £1.5 billion's worth of damage to the economy. Winds peaked at more than 120mph, damaging buildings and felling 15 million trees in the south-east of England. Millions of homes were left without power for at least a few hours, with some having no electricity for days as trees fell on power lines, disrupting supplies...*

If that wasn't enough, only a few days after on October 19th the infamous Black Monday occurred, wiping zillions from the world's stock markets overnight, sadly including most of our investments and savings. It was the largest one-day market crash in history where in one hour the Dow in New York lost 22.6% of its value, around half a trillion dollars. When events outside one's control of that magnitude take place, out of the blue, there really is nothing to do but roll with it.

The Queen herself coined an expression a few years later, which seemed to fit the bill; "Annus Horribillis!" Things couldn't have been worse. Due to the currency meltdown and subsequent capital flight, mortgage interest on our new flat escalated massively in a heartbeat. It still brings tears to the eyes; and coupled with the demise of Culture Club, the unmistakable smell of imminent catastrophe and financial change was in the air.

But there was always tomorrow!

As if on cue, the phone rang the very next morning. It was Jill Sinclair, Trevor Horn's wife, manager, and co-owner of Sarm Studios. "Hi Phil", she said introducing herself, "Trevor suggested I call you, I'd like to have a chat about management. Oh, and by the way, I've got an album project you might be interested in. Malcolm McLaren!"

Chapter 32
Artful Dodger

T he first time I met Malcolm McLaren was deep down in the basement under Trevor Horn's famous Sarm West Studios in Basing Street, Notting Hill at possibly the only time in his life the ginger impresario had ever been lost for words. A vivid and provocative character who might have walked straight out of the pages of a Dickens novel, I would soon find out was one of the most challenging and outrageously nefarious entrepreneurs I'd ever met. Here though in late 1987 the Artful Dodger of London's rock, fashion and music business world was kneeling down on the floor amongst hundreds of boxes of digital and analogue tapes, several in each hand and crying like a baby. The only thing missing from the scene was perhaps a battered top hat, a few discarded purses and a pair of moth-eaten fingerless gloves.

Jill, Trevor's formidable wife and business partner had only recently become my manager and suggested I might be hired to co-write and produce McLaren's opus *Waltz Darling* album. The project had to date already claimed the health, sanity and bank balances of several battle-weary producers, the last of whom had collapsed in the studio during an argument of biblical proportions with the tyrant, immediately after which the poor chap was dispatched to hospital in an ambulance. He lived but never came back to work for Malcolm.

I'd been interested to read somewhere of Malcolm's latest prediction that young people the world over through their fear of the shocking and scary eighties AIDS epidemic, would now want to return, en-masse to a more refined and formalised approach to social and sexual matters; to a new age of "courtly love" no less through the ritual of dance. For some reason, this concept sounded feasible to me at the time and had stuck in my mind. The waltzes of Strauss and other light classical composers were, he surmised, perfectly ideal for a more arms-length and mannered approach to encounters with the opposite, or indeed the same-sex. This was Malcolm's latest thesis for world domination in musical terms. The idea being to infuse traditional European melodies with a more modern sound for today's market. "Right down my street," I thought and although intrigued by the project and the man, right now things were not looking too hopeful.

"The cunts!" Malcolm shrieked, accompanied by a howl of desperation, "They've deliberately mixed up all my tapes, I can't find anything man! How can I ever sort all this out?" I was new to the situation but could see he was in well over his head and not used to dealing with technical details. I supposed this kind of thing was usually left to unpaid minions (unpaid minions? Mmm!) "We did loads of recording at Abbey Road with 60-piece orchestras and I can't find a fucking thing," he said, losing it again and looking up at me dolefully as if we'd known each other for years. "None of it! It cost me over sixty thousand quid!" The man sounded very hurt. It had certainly cost someone a lot of money I thought to myself, but Malcolm? Well, that was extremely doubtful. He was vulnerable though, possibly hungover and close to having a panic attack, so I attempted to console him, "Let's have a look, Malcolm. Oh, by the way, I'm Phil Pickett" I said introducing myself. "Jill asked me to come along today and see if I can help." Appearing now more like tussle-headed and chastened cockney child, there was no visible response from the impresario other than to hand me a box. On the inside, there was a scribbled note attached to one of the digital cassettes. For obvious reasons I didn't show it to him though, as it read; "Good luck with whatever you try next, arsehole, see you in Court", or words of extreme prejudice to that effect, "What does it say?" he asked sheepishly, looking up at me with a brief glimmer of hope, "I think someone's probably wiped your tapes by mistake or perhaps deliberately Malcolm. I'm going to have to call some people I know." I thought he was going to explode.

A few days later on a very hot Easter Sunday, Malcolm arrived at my studio. We were to begin work on the "Waltz" project and to co-write some new songs at the same time as hopefully sorting out the giant maelstrom of mess and confusion encountered at Sarm West. Right from the start, I realised that Malcolm, although a genius communicator and pop Imagineer par excellence really had not an ounce of musical sensibility in his bones. To him, Waltz was just a word, a concept, albeit I felt, a brilliant one. It was all about style over content, which I was initially struggling to come to terms with, until one day the penny dropped. "Can't you give it more of a beat, I mean, how are people going to dance to that?" he said, listening to one of his own tracks in a 3/4 time signature that I'd been working on. "Can't you make it more like disco man? 'Jive Talkin'', The Bee Gees, Arif Mardin, Aretha's producer, he came up with that sound didn't he?" "I know, I've worked with Arif," I reminded him. "Anyway that's 4/4" I pointed out. "Four on the floor, that's the disco dance beat, but your record is all about waltz isn't it? And waltz is in 3/4 time, 1-2-3, 1-2-3, that kind of thing." He looked at me as if I was raving mad, impervious to reason. Perhaps I was. "Stick an extra beat in there then, don't fuck around man! You can't dance to that!" "Look, I don't want to tie you down in detail Malcolm, but all of these tracks you have recorded, all the orchestral stuff you told me cost 60 thousand quid, is in 3/4 waltz-time, that's what 'Waltz' is. It's your project, I thought you understood that." He looked confused and downhearted. Evidently, he had not. "Okay then," I said, "let's forget about doing waltzes, but maybe just romantic stuff that we can personalise, change around," I suggested. "How about 'Shall We Dance' from the Rodgers and Hammerstein musical? The famous hit from the fifties was not on his radar so I played him the original. "I quite like that", he said nonchalantly; "I can't sing though, so how is that gonna work?" "Don't worry, just speak the lines in time, it'll sound cool; everyone knows the sound of your voice and it can be like a rap version, but very romantic, you know, like..."We've just been introduced, I do not know you well... shall we dance, boo boom, boom, boom etc.", "okay, we'll try it," he said, more compliant now that the ideas seemed to be working. "But first can we get something to eat around here man? I'm starving."

In those days, nothing much was open at Easter in Sheen but I went out and brought back a couple of barely edible microwaved meat pies from the local pub. "Sorry, they're really hot, I left them in a bit too long," the barman said. Hurrying back to the studio and being a lovely day, Malcolm was outside in the garden. So I gave him his pie and went inside the house to make tea. After a few minutes, there was an angry altercation going on outside and I could hear two men shouting at each other, one of them sounding a lot like Malcolm. Looking out of the window I saw one of the most incongruous sights of my entire life; a bald man, my next door neighbour, appeared to have, what looked like the remains of a pie on his head, the gravy dripping down his neck and all over the collar of his shirt. The man was vehemently protesting over my wall in a considerable degree of discomfort and humiliation.

Apparently, as far as I could make out, only a few seconds earlier, whilst minding his own business and mowing his own lawn on a perfect English summer's day, a pie, approximately the same temperature as the sun's inner core, had exploded on the top of his bald head, literally out of a clear blue sky. "I was just throwing it to the birds, man!" Malcolm drawled insistently to my, by now, apoplectic neighbour, as *Just William* might have done in the Richmal Crompton books of my childhood. Namely at those times when the outcomes of serious transgression were being "s'plained" away by William and glossed over by cocky, disingenuous bonhomie. "I didn't want it anymore, I got bored with it, man!" Malcolm explained reasonably, pouring more ire on the fire. "It was for the birds when they get hungry!" My angry neighbour was having none of it; "That's not the point, you bloody fool! You don't go hurling hot food into people's gardens," my neighbour complained. "It's outrageous and I am going to call the police," the mower-man threatened.

I suddenly saw the whole entirely random and bizarre tableau almost as one might experience a disturbingly strange dream in slow motion; on one side of the wall, a highly respectable retired doctor covered in chunks of meat and globules of gravy and on the other - Malcolm McLaren the Godfather of Punk Rock himself - both men locked in furious verbal confrontation. I wondered how much more angry the doctor might have been had he have known who the pie perpetrator actually was?

Later, back in the studio and sometime after the police had left and the fracas had died down, I was pleased with how my arrangement of 'Shall We Dance' was going. Malcolm immediately booked a New York rhythm section of some of the funkiest players I'd ever heard to fly over from America for an all night session, one of whom was apparently George Clinton's bassist, Bootsy Collins. "You won't believe these guys, Phil, they're the funkiest motherfuckers in the universe man!" he confidently assured me; "No one over here in England can play like these guys, I'm telling you!"

Malcolm asked me to take him to the bank on the way to the airport as it was apparently of utmost importance that he showed up in person to meet them with the cash. I can't remember why he asked me along, probably just for the lift, but I duly waited outside the bank in my car until he came out carrying a slim businessman's briefcase. The whole arrangement was starting to feel like an extremely dodgy drugs deal, but this is how things always seemed to be with Malcolm. On the way to the airport and during an uneasy silence, I thought it might be a good time to raise the subject of the publishing arrangements for 'Shall We Dance'. "I can talk to Boosey and Hawkes, Rodgers and Hammerstein's publishers in London if you like" I suggested. "They might give us a piece of the publishing." "Who are they, Rodgers and who?" he inquired, although I was surprised he didn't know as I thought everyone had heard of 'The King And I' with Deborah Kerr and Yul Brynner. "They're the most famous writers of musical theatre on the planet, I'm sure their publishers are going to be thrilled to know you want to cover their..." "Fuck 'em!" Malcolm interrupted, "We'll write it." "What do you mean?" I protested. "We can't do that! They'll sue our asses off. Anyway, it'll be really cool - you doing one of the best-known songs from musical theatre-land. Think about it, Malcolm. It's perfect for the "courtly love" idea of Waltz, I said, almost driving over a red light in my agitation. But Malcolm was already lost in thought. If he claimed the writing credits on the song, the earning potential would be much higher, denying the creator's royalties in the process, as long as he could get away with it. "Fuck 'em", he explained a second time, more thoughtfully. "We'll re-write it then!"

When we finally met the musicians at Heathrow, exhausted from their red-eye crossing in cattle class, Malcolm proffered the case full of cash to the tour manager who immediately disappeared to the wash room to count every last dime. That was the deal and of course, now patently obvious that with McClaren, it was the only way these guys would have ever got on the plane in the first place. Call me old-fashioned but I couldn't help wondering if there may have been something about Malcolm's payment arrangements I might be well-advised to look into a little more thoroughly in future. 'Ho hum'!

The times we spent together I was beginning to enjoy tremendously, in the restaurants and cafés of East Sheen. MC's stories and tirades were hilariously mischievous, frequently outrageous and always highly entertaining. Especially as they were all delivered in his familiar, commanding and theatrical drawl - and not giving one iota of a toss who was listening in on the conversation, while waxing forth, lyrical on the state of the music industry, politics, bands, marriage, the IRA, Thatcher, business, fashion, whatever. Deep in his cups and going for it, he would often move the subject on to how he single-handedly changed the music business, and as always his pet subject, how he was solely responsible for the invention of Punk Rock. It was all in the first person; when "I" signed with EMI, when "I" made *Never Mind The Bollocks*, when "I" took the Pistols to Virgin, with never so much as a mention of the supporting cast. A musical on Malcolm's life might have been called 'Do, Ray, Me, Me, Me, Me'.

But how could I forget?

By knowing this strange leprechaun of a man, in the morning I was meeting my idol, Jeff Beck; in my view and with supporting evidence, probably the finest guitarist the world has ever seen. And who was in the producer's chair? Yes, that's right! Me. So any other niggles, considerations and implications would just have to wait. "Did you know I also discovered Boy George and gave him his name?" Malcolm once told me over a chicken biryani in the curry house on the corner. He told me that George wasn't a singer at all until he discovered and encouraged him. "I even gave him his first break with Bow Wow Wow", he boasted. "I thought he was called 'Lieutenant Lush' in Bow Wow Wow, I inserted inconveniently. But staring into the middle distance, Malcolm was already off somewhere else and a response came there none. George will be interested to hear this, I thought.

Meanwhile, through a contact at Britannia Row Studios, I'd managed to track down Jeff Beck's roadie and guitar tech who lived in Yorkshire. Hopefully, I would be able to get some advice and tips on producing his solos on *Waltz Darling*. Jeff had quite a reputation for being a tricky sod to deal with, particularly with situations or producers with whom he was unfamiliar or for some reason didn't like or respect, so I wanted to ensure that I got everything right from the get-go. I was quite terrified actually and in awe of the man and his towering abilities; "Just make sure you get as many amps and speaker combos as you can," the roadie told me. "If Jeff says he's not feeling it, he'll often blame the sound. Then you won't see him for dust, so it's good to have as much variety as you're able to provide in that department." This seemed like a very good idea so I ordered in all the regular amps, Vox, Marshall, Orange and Fender - but at that time there was a brand new kid on the block, made by a company I'd never heard of before called Gallien Krueger. Thankfully as things turned out, I hunted one down, as it happened, the first of its kind in the country. When Jeff finally turned up to the session he was like a wide-eyed child in a toyshop. "Wow, I've heard of these, are they any good?" "They're supposed to be great," I said, hoping it was true. "Why don't you try it out?" He plugged his guitar in and started playing. I was mesmerised and star-struck. It was jaw-droppingly good and Jeff was clearly thrilled with the sound coming out of the speaker. But not anywhere near as happy as I was to hear him playing on my session. Things couldn't have started more promisingly. "Love it, thanks, man, I'll just use this then if that's okay." "Fine," I said, with a huge degree of relief and pride. "Which song do you want to start with?" "Up to you Phil, I don't mind, keep 'em coming mate." With that, he lit a fag and disappeared with his Strat and a soundproofed swoosh into the studio.

Quickly realising that he clearly hadn't heard the tracks and therefore completely unrehearsed, the guitarist proceeded to blast the control room with some of the most beautiful, flowing dexterity I'd ever heard played on any instrument. Moreover to my great personal satisfaction, he was so visibly pleased and inspired by the possibilities of the exciting new sounds he was getting out of the amplifier. And 'the sound' is everything to a guitarist. On any objective level, every solo on every track was immediately conceived, effortlessly played and majestic in its harmonic construction and flawless execution. There was a stunned silence at the end of each pass, usually accompanied by a humble and almost imperceptible, "Was that alright?" "ALRIGHT?" Way off the scale better than "alright!" I thought to myself. With exchanged knowing smiles the sound engineer and I were gobsmacked. Every note this man played was simply the best thing you'd ever heard coming out of an electric guitar. "I can do it again if you like - or change it, what do you think Phil? An embarrassment of riches came to mind. "Try something else if you like Jeff, that was bloody amazing though," I offered, still stupefied by what he had just played. We kept the original pass and kept giving him new tracks to play on. "Keep everything!" I whispered to the sound engineer.

Hard to explain to the uninitiated, but Jeff Beck's second, third or fourth attempt on the same part of the song, whilst still staggering in its complexity and beauty, was an entirely different selection of notes, timings and harmonic progressions. In most cases, it bore no relation whatsoever to what was played only seconds before on a previous take. It was a level of pure artistry and creative genius I've never really experienced before or since. Most players in that situation might partially repeat what they feel was the best aspect of the previous take and then try to build on it or improve slightly. With Jeff's uninhibited style of playing the canvass was blank every single pass and he never played the same thing twice.

As a producer working at this level must be the ultimate joy as you're just sitting there witnessing pure perfection in action. In addition to grinning like an ecstatic buffoon at every note played you have to at least try and find something constructive to say, even if only to feel you're earning your crust by helping the artist discriminate between different performances; the good, not so good and demonstrably better takes. But with Jeff, this was all pointless. After a while, superlative fatigue sets in; when everything you are hearing appears to be coming directly from musical heaven. It was embarrassing actually. If that's record production then sign me up!

Producing Jeff's solos, sublime bad-ass Harlem rhythm sections, star bassist Bootsy Collins and the world's finest orchestras at Abbey Road and Sarm West, I was being carried along on a professional high, surfing the waves of McLaren's idea-mongering. I always assumed that when it came to payment, having one of the toughest managers around in Jill Sinclair would be the ace in my hand. How wrong I was, but again, that's different story.

In truth, no one was a match for McLaren in that department. Over, what had been, a period of several months having spent countless hours working on *Waltz Darling*, Malcolm had never once actually expressed an opinion good, bad or indifferent, or indeed any thanks or recognition whatsoever for my participation in his musical venture. Furthermore, the man had never responded in any appropriate manner to my frequent but now more insistent requests for payment of some kind. I was flat broke. Coming to the end of the sessions late one evening, he asked me for a lift home to his flat in Willesden. Pulling up outside the property he smiled at me and said in a disarmingly affectionate tone; "Thanks, Phil, you've been a real help, I really appreciate it man. Don't worry about your money, I'll talk to Jill about it. Thank you again." With those words, he was gone, like a will o' the wisp. He got out of my car and I never heard, saw or spoke to him ever again.

A few days later I went back to his flat still in the futile hope of being paid, but he'd already disappeared, the circus having left town. Someone else was already living there. They told me he'd left for the Bahamas or some such place, but there was no forwarding address and all contact numbers were dead. I later learned through Phil Ramone that he'd been approached to carry on working on the project and later still, that Malcolm had taken everything to America and was cutting a swathe through the industry until the record was finally finished. *Waltz Darling* was released a little later in 1989. I ended up with a couple of co-writing credits and a 'special thanks' from Malcolm, but no hint of a production credit or payment ever ensued for my considerable efforts over many months.

During the countless hours and weeks I worked on the album with Malcolm; when he was drunk, high or sober, schemingly introspective or egregiously holding court in a club or restaurant, I found his eccentric and wildly unpredictable behaviour entertaining, frequently hilarious and endearing almost. But I can't say I ever really got to know him at all under the surface, and doubt that anyone else ever did. Beneath all the hype and bluster was a very sly fox, out for himself and preying on the unwary, the starry-eyed optimists and fools for music like me. In his view, working with him should have been enough, and looking back, in many ways I suppose it was.

With bloody difficult, megalomaniac narcissists like Malcolm, an optimistic enthusiast like me would always be on hand to come along for the ride. A shotgun enabler and facilitator of nefarious schemes, in my case, perhaps to even tell a story years on, without dwelling too long on the skulduggery of the man: Appreciating his ability as one of the true ringmasters of pop; of being able to conjure up and articulate a musical circus out of thin air by the sheer force of his personality and the originality of his ideas.

The magical experiences and stories of working with sublimely talented artists like Jeff Beck and fine orchestras at state-of-the-art studios with some of the best musicians in the world were just some of the unintended gifts that Malcolm McLaren bestowed on me, and even though I was never paid a cent for my blood sweat and tears, hopefully, I'll remember and benefit from the experiences gained long after the mortgage is paid.

For me, Gonzo journalist, Hunter S. Thompson's famous description of the music industry perfectly sums up my impression of exactly where in the scheme of things the late Malcolm McLaren inhabited, thrived and for a while, reigned supreme; "The music business is a cruel and shallow money trench, a long plastic hallway where thieves and pimps run free, and good men die like dogs. There's also a negative side."

Chapter 33
PS Love Me Do

In January 1988 I had the great good fortune to come into close contact with an individual who, growing up, had been a huge influence on my life and no doubt, billions of others. A true icon who affected others, musicians and non-musicians alike, in so many profound ways. One extremely cold Saturday I'd driven through the mid-winter wonderland of beautiful Richmond Park to my recording studio in a futile bid, yet again swearing through chattering teeth to wait for Paul, Hounslow's-own elusive playboy plumber to turn up.

After several times going AWOL, he'd faithfully promised once and for all to come and fix the central heating boiler. But to my extreme and frozen irritation, it was beginning to dawn on me that Saturday was possibly not the best day due to my plumber's regular Friday night alcoholic excursions and glandular pursuits in the fleshpots of South London. I liked coming in on a weekend usually as the phones were always quiet enabling me to finish off a few bits and pieces without constant interruption.

The previous week I'd been working on a hush-hush project for Phil Ramone, Paul Simon and Billy Joel's producer, re-arranging classic Lennon & McCartney songs from a list his office had forwarded. I was told to choose one title only and not to "ask too many questions." However, a couple of songs instantly jumped off the page: 'Love Me Do' and 'P.S. I Love You'. These were special favourites of mine and the soundtrack to much college boy smooching and earnest philandering under piles of coats in the bedrooms of blissfully unaware parents in Sutton Coldfield, circa 1963.

With a sharp intake of breath, I remembered something drastically pleasant happening during 'I Saw Her Standing There' - along the lines of Jonathan Miller's description of teenage lust and desire at the parties of his youth, and of his unrequited wish to "be severely interfered with."

Wistfully with a degree of reluctance, I managed to prize myself back to the present (1988) and noticed that out of all the songs, these two alone were published, not by ATV/Northern Songs who controlled Lennon and McCartney's priceless catalogue, but by MPL, McCartney's own company. This was apparently due to a typist's error when the rights were sold to Michael Jackson, these two titles being left out of the list. Unbelievable! Anyway, putting two and two together and having a few clues about publishing, it seemed obvious to me (and a 'fait accomplit'), that sly old Macca might have nabbed them back again. My own shifty inclinations, therefore, suggested one of these two might be worth looking at, but which one to choose?

Working late into the wee small hours at a bleary-eyed moment my keyboard sequencer must have made the choice for me - by somehow merging the two tracks into one or, more likely, I'd simply pressed the wrong button! In any event, I immediately liked the unintended medlification of these two timeless Lennon & McCartney classics and christened the arrangement 'PS Love Me Do'. The result was edgy and contemporary-sounding and the verse of 'PS' seemed to quite naturally go into the 'Love Me Do' chorus. I posted it off to Mr Ramone and keenly awaited his response.

Fast-forward if you will, now back to the present Arctic conditions outside my studio, and by this time so cold and angry I'd decided any further waiting around for the plumber was futile. On the very point of locking up, however, low and behold the telephone rang. Angrily I picked up the phone and a voice spoke; "Hi Phil, it's Paul here..." but before any further words could leave the man's lips a supercharged torrent of thermically-challenged abuse rained down on the unfortunate caller until, pausing for breath, to reload both verbal barrels, the man found a split-second to interject; "No Phil, I think there must be some mistake mate, it's Paul McCartney!"

Choking for breath I would have cried out on the spot with shame and embarrassment if I hadn't just actually swallowed my tongue whole. Throughout late childhood and into my teens and early music career, I'd grown up in complete awe of this man. An almost spiritual worship of an individual, who was possibly the 20th Century's most important composer, incomparable bassist, stylish dresser and a genius to boot. I also loved his taste in Cuban boots, Carnaby suits and gorgeous arty-looking women. Paul and his soul buddy, John, revered all of the same songwriters and artists that I had growing up; Buddy Holly, Elvis, Don and Phil Everly, Lieber and Stoller, even good old Lonnie Donegan; together the fab twosome had changed the direction and course of modern music for ever. In the process, they also changed history, putting England back on the map after it's cold grey and stingy post-War years.

Paul McCartney was my hero and inspiration for changing the course of my life and becoming a songwriter in the first place - and here he was on the other end of the line!

"Loved the arrangement of 'PS Love Me Do,' Phil, It's great! Would have never thought of that! I'm making a record with Duane Eddy and the Memphis Horns soon. How'd you fancy coming down to my place in Rye and playing the piano?" he said, all delivered in the ever-so familiar, mid-Atlantic, scouser's lilt.

As one might imagine the phone incident certainly broke the ice over what would otherwise have been a rather stilted and nervous exchange with my greatest hero, had I actually been expecting the call. I suddenly became aware of what must have seemed barefaced cheek; totally re-arranging, merging together, and even re-titling a song written by the most successful composer of all time. Thankfully though, he didn't seem to mind; "I've been called lots of things in my time but never a friggin' plumber!" said Paul, my new friend. When I put the phone down and it was finally time to go home, I locked up the studio realising I'd completely forgotten how cold it was.

Phil Ramone came out to greet me on arrival at The Mill Studio at Rye overlooking the diamond-bright English Channel. In England's Spring lanes on the way down from London, I was so terrified I'd stopped to get out of the car a few times and hyperventilate in the crisp April air. Phil was soon followed out of the studio by Paul who, walking over to my car, held out his hand and greeted me with a winsome smile; "Hello Phil, how's your heating mate?" A barely-perceptible trace of confusion flickered across Ramone's face until the reference was explained. Paul was interested in everything; asking me where I'd bought my coat, said he loved my shirt and wanted to know all about Culture Club and how they'd split up; how long had it taken to write 'Karma Chameleon', all that kind of songwriter stuff. Band talk.

"Culture Club are great, how did you get the gig?" Paul was interested to know, "A brilliant hit that was. Wish I'd written it!" which hearing Paul McCartney say something like that immediately put me at my ease with the situation; "Seriously, I haven't had a hit like that for ages, fantastic record, well-done mate." A little later we set up our equipment and slowly began learning the arrangement to 'Rockestra', the song he wanted to record with Duane Eddy.

The session itself was a buttock-clenching ordeal for me, as not only was Paul playing bass and sitting only six feet to my left at the piano, Duane Eddy was playing guitar, and some of the finest musicians in the world were also sitting in on the session. Paul had asked me to play Leon Russell's piano part on the ex-Wings classic, for which Tom Cruise's speech in *Jerry Maguire* (where he describes every day being a "pride-swallowing siege") is the only thing that comes remotely close to describing how I felt. Leon Russell, now sadly departed, was one of the finest rock pianists of all time and Paul had invited me to cover his part. It was mental!

Back in the control room listening to the playbacks with Ramone and assembled stellar company, I prayed for the ground to open up and swallow me whole. But later on, when Paul walked me out to my car at the end of the session I fully expected him to say something like; "Alright, the game's up mate, I'll get your coat. What the fuck do you think you were doing in there just now?"

But to my genuine amazement what he actually said was; "That was really great today Phil, thanks a lot, mate. Are you available to come back next week and play on me new album?
Oh, and we've still got 'P.S. Love Me Do' to record yet, I'll get the office to call you next week then."

Driving back home in the dark, I stopped the car and got out several times all over again - this time to punch the air!

As time went on, returning to The Mill several times, happily the exhilaration meter went up several notches on the mixing desk, and eventually the fear factor down a bit. Every morning on arrival, Linda, Paul's late wife would usually appear with cups of tea and "fake-bacon butties", the real item apparently being the last thing Paul struggled to give up before becoming veggie. Working with this great musician and singer at such close quarters over those few days was a rare privilege indeed, and as Ramone had remarked, the ultimate experience for a professional musician. Again, I realised how lucky I was to be working with someone who had, had such a remarkable influence not just on me but on the music of an entire generation.

There would be few people I know who could instantly overcome the sense of shy gaucheness, which I suspect that in meeting McCartney would be the case for many. But playing music together, chatting about the Beatles - something he likes to do a lot - and as a left-handed player myself, being allowed to play some of the finest collection of left-handed guitars anywhere on the planet, such intimacies seemed to transcend the impenetrably high walls of such rarefied fame and universal celebrity, at least temporarily.

Over the course of the next two weeks, we developed, what I took to be, if not exactly close, then a very warm friendship, nurtured, as is often the case, between musicians just having a laugh, doing their job away from all the ego and hype. The world's most famous left-handed bassist would often go and make you a cuppa; "Jasmine or PG?" just like one of the lads.

One day, upstairs in the long room above the studio recording area, he proudly showed me, row upon row, of a veritable phalanx of left-handed guitars, all neatly standing to attention like toy soldiers on their stands. I admired an immaculate black Gibson in row 2, right–hand side. Hands in pockets, like a father, proudly looking down at one of his offspring he said:

"Solo on 'Taxman'." "Wow, really?" I said. "Did you play that then?" "Yeah," he said, pleased to be asked.

I was in seventh (& 8th, 9th and 10th) heaven!

"What about this one?" I asked. "That was for me birthday from Les."

In immaculate, glistening mother of pearl was embedded; "To Paul McCartney from Les Paul" all the way along the classic instrument's sleek 'Holly Golightly' neck. Then, I came upon the most famous guitar of all. In pride of place was Paul's old Hoffner Violin bass. You know the one. It was set up on a three-pronged guitar stand next to a red Rickenbacker and a beautiful black Fender Jazz Bass, all left-handed.

"Is that 'The One'?" I said, "Can I have a go?" "Yeah, sure, look out though, it's still got the last Beatles' set list on the top." In true muso-style, the faded card, (the back of a No. 6 fag packet), was precariously held on by the barest, brittle and browning Sellotape upon which aeons ago, the set running order had been scribbled. It was from their last gig at San Francisco's Candlestick Park on 29th August 1966. The last eleven songs the band would ever play live were; 'Rock And Roll Music', 'She's A Woman', 'If I Needed Someone', 'Day Tripper', 'Baby's In Black', 'I Feel Fine', 'Yesterday', 'I Wanna Be Your Man', 'Nowhere Man', 'Paperback Writer' and 'Long Tall Sally'.

Picking up the fragile and originally inexpensive instrument, it felt like a feather-light plywood model aircraft, but I knew it probably had to be the most valuable guitar in the world.

"You played with this at the Birmingham Odeon in 1964," I said, "I was there!"

One Sunday afternoon a few months after working with Paul on the *Flowers In The Dirt* album and after now also having completed 'P.S. Love Me Do', I called his studio from my home and was actually surprised to get through. I'd agreed to pass on a message as a favour, something I'm usually quite wary about when celebrities are involved. But as it was on behalf of Maharishi Mahesh Yogi's organisation, I gave my word that I would at least try.

Steven Benson, the leader of the Transcendental Meditation (TM) movement in the UK at that time, on discovering I was in the loop with Paul, asked me to inform him and Linda that an Indian holy man by the name of Dr Treguna was coming to London and had specifically requested meeting Linda for a consultation on her health. Apparently at some former time she'd expressed interest in the sacred and ageless tradition of Vedic medicine.

"Look, I've promised I'll try, but he has a lot of people around him asking for lots of things all the time" I explained to Steven, "But I give you my word, I'll at least let him know if I can."

Plucking up courage and calling just after Sunday lunch at around 2.30 pm, Trevor, Paul's driver, picked up the Mill's studio phone. I explained the nature of the call and asked if he would kindly pass the message on, secretly relieved that a third-party request was being honoured and that I'd done everything I'd been asked to do.

"Why don't you tell him yourself, he's right here," Trevor said passing the phone to Paul. Before I could get my breath, to my astonishment, the mere mention of Maharishi's name seemed to unblock an avalanche of fond memories from what seemed to be a lost time in his life. "Great Phil, how is the Maharishi?" he enquired with animated interest and affection. "He was lovely to us when Brian died," he said, recalling the train trip to Bangor at George Harrison's request to meet the Maharishi for the first time on the same day the band found out their troubled manager, Brian Epstein had died from an overdose. "John fell out with everybody in Rishikesh, which was a shame," Paul said, "We nearly blew the whole thing for TM, but the

Maharishi's a really cool guy."

He intimated that John's problems and misconceptions arose out of doing intense meditation around the clock in India whilst trying to cope with the emotional and deep psychological fall-out from having tripped-out on heroin and LSD hundreds of times. Being the initially cautious messenger, I seemed to have become a catalyst to an outpouring of intimate and fascinating details about everything to do with John; how they met, John's death and how Paul found out. How he felt about it. Also, how it was he who introduced John to the avant garde, arty crowd in sixties London; And the songs; who wrote what, when and where. Bachelor adventures in St John's Wood; quite a few of them (he said!); his relationship with Yoko, George Martin – stories that seemed to flow downstream like the sudden release of a logjam in a swollen river. Prompted by my well-informed questions, (after all, I was a lifelong fan!) I simply couldn't believe the details I was hearing firsthand about my musical hero's life and times which Macca seemed more than comfortable to share with his erstwhile devotee and recent professional colleague. Ann poked her head around the door for the umpteenth time, "Sweetheart, how many more cups of tea?" she whispered while I held my hand over the receiver. He was still talking. When the call finally came to an end it was a quarter to 9 at night, pitch dark in our kitchen and at just over 6 hours, the longest phone call I'd ever made to anyone in my life.

I recall the time spent at 'Waterfalls' with great fondness and excitement, but also with a degree of sadness as, in the end, realised it could only ever be a brief glimpse of friendship with an idolised hero, perhaps even an idealised friend. "This is about as big as it gets Phil," Sinatra's, Simon's and Streisand's soundman, Phil Ramone, quietly confided one day as I had just performed John's backing vocal part with Paul on 'PS Love Me Do' (on the same mic!) He didn't have to tell me - I already knew! After a while, I even became accustomed to the rarefied atmosphere of working at Paul's immaculate studio in Rye. But finally, on leaving day, the genuine warmth of our farewells abruptly seemed to end as the darkened window of Paul's limo snapped shut on the world, its occupant cocooned again in the cool, silent, air-conditioned interior. The huge blue, Dallas-and-then-some Mercedes crunched off rapidly down the studio driveway and silently disappeared into the lanes. That was it for the time being, at least.

Two years later I was a little down on my luck due to a slight altercation with the NatWest and the Inland Revenue, which had tiresomely led to a repatriation of our beautiful Knightsbridge duplex by "The Friendly Listening Bank". In a rented house we had thus relocated to Spencer Road, Strawberry Hill. One evening, I was up very late avidly watching TV in the den to find out which song Paul was going to perform in John's memory at a special Liverpool Anniversary live concert being broadcast via satellite to untold billions throughout the world. It was the 8th December 1990 – the 10th anniversary of John's untimely death-by-bullet between car and gutter outside the Dakota Building overlooking Central Park in New York. There was much speculation from the fans, assembled talking heads and many adoring artists, including Madonna, Lenny Kravitz, Elton John and George Michael, all of whom had magnificently performed heartfelt renditions of some of the greatest Lennon & McCartney hits of all time. But – and here was the big question - which song was Paul going to perform? Which of all of their amazing catalogue would be his personal musical tribute to his closest professional ally and soul mate? We couldn't even guess, but the choice was getting smaller after each and every artist had completed yet another classic.

Paul and his band Wings, for obvious reasons, were always going to be the grand finale to the broadcast, and finally running out on stage, with customary Scouse bravado, thumbs up shouting, "How are ya?" camouflaging the underlying intense emotion of the occasion, the band struck up.

I couldn't believe my ears! It was obvious through the distinctive introduction it was going to be my arrangement of 'P.S. Love Me Do'. The previously stressful few weeks had taken their toll and I was apparently overcome with pride and joyous affirmation, "Have you got something in your eye?" Ann said walking in from the other room; "Are you okay darling?" Then she realised. "Wow, that's the arrangement you did for Paul isn't it?"

Chapter 34
The Nineties - A Better Man

After the triumphs, tears and illusions of the eighties, I was carefully trying to assemble my career again in the aftermath of Culture Club. It felt almost as if I'd fallen off the back of an express train between stations. The early nineties represented amongst other things, fears revisited, another house move, this time to the Gloucestershire countryside, a huge precursor of which was the devastating and unexpected loss of my dear Mother Eileen in September 1993. In my subsequent grief and also whilst moving house I came across an attic-full of soul searching of where to go, who to work with and what to do next against the all-too-familiar backdrop of returning financial angst and insecurity of a musician's life.

It was early 1993 when Ann and I had finally grown tired of the struggles and responsibilities of running a large family house in London and making all the pieces fit. We decided therefore to up-sticks and relocate from Strawberry Hill in Twickenham to the peace and contentment of the Cotswolds and a rented cottage in Little Rissington, Gloucestershire. As chance (or as ever, 'Karma') would have it, we found ourselves moving to the very same tiny village near Bourton-on-the-Water, close to the RAF air base in Little Rissington where my father had been stationed just after the war. This was where, prior to us being sent out by the RAF to live in Rhodesia, we lived together in a caravan. Was this some kind of healing synchronicity at work? Who knows?

Eileen had passed away after a heart attack in Spain. Bless her. To lose my mum out of the blue and to hear the news by way of a phone call from our friends, Jean and Arturo in Estepona turned my world inside out and upside down. I couldn't speak, move or do anything for a very long time. When I finally came up for air I knew I needed to escape, to get away somewhere for a while and pick up the pieces of my life. Mother and son relationships are complicated sometimes and my mum and I had our problems. Ann and Eileen often found it difficult to communicate too. But we were terribly close and I loved her to bits, still do. In May, prior to the September she died (only a week or so, as it happened after Sailor had re-launched its career in Berlin), we strolled, barefoot and hand in hand, along La Playa del Cristo, the beautiful beach outside her flat walking on into Estepona Port to have a drink with Jean and Arturo at their waterside bar, La Marinera. "Think of me as always being happy in the Spanish sun Philip," she said as we walked along the beach. I thought at the time it was an unusual thing to say which along with a few other observations and requests, in retrospect it was as if she knew she wasn't going to be around for too much longer. Here is a poem I wrote in her memory a few years later:

Eileen 1924-1993

She's a mountain road that twists and turns
To Ronda where the eagles fly
A thorny rose or tranquil fern
A thunderstorm in clear blue sky,
She's Ascot Day, a winning streak
A picnic in the shooting brake
A barefoot walk along the beach
Or 'Kismet' keeping me awake.

She's a lavish banquet at The Ritz
A Tudor monarch's regal sway,
Half a crown for egg and chips
Or 'Velvet Fog' with Mel Tormé,
She's the warning light on Bishop Rock
A sailor's rage against the dawn
Through malefic mist she's Penzance dock
A haven in a world forlorn,

The bus fare down to West Brom 'Minors'
Remembered times to savour, share
The 'Colonial Bar' on an ocean liner
Where smoke and laughter fill the air

As ever in life though, not everything was bad. There were good times, in fact, many and we loved the peace and quiet of the Cotswolds, a very soothing place for the soul to find itself in, to regroup.

Weaving in and out of this chapter of the book and my life, I apologise in advance to the reader as the multifarious projects which I instigated or was associated with during this decade, and the next all tend to merge mingle and fuse ('shake rattle and roll?') with one another. So a day-by-day, blow-by-blow account or then this and then that happened etc it is not! (But then again, neither is the entire book!)

So, after thinking that professionally everything might go up the creek in the nineties, on the contrary, the new decade contained moments of remarkable discovery, unexpected regeneration, huge professional success... and pure joy! No more so than on a scorching Men's Wimbledon Final day, July 7th, 1991 when Ann presented me (as she had done in each decade since the seventies) with our third beautiful son, Harry James Pickett. He was born at Roehampton Hospital and after a long and ultimately life-threatening labour, the little chap joined the party just as the outsider, Michael Stich was serving for the Championship having defeated Boris Becker at a local tennis court just a couple of miles up the road.

I had also discovered and was now managing a million-selling artist Keziah Jones, was about to reform Sailor and play in front of more people than in its Glam Rock heyday, (but didn't know that yet!) and towards the end of the decade I would also write and stage my first West End Musical. I'd even ended up practically living next door to my Brummie idol Steve Winwood in the Cotswolds and who was now someone I could call a friend.

Taking stock professionally, at the cusp of the nineties I was 44 and tears, tours and battle-weary, having played in practically every major venue on the planet - from Wembley Arena to Madison Square Garden via the Budokan in Tokyo and the Hollywood Bowl. Therefore, a reasonable assumption might have been my touring days were drawing to a close. I'd had a good run, but perhaps what was now on the cards from this point would be to relax for a change, sit back a bit in the studio, write a few songs, (always at the top of the list!), do the odd arrangement and production assignment and carry on from where I'd left off with the McCartneys and McLarens. Perhaps even look at management. What was it to be? The perennial question of a musician and artist; what will feed the soul, feed the family - and pay the rent?

Keziah Jones

Prior to leaving London, I was still licking my wounds after the forced sale of our luxury penthouse in Queensgate. As Mick Hucknall of Simply Red sang at the time, money was indeed "too tight to mention". So for a family outing, one Saturday Ann decided we should hop over to Portobello Road late in the afternoon and see if we could pick up some food and clothing bargains. The market sellers practically gave stuff away late in the day on Saturdays if anything perishable was left. The sights and sounds of Notting Hill never fail to enthrall however, and I'd soon dived inside a record shack rummaging through old albums and EPs. Jack, now aged 13 ran into the store looking very excited; "Dad, you've got to come out here and see this guy, he's incredible, the crowd's loving it." Having already seen one or two buskers that afternoon and pretty ropey ones at that, I was in no mood or hurry to interrupt my intended purchase of an early pristine Elvis album I'd unearthed. Jack was persistent however and practically pushed me back out onto the street. I could hear the guy, his searing soulful voice and funky acoustic guitar, but there were so many people surrounding the singer it took quite a long time to get closer. I smiled at Jack; "You're right, he's good, bloody good actually." In fact, I was galvanised to the spot. It was that feeling again. I asked someone his name and she told me it was Keziah Jones. Everything about him, his playing style, amazing voice, intense charisma and the overall look was bewitching. Talk about star quality! I was captivated.

When he'd finished his set I mooched over, tried to make an approach and find out a little more about who he was. But a very regal and almost aristocratic demeanour, combined with what could have been shyness, stand-offishness almost curtailed the halting conversation. "What do you call that kind of music?" I asked him keenly. "Blufunk" he answered economically. That was it, no pandering or trying to sell anything, he was just who he was and doing his thing.

In the end, there was not much point hanging around further so I went home without having exchanged contact details. There wasn't an opportunity and anyway, he didn't seem in any manner, engaged by my interest. It was all a little awkward but I still felt I knew quite a few people in the industry who would mightily jump at the chance to sign him and help him get up to the next level. "He was great though wasn't he dad?" Jack said on the way home. He certainly was. I was hooked and couldn't stop thinking about the guitarist and what a potential star in the making he could be. But with having to move out of our home and on to a rented place out in Twickenham in just a few weeks time, I guess there were other pressing things on my mind. So Keziah Jones got filed away as a person of interest for the time being.

After a harrowing and stressful day moving out of our flat from five floors up, with boxes still piled high in the hallway of the Strawberry Hill house we'd rented, to my astonishment I saw in the *Evening Standard* that Keziah Jones and friends were being advertised that night in a pub near Clapham Common. This realisation was accompanied by a sinking feeling in my stomach as I knew I couldn't miss the opportunity this time, as it might not come again. "I've got to go," I said. "It's important". "You've got to do what?" said Ann, understandably none too pleased, not happy at all in fact and understandably so. "It's been haunting me ever since we saw that guy in Notting Hill," I explained. "I've got one of those feelings that it could be a life-changer that's all, I'm sorry, I don't know why but I've just got to go and check him out."

This time, after his show, the artist seemed more accommodating and approachable. Not long off stage and a spellbinding performance, Keziah was having an intense conversation with a very pretty girl who looked serious and troubled. I interrupted their discussion and said I couldn't help overhearing that although loads of industry people had said they were coming down to see him play, not one of them had shown up and that the audience had been very sparse; "I think I might be able to help you there," I told them both. I assumed correctly that the young lady was his manager but there may have been something else between them too.

Keziah - his real name Olufemi Sanyaolu explained that he was from Lagos in Nigeria and on the run from his family, particularly his father, who was a very powerful businessman and tribal chief. He had been attending a private school in the UK, paid for by his father but had done a runner and was now in hiding. "My father wants me to go back and work in his company but I'll die if I do that," the young guy said earnestly. I believed him. "I need to play music and earn my livelihood this way and prove to him I can make a success of it."

I told him who I was, what I did, etc. and that I knew a lot of people in the music industry who would, I thought, be very interested. "If I ask them, I know they'll come," I said, somewhat immodestly. But it was true, they would. I was still capable of getting the attention of some of the key movers and shakers, especially if the act was unusual and considered eccentric in some way. Keziah looked at me and smiled which, not having seen him do so before, was an experience in itself. I then filmed his next appearance and by coining a huge favour through my old friend and ex-publisher Johnny Stirling, then managing South African trumpeter Hugh Masekela, Johnny kindly agreed for the thus far unknown Keziah Jones to support Masekela at the Subterrannia Club in Notting Hill. "You owe me big one for this," Johnny said.

The film, shot by talented filmmakers David and Kathy Rose came out beautifully. I then called Stewart Levine who I'd originally met with Joe Cocker in Hollywood. Stewart was also a mate of Johnny's and happened to be in town producing the mega-successful Simply Red. "You've got to see this guy Keziah Jones though," I said to Stewart; "I think he's right down your street." "I'd love to come and see him Phil, but I'm booked up for the next year. I've just got no time man!" Stewart was in huge demand now being one of the top record producers in the world so I knew it was a long shot. "Look, bring the video over to my hotel on Sunday morning," he said. "We'll have some coffee then at least I'll have a look and maybe I can suggest someone else who could take it on." "Okay great!" I said. "I'll be there."

I arrived at The Montcalm near Marble Arch, bright and early one Sunday morning as planned and stuck the video in his TV player. "You're fuckin' keen man, I'll give you that!" he said laughing. Levine sat back to watch and not even half way through Keziah's first tune, 'Free Your Soul' he said; "The kid's amazing, I've got to do this man!" looking me in the eye. Stewart sat glued to the screen and played it over again. What an instant turnaround! The man was suddenly obsessed. "Perhaps if I don't take my holiday this year we could cut the record at Bearsville near where I live." Stewart told me he was married to Quincy Jones's daughter Jolie and she'd probably be none too happy about that arrangement. "Music comes first man!" I smiled a broad grin.

"I knew you'd like him, Stewart," I said. "Like him? He's fucking incredible man, I love the guy!" I was overjoyed as it was the reaction that I knew a big part of me had expected. Now I'd be able to get some serious players on board, labels, publishers and agents.

I told Keziah the news and he seemed very impressed. Another of his rare smiles in fact. "Wow, it's like you're my manager man!" he said. "Me? A manager?" I thought, like Danny Kaye in *The Ugly Duckling*. Seriously, up to that point, I hadn't thought of my enthusiasm as management at all. I was a writer, an artist, a fellow professional, older perhaps but basically, I felt I was just doing a favour for a young artist. Someone starting out who I could see needed, and through his breathtaking talents, thoroughly deserved a break. Is that what was really going through my mind. Management?

The phone began ringing off the hook as the word of Levine's involvement spread around the industry with all of the companies and executives honing in on a slice of the action. "We want to sign him so send us a tape for the next A&R meeting," they all said.

By this time, I'd had quite enough of the A&R departments at CBS and many of the labels I'd worked with. In my experience, they had the attention span of a goldfish, the focus of a cataract patient and the trashing power of chimps.

"No, I'm sorry," I told them all. "It doesn't work like that. You have to come and see Keziah Jones play live. If you don't get it from seeing the live show, you're not the right label. Byee!" I was getting good at this! Anyway, it felt great to have the boot on the other foot for a change.

Now at forty-four with two decades-worth of writing, touring and recording under my belt, perhaps management was an option, nay, even the next logical step for me. Besides, I would always keep writing songs and producing music in one way or the other, whatever happened.

Another mate of mine was booking agent Jeff Craft who I'd invited to the Subterrannia. Jeff told me that Lenny Kravitz was about to go off on a world tour and that Keziah would be a perfect support act. Things were coming together quite naturally and of their own accord. I began to discover a propensity for the kind of promotional activity I suppose I'd always been rather good at when motivated enough. Driven by the need to succeed after some fairly rough weather in my career, to promote Keziah's shows around London I found myself trawling the Underground day and night sticking up posters for his shows; anything to fill up the clubs. I was nearly arrested by the Transport Police on more than one occasion but in the pre-internet age, and with hardly any marketing budget, fly-posting was one of the only options.

Due to my other promotional activities there were now deals from EMI (Capitol Records), Warners (East West) and Virgin coming through thick and fast, and enough stuff and shenanigans going on to fill several more books (No, no I hear you say, dear reader!) but in the end I negotiated Keziah's record contract while travelling out to Heathrow at 6 am in a limo with Ken Berry who, on his way to Tokyo, had no other time available in his diary. I took the underground back afterwards.

Ken was CEO of Branson's Virgin Records and persuaded me that Emmanuel de Buretel, at that time head of Virgin's French label, Delabel was the perfect executive to sign Keziah and spearhead the deal - and Keziah around the world. Emmanuel was so passionate about getting Keziah on his label he'd often call me in the middle of the night. The brooding Frenchman was relentless, always with serious intent, reminding me of the American TV detective *Columbo*. He just never gave up. It is probably why, almost thirty years later, Keziah is still signed to Emmanuel who now runs one of the most successful independent labels in the world, Because Music.

When Keziah eventually went on to support Lenny Kravitz, in the press pit up front during Keziah's set at Wembley, Lenny was so visibly enthralled by the amazing crowd reaction he was getting, the star suddenly dashed off backstage. Kravitz returned almost immediately, however, ushering a gaggle of Rolling Stones royalty and glittering hangers-on, including one highly animated Michael Jagger himself who was dancing around and whistling up at Keziah. "Here, he's fucking good isn't he? What's his name again?" said Jagger, in his familiar drawl, addressing me as I happened to be standing next to him. "Who's his manager anyway?" he asked. "I am", I shouted above a fresh crescendo of blufunk. "His name's Keziah Jones!"

In the early nineties Keziah's long career was thus launched, as was my new professional role as an artist manager. At first and for some time we were very successful together. But as in all other areas of an industry I'd now learned a lot about over the years, there would also inevitably be challenging issues along the way. For many involved reasons too lengthy to elaborate here, Keziah and I decided to go our separate ways late in 1993 after several professional disagreements.

Sailor's second innings

Around 1992, Keziah's career having already taken off in France, the artist was also doing exceptionally well in Japan, Switzerland, Benelux and particularly in Germany. After one of his concerts, I was at Düsseldorf Airport on my way back home to England. Just about to board my plane, I was stopped in my tracks by Rainer Haas, a concert promoter, in fact, one of the most successful in Germany. He'd started out in the sixties in Hamburg's Reeperbahn, promoting scruffy Merseybeat rockers like the Searchers, Gerry and the Pacemakers and the unknown but soon-to-be-famous Beatles.

"You are Phil Pickett from Sailor aren't you?" he said smiling as if he'd met an old friend. "Er yes", I said, "but..." "No matter Phil, allow me to introduce myself," said Haas. "I was always a very huge fan of Sailor, my favourite band from the seventies, and I would like to make you an offer to reform for some shows I am planning next year, fifty of them in fact."

Although flattered and surprised to be recognised in my manager's suit and also at the man's very direct approach (an aspect of his personality I would later learn was key to his phenomenal success), I explained that I was now managing artists and that although I appreciated his interest, there really was no chance of Sailor reforming after what had by then been fourteen years. "I think we should leave Sailor where it is Rainer," I said. "Besides, not just me, but everyone in the band is doing other things and other projects. So again many thanks for your interest, but I'm afraid it is not going to happen."

We exchanged contact details, but I knew from my side that I didn't want to turn the clock back again. Haas was very persistent however and over the next few months called me many times; "Look, Phil, with respect, you are not taking my offer seriously. I would like to invite you and your wife to come to Berlin next month as my guest. Business class and at the best hotel at my cost. Just come and see one of my shows, no obligation." "Okay, Rainer," I said. "That's a very kind offer, but it doesn't mean I will commit to doing Sailor again. I've already told you. I don't have time and neither I believe do Georg, Henry and Grant." "No, fine Phil I understand," he said confidently. "Just come!"

Ann and I arrived at the enormous Waldbühne Stadium, a relic of a bygone age, where Hitler gave many of his speeches in the 1930s; a vast imposing amphitheatre in the middle of a forest carved out of the granite rock. The place was thus a chilling symbol of the Third Reich, but these days, an "Oldie-Nacht" Emporium, having been commandeered into the service of ageing entertainers from the old enemy, Britain. Funny old world.

The outdoor auditorium was full-to-bursting, just one of three, consecutive, sold-out nights and there must have been in excess of twenty thousand people clamouring to see Rainer's show. Artists on the bill were almost exclusively taken from the sixties and seventies, such as The Searchers, The Troggs, Chubby Checker, Mamas and Papas, The Rubettes, Hermans, Hermits and Suzi Quattro; a leather-clad, diamond-studded has-been extravaganza!

I couldn't believe my eyes! Haas would have been lucky to fill the pier at Blackpool back in Britain - but here in Germany, he'd sold over 66,000 tickets and was making fortunes!

The sound system was immaculate as were the production values with impeccable world-class staging and lighting. In fact, Genesis had only just played through exactly the same equipment for their concert the previous week. "We use nothing but the best Phil, I can assure you," Rainer said. "This is not like England at all. With respect, there is a huge market here for Sailor and I am going to make you an offer you cannot refuse" (I could almost hear the strains of the Godfather accompanying when these words were uttered which was unsettling!) "What if I do?" I half-joked. "I know where you live Phil!" Rainer shot back in his German accent, by now laughing maniacally, also a worry. Handing me an address card he said; "Seriously Phil, if you agree, meet me at my bank in the morning at 10 am and I am going to pay you in advance for fifty shows next year, in full and in cash." I could not believe my ears! Was this a dream? Did stuff like this really happen? I was flummoxed, but just about holding it together.

Back at the hotel, I called Georg Kajanus. I hadn't spoken to him for a few years; later I'd also call Henry and Grant too. It felt a little like a repeat performance of turning up to the Dover Castle pub where Georg was working all those years before and waving the cheque for our first album deal. After the usual pleasantries, I asked him if he was sitting down. "I don't think you are going to believe what I am about to say, Georg." Unwittingly, by constantly rebuffing Rainer's efforts to enlist Sailor to his line-up, I'd innocently fooled him into believing it was a management ruse from the beginning, which, of course, it wasn't. Without realising it, I'd merely been upping the ante from the perfect position of not depending, or even necessarily wanting the result of the negotiation to take place. Only modesty, politics and inter-band relationships inhibit naming the price Haas eventually offered after my fourth dismissal, but I eventually found out it was several times the amount he was paying any of his other acts - and for fifty shows, in cash with every penny up front.

As Rainer had confidently predicted (as only the seriously wealthy can), the offer really was too good to refuse, almost too good to be true in fact. We would have been crazy to turn it down and in all my years in the business before or since, I'd never experienced anything quite like it.

"There's also the matter of our Nickelodeon and equipment too, Rainer" I reminded him. "It's been fourteen years since we played music on stage and we don't have it anymore." Rainer laughed again, batting away the inconsequential difficulty with a perfect cover drive for four runs, "No problem whatsoever Phil, just tell me what you want and you will have it!"

An extremely welcome surprise, the news of my coup also certainly cheered up an otherwise uneventful evening in the Marsh and Serpell households, one of whom suggested booking a room at a Heathrow hotel to split the cash. "We can't do this at the airport," Grant said; "They'll think it's a drug deal and we'll get arrested!"

Opening at the Walbühne Stadium the following year, in September 1993, Sailor, the original line-up of Georg, Grant, Henry and myself stepped out in front of a 22,000 audience at this show (and forty-nine others) and played in front of more people over the next two years than during the band's golden heyday of chart and touring successes. By now we'd also achieved two newly-recorded chart hits in Germany, both written by Georg; 'La Cumbia' and 'The Secretary.' Even at this stage of our career and after my having co-written substantial hits all over the world, Georg still insisted on writing all of the material.

In spite of initial nerves, it was unbelievable fun to be getting up there and playing music again with my old shipmates and reliving the glory days of Glam Rock with much of the band's propensity for good times and humour thankfully still intact. Performing on stage had been a very big part of my life and I hadn't realised until then how much I'd missed doing it. Sadly, however, after a couple of years Georg, being frustrated with the creative demands of a very different musical era and its audiences and who, in all fairness, never really enjoyed touring as much as the rest of us, finally decided to call it a day in 1995.

Georg was replaced at first with Peter Lincoln who, as the shows continued to flood in, admirably and with much aplomb, carried on as Sailor's lead singer for a further ten years until leaving to join The Sweet. After Peter, the baton was passed to Henry's son, Oliver, who also performed a magnificent job in ensuring Sailor stayed at the top of the bill and at the very top of its game.

What helped Sailor achieve headline act status probably more than anything else, however, was, the band's by now legendary and infamous 'Full Monty' dance routine devised by Henry's talented partner, now wife, Dee Dee Wilde. Dee Dee was a founder member of Pans People, the gorgeous dance troupe featured on Top Of The Pops during the sixties and seventies and who were every schoolboy's fantasy. Our routine was originally a product of late night, alcohol-laced musings between Henry and I, with the initial idea of walking on stage in full uniform with a replica of 'Titanic' to the strains of The Village People's 'In The Navy'. Henry characteristically leapt on the concept providing a soundtrack, to which a similarly inspired Dee Dee choreographed an elaborate, and so we were led to believe hilariously risqué dance routine.

When we first walked on with our ship and special costumes to Henry's soundtrack at the end of a regular show, none of us, including the audience, really knew what to expect. Frankly, we were all terrified. However, one scenario put forward by an anxious and unsure band member included "the end of any kind of live music career" scenario. But we ploughed on. We were already in our fifties and sixties - apart that is, from Ollie, and in completely unknown territory. Therefore I suppose it may have been considered a huge gamble. At first, there was a stunned silence from the 10,000 strong crowd but then what followed was nothing short of extraordinary. As the routine progressed everyone in the hall was suddenly up on their feet roaring with enthusiasm and laughter. In that moment we knew that the risk had been worth it. Sailor raised the roof on that, and on countless other nights. At the end of it all, we discovered that people just love being entertained.

Over the next few years our 'Full Monty' routine supercharged the gigs calendar even more and ensured from that point on that we always topped the bill wherever we played. Finally, in 2013, three years short of my 70th birthday however, seeing Ann's face looking up at her partner about to take his trousers off in front of thousands of people in Germany, a thought occurred to me that it was probably an appropriate point to hang up the "ole' dancing shoes". So far, I'd got away with it so thought it best to quit while I was ahead, just! For my part, I was done with jumping around on stage after what in the end had turned out to be a final twenty- year glory lap for Sailor.

So, looking back to the early nineties when at forty-four I thought my touring days were over - in reality, I was only just getting started! (I feel another book coming on!)

As a pleasant footnote to Sailor's second innings, in 2003 or thereabouts, along with Steven Fry, Matt Lucas and others, we were invited to perform at the Groucho Club's infamous 'Gang Show' in worthy aid of London's homeless people. Sitting enthusiastically in the front row like a couple of excited schoolgirls was my old mate Annie Lennox along with Chrissie Hynde from The Pretenders, both of whom were belting out the songs with us and at one point even dancing in the aisles! It was terrific to see Annie again and had never realised they'd been such fans of the group.

Spice it up!

"Simon Fuller left a message while you were out Phil," Ann said, after I'd just got back to the Cotswolds from one of my Sailor trips. "Bloody hell, what does he want?" I asked. "He wants you to call him, it's about an all-girl band he is managing called The Spice Girls. I think he said he wants you to work with them, he says they're going to be huge." "Oh God, I hope they can sing this time, the last few he's sent up here have been tone deaf!" I was thinking particularly of the last girl I'd written with, similar to one before, both of whom shall be nameless (hopefully), but whose idea of co-writing was plugging in a drum machine, making tea, talking on the phone and eating biscuits while I came up with the chords, melody and lyrics.

One of the girl singers unfortunately possessed the attention span of a goldfish with ADHD, so the thought of working with a whole band of similarly challenged wannabes wasn't filling me with ground shaking motivation. "Do you think they'll mind wearing wellies?" I asked Ann. With all the Gloucestershire rain we'd recently experienced and the fact that my studio was at the end of a Somme-like muddy assault course of a garden was yet another impeding factor for writing hits that was going on in the back of my mind - and I hadn't even met Posh Spice yet.

A very bubbly and keen Gerri Halliwell called back later that evening, "Can you come up to London Phil, Simon has rented a house for us and we would love to work with you, he's told us all about you and played us some of your music, which we all think is fab." "Okay, that'll be great," I said unconvincingly, but relieved they weren't coming to the wilds of Gloucestershire. I suppose I feared it would be like the last experience I'd had with one of Simon's hopefuls - multiplied this time by five.

The first time I showed up at their house out near Watford, I only met three of them, Gerri or Ginger Spice, who seemed in charge, Mel B 'Scary' and 'Sporty Spice' Melanie C. Baby Spice, Emma Bunton, was away somewhere and 'Posh' was working in Boots Chemists down the road. I would, however meet Victoria on my next visit, which was not auspicious. Anyway for now I got on with plugging my keyboards in amongst much excited girly kerfuffle and we began to try out a few ideas. They were lovely girls, very up-beat, super-positive and enthusiastic about everything, but again, not one of Simon's girl group could hold a tune for more than a couple of lines. There was just nothing distinctive, charming or even innocently redeeming about the sound they were making, except to say that they almost made up for it with their fantastic girl-power energy and being so sparky and full of life.

However, on the next visit I met 'Posh' whose vocal abilities made the other girls sound like Mariah Carey; she seemed much more self-aware, unnatural and lacking in confidence than the other Spices. Perhaps to counteract this quality she projected an above-it-all disengaged manner. I must have visibly winced when she attempted to sing the verse of a new tune we were writing as, from then on in, it was quite obvious from her haughty demeanour that our creative relationship was not destined for greatness. I should have remembered the wise words of my SODS mate, ex-Shadows guitarist, Bruce Welch, when we were doing the music for the *Top Secret* movie. Upon discussing the doubtful vocal ability of the star of the film, Val Kilmer; "When has that ever been a problem in our business?" Bruce observed wryly. In the Spice Girls case, it certainly wouldn't hold them back for a second.

"Simon, look, I'm really sorry but this just isn't working for me I'm afraid; no offence, they're lovely girls but none of them can sing, it's like pulling teeth. Can't I just stick to working with your other artists like Brian Kennedy?" I implored the taciturn impresario, "Now he can really sing."

The phone rang in the kitchen of our house at Trimleys in Gloucestershire while we were having breakfast a couple of days later. "It's going to be Gerri again Ann, can you tell her I'm... oh I dunno... rehearsing with Sailor," I begged her, as I just didn't know what to say any more. Ginger Spice could be very persuasive and pushy but however unconvincing my excuse she couldn't have tried harder to keep the association going.

When they burst on to the scene massively and internationally with 'Wannabe' only a few months later and with their debut album *Spice* selling more than 31 million copies worldwide making it the best-selling album by a female group in history, I'd like to say I was happy for them, but I wasn't. I was so distraught with myself that I could have missed such a perfect opportunity; as if that wasn't enough, Simon Fuller himself and even Gerri, had practically begged me to write for them.

Richard Stannard and Matt Rowe had done a magnificent job with the Spice Girls; I realised after then that the days of pure songwriting, around a few instruments, going on to record a demo, followed by a proper produced record at some future date, were already in the rear view mirror. Those days were gone for good and it felt like the train had left the station and I'd well and truly missed it. Now, if you called yourself a proper songwriter, you'd not only have to write the song, but go on and create a finished mastered recording. Since I'd sold my studio to AC/DC and moved to the Cotswolds, for the first time in my life, I was out of the game.

I tried to shrug it off but in truth, added to the recent loss of my mother, this perceived set-back affected me to the point where I started receiving treatment for clinical depression. This, and other factors caused a breakdown; friends tried to rally me but at gatherings felt I was the only person in the room I didn't know. It had probably been a very long time coming.

One day while unloading some my problems on an old friend legendary photographer and styling genius Jamie Morgan (who incidentally had shot and styled Culture Club's *Colour By Numbers* album cover in addition to All Saints, The Spice Girls, and countless other artists), he thought for a while and talking of me in the third person, said quietly and sagely; "But Phil Pickett never says no does he"? He was right. The Spice Girls probably represented the first time in my career that I'd turned a project down.

Musical theatre darling!

During the winter months of 1997 whilst stuck at Oxford Station in the pouring rain, I was taking shelter in the waiting room. By chance I got talking to an interesting chap called David Freeman, a Jazz FM broadcaster and music aficionado, the conversation eventually continuing all the way down to London. We got on really well and he invited me to come and do a live radio interview about my career the following week. He also mentioned that along with a local business partner Patrick Nally, they knew some big investors who were looking for someone who could write and produce musicals for West End-quality touring productions in the UK and around the world. "Being in the business Phil, you must know the kind of people we can approach to help us put the project together," David surmised.

My late mother Eileen was passionate about musical theatre and from being a little lad, regularly took me off on the coach down to London to see most of the first-run Broadway productions. For months afterwards she'd play the original cast albums to death on our Dansette record player at home. Shows like *Kismet, Oklahoma, West Side Story* and *The King And I* were her favourites and as she often accompanied the songs at the top of her voice, while dancing around the house, I guess without knowing it I became steeped in the moods and cadences of theatre music. Over the years I'd hankered after writing my own musical one day. But already in my fifties, thought by now I might have missed the chance. "I do know someone as it happens David" I said, "You're looking at him!"

Utilising my Ivor Novello awards and "Karma" credentials, Nally and Freeman took me along to a meeting the following week with the Rank board of directors in London. They told us that although there were other prospective creative teams chasing the multi-million pound contract, our small consortium was in with a good chance to create three, big budget, West End-style musical theatre productions from scratch. What had apparently helped our pitch no end was that 'Karma Chameleon' was the favourite song of the managing director's wife and their two daughters. Yet again, my good and trusty chameleonic friend was still pulling strings and prizing open career doors. It quickly dawned however that if we were ever going to land this deal, I'd need masses of help to pull off such an ambitious task. Therefore I thought who better to approach than Henry Marsh. Since Sailor had folded the first time round and again after Caribou, throughout my years touring with Culture Club and other pop ventures, Henry had concentrated on writing music for TV programmes and advertising jingles. But more pertinently with the current task in mind, he'd also received awards and written music for Shakespeare and off-Broadway productions in America, for a flamboyant, eccentric theatre director called David Bell.

Henry was thrilled to be invited aboard and loved the idea of us working together again, as I did but I also asked him if he thought David might be interested in getting involved too. I knew we would need to enlist an experienced director very soon and anyway Henry had worked with David several times over in the USA. "Ask him" Henry said positively, giving me David's number in Atlanta. "He's very busy over there most of the time, but you never know." On finally reaching Bell, I explained about the Rank Organisation and Butlins, where, amongst other entertainment chains and venues around the world, Rank was intending to promote the musicals. Initially fearing the director might be too highbrow for such an assignment, he quickly put my mind at rest; "Uh huh, I see, okay, a holiday resort, in fact several of them and playing to hundreds of thousands of people a year?" He sounded very upbeat about it all and it was turning out to be much easier than I thought. "Beats what I'm doing over here honey, even Shakespeare would have bitten someone's arm off for an opportunity like this," David assured me. "The Bard appreciated bums on seats as much as anyone ever did." We both laughed. "I'd be delighted to Phil, count me in!"

Now that Henry and David were on board I could relax knowing I'd now got the creative team in place. For the scale of family audiences Rank had in mind they had initially suggested shows based on universally known characters and stories, so our team came up with Casper The Ghost and Batman after securing the rights from the copyright holders in Los Angeles. But even at this late stage we still required a third show concept to seal the deal. Nally called me up in a state of high anxiety. "It's really important we present something that Rank will approve of by Friday at the very latest Phil, otherwise I think we could lose out."

This was a definitive deadline now and Nally was practically begging the team to wrack its brains even further for one final push, one final show to seal the deal. The trouble we were having was that most of the ideas for original shows had either been done before or were being covered by the other teams. A few days later, in fact the very morning of the Friday deadline, whilst waiting for an underground train at Tottenham Court Road, a poster guy began tearing off some old layers from a hoarding, and then... Eureka! Suddenly there it was, staring me in the face. From several years earlier, when the movie had first come out, for a few seconds the poster man revealed the corner of ancient poster for *The Mask*, starring Jim Carrey. I didn't even bother to catch the train, but instead bounded back up the escalator to ground level in order to get a signal, "Patrick, I've got it, remember, *The Mask* movie?" "Fantastic!" he said, "Let me call them right now." Ten minutes later he was on the phone again, "Well done Phil" said Nally, brimming with enthusiasm, "We're in! We've got the bloody contract! Come on over to the office in Hanover Square and let's have a glass of champagne!" Where had I heard that before I thought. I couldn't wait to tell David and Henry the news. "Book me on the next plane!" said an ecstatic David Bell, over a very bad line to Atlanta.

Composing three different shows over eighteen months, painstakingly auditioning and selecting three casts from scratch and then going on to experience the blind terror of three opening nights over a period of six months, as anyone who has ever written even ONE musical will bear out, was a health, pride and sanity-rinsing task of herculean proportions. In addition, prior to the imminent casting sessions, Henry informed me one day that as David and he were obliged to attend rehearsals for another of their shows in America, they wanted me, along with experienced choreographer, Warren Carlyle to supervise the sessions and in effect, to choose all three casts. "What, do mean, me pick all of the casts? I said, terrified at the thought. "Come on Henners, theatre is your world not mine old fruit, anyway, can't it all wait until you and David are back from the States?" "No I'm afraid not Philip, sorry, but you'll walk it, I promise you, Warren's incredibly experienced and I know you can tell a good singer when you hear one, after all, you've worked with me for years."

The response to the ad in *The Stage* had apparently been phenomenal and the project oversubscribed several times over with kids coming from all over the country. But when I finally met some of the hopefuls at Dee Dee Wilde's Dance Attic for the first day's auditions, I'd never met a more delightful and talented bunch of young people in my life. They were positively buzzing with enthusiasm and energy. Also I could tell that for everyone who had come, many from far and wide, this was a very big deal for them. For Warren, imagine Craig Revel Horwood meets Graham Norton, with theatre running through his veins and camp, ruthless humour, reigning supreme. But he certainly knew his onions when it came to dance and took no prisoners. "Watch out for the Triple Threats Philip, none of those please darling," the choreographer from hell whispered furtively. "What's a Triple Threat?" I enquired nervously, already out of my depth as the first girl stepped up on the stage. "Can't sing, can't dance, can't act!" he said. "Okay, where are you from sweetheart, what are you going to do for me today?"

Most of the kids could do one, or possibly two of Carlyle's stipulations reasonably well, but having all three was a distinct rarity. "This girl can sing, though, Warren, let's put her down for *The Mask*", I said keenly about a lovely girl from Bletchley. By now I was really getting the hang of being a latter-day Simon Cowell in the judge's hot seat and starting to relish my new role. "I agree with put her down Phil. Have you seen her move? My Chesterfield's got better pins than our Bletchley princess and I bet has better dance moves." "Come on sweetheart, dancing is dreaming with the feet, but what your doing's a bloody nightmare love!"

Our many adventures, whilst writing and recording over fifty songs and hours of supporting score would probably fill a shelf full of books but suffice to say, in time-honoured fashion, Henry and I happily survived the assault course on our friendship and senses and in the end created a body of work of which we are still immensely proud. Also we got a real boost when we heard that one of our trilogy of shows, *Casper* had been chosen by the producers to go straight into the West End, opening at the Shaftesbury Theatre late in 1999. The odds of getting a show put on in London's Theatre-land, with one's first attempt were, as David Bell assured us, a million to one; so it was perhaps a fitting end to the nineties, which in so many ways, turned out to be a surprisingly rewarding decade after all.

Casper's opening night was a glittering success and the young cast, their earlier stage-fright now well and truly behind them, were having a riotous time, letting their hair down on the dance floor at the after-show party. What little hair Henry and I still had left at the end of our colossal creative journey, accompanied, as it was, by all-but armed conflict with the show's producers, we merely waved about a bit gamely throwing a few shapes from the sidelines. Having missed seeing David Freeman at the show, I spotted him at the party and waved enthusiastically, he shouted back over the buzzing throng as he and his young family were leaving the club to get back home; "Funny what comes out of bumping into strangers on rainy Oxford platforms," Freeman said and in a flourish he was gone.

It was similarly grey and overcast next day as Ann and I drove back up the M40 through chicken shit canyon towards Oxford and yet another new home. This man-made canyon is where on a pleasant day the vista opens out dramatically across the Chilterns to reveal the gently rolling hills of the beckoning Cotswolds further north. Earlier in 1999 we had moved from our sleepy idyllic Little Rissington cottage now having bought a stylish terraced house conversion within an ex-Victorian Mental Hospital in Oxford. Several of our less politically correct friends joked that the move may have been highly appropriate. "I still miss the Cotswolds though," Ann said, wistfully gazing towards where the horizon usually was, as the wipers vainly attempted to keep up with a sudden deluge. "Harry had a lovely childhood growing up and going to school there in Great Rissy," she mused. "Out of everywhere we've lived, it has some of the happiest memories."

Once through the canyon, in those days, you could also often make out the white billowing stacks of Didcot Power Station out to the west, although due to the current inclement weather, we couldn't see that far on that day. I'd co-written and created a full-on West End Musical to be proud of but our director, David Bell had already departed the country and was back in Atlanta, not having even glanced at any of the show's reviews. Henry had pre-warned me that this was one of David's "little quirks" but it hadn't seemed quite so important back then. After Christmas the year 2000 would soon be upon us and as Ann drove us home, with me still being in a state of exhaustion from the shows to get behind the wheel, I wondered what the new century might bring.

Taboo

On January 29th 2002, Boy George invited Ann and I to the opening night of his stage musical, *Taboo*. As his show featured only two songs from the Culture Club era, 'Do You Really Want To Hurt Me' and (of course), our old friend 'Karma Chameleon', both he and his publishers and producers had kept in touch, requiring my agreement to the song's use in the show, which anyway, I was absolutely thrilled about. Knowing I'd also had my own West End show, George had frequently called for odd bits of advice on the theatre world and how it all worked which, as I had found out to my cost, was a very different kettle of fish from the music biz and just as hard to read sometimes.

We were delighted that George had put us next to his mum Dina in the audience while we all sat back and enjoyed the show. I thought it a wonderful piece of entertainment, full of George's character and style, recalling in many ways its risqué and decadent elements of some of my very favourite shows, such as *Oliver* and Christopher Isherwood's *Cabaret*.

The character representing the redoubtable Philip Sallon, doyenne of London's Gay fashion scene in the New Romantic era and who might well have been considered the John The Baptist figure in Boy George's eventual world domination was the narrator of the piece. "Every time I've seen Philip over the years, having even made a record with him once ('Housewife Superstar'), it's like he's just stepped right out of the pages of Dickens's *Oliver Twist*".

After the show, while congratulating George on his triumph at the bar, a very telling moment occurred, when a visibly shocked Sallon approached George to inform him he'd thought the actor who had played his role sounded "far too gay." "Am I that camp George? I don't think so," he complained bitterly, walking off with a swirl and a huff like Miss Piggy.

A couple of days before going to meet George at *Taboo*, in a round about and convoluted manner (which therefore came as quite a shock), Ann and I found out that our son Gus was gay. It's a hard thing to explain now, about something that is so natural and who our lovely son really is, which probably shouldn't have come as such a surprise at all. But finding out in the manner we did led to a few issues, with which, at that time, we were still trying to come to terms. On tour with Culture Club, I'd once shown George a beautiful picture of Gus taken by our friend Jan Britten, in which he had placed some cherries delicately on his ears to resemble earrings. George, upon seeing the photograph chuckled with delight; "If my dad had let me look like that when I was a kid, I wouldn't have had half the problems I've had in life!" At *Taboo's* after-show party which in impromptu-style had relocated to the Groucho as I'd invited George along with some of the cast, with huge sensitivity, compassion and kindness, George talked Ann and I down off a cliff of uncertainty and misunderstanding that, to this day, we have never forgotten. While all of his famous guests were clamouring to spend time with the star of the evening on his big night, all George insisted on doing it seemed, and for several hours, was going well over the extra mile by spending time with us, encouraging us to believe in what a great and fulfilled life Gus's could turn out to be. At that moment and ever since, to me Culture Club was not just a band I'd been involved with but something more akin to family.

Postscript
Luxury to Heartache (Part 2)

Continued from page 9...

T he big guy with the wrench suddenly turned round, the others stopping in their tracks. I jerked my head down towards the bench again; had they heard something? If not my heart, beating like a bloody hammer in my chest then perhaps my chattering teeth. I could hear activity around the van and then they were looking into the cab whilst mumbling to each other in French; someone banged on the door - hard. To avoid becoming one I lay as motionless as a corpse, crapping myself inside my son's sleeping bag.

After a while, to my massive relief, the men disappeared and after lying still for another ten minutes or so to make sure, I finally realised it was probably safe to get moving again. Tentatively, while still looking around, I started the engine and rapidly got the hell out of there and drove to the docks at Dunkirk for embarkation. Finally a few hours later, at last, I was safely home in my warm bed again.

Several months later, a detective from Interpol rang me at home. At first, I'd forgotten these scary events, put them out of my mind as one often does. According to the detective, some poor bugger had indeed been beaten within an inch of his life and was still in a coma in a Belgian hospital. My van had been picked up on the CCTV and they'd finally located me. After I recounted the vivid description of the terrifying events witnessed from my freezing cab, he thanked me for the information but fortunately I never heard from them again.

The idea for Van-Go, (with its tag line; "Express Yourself!") born as it was, out of quiet desperation from the bleeding edge of changing circumstance (which if you've made it this far, dear reader, I sincerely thank and admire you!) was my answer to coping with some of the fundamental shifts going on in our industry and the reality that it forced some of us to face. To my mind there was no use lamenting or sitting around hoping those glory years would come back. They were gone for good. Acceptance of what is seemed to be the only real, unchanging and constant attribute a musician required in a vivid and chameleonic life of extremes.

Within just a few months Van-Go became a reliable cash-making business, eventually morphing into a company that specialised in the transport of art works and art installations all over Europe. Ann and I went on to have many bizarre, amusing and often enjoyable adventures along the way, indeed quite possibly the subject of my next book if there ever is one!

When my music career seemed to be returning to rude health again a few years later and we were able to sell the venture at a considerable profit, to be honest, I was sad to see the "van go" as it had become a powerful symbol of how, when your back's up against the wall, rather than worrying yourself to death about everything, it was perhaps far better just to get out there, grab the wheel, put your foot down on the metal and get somewhere - anywhere, one a hell of a lot quicker!

Speech Day in The House Of Commons

"But that which makes her name through earth to ring,
She is the chamber to our gracious King,
The place in which the Parliament doth sit
For to determine things most requisite"

Old Ballad

During the harsh winter of 2009, Fran Nevrkla, Chairman of the Phonographic Performance Ltd (PPL) along with his publicity director, my old friend from Sailor/CBS days Jonathan Morrish contacted me to ask if I'd be willing to give a speech at the House of Commons in support of the PPL and the Musicians' Union case for extending copyright term for their members from the present fifty years to frankly as much as we could get. After all, in some countries like France for instance, it was seventy or even ninety years that after playing on an original recording, musicians or their families and heirs could go on benefiting financially from performances on records they'd made during their prime.

As it was, a lot of great musicians who'd contributed to some of the most classic records of all time, such as violinist, Pat Hale, now in his eighties, first violinist on the Beatles' 'Eleanor Rigby'. Back in the sixties, along with many others, Pat was now seeing his income from this song and others abruptly coming to an end at the very time in life he needed it most.

While considerably refreshed so I am told, I made this point quite robustly when taking part in an impromptu PPL video at Abbey Road Studios, a segment of which Prime Minister Gordon Brown and other government ministers had seen.

"Look Gordon, if I may be so bold" I said cheerfully to camera but with a degree of serious intent; "Why, with respect, does the government wish to enrich Google, the BBC and iTunes even further by taking this fine old gentleman's rightful earnings away, when all he is going to do at eighty years old, is come knocking on your door for tax payers' cash instead?"

These and other points had apparently made their mark on members of the government, including Brown, who'd seen the video.

On the big day of my speech, however, February 2nd, 2009 the whole of

London, the home counties, in fact, most of the country was brought to a standstill by a colossal snowstorm and plunging arctic temperatures.

As our car was in the garage and there were no trains running that day, I realised the only way I could get up to town was to go in our Van-Go truck. Although we had by this stage technically sold the transport business, luckily I still had the use of a van for a week or so.

Thinking of England and the fate of my musician brothers and sisters (and lest I get too full of myself - myself!) in my best Boateng suit and with Churchill's wartime words ringing in my ears, I clambered up into the cab and stoically headed off into a blizzard to carry out my mission. I felt like the last person on earth after a nuclear attack with literally no traffic at all heading up to town on the M23 motorway. Arriving at Westminster, now a beautiful Christmas card ghost town, due to the severe weather, all parking restrictions had been lifted so miraculously I managed to park the van just over the road from the Houses of Parliament. Was I really going to go through with this? In my life a familiar thought I had to admit. But really, what on earth had I been thinking about in agreeing to come here in the first place?

Going through security and by now dwarfed by the vast cavernous Westminster Hall, I was filled with foreboding. This mighty place was the medieval seat of government built by Rufus, son of William The Conqueror, rebuilt by Edward the Confessor and had been intimately involved at the heart of the nation's governance since the 11th century,

Under the cold watchful eyes of the statues of Gladstone and Disraeli, I was asked to wait in one of Pugin's mock-Gothic corridors until called through to the Committee Room. Overlooked by a huge painting of Lord Palmerston and in view of the silent and brooding grey River Thames, this was where I was to deliver my speech. I was quaking in my boots. Ministers, MPs and the press were already filing in and a liveried attendant approached in hushed tones to inform me and the PPL team that when called, we could go through in a few minutes.

At that moment the phone buzzed in my pocket. Damn! I'd forgotten to switch the bloody thing off. But for some reason, nerves I suppose, I answered it.

"Is that Van-Go?" a male voice said, "Er, yes" I answered, "but..."

"Steve here from Crawley mate, listen I've got a wardrobe needs picking up from Croydon. Do you think you could..."

"Sorry Steve" I whispered, trying to keep my voice down, "I'm, er, oh look forget it. You're going to have to call me back if that's okay, sorry mate gotta go!"

On later reflection, I don't think Steve from Croydon would have believed it for a second if I'd told him his potential wardrobe shifter was about to give a speech in the House of Commons!

At that point, the usher brought our small delegation into the chamber and after some preliminaries from Fran Nevrkla and a highly accomplished performance on the violin from Pat Hale, I rose to give my speech. It lasted around ten minutes. Strangely enough, as soon as I was up on my feet my earlier nerves had thankfully disappeared. The funnier bits I'd included for levity seemed to be working and it went down quite well from the outset.

Afterwards, Chris Smith, then Minister for Culture, and the Labour MP for Tottenham, David Lammy, gently grilled me on life in general for musicians in the modern day music industry.

"So Phil," the strikingly tall Lammy asked incredulously, "What you're saying is that four times a year a cheque arrives in the mail representing your entire income and livelihood and until you open the envelope, you have absolutely no idea how much it's going to be?"

"Yes, that just about sums it up," I said.

The MP for Tottenham paused for a while dumbfounded, scratched his head and uttered; "What a remarkable way to earn a living!"

"Yes, put like that I suppose it is," I said, "Trouble is, music's the only thing I really know much about!"

A few weeks later I received a letter from Fran and Jonathan thanking me for my involvement in the campaign and congratulating all of us who'd taken part. After a long and hard fight culminating in our visit to the House of Commons, the government had relented by finally agreeing to extend the copyright term for all musicians' performances by an additional twenty years. They even promised to review the situation again a little later on.

This, so I was told, represented at least two to three billion pounds-worth of extra earnings for musicians over the period, many of whom were scraping by on less than £15,000 a year. I later received thanks from the Musicians' Union on behalf of the UK's 40,000 musician members and also many calls from music industry friends including John Lodge from the Moody Blues thanking me for my part in the campaign.

Yo' Femi!

Just before we sold the company Ann and I were driving through Paris on a final trip in our Van-Go truck on the way back from an art installation project in Geneva. Seeing Keziah's name up in big lights outside the Olympia Concert Hall in Paris where he was advertised to appear for several sold-out nights gave us a thrill so we pulled the van over and parked up. Now and for many years, Keziah Jones had been a huge star in France and we reflected on the times way back when I'd helped kick start his career. We even recalled the day I suddenly disappeared up to town to see him after a challenging house move!

I suppose with a degree of satisfaction, bordering on wistfulness at how the thing had ended, I had often wondered how he was getting on these days.

Years ago however I'd lost all of his numbers and addresses. Was it a feeling of unfinished business? Who knew? But from the day we parted company in 1993 we'd had no contact with each other whatsoever throughout the intervening years.

I was astonished, therefore, that just a few days later while walking our dogs in front of Firle Church my phone buzzed in my pocket. It was a text from Keziah himself! He said he wasn't sure how I'd feel hearing from him again after all these years, but he was flying in from New York the following week and would I like to meet up? "Well, how about them apples?" Ann said.

When he finally bounded into the Groucho Club a week or so later, I laughed out loud. He still looked exactly the same! I was completely dumbfounded. "I'll have five quid's worth of what you've been on please!" I said. He laughed too. It was good to see him again. What Boy George once told me about Keziah was certainly true, "Black don't crack!"

We caught up on the intervening years and of our past difficulties, which were soon put in perspective. "It was the early nineties man, we were both going through lots of stuff," I explained. I'd lost my mother in 1993, Keziah's father had died around that time too, both of whom respectively had loomed very large in our lives. Also there had been many issues where we had differed over career decisions and direction. I always tried to push him into being a megastar, much too soon probably. But he always was, and still is, a genuine artist with his own time frame. The real deal for whom it was always going to take longer to come to fruition, to mature and express his uniqueness as an artist.

"Would you ever consider managing me again Phil?" he said out of the blue. I was blown away to realise that as well as touching base and breaking bread over old times, there was also a professional aspect to the meeting. I said I might need a little time to think about it but in reality, it was very cool to be asked. In the end it took very little time to arrive at a decision. Around seventeen seconds in fact! One for every year we'd been out of touch. "Seventeen years is a decent break Keziah!" I said; "Let's sail the ship home bro'!"

So in 2010 I set up a new management company, Rugged Management to handle Keziah's touring and business affairs and which very early on in the proceedings, my youngest son Harry, then only 19 came aboard to help. Not really wanting to go to University, but as I had at his age - "get out there and do something", Harry's admirable organisational skills and extremely quick thinking in addition to being thoroughly versed in the realities of the music industry quickly came to the fore. He proved to be a vital and invaluable asset not only for the company but for me personally while doing something he clearly enjoys.

***

As I write this final chapter it's now October 2015 and two days earlier, having flown down from Sao Paulo in a private Learjet, we are presently at anchor in a beautiful lagoon approximately 100 miles south of Rio de Janeiro. Today I find myself aboard the Superyacht of Alexandre, a French billionaire hotelier. Keziah Jones played a concert last night with Brazilian megastar Seu Jorge in a decaying Victorian hospital in Sao Paulo which Alexandre has bought and intends to develop into a six-star hotel. Earlier the flamboyant hotelier and I had dived off the bow of his ship and swam ashore together for a beer or two ruminating on the vicissitudes of the universe. Such, on occasion, is the life of a poacher-turned-gamekeeper songwriter manager!

These and many other adventures and experiences as a musical journeyman weaving in and out of what has come to be known and appreciated as the late 20th Century's Golden Age of Pop and its phenomenal period of sociological and commercial prominence, guided and controlled by the late, great Music Industry are what I have attempted to describe in this, my first book.

Random chances, sudden forks in the road and bizarre twists and turns of fortune typified my experiences in life and career to date, originally drawn as I was like a moth to the flame and lucky enough to get up close and personal with some of the most successful artists and songwriters of all time. Somewhere along the way this led me to a tiny rehearsal room at Nomis Studios in Shepherds Bush in 1982, where invited and encouraged by Boy George, he and I sat down and wrote 'Karma Chameleon', one of the best-known songs of all time. That twenty inspired minutes or so changed the course of my life forever.

***

Epilogue

No book of mine would be complete without a reference to my boat, my folly, my seafaring home, my Chelsea Harbour floating management office, my ship of dreams and for many years, my pride and joy. Until that is, a regrettable altercation with HMRC took place in the early nineties, after which we owned her no more. Perhaps if you like this book dear reader I shall be able to buy her back again!

Her name was and still is Aubretia. Now safely back in her berth on the Thames in Twickenham but she will forever have a place in my heart. In the late eighties with my family on board our little ship we sailed across the English Channel via Ramsgate and Cherbourg to Jersey and St Malo, then up and down the glorious canals of France. The following year Ann and I ventured back over the sea, dodging ships three times the size of Harrods and cruising on to the safe harbours, creeks and rivers of Devon and Cornwall where we spent several seasons.

As a footnote, not just to this story, but the entire book, allow me to add an enduring memory of Aubretia from a friend's perspective. In this case my dear songwriting buddy, Jon Lind and therefore from the point of view of a highly expressive, talented and charming Jewish guy from Brooklyn. He always maintains that in a fleeting metaphysical and magical moment, the following experience somehow changed the way he looked at life. He therefore always tells the following story with great animation and affection; "Mary, Joanna, Dan and I were waiting on Richmond quay, excited for the Picketts to show up in, oh I don't know, a little river boat or somethin'. It was the perfect English summer's evening, so romantic, but then this amazing little ship quietly pulls up with no fuss, a huge deck up front man, we couldn't believe it. It was so fabulous, Ann welcomed us aboard with perfectly made Pimms cups for the adults and soft drinks for the kids, while Jack and Gus are expertly handling the ropes and fenders with perfect precision like trained sea cadets. Phil, up top meanwhile, motors off down the river into the sunset, we felt like fucking Hollywood stars man! It was all too much. Then Ann appears again from the galley below, this time with a platter of tandoori chicken, with some kinda yoghourt mint, fuckin', sauce; we were like, "Are we in heaven or WHAT"?

In that moment a thought came to me. It was about fellowship and making the most out of life and despite my background and the way I am (the way we are), every now and then the world is fair. "Nowhere on the planet at any time and in any way, has life ever been better than this."

******

Acknowledgements

Thanks to Jerry Bloom and Gary Hibbert at Wymer Publishing for first approaching, then encouraging and finally beating me with sticks to finish this musical memoir.

Sincere thanks also to Keith Hayward, without whose tireless enthusiasm, 24/7 objectivity, sound advice and skilful professionalism *Calmer Chameleon* would never have hit the bookshelves in a million years!

Additional thanks to Gus Pickett, who selflessly advised his dad with constructive appraisal late into hot summer nights; particularly when approaching the deadline which come to think of it is probably the most important component of any book, musical or song.

Last (and how could he ever be least?), ultra special thanks to my friend George Alan O'Dowd a.k.a Boy George, not only for his sweet and generous foreword but also for writing a song with me that thirty-five years on still creates miracles every day.

To everyone referred to in this book, all of whom I was lucky enough to cross paths with and from many I learned invaluable lessons just by being in the same room playing music or writing songs together, I would like to wholeheartedly thank. Also countless other professionals and friends who were a great inspiration offering help, influence and advice at critical crossroads and turning points in my career and who in all manner of great and small ways helped me from the very earliest days when all I wanted to do was just get out there and write a hit song.

Of particular note and of inestimable influence in my life and career from the very beginning (in some sort of vague order of appearance) are; My father, Philip George Pickett*, my mother, Eileen Elizabeth Pickett*, Stan Greig*, Chris Barsby*, Dave Peters, Paddy Maguire* Phil Benton, Paul Warren, Pam Hirsch, 'Erskine T', Steve Winwood, Duke Ellington*, Dave Pegg, Raymond Froggatt, Stuart Reid*, Ian Ralfini, Martin Wyatt, Tony Cox, Percy Sledge*, George Young, Harry Vanda, Georgie Fame, Steve Morris, Don Powell Hunter, Laurence Myers, Robert Wace. **Georg Kajanus, Henry Marsh and Grant Serpell of Sailor.** Steve Harley, Rupert Holmes, Jeffrey Lesser, Johnny Stirling, Steve O'Rourke*, Dick Asher, Tony Roberts, James Wyllie, Phil Ramone, Ron Altback, James William Guercio, Sheena Easton, Steve Levine. **Boy George, Jon Moss, Roy Hay and Mikey Craig of Culture Club.** Helen Terry, B.A Robertson, Labi Siffre, Jon Lind, Terry Britten, Arif Mardin*, Simon Fuller, Albert Hammond, Brian Kennedy, Paul McCartney, Malcolm McLaren*, Olufemi Sanyalou (a.k.a. 'Keziah Jones') Stewart Levine,

Emmanuel de Buretel, Rainer Haas, Peter Lincoln, Graham Lyle, David Lowe, Silvio Gigante, Tim Fraser and Kim Frankiewicz. Finally Doug Flett, Frank Musker, Gary Osborne, Mike Batt, Sir Tim Rice and to each and every wonderful member of the SODS I love you all and thank you again for having me.

* deceased.

Apologies - there are more I've missed, I promise you, no less important but ran out of space... and time!

For further information and continuing conversations on aspects of this book please visit calmerchameleon.com

***

Also available from Wymer Publishing

Sailor. The Official Biography
(James McCarraher)
Foreword by Jeffrey Lesser
ISBN: 978-1-908724-52-6

A detailed chronicle of this quirky band that rose to fame in the mid-seventies and are still touring today. Based around the in-depth interviews with all the band members as well as the road crew and fans from around the world. It delves deep into the past, taking the reader back to the events surrounding the band members long before they came together and then carefully fills in every known fact throughout its pages. Complete with a full discography, chart placings and a photo section, many of which come from the band's own collection. The author was also given unique access to the record company's archives. The book has been revised and updated since it was first self-published in 2004, which helps to make this official biography the definitive word on Sailor.

Paperback (234mm x 153mm)
272 pages plus 1 x 8 page b/w photo section.

From Tin Pan Alley to The Yellow Brick Road
(Keith Hayward)
ISBN: 978-1-908724-51-9

From Tin Pan Alley To The Yellow Brick Road is author Keith Hayward's sequel to the critically acclaimed Tin Pan Alley: The Rise of Elton John. It continues Elton John's story from the start of his solo career and his breakthrough with 'Your Song' to the end of the seventies. A time where Elton achieved unparalleled success, but at a price. Personal relationships and the physical exhaustion of being one of the most in demand performers in the world are documented alongside the sometimes ruthless business side of the music world. With contributions from many people who played a big part in Elton's success, including his manager John Reid, David Larkham (cover designer), Stuart Epps, Steve James, Kenny Passarelli, Roger Pope (whom the author managed) and Kiki Dee. This is a journey through the music business - from the mid sixties through to the end of seventies - as seen through Elton's career.Complete with a comprehensive gig list that has been painstakingly researched to include gigs as far back as 1966, From Tin Pan Alley To The Yellow Brick Road is a thought provoking and engaging read that places Elton John's success within the context of the multi-faceted and sometimes complex world of the music business.

Paperback (234mm x 153mm)
Pages: 256 plus 8 page colour plate section.